T0385983

FREEDOMLAND

FREEDOMLAND

CO-OP CITY AND THE STORY OF NEW YORK

ANNEMARIE H. SAMMARTINO

THREE HILLS
AN IMPRINT OF CORNELL UNIVERSITY PRESS
Ithaca and London

First published 2022 by Cornell University Press

Printed in the United States of America

Library of Congress Cataloging-in-Publication Data
Names: Sammartino, Annemarie, author.
Title: Freedomland : Co-op City and the story of
    New York / Annemarie H. Sammartino.
Description: Ithaca [New York] : Cornell University Press,
    2022. | Includes bibliographical references and index.
Identifiers: LCCN 2021026425 (print) | LCCN 2021026426
    (ebook) | ISBN 9781501716430 (hardcover) |
    ISBN 9781501716447 (epub) | ISBN 9781501716454 (pdf)
Subjects: LCSH: Co-op City (New York, N.Y.)—History. |
    Housing, Cooperative—New York (State)—Bronx
    County—History—20th century.
Classification: LCC HD7287.72.U62 N567 2022 (print) |
    LCC HD7287.72.U62 (ebook) | DDC 334/.109747275—
    dc23/eng/20211110
LC record available at https://lccn.loc.gov/2021026425
LC ebook record available at https://lccn.loc.gov/2021026426

For the Sammartinos

My dad, my sisters, and me in our Co-op City apartment, 1983

CONTENTS

Preface   xi

Introduction: Co-op City and the
Story of New York   1

1. "The World's Greatest Housing
   Cooperative": Building a
   New City, 1965–1968   22

2. "Everyone Was Seeking a Utopia":
   Building a Community, 1968–1973   60

3. "We Remember Picket Lines":
   Cooperator Militancy, 1970–1974   96

4. "No Way, We Won't Pay": The Rent
   Strike, 1975–1976   115

5. "We Inherited a Mess!": After the
   Rent Strike, 1977–1981   148

6. "Co-op City *Is* the Bronx":
   A Middle-Class Community,
   1982–1993   181

7. "The Biggest Housing Bargain
   in Town": Achieving Financial
   Stability, 1981–1993   205

   Epilogue: Freedomland Today   223

Appendix   231

Notes   235

Index   291

PREFACE

Ada Louise Huxtable began her 1971 appraisal of Co-op City, "The motorist speeding by Co-op City on the Hutchinson River Parkway in the Bronx sees only its looming apartment towers."[1] Thirty-five years later, Ian Frazier's 2006 *New Yorker* article about Co-op City contains a similar vista, albeit from a different highway: "If you take I-95 North through the Bronx heading out of the city, Co-op City will be on your right. Its high-rise apartment buildings stand far enough from one another so that each appears distinct and impressive against the sky. In slow-motion seconds, they pass like the measureless underside of a starship in a science-fiction movie."[2] As these two examples attest, authors looking to write about Co-op City often begin by noting how it looks from the road. These stories and others then go on to marvel at Co-op City's many superlatives. With thirty-five tower buildings and seven townhouse clusters, it is the largest cooperative housing development in the world. It was by far the largest project built as part of the Mitchell-Lama program, a New York State initiative intended to provide middle-income housing that sponsored housing projects developed between the mid-1950s and mid-1970s. Approximately 15 percent of the 104,000 apartments in total constructed under New York State's Mitchell-Lama program are in Co-op City.[3] The $390 million mortgage that was issued to cover its construction costs was the largest such mortgage in the history of the New York State Housing Finance Agency. So much bathroom tile was used in the construction of Co-op City that it could have been used to build a wall five feet high from New York City to Saint Louis. If laid end to end, the pilings driven to support its massive high rises would stretch from New York City to Boston and back again.[4] If Co-op City were to secede from New York City, it would immediately become New York State's tenth-largest city. Co-op City is the largest NORC, or naturally occurring retirement community, in the United States.[5]

The reason why most stories of Co-op City begin with the view from the highway is that this is the way that most people encounter the development. Similarly, the list of Co-op City's superlatives is designed to give outsiders a sense of the scale of this "city in a city." Once writers have enumerated all the ways in which Co-op City appears as an "alien city . . . a vast, bleak, spreading mass," they often feign surprise at the normalcy of the people who live in this behemoth.[6] "Co-op City is neither the purgatory nor the heaven that its critics and champions predicted. It is a functioning community," Huxtable wrote.[7] "It may be hard for outsiders to comprehend," a resident told a reporter in 1971, "but we're a real community here."[8]

This should not be surprising, because Co-op City is a paradox—it is an extraordinary place that was built for ordinary people—middle- and working-class New Yorkers. In the words of the United Housing Foundation (UHF) that constructed it, "Co-op City is a reflection of our desire to provide good, well-built homes—real homes for people at a price they can afford."[9] This book tells Co-op City's story both from the perspective of the men and women who dreamed it, built it, and controlled it, and from the viewpoint of the ordinary people who lived in the development.

I am one of them. My parents moved to Co-op City's Adler Place town houses shortly after the conclusion of the rent strike. They moved there, as so many others did, because it was affordable and because they knew people there. Nearly my mother's entire extended family had moved to Co-op City as it opened in the late 1960s and early 1970s, happy to leave decrepit apartments and changing neighborhoods on the West Side of the Bronx. As other white families, including most of my relatives, left Co-op City in the 1970s and 1980s for more suburban precincts, my parents stayed.

I should be up-front about the fact that, growing up, I hated Co-op City. Compared to the neighborhoods my friends in high school came from— Park Slope with its gentrified energy, the cultured precincts of the Upper West Side, the risqué but cosmopolitan Village—Co-op City seemed boring, uncultured, and downright provincial. As I looked forward to college, there was nothing I wanted more than to get as far from Co-op as I possibly could. In later years, I have never trafficked in the nostalgia that so many former Co-op City-ites feel. I still remember the child and adolescent who burned with a desire to leave that place, which felt like it was in the middle of nowhere—with no connections to anything real, exciting, or worthwhile.

And yet it was home. In some ways, it still is. When I go back to visit, I do not see the towers that surround me as alien or dehumanizing. I do not get lost in Co-op City's meandering paths and cul-de-sacs. The words "Building 11" or "Section Five" do not strike me as cold and bureaucratic but rather as the places where my friends and family lived. While doing research for this book, I spoke with an old friend who said that he loves dystopian films because they remind him of home. I knew exactly what he meant.

I spent years trying to get away from Co-op City, and I got as far as Germany, where I lived for several years in Berlin while doing research for my dissertation, which later became my first book. While there, I often found myself trying to describe where I was from to Germans whose image of New York did not extend far beyond its tourist highlights. I would say that Co-op City looked a lot like Marzahn, the massive East German housing development located in the northeast quadrant of the reunited city. Investigating the physical similarity between Co-op City and Marzahn ultimately resulted in an article that examined the two housing developments as exemplars of the global architectural and sociological phenomenon of late modernism.[10] In researching that article, I discovered a history of Co-op City that I had never known anything about. Even though many of my relatives had moved there when the cooperative first opened, I had never heard anything about the United Housing Foundation, the nonprofit group that constructed Co-op City. Even though I grew up playing with the children of the leaders of the rent strike, I had only ever dimly heard of it. Even though my childhood and adolescence spanned the period of white flight, by the end of which most of my relatives had moved out and my youngest sister would be one of only two white students who graduated from IS 180 in 1995, I had never realized that this was anything more than a series of individual decisions by families to leave. As I finished working on the article, I realized I was not done researching Co-op City.

I quickly found that not only did I know very little about Co-op City's history, but I could find very little that had been written about it by historians. Co-op City's very location, on the fringes of New York's northern frontier, a subway and a bus (or an express bus) from Manhattan, means that most New Yorkers and certainly most scholars never venture there. Furthermore, Co-op City fits awkwardly or not at all into the standard narrative of New York City—one that charts the city's decline amid the urban crisis of the 1960s and 1970s and its rebirth as a city of wealth and the "creative class" living in gentrified neighborhoods in now-iconic Brooklyn. Scholars have come to appreciate the complexity of urban renewal, and they have also come to study those whose lives were upended by gentrification, a shock that could be just as jarring as Robert Moses's construction projects. But other areas—untouched by the toppling hand of privilege—still languish far from the eyes of scholars.[11]

Co-op City is a standard-bearer for these neighborhoods. It was the home of tens of thousands of working- and lower-middle-class people in 1970, and even if the color of these people's skin may have changed in the ensuing five decades, their social and economic position has not. New York today is a deeply unequal city, and the need for affordable housing is as urgent as it has ever been. It is no less urgent to understand the complex history and ambivalent lessons of this huge—literally and figuratively—attempt to provide housing to people of moderate means a half century ago.

I hope that this book has a meaning that goes beyond my own particular story; but it is also a deeply personal book. As such, it is filled with deeply personal debts. I must begin by thanking the archivists at Cornell University's Kheel Center for Labor-Management Documentation & Archives, including Patrizia Sione and Steven Calco, who not only helped me gain access to the United Housing Foundation files but also helped find some of the fabulous pictures that I was able to include in this book. Archivists at the New York City Municipal Archives, the New York State Archives, and the Bronx County Historical Society, especially Steven Payne, and the Lehman College Bronx Oral History Archive were similarly helpful. Countless librarians at the Baychester branch of the New York Public Library helped me access volume upon volume of the *Co-op City Times* and *City News*. The Baychester Library was a haven for me as a child, and it felt like coming full circle to return to it while writing this book. Oberlin College provided generous support in the form of a research status leave, where I first developed the idea of this book, and two grant-in-aid fellowships to fund archive trips.

Many former residents of Co-op City were generous enough to share their time and their memories with me. For that I am extremely grateful. Frank Guridy, Michael Agovino, and Judith Perez Caro are three former Co-op City residents who have written about Co-op City and were generous enough to read the manuscript, share their impressions, and talk though some of my conclusions. Greg Myers contributed several of his own personal photographs, which adorn these pages. Michael Horowitz, former editor of the *City News*, and Bernie Cylich, Co-op City "pioneer" and Riverbay board vice president, were generous enough to share their thoughts on parts of the manuscript. Co-op City residents have a reputation for their contentiousness, but all the ones I spoke with were unfailingly generous.

Michael Kennedy, my research assistant at Oberlin, went above and beyond—collating research materials, transcribing interviews, and creating the demographic graphs that appear in the appendix. His insights helped shape this project throughout. Michael McGandy was a tireless champion of this project and a helpful and patient editor. Thanks as well to Karen Hwa, Cornell's tireless production editor, and Sandy Sadow, for her help with indexing the manuscript. I am also very indebted to the feedback provided by the two reviewers of this manuscript. Brian Purnell, who agreed to be identified, was particularly generous in discussing the manuscript with me in a later and extremely helpful conversation.

American urban historians may have been perplexed by the fact that a German historian decided to write a book about the Bronx, but they always responded to my work with kindness and curiosity. I am so grateful to Peter Eisenstadt, Robert Fishman, Benjamin Holtzman, Suleiman Osman, Susanne Schindler, Robert Self, and Adam Tanaka for clarifying conversations at various stages of this project. My colleagues at Oberlin, and especially my fellow historians, have provided me with an intellectual and professional home that I can't begin to thank them for. Oberlin is what it is because of its students. Their curiosity, generosity, and willingness to examine historical questions with the seriousness and moral urgency they deserve have pushed me to be a better scholar and better person. I particularly need to thank those who took several iterations of History 479: Readings in Twentieth Century Urban History, for listening to my inchoate thoughts about this project and helping me think through its significance and conclusions.

Eli Rubin and I first met because of our shared interest in modernist housing. His enthusiasm for Co-op City the first time we visited together helped me realize that I had a story worth writing. I am grateful for that and for his close readings of and long conversations about each and every chapter. He is an intellectual partner, a life partner, and he is very meaningful to me. Like me, Lucien and Ezra cannot remember a time before they became acquainted with Co-op City. Seeing the development through their eyes has opened my eyes to another side of the cooperative, just as they have expanded my perspective and my heart in countless other ways. There are many Rubins—Nancy, Neal, Isaac, Oliver, and Eloise—who have no connection to Co-op City but have become an invaluable part of my life and my family during the time that it took to bring this project to completion. As such, they have earned an important place in these acknowledgments.

Finally, this book is dedicated to my parents and my sisters. If my parents, Anthony and Pearl Sherman Sammartino, had not chosen to move to Co-op City, this book would not exist. My father died just as this book neared completion. As an Italian and a Brooklynite, he never felt altogether at home in Co-op City, but his delight in the place's idiosyncrasies is part of what made me want to learn more about it. My mother, always one to downplay her experiences, never understood why I wanted to write a book about Co-op City, but I hope that she can recognize, as I do, her influence and her perspective on every page. My sisters, Tory and Gabry, shared our apartment (and for too many years, a single bedroom). Their stories are theirs to tell, but conversations with them have immeasurably enriched my understanding of the place we all called home.

FREEDOMLAND

Introduction
Co-op City and the Story of New York

Shortly after nightfall on July 13, 1977, New York City was plunged into darkness. The blackout is remembered by many New Yorkers as the city's nadir. Looting and vandalism hit neighborhoods across the city, in poor areas like Morrisania in the Bronx, middle-class neighborhoods like Flatbush in Brooklyn, and even the wealthy Upper East Side of Manhattan.[1] One firefighter described the Grand Concourse in the West Bronx, where so many of Co-op City's original residents had come from, as a "battlefield." In fifteen years on the force, he said that he had never before seen fires rage on both side of the boulevard.[2] New York City's electric utility Con Ed declared the blackout an "act of God," nothing more than a lightning strike at the wrong place at the wrong time. Mayor Abraham Beame nevertheless accused the utility of "gross negligence" and spoke out against the violence and vandalism, decrying the fact that "we've been needlessly subjected to a night of terror in many communities that have been wantonly looted and burned."[3]

In 1975, New York City had barely escaped bankruptcy. Now, less than two years later, the blackout appeared to reveal the anarchy and crime that lay just under the city's thin veneer of civility. The "orgy of looting and pillage" that engulfed New York was, in the words of one reporter, "a prophecy fulfilled."[4] The author James Goodman later summarized, "Back in the 1970s, New York had been in desperate straits, wracked by stagflation, strikes, arson, drugs, graffiti, cynicism, a serial killer, stinking subways, white flight, high crime, fiscal crisis, and racial strife."⁵ The summer of the blackout was also the summer that New Yorkers were terrorized by the "Son of Sam" serial killer, a former Co-op City resident, who killed eight New Yorkers and wounded seven others before he was finally apprehended that August. Even good events had their dark side that year. During game two of the World Series in Yankee Stadium, a helicopter shot of the surrounding neighborhood revealed a fire burning out of control in a nearby elementary school. "Ladies and Gentlemen," Howard Cosell announced, "the Bronx is burning."⁶

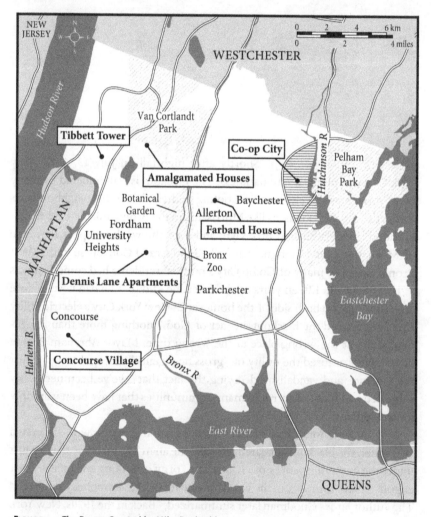

Figure 1.   The Bronx. Created by Mike Bechtold.

In 1977, the Bronx may have been the premier literal and figurative symbol of urban decay. But there was an exception, and it was a huge one: Co-op City. When the power failed, Mayor Beame was actually in Co-op City, giving a speech in a synagogue as part of his reelection campaign. Before he was hurried out by his aides, he joked that the blackout was not related to Co-op City's failure to pay its electric bill.[7] This joke did not sting as it might have even a few weeks earlier. The very week of the blackout, Co-op City and the State of New York agreed to a final settlement to the largest rent strike in US history, which had lasted from June 1975 to July 1976. As part of this settlement, the state agreed to cede operational control of the development to Co-op City's residents.

As the lights began to go out across the city, one area at a time, a group of teenagers in Building 2 looked out as the nearby Boston Secor housing project went dark. They began to chant "Co-op, Co-op," hoping that they too could enjoy the blackout. Two minutes later, their chants were answered as the entire cooperative lost power.[8] Volunteers worked under the guidance of Co-op City security to keep the cooperative safe, escorting returning residents home from the garages.[9] Elevator operators climbed the hundreds of stairs to the roofs of the tower buildings to manually move the elevators to allow trapped cooperators to escape.[10] Others, armed with candles and flashlights, assisted residents in the lobbies, while still others comforted those stuck in elevators when the lights went off or helped elderly and infirm neighbors. There was no looting and only three reports of attempted robbery (two of which were foiled) in the entire community of over fifty thousand residents. Residents who did not want to trudge the many flights to their apartments gathered in and around the lobbies on the warm summer night. Capri Pizza in Section One gave out free pizza and soda to neighbors who had helped retrieve their delivery truck.[11] Residents came downstairs with flashlights and portable radios.[12] One former resident recalled sleeping outside on a mattress that his mother threw down from their twenty-second-floor apartment.[13] Kids played with glow-in-the-dark Frisbees. The entire affair had something of a block party atmosphere.[14] Co-op City was one of the last places in the city to have full power restored, which did not happen until the following evening. However, by 10:15 on the first night, emergency power had been restored to the elevators and for other essential services.[15]

The 1977 blackout was not the first time that Co-op City had appeared as an exception to the urban crisis that engulfed New York in the second half of the twentieth century. The development had, in fact, been conceived of for just this purpose. It was the largest and most ambitious development constructed by the United Housing Foundation (UHF), a cooperative-housing developer that was responsible for over 5 percent of the housing constructed in New York between 1945 and 1975.[16] Planning for Co-op City, comprising over fifteen thousand apartments, began in 1964, and city and state officials viewed it as an effort to keep middle-class families from moving to the suburbs. However, the aims of the UHF for the development were even loftier. The UHF marveled at the development's planned tower buildings: "Height . . . man's ability to move up to clouds and outer space . . . is something new for our species! . . . The views of our City, a wondrous and growing phenomenon, will enchant our future Tower residents."[17] And most importantly, the UHF sought to use Co-op City and similar cooperatives to create "a better society." In a 1971 publication designed to celebrate twenty years of its existence, the UHF explained its aims: "Co-operative housing as a way of life extends beyond buildings. It includes the development of a cooperative community with shopping centers, pharmacies, optical dispensers, furniture stores, [and an] insurance company. The approach is best typified by the statement of the purpose of United Housing Foundation: 'All that we do is directed towards utilizing the methods of cooperation to enable people to enjoy a better life and to achieve a better society.'"[18]

In its first years of existence, Co-op City appeared poised to fulfill its promise. Even as it was decried by architects and urban planners as a set of "scattered towers [that] stand on wasteland, hemmed in by a hopelessly polluted and commercialized ilet [sic] . . . a gross debasement of the masses," it nevertheless remained very popular with potential residents, who flocked to get on its waiting list as soon as it opened to the public in 1965.[19] As whites left the city in droves in these years, Co-op City was an exception: a neighborhood to which middle-class, white New Yorkers wanted to move. Although Co-op City did not keep records of the racial makeup of the development, estimates and census records indicate that approximately 75 percent of its initial population was white, the overwhelming majority of whom were Jewish. These figures nearly matched the racial dynamics of New York City as a whole, where census figures indicate a city that in 1970 was 78 percent white.[20] At a time when racial turmoil may have roiled the rest of New York, former residents of all ethnic and racial backgrounds saw Co-op City as a relatively successful example of integration.

Cost overruns plagued the development from the start, and as the extent of Co-op City's economic problems became more evident, as reflected in a series of increases to residents' monthly carrying charges starting in 1970, Co-op City residents began to organize in opposition both to the UHF and to the state that held the development's mortgage.[21] This organizing culminated in the rent strike of 1975–76, which was led by a young, fiery, self-described Maoist named Charles Rosen. The strike, which commanded the support of approximately 75 to 80 percent of residents, overlapped with New York City's own financial crisis. The city's crisis ended with devastating cuts to city services, including fire stations, hospitals, and schools, which a wave of protests and strikes were largely powerless to stop. In contrast, Co-op City's strikers achieved full resident control of the sixty-thousand-person cooperative. A conclusion to the strike, negotiated by Rosen and his allies, was ratified by 74 percent of households who voted in a referendum.[22] Once again, in July 1977, Co-op City appeared exceptional, and there was reason to believe, as many Co-op City residents did, that the development would continue to thrive, even as the rest of the Bronx burned.

It was not to be. As Co-op City residents soon found, control of Co-op City meant responsibility for Co-op City's debt. Hundreds of millions of dollars needed to repair construction defects added to the nearly half-billion-dollar mortgage. This was a bill that the middle-class residents of the cooperative could ill afford. As debt continued to mount, residents found themselves paying yet higher monthly carrying charges. In part as a result of Co-op's financial instability, and in part owing to the racial dynamics that prompted white flight elsewhere in New York and around the United States, white families began to move out in increasing numbers in the late 1970s and 1980s. By the mid-1980s, crime had begun to rise, and test scores in the development's schools had begun to fall. It may have taken an extra decade or two, but it appeared to many in Co-op City that New York's urban problems had finally reached the Bronx's northeastern corner. Meanwhile, New York's 1980s and 1990s renaissance, anchored in finance capital and the gentrification of the kinds of neighborhoods Co-op City's residents had left, passed Co-op City by. Co-op City was too remote from the city's core, its cooperative ownership structure did not offer the possibility of a financial windfall, and its housing towers were scorned by gentrifiers longing for "character" and Old World charm. Co-op City, the largest and most lasting symbol of New York's institutional commitment to assist its poor and middle class in the decades after World War II, existed uneasily in the regime that took over the city in the final decades of the century.

In retrospect, Co-op City's apparent crime wave of the 1980s was more a reflection of anxieties about its racial transition than the actual—tangible but not huge—increase in crime, which began to decrease in the following decade as crime declined across New York. Furthermore, in part because of its own stabilizing finances, and in part as a response to the fear that Co-op City's size and crusading residents inspired, New York State began in the late

1980s to pursue a less punitive approach toward Co-op City, investing money and pursuing policies that allowed carrying charges to stabilize. The neighborhood is now a stable, middle-income pocket of the city. For all the ways that Co-op City has changed markedly since its first occupants moved in, the median household income of its residents has been near the median of the city for its entire existence (see appendix, figure 27). The people who live there enjoy the privilege of affordable housing in an increasingly unaffordable city. The Co-op City of today would be unrecognizable to the UHF that built it in the mid-1960s, but it nevertheless remains affordable for New Yorkers of moderate means in a city with all too few places for them to call home.

The construction of Co-op City was the apotheosis of a vision of affordable housing that stretched back to the teeming tenements of the immigrant Lower East Side in the early years of the twentieth century. Radical Jewish unionists at the ILGWU (International Ladies Garment Workers Union) and the ACWA (Amalgamated Clothing Workers of America) were interested improving the lives of workers beyond the factory floor. Even before World War I, they saw cooperatives as a way to translate the collective action of workers to the consumer realm.[23] After the war, union interest in cooperatives grew, with Sidney Hillman, president of the ACWA, proclaiming in 1919 that consumer cooperatives "will bring a large measure of democracy and human happiness into industry."[24] At the same time, New York housing activists became interested in the European innovation of "limited dividend" (also known as "limited profit") housing. In limited dividend housing arrangements, private developers agreed to limit their profit and the rent paid by residents to prescribed maximum levels, and in exchange were provided with either direct subsidies or state tax exemptions.[25] Housing activists such as Catherine Bauer brought this funding scheme to American shores, where it was first used in 1924 for Sunnyside Gardens in Queens (developed by the City Housing Corporation) and then enshrined in the 1926 New York State Housing Law.[26]

Taking advantage of this new law, in 1927 a series of housing cooperatives for mostly Jewish left-wing or union workers opened in the Bronx: the United Workers Cooperative on Allerton Avenue (known as the Coops), the Sholem Aleichem Houses near the Jerome Park Reservoir, the Farband Cooperative on Williamsbridge Road, and the largest and most ambitious of them all, the Amalgamated Houses off Van Cortlandt Park.[27] The last of these was spearheaded by Abraham Kazan, who would later head the UHF. Kazan was born in 1891 and was part of the great migration of Jews from the Russian Pale of Settlement to the United States. Like many Jewish immigrants, Kazan found a home on the political left. In particular, he was drawn to an idiosyncratic mix of trade unionism and anarchism, in which cooperative housing was a natural fit. In the historian Peter Eisenstadt's words, while other unionists dreamed of political power, "for Kazan, the creation of cooperatives was an end in itself. . . . Create successful cooperatives first, he argued, and the political support would come."[28]

Kazan's ambitions were much larger than the Amalgamated Houses; he hoped to create an entire cooperative sector of the economy. Such dreams were made both more urgent and less attainable by the Great Depression two years later. Kazan took the opportunity of a national conversation about the need for affordable housing to agitate for cooperatives that would both provide housing to the needy and teach them the ideas of self-help and self-reliance through mutual assistance.[29] Although Kazan and others came tantalizingly close to national funding for cooperative construction, under pressure from private housing developers the 1934 and 1937 National Housing Acts did not include provisions for cooperative or co-owned housing. Instead, both acts focused their efforts on single-family homeownership mortgage guarantees and tax incentives for the working and middle classes and public housing for those who could not afford to own their own homes.[30]

Even without federal support, New York City committed to assisting a broader swath of New Yorkers to afford urban apartments during the Depression and World War II. The New York City Public Housing Authority (NYCHA) allowed working-class families to apply for public housing. Politicians also authorized the construction of several middle-class housing developments sponsored by the Metropolitan Life Insurance Company—Peter Cooper Village and Stuyvesant Town on the East Side of Manhattan, the Riverton Houses in Harlem, and Parkchester in the East Bronx.[31] Despite these efforts, the housing situation in America's largest city was revealed to be dire once the war concluded.[32] According to one analysis, New York had a shortage of 430,000 housing units, with much of the available housing judged substandard.[33] Large-scale labor protests in 1946 led Mayor William O'Dwyer to reinstate public housing for a broader population.[34] O'Dwyer also took measures beyond public housing to encourage the construction and maintenance of affordable housing. Taking advantage of the 1926 law already on the books, his administration also offered limited-dividend housing subsidies to a range of developments. Cooperative developments such as Electchester, built by Harry Van Arsdale Jr., president of the New York City Central Labor Council, and Local 3 of the International Brotherhood of Electrical Workers in New York City took advantage of these funds. Built in 1949, Electchester contains 2,400 units in thirty-eight six-story buildings.

The 1950 Queensview Cooperative in Astoria was aimed at a similar demographic. It contains 620 apartments and was the brainchild of a number of NYCHA veterans.[35]

Struck by the great need for affordable housing and seeing an opportunity to bring his cooperative vision to a greater number of people, Kazan founded the United Housing Foundation in 1951, with the backing of a coalition of labor groups, including the ACWA and sixty-one other unions, civic organizations, and housing cooperatives.[36] Unlike the Amalgamated Houses or previous cooperative housing ventures, the UHF was explicitly apolitical and did not reserve apartments for union members.[37] The UHF's first project was a one-building addition to the original Amalgamated Co-ops in the Bronx, which was completed in 1955 with space for 123 families.[38] Each successive UHF development was larger than the previous one.[39] After forays into housing in Manhattan, such as Penn South, which comprised a total of 2,820 apartments in ten buildings and was completed in 1963, the UHF moved back to the outer boroughs for its largest pre-Co-op City project, Rochdale Village, a 5,860-unit development in eastern Queens, on land that had previously been home to the Jamaica Racetrack.[40] Altogether, in the 1950s and 1960s, the UHF was responsible for more than half the publicly subsidized, limited-income housing built in New York City, including Co-op City, its last and largest development.[41]

The UHF was part of a broader program of postwar urban liberalism that built upon the political coalitions of the New Deal era. Urban liberalism was not unique to New York; however, it reached its fullest flower in America's largest city. During the years between the end of World War II and the financial crisis of the mid-1970s, New York City government expanded to offer a wide array of social services to its residents. New York's largesse was indebted to the power of its large and politically engaged labor movement, as well as a long tradition of urban activists and policy makers with transatlantic connections and influences.[42] These factors combined to foster a "homegrown version of social democracy that made life in New York unlike anyplace else in the United States."[43] New Yorkers could benefit from free college at the City University of New York (CUNY), a network of high-quality public hospitals and medical clinics, a vast and modestly priced public transportation system, expansive municipal welfare provisions, and publicly subsidized arts institutions. All these things existed in other US cities, but in its size and generosity, the level of social investment in New York was unmatched.

Nowhere was the uniqueness of New York's social democracy more apparent than when it came to housing. In cities from Los Angeles to Detroit, the white middle and working classes were encouraged instead to purchase single-family homes within the city and its suburbs. Meanwhile, public housing was reserved for the most destitute. This bifurcated approach was enshrined on the federal level in the 1949 Housing Act, which provided funding for slum clearance and the construction of public housing, as well as monies to extend the federal mortgage insurance program for single-family homes.[44] The result of this approach was the massive expansion of American suburbia. New York was not untouched by the national move to the suburbs. Over the 1950s, New York City's suburban population grew by 2,180,492, while its urban population declined by 109,973. Nassau County on Long Island, home to Levittown and other sprawling new suburbs, grew by 141.5 percent. By the end of the decade, metro New York's suburban population exceeded its urban one for the first time.[45]

However, unlike many other cities, New York did not wholeheartedly embrace either the suburban solution for the middle class or the assignment of public housing for only the very poor. Instead, the city offered a grab bag of approaches to affordable housing for residents of modest means. One approach was a massive push to construct new public housing, with 75,403 new apartments built in the 1950s alone.[46] While public housing became a symbol for the failures of urban governance in Chicago and other cities, NYCHA navigated a relatively successful path in its attempt to provide housing for New Yorkers.[47] In 1950, New York State also took over and made permanent the rent control measures that had previously been a wartime measure of the federal government.[48]

Cooperative housing was another initiative—this time in a partnership between the city and state—that was fostered in New York to provide affordable housing to the middle class.[49] Already in the 1920s, cooperative housing had taken advantage of state-sponsored limited-dividend financing. Building on the 1926 law, in 1955 New York State passed the New York State Limited-Profit Housing Companies Act, which came to be known as Mitchell-Lama. This New York State legislation, sponsored by State Senator MacNeil Mitchell and Assemblyman Alfred Lama, offered state funds for limited-equity rental and cooperative housing construction.[50] Mitchell-Lama provided tax abatements, below-market mortgages of up to 95 percent of construction costs, and a guaranteed 6 percent (later 7.5 percent) return on investment.[51] Limits were placed on profits and rents as well as the design of Mitchell-Lama projects.[52] Meanwhile, Mitchell-Lama renters or cooperators who earned more than roughly seven to eight times their rent were subject to surcharges.[53]

Four year after Mitchell-Lama was initially passed, new governor Nelson Rockefeller poured money into its coffers. Rockefeller explained the importance the program in the following terms: "The lack of urban housing for middle class families is a persistent municipal problem for New York City and every major city in the State and the nation. This income group from which the City largely draws its civic leadership and economic support, has been forced into the suburbs to find adequate homes."[54] As this quote suggests, the vast majority of Mitchell-Lama funding went to New York City.[55] Until the Mitchell-Lama program ceased construction in 1974, it was responsible for 138,000 apartments in New York City, and the UHF was the largest single contributor to that number.[56] Altogether, over Rockefeller's tenure as governor, which spanned the 1958–59 to 1973–74 budgets, state outlays for housing increased almost 291.5 percent, considerably more than the 203.5 percent overall increase in funding to state agencies.[57]

To pay for this massive expansion in state-funded affordable housing, Rockefeller created the State Housing Finance Agency in 1960, financed by public "moral obligation" bonds.[58] "Moral obligation" bonds were a new financial instrument invented by Rockefeller's administration. Tenant rents or cooperative carrying charges would pay off the bonds; however, if they failed to cover bond payments, the state itself had a "moral obligation" to pay the bondholders. The phrase "moral obligation" was intentionally murky. Because the state did not have a legal obligation to pay "moral obligation" debt, these bonds did not count toward the state's statutory debt limit. They were, thus, a way for Rockefeller to circumvent the financial strictures of an increasingly skeptical state legislature.[59] At the same time, the phrase "moral obligation" was meant to reassure investors that although New York State was not legally responsible for these bonds, it recognized a "moral obligation" to pay bondholders in the case that problems with Mitchell-Lama projects led it to be unable to make debt service payments. This was a theoretical risk in 1960. However, during the Co-op City rent strike fifteen years later, it became an all too real possibility.

The UHF required not just the financing provided by Mitchell-Lama; it also needed a powerful patron, and it found one in Robert Moses. New York's "master builder" dominated urban construction in New York City and State in the postwar period, holding at one point the titles of parks commissioner, chairman of the New York State Power Commission, as well as ten other offices.[60] Moses believed that new buildings to replace dilapidated inner-city neighborhoods would have a transformative effect on poor and middle-income New Yorkers.[61] It was on this point that he and Kazan would find common ground. Co-op City would turn out to be the last major project that Moses or Kazan had a role in building.

Moses had a particular interest in housing. During World War II, he helped push through the Metropolitan Life Insurance Company's middle-class housing developments. In each of these developments, as well as the public housing completed during his tenure, Moses followed a "towers in a park" model.[62] This was also the preferred construction model for the UHF's developments. For Moses as well as Kazan's UHF, vertical construction was primarily appealing for its potential to reduce construction costs. Kazan and Moses alike were vocally dismissive of the utopianism and architectural determinism of Le Corbusier and other European modernists who pioneered the idea of using housing towers to create a "radiant" new city. Nevertheless, like many planners on both sides of the Cold War, they shared the belief that such developments could literally lift the poor and middle class from the social ills of the tenements.[63]

Moses was famous not merely for what he built, but also for what he destroyed.[64] The Federal 1949 Housing Act provided Title I funding for slum clearance. Moses used this money on a massive scale in New York to destroy old working-class neighborhoods and construct new housing in its stead. The provisions of Title I insisted that only public housing be built on land where slums had been razed. But Moses was able to bend the rules more than most and used these funds not just for public housing but for middle-class developments as well. By 1959, on the site of homes formerly occupied by one hundred thousand people, many of them poor minorities, sixteen Title I projects had been built in Manhattan and Brooklyn to house the white middle class.[65] Moses was also a supporter of NYCHA and orchestrated the construction of vast stretches of public housing, which replaced tenements in Harlem, the Lower East Side, and other sections of the city. Neither Moses nor Kazan shed many tears for the homes that were destroyed to make way for either public housing or middle-class cooperatives. In a typical formulation, Kazan dismissed the Lower East Side where he had spent his youth "as a breeding ground of disease and other social problems. . . . For generations the words 'Lower East Side' have been synonymous with 'miserable slum.'"[66] A UHF publication from 1971 celebrating the first twenty years of the foundation's history recalled protests against the destruction of tenements to make room for a planned cooperative development as "obstacles" that stood in the way of an "immeasurably brighter" story of cooperative housing success.[67]

Yet if the UHF could easily be caricatured as a heartless proponent of slum clearance, it also articulated a utopianism that far exceeded the practicalities of brick and mortar. As Harold Ostroff, then executive vice president of the UHF, explained in a 1966 speech to the National Association for Housing Cooperatives, "The purpose of cooperation is to give people the opportunity to appreciate Grand Opera and Shakespeare. But before they can appreciate these things," he added, "they must have decent homes, enough food, security and so forth."[68] Cooperative living was not just about providing a firm material basis from which residents could explore the world of high culture. Ostroff and others within the UHF leadership also believed that cooperatives were transformative themselves. The UHF hoped to create an alternative economy and culture that would "eliminat[e] the profit system. Eliminate it, that is by putting the interests of people first."[69] Cooperative housing would provide both the material and ideological means of giving people the tools to "change society in a fundamental way."[70] In 1967, Ostroff testified in Congress at a hearing on urban crisis: "The city has been pictured as a place where people have no roots, where people are part of a 'lonely crowd.' This is generally true but not in cooperatives, where people have invested their funds and share responsibilities of ownership. . . . Where there are cooperatives, the local police station will advise you there is little juvenile delinquency or crime."[71] The UHF's statement of purpose summed up its mission: "All that we do is directed towards utilizing the methods of cooperation to enable people to enjoy a better life and to achieve a better society."[72]

The UHF leadership were simultaneously hard-nosed political players, able to navigate the treacherous waters of municipal politics, and dreamers, who sought to use cooperative housing as the nucleus of a better world. Co-op City was their greatest attempt to both solve the city's affordable-housing crisis and construct a post-capitalist future for its people. In this combination of utopianism, practicality, and paternalism, the UHF was the apotheosis of the social welfare consensus in New York City politics during the middle years of the twentieth century.[73]

If Co-op City was built at the close of one era of New York City's development, its residents would live, and its history would be written—or more precisely overlooked—in a different one. Co-op City has received barely a mention in histories of the city. Although Co-op City was Robert Moses's final large project in New York City, the development is all but ignored in Robert Caro's magisterial biography of Moses.[74] Even more recent work that has sought to recuperate Moses's reputation has referred to Co-op City only in passing.[75] Histories of the Bronx generally confine their brief discussions of Co-op City to how it affected other parts of the borough rather than as a place in its own right.[76] Roberta Gold's inspiring history of New York's forgotten tenant activism spends a scant three pages on Co-op City, despite the fact that Co-op City's residents were responsible for the largest rent strike in US history.[77] Kim Phillips-Fein's superb account of the New York City fiscal crisis sheds light on how New York's less fortunate residents resisted the city's turn to austerity in the mid-1970s. She mentions Co-op City once, in passing, and does not discuss the rent strike at all, even though it virtually coincided with New York City's financial crisis and occurred for similar reasons, and (as chapter 3 will discuss) the two crises each played a role in the other's misfortune.[78] Matthew Lasner's excellent study of cooperative and condominium housing similarly spends less than a page on Co-op City.[79] Even Joshua Freeman's history of social democratic New York confines its discussion of Co-op City to four pages.[80] Given Co-op City's sheer size, much less its status as one of the most ambitious urban projects in American postwar history, its absence from the history of New York is both striking and curious.

The reasons for Co-op City's failure to penetrate these histories of the city lies in a combination of factors, including both the changing fashions in urban planning and, relatedly, the dominant narratives of American urban history. Just as Co-op City was first conceived in 1964, urban planners were in the process of revising their ideas about the purpose of planning and the ideal of the city. The new vision of the city that captured the minds of planners is often associated with the figure of Jane Jacobs.[81] Contrary to the diagnosis of urban catastrophe that motivated the proponents of urban renewal, Jacobs argued that the true scourge of the city was urban renewal itself, whose bulldozers destroyed vibrant communities. Jacobs attacked urban renewal on several fronts. First, she defended the diversity and sense of community in older neighborhoods. Second, she argued that the high-rise towers the UHF was so proud of lacked the human scale that these established neighborhoods possessed and which was essential to the development of a sense of community. Finally, she criticized the "totalizing," indeed totalitarian, ethos that governed urban renewal and neglected voices from the communities affected by municipal projects. Jacobs's 1961 manifesto, *The Death and Life of Great American Cities*, is a book with a very particular moral charge: urban neighborhoods were vibrant but fragile, and large-scale development could and often would destroy them. Thus, Jacobs argued, the true task of an urban planner should be preservationist. Urban renewal projects, she argued, would hinder rather than help the "spontaneous unslumming" process that represented the source of true urban regeneration.[82]

Jacobs was both ideologically and practically at odds with no one more than Moses. Jacobs dealt Moses his first major defeat when she and other local activists opposed his plan to build the Lower Manhattan Expressway through Greenwich Village in 1962. More important for her cause than this specific victory, she managed to channel an inchoate opposition to urban renewal's means and aims, changing the culture of urban planning to one that had to take into account the voices of residents and resisted the combination of paternalism and utopianism that had marked urban renewal initiatives spearheaded by Moses and others.[83]

The UHF was also a target of Jacobs's scorn. Peter Eisenstadt has argued that there is no necessary reason why Jacobs could not have found some common cause with the UHF.[84] The UHF and Jacobs shared a commitment to urban living, as well as a belief that communities develop and grow spontaneously. However, Jacobs and the UHF saw each other as bitter enemies. In *The Life and Death of Great American Cities*, Jacobs reserves particular contempt for the UHF's Lower East Side cooperatives. She criticizes the Amalgamated Houses for closing off their central promenade with a padlock. And she chastises the affiliated cooperative supermarket for its lack of friendliness, claiming that "a store like this would fail economically if it had competition."[85] Yet the pettiness of these complaints leads one to suspect that her opposition to the UHF may have had as much to do with Kazan's alliance with Moses as with the UHF's own work. UHF leadership, never ones to back down from a fight, critiqued Jacobs in similarly outlandish terms. George Schechter of the UHF stated, "If people live out on Jane Jacobs' streets, it is because the inside of their buildings are so unpleasant."[86] Whatever the potential for an alliance between the UHF and Jacobs in theory, in reality they were on opposite sides of the battles about the aims and methods of urban planning that raged in the 1960s.

Co-op City was not an urban renewal project. Built on the site of a former amusement park and an unoccupied swamp, it displaced no residents and was not intended to remake the center of the city. However, from the time of its first proposal, it has been a lightning rod for critics, who saw in its towers and open plazas the image of modernist alienation that they associated with the heavy hand of urban renewal. The alliance with Moses had been crucial in allowing Kazan to build the UHF into the housing behemoth it had become by the mid-1960s, but that alliance ultimately became a burden for the reputation of the UHF and the projects it constructed. Once Moses fell out of favor, the UHF did too. Rather than seeing the UHF as a champion for the needs of common people, architects and activists of the 1960s alike saw it as a symbol of everything that was wrong with the establishment and its urban vision. During a 1968 visit by Moses, Yale architecture students used Co-op City as Exhibit A for the failures of urban renewal, describing the development as "an example of the bleak, inhuman, uninhabitable masses of stone, the products of a society so distorted in its values that it can offer nothing but ugliness to its less fortunate members."[87]

Many artists, intellectuals, and professionals who deliberately avoided the siren song of suburbia were entranced by Jacobs's romantic vision of the

lively and authentic urban neighborhood.[88] Moreover, not only have urban-
ists and liberals embraced Jacobs's vision of a thriving metropolis; they have
adopted her bogeyman as well. By the 1970s and continuing to today, urban
activists and later urban historians blame urban renewal for a grab bag of
sins. The aesthetic failures of the mid-century urban renewal regime were
seen as the outward manifestation of an internal moral bankruptcy, a lack of
respect for the people who lost their homes and neighborhoods to freeways
or failed to benefit from the placement of public pools and parks. Urban
renewal had "destroyed working-class neighborhoods, uprooted and dislo-
cated communities, reinforced racial segregation, spurred suburbanization,
and furthered deindustrialization. . . . [It] reinforced the consolidation of a
spatial understanding of race, whereby cities came to be seen as black spaces
and suburbs as white ones, each severed from the other socially, physically,
and economically."[89]

The rejection of urban renewal by the left has provided a convenient ally
for those who had other reasons for disliking the social democratic city.[90] As
early as 1964, Martin Anderson's *The Federal Bulldozer: A Critical Analysis of
Urban Renewal, 1949–1962* asked skeptically whether government antipoverty
efforts had achieved their intended effect, ultimately concluding that the millions of dollars poured into urban renewal projects had merely relocated
slums, not eliminated them.[91] This critique picked up steam as the urban crisis worsened in New York and elsewhere later in the 1960s and into the 1970s
and became hegemonic in the wake of New York's near bankruptcy in the
fall of 1975. A consensus on the right found that New York's fiscal crisis was
evidence of the failure of urban liberalism—the power of public employee
unions, the extent of the welfare apparatus, the tolerance for disorder, and
the predilection for borrowing money rather than practicing sensible austerity. In the words of William Simon, treasury secretary under President
Gerald Ford, the city's financial collapse was a "terrifying dress rehearsal of
the fate that lies ahead for this country if it continues to be guided by the
same philosophy of government."[92] The expenditure of municipal dollars on
social programs was both a waste of resources, since government could not
solve poverty or social disorder, and, even worse, itself contributed to the
destabilization of the city.

In place of this discredited model of urban liberalism, right-wing think
tanks such as the Manhattan Institute and the Heritage Foundation pushed
forward what they referred to as a "new urban paradigm" based on "school
vouchers, workfare, privatization and government supported 'faith based
initiatives.'" Instead of "social engineering," conservative activists lauded
"free market 'choice,' civic order, and privatized social provision."[93] It is no

small historical irony that Jane Jacobs's left-wing optimism about the city left to its own devices found unlikely allies among neoliberals in academia and government.[94] In both cases they made the determination that mass housing developments such as Co-op City were misguided and doomed to failure, and in both cases they instead lauded and supported the efforts of private individuals and groups to remake urban neighborhoods.[95]

Even if many urban historians do not subscribe to the social or political vision of the Manhattan Institute, their work often shares a similar assumption about the supposed demise of postwar urban liberalism. If histories of the 1950s and 1960s are often about the challenges and ultimate demise of urban liberalism, histories of the ensuing decades have grappled with the costs and benefits of the ensuing post-liberal era. A number of histories of the 1970s demonstrate how the nation as a whole underwent a powerful ideological reorientation in that decade.[96] According to Thomas Borstelmann, this transition was marked by two interlocking trends: "One was a spirit of egalitarianism and inclusiveness that rejected traditional hierarchies and lines of authorities, asserting instead the equality of all people. . . . The second powerful undercurrent was a decisive turn toward free-market economics as the preferred means for resolving political and social problems."[97] Some scholars use the term "neoliberal" to refer to the governance structure that resulted from these shifts. According to David Harvey, "Neoliberalism is in the first instance a theory of public economic practices that proposes that human well-being can best be advanced by liberating individual entrepreneurial freedoms and skills within an institutional framework characterized by strong private property rights, free markets, and free trade."[98] Within the sphere of urban politics, neoliberal cities seek market solutions to social problems (to the degree they even recognize social issues as problems requiring solutions), viewing government as inefficient and corrupt compared to the invisible hand of the marketplace.[99] While the term "neoliberal" has been rightly criticized for its vagueness, the concept of neoliberal urbanism is a useful heuristic for isolating some of the most important pieces of the 1970s transition, including the rejection of large, government-sponsored projects like Co-op City.

In the wake of the austerity politics of the late 1970s, New York City, the onetime headquarters of postwar urban liberal politics, was transformed into a glittering neoliberal city characterized by finance capital, gentrification, and an increasingly intense affordability crisis for its poor and middle-class residents. Recent studies have examined the complexity of such transition and have developed a more nuanced sense of its causes, processes, and effects than have its cheerleaders in the Manhattan Institute and other precincts of the right, particularly in a body of work that has now developed to study gentrification, and which has sought to examine how the iconic residents of the neoliberal city, the so-called members of the "creative class," challenged pre-existing social and political hierarchies and alliances and generated new ones.[100]

It is within the domain of the history of race relations, in particular, that historians have offered the most brutal critique of the modern American city. On the one hand, in the aftermath of white flight, Blacks achieved positions of real political power in the nation's large cities.[101] However, these years also witnessed new forms of racial inequities and new racial cleavages. Even more than the years of New Deal liberalism, in the post-liberal era, the hypocrisy and racism of northern whites were on full display in battles over school busing and housing integration.[102] Many white ethnic members of the working class in these years grew more conservative, seeing themselves more as homeowners needing to defend their meager investments and less as workers, interested in using unions as vehicles of social mobility.[103] Meanwhile, during the course of the war on drugs and the expansion of mass incarceration, the Black proportion of the overall American prison population rose from one-third in the 1960s to over one-half by the end of the 1980s, the result of an understanding of "black urban poverty as pathological—as the product of individual and cultural 'deficiencies.'"[104] Responding to the persistence of racism and disillusioned by the slow pace of racial justice, minority groups asserted their rights more forcefully, often turning away from integrationist approaches of the past.[105]

As this sketch implies, historians of postwar urban America and New York generally accept the premise that the political and social world of postwar liberalism shattered at some point in the 1960s or 1970s, when it became supplanted by something new. Historians disagree about what, exactly, is most important about the transformation of the American city in the later part of the twentieth century: Is it the economic shift from a welfare-state politics to one that stresses self-reliance and public/private partnerships? Is it about the shift from cities dominated by whites to ones with a more racially diverse leadership? Is it about the heightened tensions between a more assertive and diverse minority population and a defensively minded ethnic white working class? Is it about the "revitalization" of the city by a new "creative class" of entrepreneurs, artists, and intellectuals? Was the postwar city killed by an unresponsive and callous federal government? Or did it die as a result of natural causes—that is, of its own internal dynamics? However much historians debate the contours and causes of the 1960s/1970s urban paradigm shift, the fact that such a shift occurred is generally accepted as fact.

It is hard to locate Co-op City in the landscape of the neoliberal city. Co-op City is situated neither in the urban core nor in the suburbs. Its residents are not the up-and-coming creative class revitalizing moribund neighborhoods, but nor are they the poor who have been displaced by these would-be saviors. While some of Co-op City's white residents did become more conservative during the school fights of the early 1970s, it was more common for them to look for compromise. Co-op City's Black Caucus similarly eschewed conflict and generally sought accommodation with the white majority in the development. Even during the development's most anxious days in the 1980s and 1990s, it never faced the disinvestment of the state or reached the depths of despair common in other precincts of the city. Co-op City's story is not one of urban collapse or the flight from the city. Nor is it the story of urban renaissance paid for by federal grants, gentrifying artists, or public-private partnerships.

The few mentions of Co-op City in the existing literature generally try to shoehorn it into a narrative about the inevitable demise of postwar urban liberalism, of which Co-op City is a highly visible monument, rather than offering a true accounting of the actual history of Co-op City as a community. For example, the Bronx historian Evelyn Gonzalez casts the development's early occupants as "fearful white Jewish" villains whose move to Co-op City undermined the "rich and integral fabric of Bronx neighborhoods."[106] However, as chapters 1 and 2 will demonstrate, Co-op City's early history was at one and the same time defined by white flight and an earnest attempt to create a multiracial community. Roberta Gold's history of tenant activism linked Co-op City's rent strike to the fact that its planners "paid little heed to [the] principles of progressive planning," explaining that "its gigantism fostered class segregation."[107] And yet, as chapters 3 and 4 of this book reveal, there is no evidence that tenant activism was in any way hindered by a lack of "progressive planning" or that class segregation was a serious problem in this exclusively working- and lower-middle-class development. If anything, the opposite was true, as densely packed high-rises proved an ideal terrain for political organizing. Although sympathetic to its ambitions, Joshua Freeman calls Co-op City "a literal and figurative quagmire," the "Vietnam of the cooperative housing movement."[108] Yet if Co-op City did indeed signal the end for the UHF, the reality for the people who lived in it is substantially more complex.

The history of Co-op City reveals that the transition to the neoliberal city said to occur in the aftermath of New York's mid-1970s fiscal crisis was neither as abrupt nor as complete as many historians believe.[109] The persistent insistence of Co-op City's residents that the development could and should be a color-blind, multiracial community provides one example of the complexity of this transition. Co-op City's demographic history roughly parallels that of New York City, from being a majority white development in the early 1970s to becoming majority nonwhite within the ensuing two decades. Yet its transition was generally less fraught than the changes in many other outer borough neighborhoods in which a population of working- and middle-class ethnic whites was supplanted by new groups. In part that was because unlike elsewhere both in New York and in other cities, Co-op City residents were not homeowners, and new residents were not of a different class background from older ones. The relative class homogeneity in Co-op City played a role in modulating its racial transition.

Across this demographic transition, Co-op City's leaders and many residents continued to vocally and enthusiastically support the idea that Co-op City was a place in which people of all racial backgrounds could live harmoniously with one another. In the mid-twentieth century, such racial liberalism was embraced by both Jews and Blacks who saw in it the potential for their acceptance or integration into mainstream (read: white) American society. According to many historians, racial liberalism was supposedly tested and supplanted as part of the collapse of urban liberalism in the 1960s and 1970s, as white ethnics became more conservative, interested in defending their meager privileges against supposedly undeserving minorities, and as the leaders of nonwhite groups became frustrated with the failure of racial liberals to make sufficient progress against prejudice and segregation.[110]

Yet racial liberalism endured in Co-op City long past its supposed expiration date. Black leaders in the 1980s referred to Co-op City's multiracial harmony in terms that were little changed from those that white leaders used two decades earlier. Academics tend to dismiss "color blindness" as, at best, naïve, and at worse as an alibi for ignoring continuing racial disparities and prejudice. It is undoubtedly true that pretending that any community or any policy can truly be race neutral ignores the structural legacies and realities of racism in the United States.[111] It is also undoubtedly true that the rhetoric of racial liberalism in Co-op City could easily curdle into a facile refusal to take seriously ongoing racial disparities in New York City and beyond. And yet it is also important to take seriously the durability of the appeal of such a rhetoric across time and among people of different racial backgrounds in Co-op City, as well as take seriously how this rhetoric both helped and hindered race relations in the community. Racial liberalism enabled Co-op City residents to build a multicultural community that they are justifiably proud of, but it also made it hard for them to talk about the ways in which this community fell short of that ideal.

The history of Co-op City reveals that the contestation between postwar liberalism and neoliberalism in the American city is ongoing in other ways as well, its temporality both jagged and uneven. On the one hand, the "moral obligation" debt financing that funded Mitchell-Lama projects was a precursor to the public-private funding model that would come to be seen as a hallmark of neoliberalism, revealing the roots of neoliberalism in the era that it supposedly supplanted. On the other, the continued persistence of urban liberalism in New York was due in no small measure to the activism of New Yorkers who fought both economic crisis and state-sponsored austerity measures and continued to subscribe to the urban liberal belief in the obligations owed by the city to its residents. Nowhere was this activism more visible and, arguably, more successful, than in Co-op City.

Co-op City's rent strike in 1975–76 coincided with the city's broader fiscal crisis. It was one of a series of protest movements against the coming austerity regime by the ordinary New Yorkers who had previous benefited from the city's largesse—the students who attended the CUNY system and used it as a ladder to the middle and upper classes, the municipal employees who had found job security and stability working for the city's sprawling bureaucracy, and the neighbors stunned by planned cuts to municipal services like the fire department and local libraries.[112] Co-op City residents in many cases overlapped with these groups—they were disproportionately likely to be employed by municipal unions, and if they had attended college, that college was most likely part of the CUNY system.

And yet if it proved surprisingly easy to curb the power of the city unions and the city colleges, Co-op City was significantly more difficult to tame. The irony was that Co-op City's massive indebtedness gave its residents considerable power during the rent strike. The ability of the strike's leadership—Steering Committee III (SCIII)—to withhold mortgage payments during the strike threatened the State Housing Finance Agency with bankruptcy. Co-op City was literally and figuratively too big to fail. SCIII used this leverage to force the state to the bargaining table and after thirteen long months win control of the development. However, once SCIII had assumed control of Co-op City, it also assumed control of Co-op City's debt. This debt became a millstone around the necks of Co-op City's residents, now chastised by their creditors for their irresponsibility and still unable to avoid the torturous rent increases that led to the rent strike in the first place. Co-op City became a symbol of the evils of debt, while the development simultaneously became a victim of the politics of austerity that placed debt service (of a debt that spiraled further as the depth of construction defects became known in the following decade) above all other virtues, including the provision of a place to live. Co-op City's achievements in the rent strike appeared increasingly tenuous in the ensuing years. Co-op City's financially precarious situation has meant that it has been dependent both on state support and on the desire of people to live in the development. Co-op City may have been a social democratic island, but it was situated in dangerous, neoliberal waters.

Nevertheless, Co-op City's middle- and working-class cooperators weathered New York's neoliberal transition in a way that residents of other neighborhoods often did not. The Co-op City-ites who fill its towers and town houses are the people who clung to urban liberalism long after its supposed demise. Because of Co-op City's cooperative ownership structure, residents could not be forced out by speculators, but nor could they themselves reap windfall profits for "buying at the right time." In Co-op City, the vagaries of homeownership decisions made at an earlier time and for different reasons did not separate winners and losers as it did in some other neighborhoods. Moreover, irascibility was written into Co-op City's DNA. Even as the mass rallies on Co-op City's central Greenway faded as the 1970s turned to the 1980s, lawmakers continued to receive letters and Riverbay leadership continued to drive a hard bargain, ensuring that Co-op City remained affordable as so many other places in the city did not. Co-op City stands for the persistence of urban liberalism in the form of brick and mortar—defiant and uneasy—within the new New York.

CHAPTER 1

"The World's Greatest Housing Cooperative"

Building a New City, 1965–1968

On May 14, 1966, a group of New York City and State luminaries gathered in a swamp in the northeast corner of the Bronx to celebrate the groundbreaking of what Governor Nelson Rockefeller termed "the world's greatest housing cooperative."[1] Rockefeller, Bronx borough president Herman Badillo, labor leader Harry Van Arsdale, and the management of the United Housing Foundation, including Abraham Kazan, Jacob Potofsky, and Harold Ostroff, attended. George Meaney, president of the AFL-CIO, who was recuperating from recent surgery, sent a taped message of congratulations.[2] President Lyndon Johnson heralded Co-op City as "a significant development in the efforts to improve the quality of our national life."[3] The *New York Times* thanked Co-op City's founders for providing a "new lesson in creative unionism for social progress."[4] Using his customary bluntly colorful language, Robert Moses slammed the critics of the project: "Anybody with good vision, an abacus and a command of simple English can tell you that rehabilitation of existing decayed, scrofulous, rat-infested tenements is a salve, not a cure, a gesture not a confrontation."[5] Co-op City was, Moses proclaimed, a "name to conjure with."[6] A commemorative photo immortalized the smiling VIPs, shovels in hand, surrounded by a mixed-race group of children. They had much to smile about.

For the UHF, Co-op City was a chance to build "the most beautiful instant city in the history of civilization; 60,000 people in one community at one

FIGURE 2.   Co-op City groundbreaking ceremony, with a smiling Governor Nelson Rockefeller at center of photo, 1966. Amalgamated Clothing Workers of America Records, Kheel Center, Cornell University. Photograph by Sam Reiss.

time . . . a cooperative community."[7] Co-op City was three times larger than the UHF's Rochdale Village, which had been completed one year earlier. When finished, Co-op City would be a "city within the city" roughly the size of Santa Barbara, California, or Laredo, Texas.[8] For Rockefeller and Moses, Co-op City offered the chance to make a significant dent in New York's crisis of affordable housing, as well as its burgeoning social crisis. For its future residents, it offered spacious apartments with hardwood floors, views of the surrounding city, and modern amenities like central air conditioning. As Rockefeller, Moses, and Kazan celebrated their triumph, they could not have realized that this project would be the last of its kind, nor that Co-op City would find itself bedeviled by financial and social issues. Co-op City was the apotheosis of a model of urban planning that emphasized a partnership between labor and the state to create large-scale development projects. It was an approach that would not survive much longer than this cool May morning.[9]

Just a sign of the headwinds that Co-op City would face had already become apparent in the planning process itself. The project's plans met a hostile reception both within the New York City Planning Commission (CPC) and among outside critics. Many of these criticisms focused on the aesthetics of the development—especially its reliance on the "tower in a park" model, and the UHF's lack of interest in emphasizing street life in the development. Other critiques stressed the transportation issues generated by its remote location—there was no subway line that reached Co-op City, and planned bus connections appeared inadequate. Finally, a few planners and housing activists complained that the UHF's stated intent to serve only a middle-class public would both fail to impact the city's affordable-housing crisis and would render the development itself too economically and ethnically homogeneous.

After Co-op City won approval, with a few aesthetic modifications to mollify its critics, it would face still more problems. The loudest concern of Co-op City's critics, namely that no organic community would develop in the sterile high-rises, would prove to be entirely overblown. However, bigger storms were on the horizon. First, the development would be under near constant financial strain, generated by the combination of rising interest rates on Co-op City's massive mortgage and inflation in the prices of the goods and services needed to build the development. Second, in a troubling sign, on the same day that a front page article in the *New York Times* announced the contract signed between the UHF and New York City for the construction of Co-op City, another article on the front page noted the 52 percent rise in crime in New York's subways and a 9 percent rise in crime for the city was a whole.[10] The four years between the signing of the contract and occupancy would be eventful and troubling ones for urban America. The Co-op City that opened to residents in December 1968 did so in a very different New York from the one its founders envisioned in January 1965.

For centuries, the site that would later become Co-op City had been occupied by Native Americans, who dug for oysters and clams in the marshy ground and caught fish along its creeks.[11] The first contact with Europeans came when Dutch settlers arrived and bought this territory in 1643, along with much of what would become Westchester County, for axes, knives, and beads that were worth less than $9,000 in today's money. The Dutch named this new territory Vredeland, or Freeland. Shortly after the arrival of the Dutch, the English widow Anne Hutchinson, who had fled religious persecution in the Massachusetts Bay Colony and settled nearby, was killed by Native Americans.[12] Twenty years after this inauspicious start, the king of England deeded a large tract of the North Bronx, including present-day Co-op City and Pelham Bay, to Sir Thomas Pell, which Pell, in turn, allotted to ten families. By the early 1900s, the land was occupied by a small number of people, who were mostly involved in fishing. During the first half of the twentieth century, developers drew up a variety of plans for projects to occupy this area. In the 1920s, a racetrack was considered; in the 1930s, an airport was proposed.[13] However, the first major development to actually occupy the site was the Freedomland amusement park, which was owned by Webb & Knapp, a real estate company controlled by William Zeckendorf, a prominent and well-connected developer. Freedomland, which was designed by a former Disney associate, C. V. Woods, and devoted to displaying the panorama of US history, opened in 1960. It featured such historical themes as Chicago at the time of the great fire, San Francisco at the time of the earthquake, a section representing a Civil War battlefield, and another attraction that represented the mining towns of the Southwest.[14]

The park was hated by journalists and intellectuals, including Walter Muir Whitehill, who decried its "veneer of pseudo history."[15] After some initial popularity, it appears that much of the public agreed. Anticipated first-year attendance was cut by two-thirds, and by 1964 Freedomland was forced into bankruptcy. Its owners had sold their stock to Webb & Knapp in lieu of rent, and so when Freedomland closed, Webb & Knapp found itself in serious financial trouble.[16] Zeckendorf approached the UHF in June 1964 with a proposal: the UHF could purchase 415 acres of land, including the site of Freedomland as well as the surrounding marshes, for use as a housing development.[17] However, even before he could make the sale, Zeckendorf himself went bankrupt, and ownership passed to the Teamsters' Pension Fund, which had invested in the project. The Teamsters had little use for a troubled parcel of swampland in the northeast Bronx and were desperate to find a buyer.[18]

At this very moment, the UHF was looking for land for a development to follow up on its recently completed Rochdale Village cooperative. The UHF's original plan for its next project had been for a fifty-five-hundred-unit complex in an area bounded by Delancey, Allen, Pitt, and Houston Streets on the Lower East Side. This plan had foundered, because of opposition from the five thousand residents of the area who would have faced relocation. The city was still smarting from the fight over the Lower Manhattan Expressway three years earlier, and it refused to authorize a project that would result in such large-scale displacement.[19] Impressed by the opportunities offered by the Freedomland tract's size and the fact that there were no residents there who have to be relocated, the UHF enthusiastically began to draw up plans, which initially featured twenty thousand apartments and accompanying facilities.[20]

According to the UHF's vice president George Schechter, Robert Moses "was the marriage broker" who arranged the sale of the Freedomland site and its surrounding marshes to the UHF.[21] After receiving assurances from Mayor Robert Wagner that the city was willing to assist the project, the UHF signed a contract in January 1965 to purchase this parcel of land to create the Co-op City housing development. By this point, the plan for the development was 25 percent smaller than originally discussed, owing to resistance from the city regarding the size that the UHF initially planned.[22] The project had been scaled down in another way as well. The UHF's architect, Hermann Jessor, originally considered incorporating the swampy ground of the site into his plan by creating a "miniature Venice." The costs for such an ambitious plan, however, proved prohibitive.[23] Instead, like UHF's previous developments, the project consisted of high-rise towers grouped into a number of superblocks and connected by a central green space, with a waterfront park planned for the Hutchinson River shoreline. Even if scaled down from twenty thousand apartments, Co-op City was still massive. With a planned 15,372 apartments in a combination of 35 high-rise towers and 236 town house apartments, the number of apartments planned for Co-op City was larger than the number of apartments (15,061) constructed by the UHF in all its previous projects combined. In addition to housing, the original plans called for three shopping centers, each with fifty thousand square feet of retail space, an "Educational Park" (containing four elementary schools, two intermediate schools, and a high school), a fifth elementary school not on the Educational Park grounds, a firehouse, a police station, community centers, and a branch of the New York Public Library. The development would also boast its own air conditioning and power plants.[24] Once it was completed, UHF officials claimed, Co-op City would be the largest planned development on the planet.[25]

In February 1965, the UHF applied to the New York City Board of Estimate, then the body responsible for budgetary and land-use decisions, for approval of the project, along with a thirty-year, 50 percent local tax abatement.[26] At the time, the UHF believed that cooperators would pay a modest down payment of $450 per room and then monthly carrying charges of between $22 and $23 per room, which would cover both mortgage service and operating expenses. The $10 million cost of utility improvements and street construction necessary for the development would be shared by the city and the UHF, with the city bearing the responsibility for approximately

70 percent of the cost, and the UHF shouldering the remaining 30 percent, although the details of this arrangement were left to be worked out later.[27] Co-op City would also enjoy a 50 percent city tax abatement for its first thirty years of existence.[28] On July 14, 1965, the UHF signed a $250.9 million mortgage through the New York State Housing Finance Agency (HFA) for the construction of the property.[29]

Concerns about the lack of amenities and infrastructure for the "Freedom-land Tract Housing Development" began shortly after the project was first proposed in August 1964. In a memo, the City Planning Commission Division of Public Improvements noted that it would be necessary to establish bus connections to the nearby Dyre Avenue subway station (the current No. 5 train) and the Pelham Bay subway station (the current No. 6 train).[30] Two months later, in October 1964, the CPC noted just how difficult and necessary it would be to connect Co-op City's future residents to the subway system. Co-op City was expected to have little in the way of local jobs, and 90 percent of the wage earners in the cooperative were expected to commute elsewhere in the Bronx or Manhattan via public transit. However, the nearest subway line, the IRT Seventh Avenue–Dyre Avenue Line, was a half mile from the nearest portion of the site. Moreover, to get there required crossing over Interstate 95. Not only that, but this train and the nearby Pelham Bay Line were already over capacity. Adding another twenty thousand commuters, as planners assumed, would significantly tax these already stressed resources.[31] On this point, if on no other, the CPC and the UHF were in complete agreement.[32] Even Moses stated in his speech at Co-op City's groundbreaking, "I wish I could honestly say Co-op City had entirely adequate approaches and transportation. A subway extension is not in the foreseeable future."[33]

If all parties believed that Co-op City's dearth of public transportation was a significant problem, the UHF fiercely objected to every other critique leveled by architects and urban planners. There was much for the UHF to rebut, as Co-op City faced a firestorm of criticism from architects before even one dollar had been spent or one shovel had broken the earth. Most of the critiques focused on the development's monumental scale and lack of architectural interest. These criticisms began in the CPC itself. On November 24, 1964, Charles Smith, a CPC official, wrote a devastating critique of the original plan submitted by Jessor and the UHF one week earlier. First, he objected to the fact that the proposal included only two types of building—a tower and a slab. Second, this monotony was exacerbated by the arrangement of the buildings in superblocks, which only "emphasize[d] the oppressiveness of the slabs." Third, Smith noted that the plans appeared to include only a minimal number of consumer amenities. And finally, the development did not open up to the surrounding area and was disconnected from the surrounding street grid. In summary, Smith wrote that "this scheme is completely oblivious to the need for variety of building type, meaningful spatial relationship and use of space, and visual interest." To emphasize his point, he noted sardonically that "the best sign of encouragement comes from the architect himself [Jessor] in his note 'ENTIRE LAYOUT SUBJECT TO COMPLETE CHANGE.' To this I add: 'OF HEART?'"[34]

Once the plan for Co-op City became public, outside architects chimed in with similar critiques. In February 1965, one month after Co-op City signed its preliminary contract with the city, Percival Goodman, a Columbia University architecture professor, condemned it as a "disgrace of humanity. . . . Just because it keeps the rain off doesn't make it worthy to live in." Goodman was speaking on behalf of the Committee for Excellence in Architecture, for whom Co-op City's architectural banality rendered it an illegitimate "negation of the ideals of the great society."[35] Goodman was not alone. At an April 28 public hearing, the American Institute of Architects (AIA) charged that the spirits of Co-op City's residents "would be dampened and deadened by the paucity of their environment."[36] At the same hearing, Giorgio Cavaglieri, president of the Municipal Art Society of New York, described the plans for Co-op City as a "plain dormitory."[37] Peter Scheles of the National Council on Planning and Architectural Renewal called the proposal a "monumental failure."[38] These architects believed that to construct a massive new housing development and expect a true community to develop within its confines was naïve at best.

The UHF defended its reliance on the "towers in a park" model and praised the development's low cost as worth the sacrifice in aesthetics. Ostroff argued, "Now where is the hue and cry about what's going on in the so-called good architecture for our very high-cost housing in the City of New York? I very seldom see any of these same people coming down and protesting what's happening on Madison Avenue and on Third Avenue and on Park Avenue. . . . Why must all of these things always be borne by those least able to do it?"[39] Indeed, the UHF seemed to take an almost perverse pride in Co-op City's lack of charm. A 1966 article in the UHF publication Co-op Contact sarcastically asked residents of UHF Co-ops to send a postcard if they would agree to increase their monthly rent by two dollars per room to pay for aesthetic improvements, stating, "When housing is designed for the use of families of modest means . . . the first and primary consideration must be for providing the best possible housing at the lowest possible price. . . . Perhaps the professional planners and architects are too far removed from people of modest means to really know what their needs and desires are."[40] "We are willing to pay for something practical," Jessor added, "but we are unwilling to pay for art."[41]

For the UHF, architecture was beside the point. As Ostroff put it, "We do not subscribe to the theory that people become frustrated, alienated or dehumanized by the size and shape of buildings. What is important is for people to have the opportunity to live in dignity and self-respect with their neighbors."[42] Schechter responded to the critics of Co-op City's aesthetics with the claim that they "never understood that it isn't buildings that dehumanize people— the problem is whether the people have a sense of community."[43] Several years later, in the pages of the *Co-op City Times*, Co-op City's first director for community affairs, Don Phillips, dismissively referred to the housing as mere "bones," which required "community flesh" to become real.[44]

A second set of concerns voiced by Co-op City's early critics focused on the absence of the amenities necessary for the development of a thriving community. After the CPC approved the UHF's plans, Cavaglieri wrote an addendum to his earlier critique, in which he emphasized that the number of commercial establishments, in particular, was "not enough to assure that there will be centers of real life and activity which are necessary in this community."[45] In similar terms, the American Institute of Architects stressed the importance of creating a walkable commercial hub for the new development. Rather than shopping centers surrounded by parking, the AIA recommended the development of a pedestrian "downtown." Such a downtown, the AIA claimed, would serve as "the 'Action'—the place to rub elbows with people as is ardently desired and sung about by our youths." It would not only "bring children closer to their families," but "the convenience and ease of walking will feedback and proliferate in geometrically increasing revenues to all enterprises."[46]

The objections of both the AIA and Cavaglieri were motivated by the work of Greenwich Village–based urbanist Jane Jacobs on the ideal urban community.[47] Of course, as a newly constructed development, Co-op City could not hope to live up to Jacobs's aesthetic preference for small-scale, older buildings. In two ways, however—the emphasis on walkability and the stress on commercial institutions as the center of community—the AIA believed it could be made to conform to Jacobs's definition of urbanity. In his statement to the CPC, Ostroff recognized the appeal of Jacobs's ideas.[48] He and Jacobs shared a sense of scorn for those who believed that architects and urban planners could create community out of whole cloth, and each of them instead stressed that human values required the actions of residents.[49]

However, there was a fundamental difference between what community meant for Jacobs and what it meant for the UHF. Jacobs's famous passage about the "ballet of the good sidewalk" in Greenwich Village describes it in the following terms:

> I watch the other rituals of the morning: Mr. Halpert unlocking the laundry's handcart from its mooring to a cellar door, Joe Cornacchia's son-in-law stacking out the empty crates from the delicatessen, the barber bringing out his sidewalk folding chair. . . . It is time for me to hurry to work too, and I exchange my ritual farewell with Mr. Lofaro, the short, thick-bodied, wide-aproned fruit man who stands outside his doorway a little up the street, his arms folded, his feet planted, look-ing solid as earth itself. We nod; we each glance quickly up and down the street, then look back to each other and smile. . . . All is well.[50]

For Jacobs, urban community was experiential. The spontaneous encoun-ters of urban life were what generated authentic communities, and there was no more important site for these encounters than the small-scale com-mercial byways of the street. Commercial activity was important because it provided opportunities for neighbors to meet one another and interact with shopkeepers, whose presence provided the backbone for the development of community.

For the UHF, the experience of shopping that was so important to Jacobs was nearly irrelevant. Ostroff emphasized the political education afforded by cooperative consumerism: "As producers many men and women have learned the values of acting together to improve their social and eco-nomic positions. More and more people are learning they possess another power—as consumers. Workers must also be organized as consumers if the gains they make as producers are going to be real."[51] Cooperative activists at the UHF and elsewhere instead stressed that shopping was a political act, and were proud of the fact that Co-op City would be occupied by a host of cooperatively owned stores. Jacob Potofsky, president of the Amalgam-ated Bank, which worked closely with UHF, explained that the resident of Co-op City should "buy in our co-operative food stores. He buys his furni-ture in a co-operative furniture store. He buys his cosmetics and drugs in a co-operative drug store. . . . He opens his account in the Amalgamated Bank, which is union owned. . . . We have our own insurance company."[52] Furthermore, cooperative consumption was important because it allowed cooperators to save money. As one article explained, "The stimulation of cooperative food societies, credit unions, a furniture center, pharmacies and optical centers and similar efforts are considered by Foundation leaders to be not only sound projections of the cooperative philosophy but also sources of continued savings for members"[53]

In addition to shopping in an appropriate manner, the UHF believed, residents required training to develop the right kinds of cooperative behavior in order to create the kind of community they prized. *Cooperative Housing,* published by the National Association of Housing Cooperatives, of which the UHF was by far the largest member, explained the role of the orientation sessions offered by the UHF to new families at its cooperatives: "The families who come to these orientation sessions are attracted by something else. Even if they don't know what co-ops are, they have an image of a "co-op" community as a pretty good place to live—where people treat each other with respect as well as having something to say about the place. . . . UHF leadership is determined to create a new kind of co-op owner in Co-op City (as well as in other co-op communities it has sponsored)."[54] In other words, the UHF was less interested in social engagement as such and more interested in teaching its members to engage with one other appropriately to create a better kind of communal bond.

This idea of an educated and politicized community stood in a certain amount of tension with the more organicist views of community sometimes articulated by UHF officials. For example, as expressed in an article in the *Co-op City Times,* the UHF's newspaper in the development, in 1967, commercial and other public spaces were the outcome of a community-building process, rather than the arena where communities were forged:

> People entering for the first time cooperative communities like Co-op City often wonder why everything isn't all figured out ahead of time: swimming pools, churches, synagogues, nursery schools and the like. The answer rests in understanding how dynamic communities are built. Without a doubt, the UHF with all its experience and "know hows" could do everything before the first resident moves in. But an added element in the Foundation's experience . . . related to its understanding of what Cooperation itself is all about . . . is that the community is a stronger and more vital one when the people who live in it take the responsibility and have a major share in planning and organizing community activities.[55]

However, in each case—whether community was built by educating cooperators or by the alchemy of cooperators coming together to determine their best interests—the UHF rejected the belief that Co-op City's admittedly sterile architecture determined its fate. Furthermore, it insisted that Co-op City neither required nor wanted a "downtown" to serve as the "Action," as formulated by the AIA. The "Action" they wanted was not the shopkeeper engaging with the shopper, but a community election. As Ostroff sought to explain to the CPC the "true democracy" that developed in UHF cooperatives, he described a recent election in Rochdale Village: "Over 3,600 individual people representing their families came down and voted. . . . Atmosphere there was something that would warm anyone's heart because here you saw people living truly together, taking a part in the destinies they had to face and trying to solve some of their own problems together."[56]

Like its critics, the UHF was also interested in the walkability of its developments. However, rather than emphasizing the urban flaneur's leisurely stroll through city streets, the UHF emphasized the ease of getting from one place to another and the possibility of avoiding busy urban thoroughfares. An article in *Cooperative Housing* explained, "[The street] tends to divide families . . . from each other. Children can only have a little backyard instead of having use of a large central green. . . . Adults tend to drive away to other parts of the city rather than staying home and enjoying their own property. Such a community is 'street' oriented rather than 'community' oriented. Public streets tend to fragment a community. They should be minimized in the heart of a real residential community."[57] While Jacobs saw the city streets and bustling sidewalks as the site of community formation, the UHF believed that streets and communities existed in opposition. The goal in each case was community, but the means of getting there and the aesthetics of the resulting neighborhood were substantially different.

Finally, the social makeup of the community received some scrutiny from Co-op City's critics. While the UHF hoped to build a quasi-utopian bridge to a better world on the Freedomland site, the goals of the CPC were substantially more prosaic. It saw the UHF as a tool toward creating adequate, affordable housing. The city hoped to broaden the development from a middle-class preserve to one that provided subsidized housing to a mixed middle-class and poor constituency. As early as November 1964, Richard Bernstein at the CPC commented with concerns about the lack of ethnic diversity in the development. He noted with alarm that previous projects created with public funding had only 3 percent nonwhite occupancy, and he argued that "if we are striving for integrated communities . . . every available type of financing technique must be used to achieve a varied range in rentals."[58] From the point of view of Bernstein, racial and economic diversity were inextricably linked. In the words of another memo from the CPC, "economic integration may well be the only positive approach to ethnic integration."[59] In order to achieve ethnic integration, Bernstein and the CPC were perfectly willing to jettison the UHF's insistence on an exclusively middle-class cooperative.

It should be no surprise that the UHF strenuously objected to Bernstein's conclusions. In fact, rather than seeing economic homogeneity as a weakness, the UHF saw it as an absolute requirement. The leaders of the UHF were not opposed to a racially diverse community, but they were fundamentally opposed to using economic diversity as a means to achieving it. As an article in the *Co-op City Times* stated, "The general philosophy of cooperatives—based on the traditional self-help ideas of the Rochdale Pioneers—has been antagonistic to programs which 'do something for others' without involving repayment or the assumption of individual responsibilities. . . . Cooperators, while sympathetic with the goal [of rental assistance,] point out that the very idea of cooperation is inimical to such programs within cooperatives."[60] For the UHF, the important thing about Co-op City was that it was a cooperative. One of the UHF's bedrock principles was that all members bought into the cooperative on equal terms, as this was the requirement for their ability to share ownership equally. However, for city and state officials, Co-op City's importance lay in the fact that it was affordable housing. The alliance among the UHF, New York State, and New York City that had persisted over the past decade was based on the fact that these two goals—affordability and shared ownership—had dovetailed over that period. However, neither side had changed what it wanted—the UHF would never be convinced that it was building mere housing, and the state and city would never fully support the cooperative model as a goal unto itself. Now, these two goals appeared in conflict.

These tensions and the objections of both the planning establishment and the architectural community were not enough to overcome the combined support of Moses, Mayor Wagner, and Governor Rockefeller. On May 12, 1965, the CPC unanimously approved Co-op City's plan with no major alterations. Contrary to the accusations of the AIA and others, the CPC found that the development was not designed on an "inhuman scale."[61] In response to the concerns about transportation, rather than calling for an extension of subway service, the CPC recommended instead an industrial park be built nearby that might provide jobs to residents. It rejected concerns about economic homogeneity, stating that there would be a wide range of rental prices (which proved false). It used the example of Rochdale Village, which was 20 percent nonwhite, a percentage similar to that of the city as a whole, to claim that Co-op City would be racially diverse. And it more broadly rejected the suspicion, even voiced by its own staff, that large-scale housing developments should be abandoned in favor of smaller projects, stating that "these matters have been studied over a period of years and should be the subject of continued comprehensive and intensive study. In the meantime, we must try to build housing accommodations as best we know how, to meet the urgent needs of our citizens for decent living."[62]

The approval of Co-op City by the CPC may have been a foregone conclusion, given the political support the project had at the highest levels of state and city government. However, what emerged from the initial planning process was a sense that this approval was begrudging at best. Co-op City flew in the face of many of the emergent principles of architectural planning in the mid-1960s: it was huge when small scale was prized; it emphasized politics and education in its understanding of social relations at a time when a consumer model was ascendant; it was homogeneous (economically if not necessarily racially) at a time when heterogeneity was increasingly important; and it was located on the fringe of the city, just as the urban core was beginning to be rethought and revitalized. As such, it was intensely disliked by many within the planning and architectural establishment. In 1965, these planners and architects did not have the clout to stand in the way of major political figures such as Rockefeller, Moses, or the big-labor supporters of the UHF. However, Co-op City's critics were ascendant, and the luminaries who gathered for Co-op City's groundbreaking were not.

Controversial as approval from the city had been, once it was in hand, the UHF began to advertise for Co-op City's future residents. As it had done with previous developments, the UHF spread the word among the city's labor unions. Furthermore, in an attempt to reach as wide a pool of applicants for the massive development as possible, advertisements were also placed in city newspapers. A display in the lobby of the union-owned Amalgamated Bank headquarters in Manhattan was designed to stimulate interest in the new development.[63] In any case, the UHF did not need to do much to drum up interest in Co-op City. On February 10, 1965, the first day the project was announced, 1,698 people lined up outside the UHF's offices on Grand Street. Less than two months later, the UHF boasted 14,700 applications for the 15,372-apartment development.[64] The following year, the UHF opened a new office, at 309 West 23rd Street, solely to process Co-op City applications. Applicants could write or call and request an application, which they then sent in by mail, along with a $500 check toward their apartment equity deposit. Co-op City apartments were open to all—regardless of race, job, or current living situation—provided that they could pay the $450-a-room equity deposit to enter the cooperative and met Mitchell-Lama income guidelines mandating that they earn no more than seven times the carrying charge on Co-op City's apartments, which in 1965 was projected to be $22 a room.[65] Once a set of buildings began construction and apartments

FIGURE 3. Co-op City application office, 1960s. Amalgamated Clothing Workers of America Records, Kheel Center, Cornell University.

FIGURE 4. Co-op City application office, 1960s. Amalgamated Clothing Workers of America Records, Kheel Center, Cornell University.

were ready for assignment, applicants came in person to select an apartment and pay the balance of the equity they had due.⁶⁶

The UHF began to construct its utopia in the marshes of the northeast Bronx. As part of this process, on the other side of the city, a total of five million cubic yards of sand was dredged offshore from Coney Island and taken by barge to a staging area on City Island, off the mouth of the Hutchinson River. From there it was pumped under and up the river to the building site, to complete the landfill on the marshy parcel. Meanwhile, huge pilings were driven down to the rocks under the swamp in order to support the enormous weight of Co-op City's residential skyscrapers.⁶⁷

While the dredging would go on for two years, construction proceeded quickly. By late 1966, the first of the towers began to rise. And by April 1968, pilings for all thirty-five high-rises had been driven.⁶⁸ But however fast the construction process was, it was not quite fast enough, as two issues that had not been on the horizon during the initial planning process—the worsening crisis of the West Bronx and the worsening economic crisis of the nation—would arise in the years between the initial planning process and Co-op City's first occupants in December 1968. These issues would each leave an indelible imprint on Co-op City.

FIGURE 5.   Co-op City site, January 1967. New York City Municipal Archives.

Between Co-op City's planning process and the period when the development began to actively solicit residents, John Lindsay was elected mayor. Lindsay later became a lightning rod for critics who saw him as responsible for the social and labor conflicts, as well as economic chicanery, that ultimately consumed his mayoralty.[69] However, at the beginning of his tenure, Lindsay represented a sense of change and optimism in the city. A progressive Republican, Lindsay came into office with the support of the Manhattan white elite and the city's poorer minorities, and was often viewed suspiciously by working- and middle-class white New Yorkers, especially those who lived in the outer boroughs.[70] He was also unafraid to confront the unions that made up the leadership of the UHF and much of the population that lived in its cooperatives. And finally, Lindsay was suspicious of Robert Moses and the urban renewal "bulldozer" policies that he, and the UHF, championed.[71] As a result, it was probably no surprise that the new Lindsay administration would come into conflict with the UHF and its plans for Co-op City. This conflict primarily focused on issues of race—both the racial makeup of the development itself, which had been a concern during the initial planning process, and the impact that the departure of Co-op City's middle-class Jewish residents would have on the neighborhoods they left behind, which had not. As Lindsay administration officials realized that Co-op City would contribute to white flight from the Grand Concourse, they would come to see the problem of white flight in general in different terms. Rather than attempting to keep whites in the city, even if they moved to new neighborhoods—the policy that had been followed prior to 1965—some officials within the Lindsay administration would begin to see neighborhood preservation as key. They believed it was crucial to keep neighborhoods racially and economically mixed, and Co-op City's attraction for the Jews of the West Bronx was a major threat to this goal.

During the CPC approval process, one of the UHF's selling points for Co-op City was that it would keep New Yorkers from leaving the city altogether, while allowing them to leave decrepit apartments. In his statement at the April 28, 1965, CPC hearing, Ostroff insisted that "if we are to become a City truly integrated economically, racially and in every other way, we must find a place for our younger middle-income families to remain in decent housing in decent surroundings in our City. Otherwise all we will be doing, in effect, is encouraging the building of Levittowns all around the City of New York, rather than to create communities within the City of New York."[72] The CPC agreed. Bernstein's otherwise quite skeptical 1964 analysis of the plan for Co-op City began with the "basic assumption . . . that a substantial number of future residents of Freedomland represent an increase in population in New York City, either as in-migrants or persons who, if such facilities were not supplied to them, would leave the city."[73] For Bernstein and the CPC more generally, the fact that Co-op City would counteract white flight from the city was one of its great strengths. Governor Rockefeller agreed as well, and his support for the expansion of funding to the Mitchell-Lama program was based on his belief that it was necessary to keep the middle class from leaving New York.[74] Furthermore, the UHF and CPC planners alike appreciated that the Co-op City plan did not involve removing existing communities from the building site, since it was occupied solely by the defunct Freedomland amusement park and a swamp.[75]

The only person to offer a starkly different perspective was Roger Starr, executive director of the nonprofit Citizens Housing and Planning Council, who testified before the 1965 CPC hearing on Co-op City. Starr was otherwise a supporter of the project, dismissing concerns about architectural monotony as unrealistic. But he was deeply worried about the apartments that would be left vacant by residents who departed for Co-op City: "What will happen when the people move out of those apartments and into Co-op City is that the landlords . . . will unquestionably try to get 15 percent rent increases . . . and this will mean that the new arrivals will have to overcrowd them illegally."[76] Despite the best intentions, the construction of Co-op City, Starr implied, would only worsen rental situations elsewhere in the city. Yet even here, Starr was not speaking about the viability of neighborhoods per se, but rather about the affordability of apartments. Even Bronx borough president Herman Badillo, who would later become the public official most concerned about Co-op City's impact on the rest of the Bronx, said nothing about this concern at the spring 1965 hearings. Instead, his testimony focused on the need for adequate community facilities to be provided in Co-op City and the surrounding area, the desire for a local industrial area to provide jobs to residents, and the need for improved transit facilities.[77]

Soon after the CPC issued its approval in May of 1965, public officials and others would begin to pay more attention to the neighborhoods of origin of Co-op City's applicants. While in 1965, officials spoke of Co-op City as a means to counteract white flight—an implicit acknowledgment that it would be populated mostly by white residents—less than a year later, city officials began to be concerned about what the departure of so many white residents would do to the neighborhoods they left behind. In early 1966, Deputy Mayor Robert Sweet sounded the alarm that this massive exodus of Jews would significantly destabilize the already precarious neighborhoods that they were leaving.[78] In particular, he expressed concern about the West Bronx neighborhood near the Grand Concourse and Fordham University.

Today it has become conventional wisdom that the migration of Jews from the Concourse to Co-op City "helped undermine the rich and integral fabric of Bronx neighborhoods."[79] So what were these neighborhoods, and who were these Jews? And is this conventional wisdom actually correct? The actual story is, as always, more complicated.

For much of the twentieth century, the West Bronx had been a symbol of prestige, especially for the Jews who inhabited the neighborhoods

FIGURE 6.   Apartment building at 1116 Grand Concourse, between McClellan and 167th Streets, in 1968. Courtesy of the Bronx County Historical Society Research Library.

surrounding the Grand Concourse, which bisected the west side of the borough from roughly north to south. The Grand Concourse is located to the west of Webster Avenue and stretches from Franz Sigel Park upward to the Mosholu Parkway. Large, art deco apartment buildings lined the boulevard that the 1939 WPA New York City guide called "the Park Avenue of middle class Bronx residents."[80] Through the 1950s, these residents were overwhelmingly white and mostly Jewish, with a smattering of Irish and Italians.[81] Jews had moved to the area in the interwar period, when new arrivals, often following friends and family in chain migrations, "constructed a moral and associational community" that mirrored what they had left in their older, poorer past.[82] For them, the move to the Bronx was a story of upward mobility. To live on the Concourse or even in its surrounding walk-ups was a sign that you had arrived. One observer acerbically described the Jews of the Concourse: "To confirm their faith in themselves and in America's promises, they become conspicuous consumers of silver foxes, simultaneously of learning, gift-shop monstrosities, liberal causes, and gargantuan pastries."[83] As Alfred Kazin explained in 1951, comparing the poorer Jews in the East Bronx with those of the Grand Concourse neighborhood, "It was the ambition of almost every East 'Bronxer' to some time reach the point in life where he can afford to become a resident of the West Bronx."[84]

The neighborhood's street life and temporal rhythms were set by both religious and secular Jewish culture. One resident described how the Concourse would transform on the Jewish High Holy Days. "On three days in early autumn the sidewalks were virtually obscured by families heading home from temple . . . the men in sleek black Homburgs carrying their prayer shawls in blue velvet containers embroidered with the gold Star of David. The tableaux on the street seemed to mirror the rituals that had been enacted in the synagogue just moments earlier."[85] The writer Vivian Gornick recalled that during her youth in the West Bronx, there "was Jewishness in all is rich variety. Down the street were Orthodox Jews, up the street were Zionists, in the middle of the street were shtetl, get-rich-quick Jews, European humanist Jews."[86]

By the postwar period, such Jewish enclaves were increasingly rare in New York City. As restrictive housing covenants that excluded Jews were increasingly phased out, more New York Jews moved to the suburbs after World War II. Those who stayed in the West Bronx mostly did so for two reasons: they wished to live in an urban Jewish community, or they could not afford to buy a house.[87] As Constance Rosenblum writes, "Despite its lustrous reputation, the Grand Concourse never represented an unbroken strip of elegant buildings occupied by happy and prosperous families. . . . Interspersed with those handsome Art Deco apartment houses and in many stretches outnumbering them stood large numbers of five-story and six-story walkups, home to families of far more modest means."[88] The values of the neighborhood were uniformly middle class—emphasizing education, community, family, and stability. But many of the people who lived there were of a more tenuous economic status, especially after the wealthier among them began to depart for Westchester and Long Island.[89]

The sense of anxiety in the once-secure precincts of the Concourse only increased as the neighborhood became both poorer and less white. In the West Bronx neighborhoods from which much of Co-op City's initial population was drawn, between 1940 and 1970, the percentage of whites dropped from 90 to 47 percent, the percentage of Blacks rose from 6 to 28 percent, and the percentage of Puerto Ricans rose from 3 to 25 percent.[90] Many of these new residents were poorer than the white residents who had lived in the neighborhood earlier. Furthermore, crime began to rise as well. For many longtime residents of the Grand Concourse, the first sign of the changing neighborhood came slowly, with the rise of "unfamiliar smells," "unfamiliar faces," and graffiti.[91] In 1965, a large cooperative development, Concourse Village, opened on the lower Grand Concourse, close to the Black and Hispanic neighborhoods in the South Bronx. Shortly thereafter, a doorman was murdered a block away. While the two events were not related, they were soon linked by wary residents.[92] Increasingly residents began to trade stories: "The local deli was held up at knifepoint. The owner of a candy store was held up, this time at gunpoint. Heroin produced bands of glassy-eyed kids who roamed the landscape, willing to do anything or hurt anyone in exchange for a fix."[93]

According to the Bronx historian Jill Jonnes, 1965 to 1966 was something of a turning point in this regard. She notes that a 1965 *New York Times* story about the Grand Concourse's changing demography was "affectionate and lighthearted," while a year later, another article on the same topic began by quoting a rabbi stating, "The neighborhood is deteriorating, there's no getting away from it."[94] For Jewish residents of the West Bronx, this was a replay of what had happened in other heavily Jewish neighborhoods in New York City that had changed in similar ways.[95] This was, of course, the moment that Co-op City began to solicit applications.

Housing turnover for the West Bronx areas of Morris Heights and High Bridge rose from 2 percent in 1964 to 8 percent in 1969, the first full year that residents could move to Co-op City. In the two districts, an astonishing

11 percent and 7 percent of households respectively filed applications to move to Co-op City.[96] By 1969, so many Concourse residents were moving to Co-op City that Sachs Quality Furniture store on the corner of Fordham and the Concourse created a four-bedroom "room-for-room" replica Co-op City apartment for shoppers to tour.[97] Nonetheless, journalist Roberta Brandes Gratz's claim that the development "drained other neighborhoods of the middle class" is too simplistic.[98] A 1972 HUD study on the effect of Co-op City on the rest of the Bronx found that Co-op City may have been responsible for the loss of many elderly Jews from the Concourse neighborhoods, whose options to move were generally more limited than their younger neighbors. However, it also found that many West Bronx Jews had planned to leave before Co-op City was planned, and if Co-op City encouraged this exodus and gave it a focus, charges that it alone dealt the fatal blow to the West Bronx are overblown.[99]

While Gratz and others blame Co-op City for the Grand Concourse's problems, in the stories of those who moved, it was the deterioration of their neighborhood that motivated them to leave, not the other way around. Many applicants echoed the words of Ben Schumann, a seventy-year-old union member, who wrote to ask for a place in a UHF cooperative because his "neighborhood is now unsafe for us to be out after dark. The house has deteriorated and [is] fast becoming a slum house—elevator breaks down and it takes 3 days before it is repaired; the halls, plaster peeling and not cleaned for many weeks. Many tenants have been mugged and robbed in lobby—apartments broken into—boiler breaks—therefore no hot water or heat for almost a week."[100] One new arrival to Co-op City explained that in her old neighborhood, "I was a prisoner in my own home. I felt fearful about travelling, going to the store, sitting on a bench, riding in an elevator or even relaxing in my own living room."[101] The UHF was frank that "large numbers of the applicants for Co-op City came from deteriorating areas of the city, particularly from sections of the Bronx."[102] In a 1971 survey of Co-op City residents, 44 percent cited neighborhood deterioration as the primary factor that encouraged them to move to the cooperative.[103]

There is no way to hear these quotes without wondering to what degree "deterioration" was a euphemism for race. Certainly, one does not need to look far to find evidence that many West Bronxites associated the arrival of Blacks and Puerto Ricans in their neighborhood with rising crime. One seventy-year-old who moved to Co-op City explained why he left his apartment just off the Concourse: "For over thirty years it was nice. Then, it began to change. Some people died, some moved away, *schwartzers* [Blacks] moved in and mugging, vandalism, crime was terrific."[104] Another applicant who wrote to the UHF in 1967 seeking a new apartment pleaded,

My neighborhood has completely folded up. I am the only white girl on my floor and I tremble with fear whenever I have to step into the hall. . . . Block-busters are so intent on flooding a white neighborhood with a deadly but terrible element who just happen to be Negroes in an overzealous effort to scare white people of their neighborhoods and drive them out of their homes. . . . It has happened in my house, out of 28 families, only 4 are white now. It was all white when I moved in.[105]

Statistics also show that however much many Jews on the Concourse may have been relying on racial stereotypes, crime was on the rise in the West Bronx. In the zip codes that made up the Concourse neighborhood, felonies rose 69 percent just in the year between 1968 and 1969. In the first ten months of 1969, the Forty-First Precinct, which covered the Bronx's nearby Hunts Point neighborhood, ranked first in New York City for reported burglaries, third for murders, and fourth in assaults.[106] A Bronx Planning Commission study of the elderly living on the Grand Concourse found that over one-third of them had been mugged at least once.[107] In their minds, what these Jews were escaping were crime and physical decay, not race per se.[108] Meanwhile, many early residents of different racial and ethnic backgrounds would be proud of Co-op City's status as a "melting pot"—Jews from the Concourse among them.

If these West Bronx Jews believed they were fleeing urban crisis, for city officials, the desire of middle-class whites to leave their neighborhoods was itself the crisis. On March 22, 1966, during the interlude between the approval of Co-op City's plans by the CPC and the official groundbreaking ceremony, Barney Rabinow, a CPC city planner, visited the Co-op City application office. He noted that there were already 4,500 applications for the 15,372-apartment complex. Of those, 3,397, or 75 percent, were from the Bronx. Rabinow noted that there were several areas where applicants were particularly heavily concentrated, including some blocks with as many as fifty applicants and some buildings with five to ten applicants each. The area of greatest applicant density ran the length of the Concourse, from Highbridge up to Woodlawn Cemetery.[109] One day later, Deputy Mayor Sweet wrote to William Ballard, chair of the CPC, with alarming-sounding news: "It is estimated that of the 15,500 families which will move to Co-op City as many as 11,000 may well be drawn from the middle-class predominantly Jewish community of the West Bronx generally south of Fordham Road.

Such an exodus would trigger other similar families to leave the area and induce an over preponderance of low income Negroes and Puerto Ricans to move in. Rents will increase; crowding will increase; voluntary philanthropic agencies will leave and a disadvantaged population will be left to create a spreading slum ghetto."[110]

Over the course of less than a year, Co-op City had gone from being seen as a corrective to white flight to being seen as its cause. In 1964 and 1965, during the initial planning process, the goal of the CPC had been to keep middle-class whites in the city. By 1966 and 1967, some officials were beginning to see urban crisis in neighborhood terms—the destabilizing effects of a mass exodus of Jews from the Concourse would cause the decline of the neighborhood and hence of the borough as a whole. This was not a universal opinion. In 1967, Jason Nathan, head of the New York City Housing and Development Administration, stated that "white areas are going to change anyway. . . . If we are going to keep middle class families of all races in the city, we have to provide them with adequate housing choices. Co-op City . . . [does] that."[111] Increasingly, however, officials believed that their task was "to find some way to keep enough whites from moving so as to forestall the economic forces that produce slums."[112] And increasingly they sought to do this in ways that were targeted to specific neighborhoods. Sweet wrote that "the problems faced by the West Bronx [were] to be expected in a number of other areas of the City. . . . It is recommended that a committee be formed . . . [to] formulate a positive program for dealing with such areas."[113] Several months later, Morton Isler of the CPC stressed that the city needed to provide loans and grants to renovate decaying buildings and expend more resources in code enforcement.[114] From the perspective of city officials in 1966 and 1967, it was not enough to keep middle-class whites in New York City; it was necessary to keep them in their neighborhoods. Co-op City may have been a boon to the former goal, but it was clearly a hindrance to the latter one.

At the same time, concerns about Co-op City's own racial makeup, which had been voiced in 1964 and 1965 during the initial planning process, began to mount. At Co-op City's groundbreaking ceremony in May 1966, Bronx borough president Badillo "expressed deep concern that Co-op City not become an isolated community."[115] Badillo was blunter in private remarks to Lindsay: "Everybody knows that the word 'co-op' is a synonym for 'Jewish housing.' . . . Puerto Ricans and Hispanics don't understand co-ops and don't have the money for co-ops, and neither do blacks. Therefore, if you're building a co-op, if you don't have any rental apartments, you are, in effect, creating a white enclave."[116] As a result of this meeting, Lindsay and Badillo expressed concern to the UHF that Co-op City demonstrate the appropriate degree of balance in terms of the "ethnic and economic status" of the complex.[117]

The UHF was not averse to ethnic diversity. Unlike other middle-class developers in New York, such as Met Life, which explicitly refused to accept Black tenants, the UHF was "happy, even eager to adopt non-discriminatory house policy" as far back as the 1940s and 1950s.[118] In 1956, Henry Lee Moon, director of publicity for the NAACP, resident of a union cooperative in Queens, and a future board member of the UHF, was quoted in the *Co-op Contact*, "It's good for a child to grow up with knowledge and consciousness of people of various races, creeds, religions and backgrounds."[119] Looking back on the history of cooperatives, the *Cooperator* magazine proclaimed, "No one is excluded. The Finns, The Bohemians, the Jews, the Negroes, the Puerto Ricans, the Italians, the Irish, the English, the Chinese. . . . We've seen brotherhood work all year round in the cooperatives; from *that* perspective we have many things to teach our brothers who have not yet entered the cooperative fold."[120] Despite this rhetoric of inclusion, and although anyone with the required equity deposit could apply to their cooperatives, the fact that information about the cooperatives primarily spread by word of mouth, starting with labor unions, and the fact that the cooperatives were located primarily in Jewish neighborhoods, meant that in practice most residents of UHF cooperatives were Jewish, or involved in the labor movement, or both.[121]

By the 1960s, the UHF's leadership had come to recognize the gap between the rhetoric of integration and the homogeneous population that actually lived in their cooperatives. In Rochdale Village, which was planned in the late 1950s and opened for residents in 1961, the UHF consciously planned to encourage integration. The centerpiece of this effort was the building of several schools, which served both Rochdale's predominantly white residents and the surrounding predominantly Black neighborhood. UHF leaders hoped that the fact the cooperative was more than twice the size of any of their previous developments would mean there would be more space open for applicants who did not arrive through word-of-mouth recruitment in labor circles. Because Rochdale was located near heavily Black Jamaica, Queens, the UHF hoped that more Blacks would be encouraged to apply. Moreover, the UHF advertised widely in the hopes that it could obtain a balanced applicant pool without the use of strict quotas.[122] While hard numbers are impossible to come by, Rochdale was approximately 80 percent white (mostly Jewish) and 20 percent Black when first occupied in 1963, a percentage that mirrored the demographics of New York as a whole in the 1960s.[123]

Kazan and other UHF officials repeatedly described Rochdale as a model for urban integration. In Rochdale, "children share the same play areas, attend the same schools . . . adults participate in the same community activities. . . . Volumes of all kinds of theories are being written about how to achieve better human relations. However, if we could concentrate our efforts on one phase—housing—we would be attacking the root of our other problems."[124]

At Co-op City's ceremonial groundbreaking, Amalgamated Bank's Potofsky proudly announced that residents of this new community "come from all walks of life . . . represent all races, creeds and colors . . . [and] use the same schools, the same stores and the same churches."[125] Repeatedly, Co-op City officials emphasized that "Co-op City is an open city, open to all people with various backgrounds both racially and ethnically."[126] The much-publicized awarding of the first apartments included a Black family, the "Leroy Smiths."[127] The UHF's application did not contain any questions that referenced race or religion.[128] An article about the application office that appeared in the Co-op City Times in 1967 exulted that "one of the delights of the eye is to notice the number of applicants of various ethnic backgrounds and occupations."[129] In interviews with multiple Black residents who applied and moved in to Co-op City in this period, none of them spoke about encountering racial prejudice in the application process. However, this was not Rochdale, which had been conceived in 1961 and first occupied in 1963. Whereas integrating Rochdale had been a tentative partnership between the UHF and the city, when it came to Co-op City, the UHF found itself at loggerheads with municipal officials and public pressure groups.

After the May 1966 meeting with Badillo and the UHF, Lindsay demanded regular reports on the location and ethnic makeup of apartment applicants. The UHF acquiesced to this demand.[130] When pushed to address the question of diversity, UHF leaders were "defensive and testy about the whole subject—repeating again that it is an open project, that more people could really afford to live in Co-op City, but how do you reach them?"[131] However begrudgingly, the UHF did make genuine efforts to reach an audience beyond the Jewish labor circles it usually appealed to. When a coalition of citizen groups in the Bronx called "Citizens Concerned about Co-op City," led by the NAACP, lobbied the UHF in 1967, the latter agreed to place advertisements for the development in the Black and Spanish press as well as send flyers to churches and other organizations prominent in the Black and Hispanic communities.[132] The UHF also distributed literature through the Urban League's Open City service.[133] At the same time, it balked at demands from community groups to reserve 33 to 40 percent of apartments for nonwhite applicants.[134]

More than anything else, the UHF was insistent on keeping its developments economically homogeneous. It vehemently resisted any attempt to rent apartments at a subsidized rate to those who could not afford the required $450-a-room equity deposit to secure an apartment. Marion Sameth, a member of the Citizens Housing and Planning Council and a supporter of the Lindsay administration's initiatives to integrate Co-op City, noted that the possibility of taking in welfare families at the new development "seems to be a very sore subject" for the UHF.[135] Sameth was correct. The UHF commitment to racial diversity was always secondary to its commitment to cooperative living and cooperative ownership. As UHF leaders saw it, to allow renters into a cooperative would destroy the very cooperative relationship that they considered the UHF's reason for existing. In an article in *Cooperative Housing* magazine published in 1965, Ostroff explained, "The members of a housing cooperatives are more than tenants. They are at the same time stockholders—the owners of a cooperative enterprise. . . . As members of a cooperative they are a part of the cooperative movement and again are invited to use the methods of cooperation in every way possible to help themselves."[136] In 1967, legislation was passed in Albany that enabled the state's Division of Housing and Community Renewal to purchase up to 20 percent of the housing in any Mitchell-Lama cooperative, with the idea that the state would then re-rent these units to low-income residents. The law required the assent of the sponsoring organization, which the UHF refused, stating that it preferred a "voluntary" approach to integration. It would advertise widely in the hopes of attracting a more diverse pool of residents, but it refused to lower the equity deposit or carrying charges that residents would pay.[137]

The idea that all members of the cooperative contribute a proportionate economic share was one that the UHF was unwilling to compromise on. In the case of Co-op City, this meant that each family was responsible for a onetime equity payment of $450 a room and then an ongoing carrying charge that was initially set at $22 a room.[138] The UHF was itself willing to make a limited number of loans to prospective cooperators, as well as assist some cooperators with receiving loans from banks and credit unions.[139] However, the UHF did not widely advertise its loan assistance programs and only informed prospective residents about them once they had submitted an application.[140] Therefore, those who were not already acquainted with the loans—in other words, those who were not associated with Jewish labor circles—may not have even applied because they did not know about the possibility of loans to assist with their equity deposit.[141] And even with this assistance, the development was out of reach for many poorer New Yorkers.

The UHF stance in the late 1960s remained the same "color-blind" but "income-sensitive" position that it had been since the organization's founding in 1951. If Black or Latino families could pay the same equity deposit, they were more than welcome to move to Co-op City; but if they could not, the UHF refused to do anything to accommodate them in the interests of creating a racially diverse community. However, what had appeared a progressive stance toward race relations in the early 1950s now appeared hopelessly inadequate and shortsighted by the standards of the Lindsay administration and the public pressure groups that pushed the UHF to adopt more proactive means of encouraging racial and economic integration.

For the Lindsay administration officials and outside groups interested in fostering residential integration in Co-op City, the UHF's claims to racial innocence were preposterous and self-serving. After all, a whole system of racial privileges—including access to the very unions from which the UHF drew much of its support—explained why whites might be more able than their Black and Puerto Rican neighbors to save the equity deposit that served as the key to access to Co-op City's low monthly carrying charges.[142] At the same time, neither the state, the city, nor any of these outside groups offered to front equity deposit funds to racial minorities. As the following chapter will discuss, in the end, Co-op City's racial demographics would be similar to those of the city as a whole. For the Blacks and Latinos who did move in, their class parity with their white neighbors was a source of pride. And for white residents, the fact that racial minorities in Co-op City were of the same class status would be one of the things that paved the way for their relative acceptance.

The UHF was not blind to the fact that there was a relationship between the appeal of Co-op City and the decline of the Grand Concourse. In Ostroff's words, "a lot of people are trying to escape from something. They are running, as so many have been running, from changing neighborhoods."[143] However, the Lindsay administration and the UHF saw the situation in fundamentally different terms. When the Lindsay administration looked at the Grand Concourse, it saw a neighborhood abandoned by middle-class white flight. As one city official put it, Co-op City had created a "vacuum in the Grand Concourse."[144] When the UHF looked at the Grand Concourse, it saw the slumlords it had been fighting for decades, who were trying to take advantage of renters. The Lindsay administration wanted to help the Grand Concourse neighborhood. The UHF believed it had a responsibility to help these people who were fleeing, and not the neighborhoods they were fleeing from.

The UHF felt pressure from other quarters. Many of Co-op City's initial Jewish residents were proud that the development was racially integrated;

however, they wanted racial integration without the barest hint that this could lead to an influx of poorer residents or crime. When the *New York Times* erroneously reported that the city was thinking of buying space in cooperative housing for poorer Black and Puerto Rican families, the Co-op City application office was deluged with hundreds of calls from applicants asking about the report, and fifty even withdrew their applications, despite reassurances that Co-op City was not part of this program.[145] For these Jews, who were a generation at most removed from the immigrant slums and who had watched their own neighborhoods decline, the idea that Co-op City could suffer the same fate was their worst nightmare. Even if many of them were not committed to the same cooperative ideals that motivated the UHF, Co-op City's Jewish applicants shared the belief that while racial integration might have been desirable, economic integration was not.

This tension between the desire of the UHF and many of Co-op City's applicants for integration on their own terms, and the desire of the city to use Co-op City to foster integration, played itself out in the ongoing discussions about the community's schools. It is not surprising that education became the battlefield for discussions of race in Co-op City. After the *Brown v. Board of Education* decision in 1954 mandated the dismantling of legally segregated schools, schools became a major flashpoint across America.[146] While New York did not have the official Jim Crow policies of the South, the nation's largest city had a school system that was often just as segregated in practice. Owing to a combination of opposition from white parents, the move of white New Yorkers to the suburbs, the growing power of New York's teachers' union, and the Board of Education's hidebound bureaucracy, New York's schools were even more segregated in the mid-1960s than they had been a decade earlier.[147]

In Rochdale Village, school integration had been both a UHF priority and an accidental reality. Because of the delayed completion of new schools in the area, Rochdale's mostly white students went to school in the surrounding, majority Black, South Jamaica neighborhood. Eisenstadt claims that, at least until 1968, school integration between Rochdale and South Jamaica was relatively successful.[148] Nevertheless, from the outset, the UHF had a different plan in mind for Co-op City. Rather than integrating Co-op City's students into schools in the surrounding (mostly white) neighborhood, the plans for Co-op City included an "Educational Park," in which the development's elementary, intermediate, and high schools would be located on a single campus within the boundaries of the cooperative. Furthermore, unlike Rochdale's schools, which were intended both for the development's residents and for their neighbors, Co-op City's schools were originally designed solely for the residents themselves, along with the residents of the nearby NYCHA Boston Secor Houses. In part, this was a gesture toward Co-op City's much greater size. A development of fifteen thousand families would be enough to populate several schools on its own. It was also a result of the mid-1960s enthusiasm in some quarters for the "educational park" model.

At the time that Co-op City was being planned, the New York City Board of Education was looking for a place where it could try out the new model of educational parks, in which multiple schools populated by students from kindergarten through high school occupied the same campus. A study of the education park carried out by the Corde Corporation explained the many benefits of the concept. In particular, it stressed that the greater size of the educational park allowed it to benefit from the "greater potential for the integration of its students. . . . The larger the attendance area, the greater the chance for student diversity and for flexibility of feeder patterns."[149] The educational park also offered the possibility of taking advantage of economies of scale. "For example, two elementary schools located on the same site can share one auditorium. The saved space can be devoted to a use neither school could have had if separated"[150] New York City Board of Education officials initially saw the educational park model as a tool for racial integration, bringing together students from multiple neighborhoods to a neutral site. However, the board was also forced to abandon the site it was most interested in, Ocean Hill–Brownsville, owing to community resistance, led by the Reverend Milton Galamison, who would later famously lead the movement for community control of education in that district.[151]

Yet if the educational park concept was rejected by Ocean Hill–Brownsville, it was eagerly embraced by the UHF for Co-op City. The emphasis on size as a positive good was something the educational park concept shared with the UHF's model of urban housing, and would ultimately be part of what endeared this concept to the planners of Co-op City. The Northeast Bronx Educational Park was to be Co-op City's crowning achievement. It would offer an elite education and also be the center of community life. The Educational Park was so important that when construction delays began to mount, the city would borrow funds from the state to allow the UHF to build the park itself, becoming the first private entity to build public schools in New York City, an arrangement that required special permission from the state legislature.[152]

Several features made the UHF especially interested in the educational park concept. First, Co-op City's residents were promised the very latest in educational trends: "individualization of learning—open classrooms,

FIGURE 7. The Northeast Bronx Educational Park under construction, December 1970. AP photo / Jim Wells.

flexible groupings of pupils and modern educational techniques and technologies."[153] UHF leaders waxed rhapsodic about the possibilities available when students were grouped by ability rather than age: "Elementary school children who were talented in music would be integrated into the orchestra, bands and choral groups of the senior high school. Mathematical geniuses would leave their elementary age classmates and work together with older students on a par with them in mathematics. Similar ability groupings would be established for language skills, the arts and other fields of talent."[154] The UHF also appreciated the new amenities that were to be included in the Educational Park, including "an observatory, a planetarium, a museum, swimming facilities and a small theatre."[155] Because the Educational Park would otherwise produce cost savings through the use of shared facilities across schools, the budget for the Northeast Bronx Educational Park, located in Co-op City, even with these amenities, was no more than $2.5 million above the cost of building the schools individually. And both the city and the UHF considered the extra costs justified because of the "great many additional community facilities that would not be included in separate schools."[156] As this statement implies, the educational park was designed to be much more than a collection of schools; it was also expected to be "a center of community pride and of community service, thus contributing to the effectiveness of the integrated school experience."[157] For the UHF leadership who saw the idea of pedagogy as intrinsic to their very vision of community, the idea of a school serving as a center for the community was deeply attractive.

Finally, Co-op City's Educational Park was not only appreciated for what it included. It was also appreciated by the UHF, and by many residents, for what—or rather *whom*—it did not include. One of the original appeals of the educational park concept was that it was a means toward integrating neighborhoods with each other. According to one critic at the Board of Education, with the planning for the Northeast Bronx Educational Park, the concept had shifted from "integration" to "quality education"—in his eyes a justification for continued segregation.[158] Co-op City's promotional materials stressed the existence of the Educational Park in a "centrally located campus setting"—emphasizing its bucolic appearance and convenience to Co-op City residents, and Co-op City residents alone.[159] While Co-op City officials did note that "students were to be integrated racially and ethnically," it was unclear exactly what this meant in practice, and the UHF provided no clear plan for achieving such integration.[160] When the New York City civil rights commissioner, William Booth, recommended locating the Northeast Bronx Educational Park outside of Co-op City, Ostroff and Jessor reacted vehemently.[161]

A second set of developments intertwined with these social concerns and would also prove to be equally, if not more, important for Co-op City's future. Co-op City's affordability was based on assumptions made in 1965 and 1966 about the cost of labor and the interest rate on its mortgage bonds—assumptions that proved very quickly to be overoptimistic. In 1968, as construction was in full swing, Ostroff reported that costs were already spiraling out of control in the construction of the town houses.[162] The town houses were always a thorn in the UHF's side—as smaller structures, they were more expensive to construct per unit than the skyscrapers that the UHF favored, and the UHF had only authorized them as an experiment to see if they could be used to attract more families with young children.[163] Ostroff sought ways to cut costs for the town houses, including converting them from "fully fireproof" to "semi-fireproof" structures.[164] However, the town houses were not the only cause of construction overruns. The landfill of the site required an additional three hundred thousand cubic yards of fill above the original estimates. By 1968, rising interest rates had become a problem as well. Co-op City was financed by HFA mortgage bonds, which were sold on the open market. HFA mortgage bonds sold in 1968 at an interest rate of 5.2 percent rather than the 4 percent originally forecast and the 3.75 percent they had been at as late as 1966. As a result of all of these unforeseen expenses, in mid-1968 the UHF estimated carrying cost increases of $3.00 or $3.50 above the originally planned $22 a room.[165] On September 16, 1968, Ostroff warned the UHF board to expect the cost of newly contracted work to "be considerably higher than originally estimated in the early part of 1966."[166]

The UHF's financial woes continued in 1969. New union contracts in the building trades meant that labor costs would increase between 41 percent and 51 percent for masons and bricklayers. In September 1969, Ostroff estimated that this meant that the cost of construction for Co-op City would be about 15 percent higher than anticipated in 1965, going from $267 million to $307 million. Moreover, the ongoing dramatic increases in interest rates meant that financing charges, which had been estimated in 1965 as $6.7 million, would have to be revised to $32.9 million, an increase of nearly 400 percent. The impact of the revised estimates was a $69 million or

FIGURE 8.   Apartments under construction. Undated. Amalgamated Clothing Workers of America Records, Kheel Center, Cornell University.

26.5 percent increase in the total cost of the Co-op City project.[167] A thirteen-week strike by elevator operators in the same year did further damage to both Co-op City's budget and its timeline. The lost rental income totaled only $300,000; however, Ostroff noted that the delays caused a rise in construction costs that was far higher.[168] Two days before the first cooperators moved in, Ostroff begged the CPC to allow the UHF to cut parking facilities to save money. "I most urgently plead that the Planning Commission at this time does not force us into additional capital expenses since the present cost of money provided by the New York State Housing Finance Agency is fast approaching 7%." The CPC refused.[169]

To hear Ostroff and others in the UHF tell it, Co-op City's cost overruns were a function of factors beyond its control—the inflation in the cost of goods and services, the demands of the CPC, and rising interest rates. Yet this was not the full story. Kazan later admitted that it was his "regular practice to understate construction costs on all projects. . . . Kazan [said] that if he projected construction costs realistically in his original applications [to the DHCR—the state Department of Housing and Community Renewal], he would lose bargaining power when it came time to negotiate with subcontractors and suppliers."[170] In other words, Co-op City's cost estimates (and the carrying charge figures based on them) were never realistic to begin with. The DHCR's own cost estimates were consistently higher than those Kazan provided; however, because it was fearful that higher cost estimates would lead to problems marketing the apartments, the DHCR remained silent.[171] But the understating of its costs was not the only way in which the construction of Co-op City diverged from best practices.

Construction in New York was never entirely free of corruption; however, the financing model of Mitchell-Lama housing in general, and UHF housing in particular, may have made it particularly susceptible to graft. According to the Mitchell-Lama Law, Mitchell-Lama housing allowed developers to pay for their developments with construction bonds backed by New York State (and, later New York City). This allowed builders to obtain lower interest rates than if they were solely reliant on private financing. Mitchell-Lama also reduced the tax burdens of private and nonprofit developers, offering an incentive to encourage them to build middle-income housing. The journalists Jack Newfield and Paul DuBrul claimed that since the Mitchell-Lama funding model meant that the state and the city bore the costs of construction, "builders had little incentive to resist [cost] increases. The city and state guaranteed them a fixed profit and were always willing to enlarge the mortgage as the project moved ahead."[172] Even MacNeil Mitchell and Alfred Lama, the sponsors of the initial state legislation, were themselves involved in kickback schemes related to Mitchell-Lama projects. While Co-op City was under con-struction, the State Investigation Commission held hearings on corruption in Trump Village, a Mitchell-Lama project run by Fred Trump.[173] Beyond kickbacks and other financial shadiness, the Mitchell-Lama structure also affected the quality of the apartments in other ways. Depending on whether the particular development was state or city financed, the state or city was required to "sign off" on construction jobs. According to later residents dis-mayed at the defects in their apartments, this was often done with "indecent haste," driven by the desire to fill buildings as soon as possible. Furthermore, oversight was often lacking because of a revolving door in which many pub-lic officials "graduated from public employment to jobs with the very hous-ing companies they had been supervising."[174]

If corruption was endemic to the Mitchell-Lama program in general, the UHF had a particular set of issues. Indeed, Co-op City's very origin story reflected the cozy world of real estate developers, big labor, and public offi-cialdom. The parcel of land on which Co-op City was situated had once been owned by the Teamsters Union. They had sold it to William Zeckendorf, who had built the Freedomland amusement park on the site. When Freedomland failed and Zeckendorf's firm, Webb & Knapp, declared bankruptcy, the land reverted to the Teamsters. One way of looking at the UHF purchase of the property was that the UHF was taking advantage of an opportunity to cre-ate much-needed affordable housing. From another perspective, however, the UHF was also saving Zeckendorf and the Teamsters a substantial head-ache. Furthermore, the entire parcel was not sold to the UHF. The Teamsters retained a small portion, on which they built a gas station. Later on, Charles Rosen, the 1975–76 rent strike leader, would accuse the Teamsters of keeping the "solid rock and dump[ing] the swamp on the UHF."[175] Rosen's implica-tion was that the Teamsters had kept the good part of the site to themselves while saddling the UHF with the massive landfill costs required to make their portion realize its value.

Technically speaking, the UHF did not construct Co-op City or any of its other real estate projects. Rather, it used Community Services Incorporated (CSI) as its general contractor. As a nonprofit, the UHF did not pay taxes, and there was no public oversight regarding the salaries it paid to its officials. CSI was both a for-profit company and a wholly owned subsidiary of the UHF. Kazan established CSI in 1950, a year before the founding of the UHF. CSI would "hire and supervise subcontractors and receive a 1 percent devel-oper's fee on completion of each project."[176] CSI's initial board consisted of Abraham Kazan, Jacob Potofsky, Louis Stulberg, Robert Szold, and Harold Ostroff—the very same men who sat on the UHF's board.[177] The UHF then would create a corporation to manage each of its cooperatives. In the case of Co-op City, this was the Riverbay Corporation. Following the practice used with other cooperatives built by the UHF, Riverbay then hired CSI to manage the construction process.[178] The leadership of the UHF also controlled Riverbay—indeed the very same men who controlled the UHF and CSI also sat on Riverbay's board. To make matters worse, Riverbay hired consultants from CSI/UHF without competitive bidding. Moreover, Co-op City's construction funds, which ultimately ran to nearly half a billion dollars, were held in Amalgamated Bank, which was controlled by Potofsky, who sat on the boards of the UHF, CSI, and Riverbay. According to George Schechter of the UHF, this unusual organizational structure was a cost-saving measure: "We dealt with ourselves to save money. We didn't want to farm out work to other profit-making agencies. We didn't collect any commission, just an allowance for the overhead of selling apartments. We made a profit on some of our operations and we did pay taxes. But, it was all washed out in the end."[179] However true this may have been, this was also an environment—featuring cross-cutting lines of authority and absent any transparency—tailor-made for corruption. As the state official in charge of overseeing Mitchell-Lama construction was himself a former UHF employee, this unusual arrangement received little to no oversight.[180]

One example of the irregularities that resulted from this arrangement was the construction of Co-op City's power plant. A power plant had been a feature of Rochdale Village, and Community Services hired Kazan's nephew Leon to design a similar power plant for Co-op City. Ostensibly this was an attempt to avoid Con Edison's exorbitant rates. However, the plant was a boondoggle that never actually worked during the time that the UHF controlled the development. A cooperator lawsuit claimed that it had been "designed and constructed in an ineffective and unsound manner." The rent strike leader Rosen would even maintain that turbines ordered for Co-op City's power plant wound up in a different UHF cooperative.[181] This was not the only example of potential corruption. Rather than CSI buying appliances directly from the manufacturer, as would have been customary for large housing projects, CSI hired a subcontractor whom they paid for 20,000 stoves and refrigerators for this housing development of 15,372 apartments.[182] The UHF paid CSI a $2 million flat fee for undefined "home office overhead."[183] In 1968, CSI footed the $15,000 bill (the equivalent of over $100,000 in 2020) for Kazan's retirement party.[184] The UHF placed Co-op City's liability insurance with the Urban Insurance Company, with CSI as its broker. According to Louis Nizer, who would become the cooperators' lawyer in their suits against the UHF in the 1970s, this was a way for the UHF to make a "secret profit."[185] During the rent strike, Rosen claimed, "all the deals between the UHF and its subsidiaries cost us millions of dollars. No one will ever know the exact amount because it was hidden from us, because there are all these interlocking directorates and because there was no audit. But I believe each of the rent increases we have paid was the direct result of all this internal theft. The UHF and [CSI] got rich off this development."[186] Later, Rosen would repeat, "they ran this place like a corner candy store. There is no way to even begin to discover how much was stolen."[187]

Whether cost overruns resulted from UHF corruption, factors beyond its control, or a combination of the two, the UHF was well aware that higher costs would ultimately result in greater costs to cooperators, a result that it desperately wished to avoid. Even at the very beginning of the planning process, CPC planners noted the UHF's insistence on maintaining an "arbitrary carrying charge of $21 or $22/room . . . a figure [that] in all likelihood precedes the economic analysis of the project."[188] As costs began to rise, the UHF's leaders were not concerned with what this would do to the city or state's bottom line. On the other hand, they were very worried about how rising costs would impact cooperators. A growing mortgage would ultimately result in growing cooperator carrying charges, and this threatened their very raison d'être as providers of affordable housing. As early as 1969, UHF leadership were having panicked internal discussions that rising costs would mean a minimum of a 16 percent rise in carrying charges.[189] In an attempt to brace newly arriving residents for these increases, the *Co-op City Times* explained the predicament that the UHF found itself in and asked cooperators to take responsibility, comparing Co-op City to a family, which "must live within [its] income or find additional money."[190] This explanation would not be satisfying to the development's new residents. The UHF and the cooperators—sometimes working together and ultimately in opposition to one another—would continue to search for ways to limit cooperator carrying charges.

The UHF's options were limited. In 1969, the UHF was able to convince Mayor Lindsay to authorize an increase in Co-op City's tax abatement from 50 percent to 80 percent, which kept resident carrying costs from almost doubling to a prohibitive $38 per room.[191] But the state and the city were unwilling to take more aggressive actions to assist with cost control, such as forgiving part of the mortgage itself.[192] Although this leaves few traces in UHF records, it is clear that the UHF/ CSI also cut corners in the construction process. Based on an HFA recommendation, CSI ordered two-ply rather than four-ply roof insulation. CSI also used high-voltage underground cables with a covering that was untested in Co-op City's marshy soil. Bernie Cylich, a union electrician who later moved to Co-op City and eventually became a member of the Riverbay board, later recalled that contractors used insufficient plaster in an attempt to save money, although it was unclear if this was at the recommendation of CSI or not. The desire to complete apartments as quickly as possible also meant that contractors often cut corners—Cylich recalled seeing masons allowing mortar to fill weep holes in their haste to move on to the next row of bricks, which would ultimately compromise the ability of buildings to shed water.[193]

As early as 1973, cracks began to appear in the walls of top-floor apartments in all thirty-five high-rise buildings.[194] By 1974, parents, staff, and students at the Educational Park's Truman High School would hold boycotts to protest construction defects, including water "gushing" into the home economics room owing to a poorly constructed roof. While a neighboring room at the school was converted into a "'green house,' utilizing the damp, humid conditions in this room," not all errors could be compensated for so easily.[195] A construction audit completed by the engineering firm Perkins + Will in the late 1970s would note that although the UHF/CSI had no experience building in the tricky conditions presented by Co-op City's landfill-on-top-of-a-swamp, "we are not aware of any report or study of maximum design water levels at the site or correspondence indicating that such a study should be made." The study found myriad construction defects, ranging from a poorly constructed landfill that led to methane gas escaping, the need to replace thirty-two miles of pipes throughout the development, sinking pylons for the high-rise buildings, and other major problems.[196] While tax abatements and the lowering of construction standards could help on the margins, Co-op City's ballooning mortgage would ultimately have to be paid. By the 1970s, despite the UHF's desperate pleas, neither the state nor the city had the will or the means to help. Costs would be passed down to the cooperators themselves.

By the time that the first cooperators moved into the development in late 1968, the tenuous alliance between the city, which wanted affordable housing, and the UHF, which wanted to build a cooperative community for people of modest means, was badly strained. The Lindsay administration's goal of an economically and racially integrated community that fit in with the existing urban fabric was diametrically opposed to the large-scale, economically homogeneous community that the UHF had built in Co-op City. Lindsay was no longer interested in large-scale urban development projects, especially those related to housing. Instead, he came to support "scatter site" public housing, with an eye toward integrating subsidized housing with existing communities, and he would shy away from constructing middle-income housing altogether.[197] Meanwhile, as Co-op City's construction came to a close several years later, Ostroff would admit defeat: "Without [new systems for the construction of large-scale housing], I would strongly urge our organization not to get involved in any new work. Our experience at Co-op City during these past six years . . . is the best reason I can use to document this opinion."[198] Ostroff was true to his word. After their failure to find adequate economic models for planned developments in South Brooklyn and Jersey City, Co-op City would be the last development built by the UHF.

During the years of Co-op City's planning and construction, an increasing number of critics argued that the development was morally and aesthetically suspect. It was ugly and poorly planned, it had a deleterious effect on the rest of the Bronx, and it was beset by corruption and financial irregularities. It was inauthentic and even un-urban. Ada Louise Huxtable in the *New York Times* would write in 1968 on the eve of the arrival of Co-op City's first residents that the development "stun[s] those trained to think in urban terms." She accused the UHF of creating "a bumper crop of human failures through environmental failure."[199] In the pages of *Progressive Architecture*, Ulrich Franzen would call this development (built by socialist-leaning unionists) "silent majority architecture," designed for the complacent masses who had elected Nixon.[200]

It came as a surprise to many of these critics that Co-op City's first cooperators greeted their new homes and their new community with a breathtaking degree of enthusiasm. An article in *Newsweek* revisited the AIA's warning that "the spirits of the tenants . . . would be dampened by the paucity of their environment" and wrote that "as Co-op City's current residents prepared to celebrate the development's second anniversary this kind of warning seemed somewhat beside the point." The article went on to explore the "pioneering gusto" that was turning the development into a community.[201] It appeared that the UHF had been proven correct: high-rise architecture was no impediment to the development of community in Co-op City.

CHAPTER 2

"Everyone Was Seeking a Utopia"

Building a Community, 1968–1973

On February 8 and 9, 1969, a snowstorm paralyzed New York City. As fifteen inches of snow fell, the city declared a snow emergency, closing roads and calling off sanitation pickups. In contrast to the response to a storm of similar magnitude that hit the city in 1961, the response to the 1969 storm was a debacle. For many observers, New York's poor handling of the February 1969 snowstorm was a microcosm of the broader crisis of the city. Mayor Lindsay faced searing criticism about the fact that up to 40 percent of snowplows were out of service for a week after the snow fell, while the hodgepodge of city agencies responsible for the cleanup argued among themselves. Budgetary constraints were to blame for the city's "antiquated" removal equipment and its failure to provide enough manpower to deal with the snow removal problem at the outset. The mayor was out of town when the storm hit and did not put emergency plans into action quickly enough. A lack of advance planning forced the city to improvise a response, which was often slow or ineffective. According to John J. De Lury, president of the Uniformed Sanitationmen's Association, the Lindsay administration "tried to play it by ear and they were tone deaf."[1] According to the reporter Richard Phalon, even the move of New Yorkers to the suburbs played a role in the fiasco, as this demographic shift meant that an additional three hundred thousand commuters came to Manhattan each day compared to twenty years earlier. The increase in car traffic along with the decline in the use of public transportation meant that there were many more vehicles on the road. Hence, Phalon explained, the entire transportation network was "more fragile" and vulnerable to extreme weather events.[2] The consequence of the city's poor response appeared to be the loss of governmental authority and the breakdown of social order, as garbage and snow piled up and residents refused to obey emergency signs, laughing in the face of city authorities and significantly complicating cleanup efforts.[3]

As depicted in the pages of the *Co-op City Times*, the fledgling development was an island of care and competence in the sea of chaos created by the storm and its aftermath. On the day of the storm, nearby Interstate 95 shut down owing to a combination of the swiftly falling snow and vehicles abandoned by their drivers as conditions deteriorated. Co-op City had only opened to its first residents less than two months earlier, and some of these new cooperators went to the highway to assist drivers who had skidded off the road. They brought the tired travelers to Building 1, where "cooperators rushed into the winds to carry in babies, to assist the elderly and to offer a welcoming hand to all."[4] Tables were set up in the lobby laden with soup, coffee, and sandwiches, while stranded travelers were offered beds or couches to sleep on. Meanwhile, teenagers walked up and down the highway with provisions for those stuck in their cars. At a time when New York appeared to be an ungovernable metropolis, the *Co-op City Times* proclaimed the new development a "city of hope."[5]

The story of the February snowstorm quickly passed into UHF mythology. A year after the storm, the *Co-op City Times* quoted the reminiscences of residents of Building 1, who exclaimed, "This brought us all together; this is where it all started," and "We had all just moved in, so it was just 'hello-goodbye' until then. We really made a lot of friends during the storm. It was great teamwork." The storm had even brought residents and UHF managers together, with kids pelting Don Phillips, the director of community affairs, with snowballs.[6] What the city could not do, the *Co-op City Times* seemed to say, Co-op City would do for itself—caring for residents and even travelers passing by. Furthermore, the very process of doing this had forged a cooperative community. One Building 1 resident was quoted as saying, "The greatest thing is what happened to us as we responded cooperatively to the needs of our fellow men. Working cooperatively with our material resources can build cooperative housing, but working together with our hearts, our hands, our young and our old, builds what's most important[,] a 'cooperative community.'"[7]

Over the next several years, the initial sixteen families, who arrived in December 1968, were joined by thousands of others. As they did so, the UHF sought to turn these neighbors into a community. In the minds of the UHF, the goal of providing affordable housing was only one purpose of cooperative housing. The *Co-op City Times* explained,

> United Housing Foundation officials have long held that the answer to our cities is not mere good housing, that the *way people live* in their new communities is the key to a "new city." Cooperative Housing, they say, has made its greatest mark when its residents have embarked on programs to build the sense of neighborhood, developing the sense of "hello, friend," stimulating the desire of cooperators to make music together. Educational activities for children and adults, cultural and musical programs, club groups, workshops for carpenters, baseball leagues . . . all these and many more . . . build the fine thread of association, friends and activities that one associates with a home community, a family community.[8]

As it would turn out, not every challenge that the UHF and Co-op City's new residents faced would be as easy to respond to as February 1969's blanket of snow.

This chapter will explore how Co-op City's first cooperators built a community and the controversies that tested it. The largest tensions within the development stemmed either from race or generation, or a combination of the two. These tensions had at their root a fundamental conflict between the vision that inspired many residents to move to Co-op City and the fears that they harbored of their new neighborhood becoming like the slums that they had left. On the one hand, Co-op City was explicitly designed with young families in mind, who signaled to many the vitality and promise of the cooperative vision. On the other hand, the presence of many young people brought with it disorder and, occasionally, petty crime, and this could be read as a symbol of neighborhood deterioration. White, Black, and Latino cooperators wanted Co-op City to be an escape from the prejudices that they saw as endemic in their older neighborhoods. But, for some cooperators, the presence of Blacks, in particular, led to the fear that Co-op City would become a slum. The sight of teenagers and the sight of Black residents awakened hopes and fears at the same time. Both these hopes and these fears were a result of the fervent desire of so many Co-op City residents of all ages and all racial backgrounds for a clean break with the past.

Given the contradictory emotions invested in diversity of multiple kinds, it was no surprise that it was this set of conflicts that motivated the most consequential debates that stressed Co-op City during its first years: the tensions around minority representation in the development's political structure, generational strains and anxieties regarding public space and vandalism, and the relationship between Co-op City and the rest of the Bronx. Co-op City gradually came to something of an accommodation in each of these controversies. However imperfect, it was possible to see the outlines of a multigenerational and multiethnic community emerging in the early 1970s in Co-op City, a time of much more devastating generational and racial conflicts elsewhere in the city and the nation.

The Co-op City that the first residents moved into was largely a construction zone. It would take another three and a half years for the final cooperators to move in, in March 1972.[9] When the development was complete, it would contain 15,372 apartments, arrayed in a combination of thirty-five high-rise towers and 236 town house apartments, divided into five sections. These five sections were divided into two areas, the larger of which occupied 220 acres. This larger area comprised four of Co-op City's five sections, surrounding a central "Greenway" park. The fifth section occupied an eighty-acre site, which was separated from the other four sections by a bend in the Hutchinson River. The original plans for Co-op City included a riverfront marina in this area; however, the marina was never completed, and instead Section Five was connected simply by a dangerous stretch of road.

In all five sections, both the high-rise and town house buildings led directly to cul-de-sac interior streets, creating a development that was easily walkable. It was also disorienting for many visitors and new residents, who found themselves surrounded by seemingly identical towers and slabs. To provide a sense of orientation, the street names for each of the five sections began with a different letter. The streets themselves were named for a variety of writers, scientists, and socialists. Section One, for example, featured Dreiser Loop, for the novelist; Debs place, for the socialist politician; DeKruif Place, for the scientist; DeFoe Place, for the author; Darrow Place, for the lawyer; and Donizetti Place, for the composer.[10] These names displayed the values of the UHF: they were aspirational, and while they were largely, but not exclusively, American, they were otherwise unconnected to any one place or one history. Insofar as the very word "utopia" is derived from the Greek for "no place," these names were utopian. They conveyed the UHF's belief that its cooperatives stood for progress: scientific, social, cultural, and political.

Co-op City's apartment buildings occupied only 15 percent of the land area of the development.[11] The rest of the space was open, or utilized by a variety of establishments. There were three community centers, one in Section One, one located between Sections Three and Four, and one in Section Five. These community centers featured a variety of goods and services

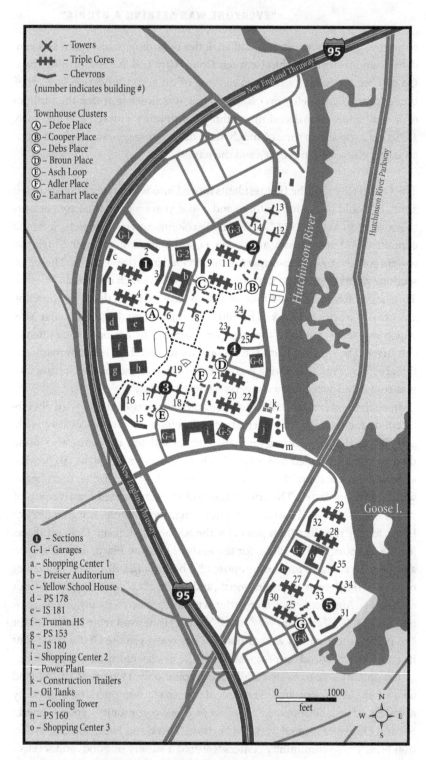

FIGURE 9. Co-op City. Map created by Mike Bechtold.

for Co-op City's residents, including both commercial and noncommercial spaces. There were several cooperative supermarkets, a cooperative pharmacy and optical store, an Amalgamated Bank, a credit union, kosher butchers and delis, a few restaurants, clothing and shoe stores, a movie theater, and other shopping and recreational establishments.[12] There was a branch of the New York Public Library located in Community Center 2 (between Sections Three and Four). Each of the community centers also had fifty rooms for community meetings, which were leased to clubs, educational groups, and voluntary associations. The centers also provided a location for religious communities, including synagogues and churches, and for the cooperative administrative offices. The high-rise towers provided community facilities as well, including a cooperative nursery school located off the lobby of Building 15, and rooms for a variety of medical offices. The development had its own fire station. It had eight six-story garages, which provided parking for eleven thousand cars. Although it would not open fully until 1973, there was an Educational Park featuring two elementary schools, two intermediate schools, and a high school, located just off the central Greenway. There was also an additional elementary school, located in Section Five, across the river bend from the first four sections. The remaining land was used for parks, including the central Greenway, sport facilities, gardens, bike paths, and playgrounds.

The UHF officially refused to publish demographic statistics of the residents of Co-op City. However, it is possible to piece together some information about the people who initially moved to Co-op City in the late 1960s and early 1970s. Throughout the period between Co-op City's initial proposal and its initial occupancy, the UHF fought to keep the development exclusively middle class. It largely succeeded, in part owing to the requirements of the Mitchell-Lama program. Mitchell-Lama regulated the maximum allowable income for Co-op City residents according to a formula that roughly came out to six times (for a family of three or fewer) to seven times (for a family of four or more) the apartment's carrying charge. Based on this formula, a family residing in a five-room apartment could have a yearly income of no more than $13,506 or $15,757, depending on the size of the family. Residents who earned more than this amount were subject to surcharges amounting to 5 percentage-point steps at 5 percent intervals of income above this level.[13] While there was no lower bound for income, the requirement that Co-op City residents pay a $450-a-room equity deposit up front meant that the cooperative was largely off limits to poorer New Yorkers.

Because of both the equity deposit and Mitchell-Lama income regulations, Co-op City's initial residents earned incomes in a relatively narrow band, with most residents occupying the hazy space between the working class and the lower middle class, with a large percentage employed in unionized professions such as education and the garment industry.[14] In 1970, the mean total annual income of Co-op City residents was $8,325, and the median was $8,500, which was almost identical to that of the borough as a whole.[15] Some 65 percent of families had an income between $5,000 and $10,000, and over 80 percent had a total household income between $3,000 and $12,000. The majority of those at the bottom of the income bracket were retirees, who were eligible to receive a carrying charge subsidy allocated from the surcharges paid by those who earned over the Mitchell-Lama maximum.[16] The most common professions included office workers, federal, state, and city employees, pharmacists, garment workers, and accountants, with a smattering of physicians and lawyers at the top income rungs.[17]

Upward of 70 percent, or over thirty thousand, of Co-op City's initial residents were Jewish.[18] Co-op City's Jewish population placed it within the ranks of some of the largest Jewish cities in the United States and the world. According to sociologist Kenneth Brook, in the early 1970s there were only twelve cities in the United States that had more Jews than Co-op City, including Los Angeles, Philadelphia, Cleveland, and Detroit. Meanwhile, Co-op City would have ranked among the top twenty-five Jewish cities in the *entire world*.[19] While Co-op City's Jewish population was double the percentage of Jews in the Bronx, it was also not quite the white, Jewish enclave that the Lindsay administration had feared. Although Section One was almost entirely Jewish and made up of the first people to submit applications in 1965 and 1966, as word spread, Co-op City's applicant pool became more diverse. In 1968, Ostroff boasted that "we're getting 20 percent nonwhite applicants, which I think is pretty good. We'll have a very well-integrated city."[20] Later sections had a larger percentage of Black and Latino residents, especially Section Five, which was the last section to be occupied. By the time Co-op City was fully occupied, 20 to 25 percent of residents were either Black or Latino, the latter mostly Puerto Rican.[21] According to census statistics, New York in 1970 was 76.6 percent white, and the "white non-Hispanic" population was estimated at 64 percent. In the end, Co-op City was only slightly more white than the city as a whole (see appendix, figures 25 and 26).[22] Just as the UHF had insisted, its Black and Latino residents were drawn from the same middle-class demographic as its white residents, and their reasons for moving to Co-op City were largely similar.[23]

Many of the Jews who moved to Co-op City came from the West Bronx neighborhoods around the Grand Concourse, and they identified the changing nature of their old neighborhood as the primary reason that they left. Five years after Co-op City opened, Irving Rosenfeld called on his neighbors to "let us not forget that most of us came here from congested, deteriorated crime-ridden areas or areas about to become so. The shelter of Co-op City is like wearing fleece-lined boots on an icy street on a freezing day. . . . This giant housing complex . . . rescued many thousands of families from terror, fright, gloom and fume."[24] Safety and the desire to leave dangerous neighborhoods were also important to nonwhite arrivals. One early Black resident would later explain that her parents were motivated by the fact that "Co-op City was an economical, safe, and good place to raise children."[25] Another Black woman who moved to the development as an adult also stressed how important it was that this was a neighborhood that "was going to be safe."[26] A Black man whose family moved to Co-op City when he was a young teenager explained that his mom wanted to leave the Hunts Point neighborhood in the South Bronx because she feared growing crime and prostitution and "didn't want [him] growing up in that element."[27] The future Supreme Court Justice Sonia Sotomayor wrote that her family moved to Co-op City in 1970 when she was a teenager because "my mother was eager to get us into a safer place because the Bronxdale projects were headed downhill fast. . . . Home was starting to look like a war zone."[28]

In addition to these fears about neighborhood deterioration, the very fact that so many people one knew were moving was itself a reason to move. Many Jews moved to Co-op City with friends or family from their West Bronx neighborhoods. For example, my mother's family had mostly lived in walk-up apartments within a few blocks of one another, close to the Concourse. My great-grandmother, along with my mother's parents, her brother, his wife and their two kids, three of her aunts and uncles, their spouses, and no fewer than eight of her cousins moved to Co-op City within the course of three years. They were joined by several more distant relatives as well. This kind of familial migration to Co-op City was typical and echoed the earlier chain migrations that had brought Jews to the Concourse and other outer-borough neighborhoods.[29] Chain migrations were not limited to Jews. In my interviews with former Co-op City residents, without exception all of them who moved in during the initial occupancy period—regardless of their racial background or where they had lived before moving to Co-op City—mentioned finding out about the cooperative from a friend or family member. In her memoir *My Beloved World*, Sotomayor recounted that after her family came to Co-op City, "It started to look like a good idea to everyone else. Alfred, married and with kids by then, ended up in a building not far from us. Eventually Titi Carmen arrived with Miriam and Eddie; Charlie with his new wife Ruth; and finally Titi Gloria and Tio Tonio came too. Titi Aurora had beaten them all to the punch: as soon as we were settled, my mother's sister moved in with us."[30]

New arrivals appreciated the fact that Co-op City offered a great apartment for a low price. One new arrival who came from the Grand Concourse wrote that "pricewise, you couldn't beat the deal. You were paying less and getting more."[31] Another stated that she was "glad to get a bargain."[32] Moreover, through advertisements and word of mouth, they got the sense that Co-op City was "supposed to be some kind of shining jewel."[33] A woman who came as a five-year-old explained how impressed the family was by the advertisements of "huge, gorgeous, modern apartments, with luxury everything. If you were moving to Co-op, you were moving up."[34] Debra Genender, who also moved as a small child, explained that Co-op City seemed to be "an up and coming community."[35] To one cooperator, "Co-op City [was] like the promised land for the middle-class, retirees, and small families."[36]

New residents enthused about their Co-op City apartments—they were new, large, filled with modern amenities, and often had a great view. Just as the UHF had insisted, the existence of air conditioning was a major boon to residents. Helen Schwartz recalled that "there was air conditioning, free electric."[37] Sotomayor wrote that her apartment "had parquet floors and a big window in the living room with a long view. All the rooms were twice the size of those cubbyholes in the projects."[38] Lynn Sjogren, who moved from a walk-up on Davidson Avenue near the Concourse, explained that "the kitchen on Davidson was so tiny, but here we had room—an eat-in kitchen."[39] Judy Rabinowitz, another early resident, stated in 1969 how much she enjoyed her new home: "The apartment is great. There's air-conditioning and the kitchen has a lot of cabinets. There are a lot of closets, and there are parquet floors and the rooms are a nice size."[40] Ann Herskowitz recalled, "I never remember being so excited about anything. We hadn't seen the apartment until we walked in and we ran around exploring every nook and corner of the beautiful six room apartment."[41] According to Anne Sullivan, when she arrived in Co-op City on her moving day, she was met in the elevator by her excited movers, who exclaimed, "Wait till you see what you've got!" On a clear day, she could see from her twenty-fourth-story window all the way to LaGuardia Airport. The apartment was spacious, and she felt like she "had died and gone to heaven."[42] Mrs. Albert Sanchez echoed her: "Sometimes we're above the fog. . . . I love this apartment."[43]

Among the many reasons for moving to Co-op City, a deep commitment to cooperative living was rarely mentioned. Although Co-op City's early residents

FIGURE 10. New residents observing the view. Undated. Amalgamated Clothing Workers of America Records, Kheel Center, Cornell University.

were drawn almost exclusively from the left of the political spectrum, as was common in UHF buildings and other limited-equity cooperatives, creature comforts and safety far outweighed the ideological appeal of the UHF's cooperative vision.[44] The UHF was largely undisturbed by this fact, reasoning that "even if [new residents] don't know what co-ops are, they have an image of a 'co-op' community as a pretty good place to live—where people treat each other with respect as well as having something to say about the place."[45] The UHF, further, believed that it could train people for cooperative living. At the UHF's behest, Herman Liebman, former education director of the Amalgamated Housing cooperative, organized a program of orientation meetings for new Co-op City residents. Cooperators were each to attend meetings for forty minutes at least four times in an effort to instill in them the "meaning of cooperation."[46] In 1965 alone, more than sixty orientation meetings were held for four thousand future residents.[47] These meetings were later scaled back and eliminated altogether because of cost concerns; however, this did not mean that the UHF abandoned its pedagogical ambitions.

New residents received a pamphlet titled *Co-op Living: A Guide for Members.* It included everything from practical advice about the laundry rooms and milk vending machines to a map of the development, from a history of the cooperative movement to admonishments about the need to be responsible, as "we are our own landlords." It also included some lofty advice from UHF president Harold Ostroff himself: "Co-op City is not built in a day. It will take time for things to 'settle down.' But every experienced cooperator will tell you it's worth the wait and the worry. Good things do not come easily, but by working together in a spirit of friendship, we expect Co-op City to be, before too long, a shining example of what people can do together in a housing cooperative community."[48] The weekly *Co-op City Times* contained article after article stressing the benefits of cooperative living. A Department of Co-operative Education and Activities aimed to foster this spirit among Co-op City's residents through providing financial and logistical support for social groups, lectures, concerts, and a yearly community fair. Recognizing the potential for generational and racial splits in the development, that department additionally proposed plans for intergenerational groups, in which young people and senior citizens could discuss "the generation gap," along with a "course on Black History . . . conducted for both Blacks and Whites."[49]

UHF leadership was thrilled by the community life that it saw blossoming in the new development. Don Phillips, Co-op City's community affairs director, waxed rhapsodic: "We are people! We are new babies being born to young parents, we are mothers rearing children, fathers paying bills. We

FIGURE 11.   Co-op City orientation meeting. Undated. Amalgamated Clothing Workers of America Records, Kheel Center, Cornell University.

are persons searching for a new community. . . . A community—one with meaning—comes when we invest ourselves to make something new. And that kind of investment . . . is happening. It's happening in the dozens of volunteers building new relationships, in the warm-electric feeling passing from hand to hand between girls and boys who've found new affections. It's happening! And it's warm and human."[50] Liebman, who had run the initial orientation meetings for Co-op City applicants, exulted, "After nearly 3 years of meeting with thousands of applicants . . . I suddenly walked into a living, throbbing beehive of humanity—grandparents relaxing on benches, young mothers 'schuesing' [sic] by baby carriages and oceans of children in and out of camp scattered in every cool nook and cranny, playing happily in the vast and as yet uncultivated 'good earth' completely unconscious of color or any other adult-oriented distinction that are the base of our society, everywhere, except in co-op communities."[51]

For longtime cooperative activists such as Phillips or Liebman, Co-op City was a cooperative dream come true. However, even for those who did not share their specific vision, as the months and years ticked by "Co-op City gradually transformed from a construction site to a community."[52] Beyond the possible assistance of cooperative education, two factors seemed to be responsible for the rapid formation of a sense of community: population density and the fact that everyone was a new arrival. The sheer number of apartments in Co-op City meant for one woman who moved there as a child that "everybody was always right outside your front door. With Co-op, there was always somebody around. . . . Kids were always available to play with."[53] Karen Benjamin, who moved to Co-op City as a young child, said that she "never had to make plans. You'd just go outside and people would be there to hang out with."[54] For one woman who moved in as an adult, "Everyone would say 'Hello, how are you!' . . . Because it was all new, nobody could get cliquish."[55] An elderly resident explained that "Co-op City is a good place. . . . I used to be bored, almost to death, but now I go to the club, to concerts, on trips, or just *shmooze* on the benches. Everyday there's something to do."[56] Many residents became friends with the neighbors on their floor. Others met their neighbors in the laundry rooms located in the basements of all the buildings.[57] Parents of small children met other parents of small children. Over two hundred community organizations, including ethnic clubs, political clubs, charitable clubs, social clubs, and organizations for children, including no fewer than three separate bowling leagues, attracted a wide variety of cooperators.[58] One former resident later described Co-op City in these years as "the biggest little small town in the world."[59] In 1972 one resident explained, Before I came here . . . I used to complain that 'nobody knows my name.' Now my main complaint is that everybody knows my name. The phone is constantly ringing and there's always someone on the other end asking me to raise money to fight cancer or to campaign for someone running for some kind of office, or take up ballet, for heaven's sake. It's friendly and sweet but sometimes I just like to be left alone."[60] Indeed, if there was any problem with the development, one elderly resident complained, it was that "there are so many *yentas* [busybodies] living here and sometimes I can't stand it. All they want to know is your business and to gossip about everybody. . . . There is no privacy here."[61] One of the most enduring critiques of urban renewal housing developments is that their architectural bleakness and lack of connection to established neighborhoods made them incubators of social problems and stymied the creation of functioning communities. However, the experiences of Co-op City's initial residents demonstrate that this sort of architectural determinism is just as flawed as the urban renewal regime it supplanted.

The ability to live in an ethnically mixed neighborhood was important to many Jewish Co-op City residents. Many of them claimed that they "didn't see" color, or that they appreciated living in a "melting pot," or that "children never knew if you were Jewish or Christian."[62] Esther Benjamin, who arrived as an adult in 1970, looked back on the fact that "all colors, sizes and stripes—everyone came together. We were all new in this new thing."[63] Anne Sullivan, who arrived the same year with her husband and two boys, said that they were excited about the "melting-pot aspect" of Co-op City when they first arrived.[64] Lynn Sjogren, whose family moved in when she was eleven years old, said that one of the most important aspects of Co-op City to her was the fact that "the groups I hung out with were mixed . . . it was a real melting pot, everyone played with everyone."[65] According to the journalists Jack Newfield and Paul DuBrul, Co-op City's Jewish residents "took quiet pride in the fact that they lived in 'integrated' communities with middle-class blacks and Hispanics who shared their fears and aspirations."[66]

The desire for Co-op City's Jews to live in a racially mixed community was part and parcel of Jewish racial liberalism in this era. Many Jews in postwar America held to an optimistic universalism that insisted on the equality of all individuals regardless of race. Jews were both more likely to be racially tolerant than other whites and to insist that their tolerance was an expression simultaneously of Jewish and American ideals, claiming that racial prejudice was "un-American" and antidemocratic, while at the same time insisting that their liberalism was an expression of a long-standing Jewish "struggle for universal justice and human brotherhood."[67] This Jewish commitment to racial liberalism began to fracture in the late 1960s. Some historians have noted that while more wealthy and secure "Manhattan Jews" continued to stress the importance of civil rights and racial tolerance, many "outer-borough" Jews began to embrace a "nervous parochialism" as the civil rights demands of Black and Hispanic New Yorkers increased at the same time as the city's overall crime rate. However, this divide was never absolute, with some middle- and working-class outer-borough Jews expressing a racial liberalism more in line with their wealthier coreligionists. Rather than a divide between boroughs, some scholars have suggested that the degree of racial liberalism among Jews had more to do with whether their view of their and the city's future was optimistic or not, with optimistic Jews more likely to support civil rights and integration.[68] There was hardly a more optimistic group of New York Jews than the new residents of Co-op City. Indeed, while wealthier Manhattan Jews remained wary of sharing schools and neighborhoods with nonwhites even as they continued to pay lip service to the ideals of integration, Co-op City's Jews eagerly insisted on their commitment to interracial living.[69]

Co-op City's Jews were affected by many of the factors that led other outer-borough Jews to the sentiments of racial backlash—they connected the decline of their neighborhoods with the incursion of Black and Puerto Rican residents, they were terrified of crime, and they were wary of know-it-all "limousine liberals."[70] Yet there were several factors that allowed the Jews of Co-op City to hold the seemingly contradictory beliefs that the decline of the Concourse was linked to its increasingly Black and Puerto Rican population and that Co-op City's racial diversity was part of its appeal. First was the fact that the Blacks and Puerto Ricans who moved into Co-op City were of a class background similar to that of its Jewish residents and thus less poor than the Blacks and Puerto Ricans who were currently relocating to the Concourse neighborhoods in greater numbers. The UHF's insistence on economic homogeneity appears, in this sense, to have had its desired effect.[71] As Reggie, a Black resident, said in order to explain Co-op City's relative racial peace at this time of heightened tensions elsewhere in the City, "I didn't know anyone who was on welfare or Section 8. Everyone seemed to be working hard and instilling a value in their kids. Everyone was seeking a Utopia. We were all 'haves'—no have nots."[72] Another reason was the fact that Co-op City was so overwhelmingly Jewish that its residents could experience it simultaneously as a Jewish community and as a multicultural one. Marc Bosyk, who came from a Jewish family, had a typical experience. On the one hand, he emphasized that his friends in the development were from a variety of ethnic and racial backgrounds. However, he also

noted that most of his friends were Jewish, just because there were so many
Jews there. "Everybody dressed up on the High Holy Days. There were so
many Jewish people. It was just normal. When I moved to Pennsylvania [in
1977], I realized that not the whole world was Jewish."[73] Finally, during a
series of conflicts in these early years, institutional actors, from the UHF to
an array of other community groups, worked to lower the temperature of
racial conflict. As Co-op City became less white and as its residents became
less optimistic in the ensuing years, the tolerance of some of Co-op City's
Jews for ethnic diversity generally declined. However, in the early 1970s, the
promise of racial harmony was a significant reason for Co-op City's appeal
to the Jews who lived there.

That did not mean that Co-op City's Jewish residents were free of racial
prejudice. They shared many of the usual blind spots of racial liberals.[74] Eli
Lederhendler, a historian of New York Jewry, writes of his own upbringing in
a "middle to lower-middle-class neighborhood" in terms that are reminiscent
of Co-op City: "I (and many others) lived in a kind of conditioned ignorance
where black-white relations in our city were concerned. . . . Certainly nothing explicit was ever mentioned that was anti-black. In fact, as far as I could
pick up from people of my parents' generation (relatives, friends, teachers),
there was an active desire to put things right."[75] Yet as Lederhendler notes,
this racial liberalism did not necessarily extend to a broader systemic recognition of the limits and biases of supposedly color-blind policies among either
his neighbors or New York Jews more generally.[76]

The presence of so many middle-class Black and Puerto Rican neighbors
reified the belief held by many Jewish Co-op City residents that a color-blind
society was possible without addressing the pervasive imbalances in school-
ing, housing, and employment in New York and elsewhere. An anecdote in
the New York Times is revealing in this regard. "I want you to print this," Sol
Oratofsky, the president of a Co-op City's senior citizens organization, told
a reporter while holding a sheet with the names of three Black boys who
had found a check for $314 and returned it. "Everybody says the colored
kids are the bad ones. This will show that it's not true."[77] On the one hand,
Oratofsky sought to correct the impression that Black kids were criminals.
On the other, he not only assumed that this stereotype was widely held, but
also felt that pointing out the presence of "good" Black boys was sufficient
to defeat it.

Black and Puerto Rican residents of Co-op City were also enthusiastic
about Co-op City's racial diversity. Eden Ross Lipson, a former CPC official who visited Co-op City in 1969, reported that the Black and Puerto
Rican residents were "self-conscious upwardly mobile younger families

who want larger apartments with balconies and status."[78] For these families, racial integration was crucial to their vision of the good life.[79] Alison, a Black woman who moved to Co-op City as a young child, explained, "My family moved from the South Bronx to Co-op for a better environment to raise children. . . . My father didn't want to move to Harlem, there were too many black people there. He didn't mean this in a negative way. My parents just wanted to move to a more mixed neighborhood."[80] Another Black resident said that "we were attracted to . . . the prospect that we would participate in creating a new ideal community. We saw all of us living together as neighbors, participating freely in the life of the community and leaving behind us the fears and prejudices that clouded our lives in our old neighborhoods."[81] "For a black man like myself," one resident told a reporter, "this was a chance to get in on the ground floor, instead of settling for some place that the white man had used and left."[82]

For non-Jews, the experience of living with so many Jewish neighbors was fundamental to their experience in Co-op City. Sotomayor reminisced, "If you grow up on salsa and merengue, then polkas and jitterbugs look like they jumped off the pages of *National Geographic*. . . . I noticed too that the *mishigas* [craziness] on display in the hallways of Co-op City . . . more than matched the volubility of Puerto Rican family life."[83] She also describes working in a local bakery where customers would try to engage her in Yiddish: "'What, no Yiddish? A nice Jewish girl like you?' I heard that so often that I knew the routine: my boss would explain with a little bit of Yiddish I did recognize. 'Shiksa' was technically derogative, but she said it so affectionately that I couldn't fault it. At least it wasn't 'spic'—elsewhere I'd get that often enough too."[84]

Much like Sotomayor, many Blacks felt that social integration in Co-op City was generally successful. Ofonedu (identified as such in an interview) said simply that "there was not much of an emphasis on ethnicity."[85] Sheldon explained that "the best part of Co-op City is the different mix of people. My core group of friends as a kid included two Jewish boys, one Italian and two blacks."[86] Robin Nurse, who moved to Co-op City as a child, said, "The Bronx was definitely segregated . . . but Co-op City was mixed. . . . We were mixed groups—Spanish, white, black, green, if there was somebody there that was green. But we all played together, especially in the first couple of years."[87] Bob compared Co-op City to Crown Heights, the neighborhood he had come from: "I didn't care for white people at all, but now I lived amongst them in Co-op City. What I was to learn was that we were all in the same boat, no one was better or worse than the other. . . . I know more things about Jewish culture than people expect."[88]

Despite the potency of these memories of interracial harmony, Co-op City residents of both races noted that Black-white relationships had the potential be fraught.[89] Patrice, another Black Co-op City resident, said that Co-op City was not free of racism, but that this racism was relatively mild compared with what she experienced elsewhere: "There was a tendency for members of the same ethnic group to congregate together, but I was never made to feel that there were areas of Co-op City (stores, buildings, playgrounds, etc.) that I was not welcome in due to my race or color. . . . It wasn't perfect. There were problems but when I contrast it against what I felt and observed in other parts of the city the relatively few incidents of bias seem to pale in comparison."[90] This sort of balanced perspective was common. A Black woman named Shirley would later describe how one set of neighbors immediately welcomed her and her small children to their town house complex, while another set never spoke to them.[91] Meanwhile, an article in the *Co-op City Times* from 1973 noted that "the integration of Black families in Co-op City is proceeding at different rates in different buildings," depending on the culture that developed among particular groups of neighbors.[92]

When the development opened, the political structure of Co-op City was explicitly race-blind. Residents voted for building representatives who sat on a development-wide Advisory Council. The Advisory Council officially advised the Riverbay Corporation, which had been set up by the UHF to manage the development. When the development opened, Riverbay's ten-person board of directors consisted solely of members of UHF leadership, chaired by Ostroff himself. In 1970, the board was expanded to fifteen members, two of whom were elected directly by residents.[93] Three more directly elected members were added by the mid-1970s.[94] The UHF's continued control of the development would become a source of considerable tension in Co-op City, but even the Advisory Council's makeup was not free of rancor.

In the first Advisory Council elections in the spring of 1970, no Black or Latino candidates were elected. This appeared, at least in part, to be a result of the Advisory Council's structure—two representatives were elected for each building, and the successful AC candidates were all Jewish, reflecting the fact that Jews were a majority in each building. After the results came in, E. C. Tolson from the Black Caucus wrote, "The so-called 'democratic process' which was used, proved again that the 'best man' won? People voted their 'consciences,' and not a Black or Puerto Rican candidate or any other non-white won in this racist election. If this is cooperative living, NO THANKS! We would much prefer uncooperative living in which Blacks set up a Black Advisory Council, so that non-whites will have a voice to parallel the white one elected through the so-called 'democratic process.'"[95]

The Black Caucus had been founded in September 1969, with a mission of "bringing people together and achieving what is best for all people of Co-op City," with a particular focus on children and educational issues.[96] Had the Black Caucus remained solely committed to education, it might have been uncontroversial. However, by protesting the results of the Advisory Council elections, by accusing the development of operating in a racist manner, and by threatening to make sure the Advisory Council had a "short and uncomfortable life," it invited controversy and, in its members' own words, began to be accused of being "unreasonable and irresponsible."[97]

The Black Caucus responded to these accusations with a statement:

Black Caucus is comprised of unreasonable members. We are unreasonable when others try to dictate their philosophy to us without seriously listening to ours. We are unreasonable when community policies do not include our aspirations as well as those of other residents. We will continue to be unreasonable as long as our fellow residents refuse to recognize that all concerned stockholders have the right to voice opinions and supply their solutions individually or collectively. As George Bernard Shaw wrote, "The reasonable one persists in adapting himself to the world. Therefore, all progress depends on the unreasonable man." The man who listens to reason is lost. Reason enslaves all those whose minds are not strong enough to master her.[98]

This combination of combativeness, belief in progress, and dedication to the Western canon, as represented in the quote by George Bernard Shaw, should not have been unfamiliar to Co-op City's management or its majority Jewish population, as it was a mirror image of their own values and their own brash style. It also reflected a shift within Black politics in the 1960s toward more assertive claims that Black politicians needed a seat at the table in order to have the needs of Black people represented—claims the resonated from the streets of American cities to the halls of Congress, including the formation of the Congressional Black Caucus in 1971.[99] Much like the CBC, Co-op City's Black Caucus did not deny the credibility of the Advisory Council, and instead advocated for its own inclusion. Walter Simon, the caucus's president, proposed that one-third of council seats be reserved for minority members, with a series of open town hall meetings to air concerns about the representative nature of the Advisory Council election process and about race relations in the cooperative more generally.[100]

George Schechter, vice president of the UHF, urged the Advisory Council to take the Black Caucus's proposal seriously: "You're the elected officials of Co-op City's Advisory Council and you are on the firing line now and will continue to be. . . . You have to solve this problem of minority representation in a logical and orderly way and you have to solve it now."[101] Ostroff called for patience, asking people to hear out the Black Caucus, "recognizing that there are unfortunate carryovers of prejudices and feelings that people had before they came to Co-op City. I think it is inconceivable to think that the moment they move into Co-op City all these things drop away. It will take time, and hopefully with the good effort of people . . . we can begin to try to meet some of the problems of the interracial experience in a more calm setting, possibly, and find some of the answers that we must find in our metropolitan, urban area."[102] To the degree there was a dissenting voice in the UHF to Ostroff and Schechter's call to listen to the Black Caucus's concerns and their proposal, it came from Ed Marshall, Riverbay's new director of community relations and the first Black senior member of the development's staff, who came into the job in May 1970.[103] A seasoned veteran of the cooperative housing movement, Marshall stated his concern that tinkering with the election process to assure minority representation on the Advisory Council would "be viewed as paternalistic."[104]

Some Co-op City members shared Marshall's concerns about the Black Caucus's solution. Julius Kaufman wrote,

> When, upon my request, the renting office sent me an application for an apt in Co-op City, I was delighted to notice that questions about the color of my skin, my religion or national origin not in evidence. It gave me the happy feeling that, at last, a community was being organized where bigotry and prejudice had no place and was entirely eliminated. . . . Unfortunately, my rejoicing lasted only until the question of the election of an advisory council came up. I discovered to my sorrow that we find among us a number of individuals (and I hope that the number is not too great) whose primary interest is to bring in disunity and dissention among the cooperators by injecting the question of majority and minority groups, the question of senior or junior representation, etc.[105]

On the other hand, many of Co-op City's Jewish residents recognized the legitimacy of the Black Caucus's grievances.[106] After all, there was clear evidence that cooperators had elected only Advisory Council delegates that looked like them. One cooperator suggested having meetings so that residents could meet candidates, in particular those with a different "color, religion, or country of birth."[107] Another urged white cooperators to try to respect the desire of their Black neighbors for Black representation: "No white member of the Advisory Council can fully understand the situation, the needs, the hopes and aspirations of Blacks and Spanish-speaking people. . . . An Advisory Council which has Blacks and Spanish-speaking people on it can help establish harmonious relations between ethnic groups."[108]

After a contentious town hall meeting attended by one thousand cooperators in May 1970, the Advisory Council approved a resolution that largely accepted the Black Caucus's plan to enlarge the Advisory Council, with the added seats reserved specifically for minorities, which they defined as "any non-white Jew, or any person other than the Jewish faith."[109] They further mandated that there would be a "make-up" election in June 1970 for Black and Latino cooperators to elect six additional representatives to the council. In future elections, four representatives would be elected from each building. If none of the four was Black or Latino, the top Black or Latino vote-getter would automatically get the fourth seat from the building. With this "minority clause" in place, the issue largely disappeared as a major source of conflict in the development.

Within a year, most of the Black Caucus's energies were spent on organizing dances and senior citizen and youth programming, including the establishment of the Adam Clayton Powell Early Childhood Center.[110] Political activities faded into the background. The Spanish-American Society's activities were even less confrontational, primarily consisting of sponsoring film screenings and dances aimed at the entire Co-op City community.[111] Yet solving the Advisory Council issue did not entirely defuse racial tensions within the cooperative.

Co-op City's location on the urban fringe made it attractive to those seeking to escape the city but without the means to purchase a suburban home. The UHF capitalized on this by advertising Co-op City as a "blend of urban and suburban living."[112] Despite the urban origins and values of the UHF, Co-op City's ads often emphasized its remoteness from the city around them—stressing that it was a "park city on [a] river front without interior traffic roads," with "panoramic views over park and marine surroundings."[113] Surrounded by the Hutchinson River Parkway, the Hutchinson River, and Interstate 95, the development was an island in the Bronx—in the words of architect and urban planner Oscar Newman, "a self-imposed ghetto."[114]

This isolation was experienced by Co-op City's residents as something of a mixed blessing. One of Co-op City's main attractions was the fact that it was safe compared to the neighborhoods that many residents had left behind. Some residents exulted in the fact that "it is a most glorious feeling to be able to walk on the streets at any hour of the day or night and enjoy fresh air without fear of being attacked by a punk."[115] A survey conducted by the New York City Office of the Aging found that although 65 percent of elderly Co-op City residents left the development at least once per week, "such journeys are made with fear and kept to a minimum."[116] However, many Co-op City residents were worried that this safety had been attained at a price and were more ambivalent about being cut off from the rest of the city. This ambivalence was captured by new resident Lillian Gluckman, who explained in 1969 that "I like best the idea that this is a new community—completely self-contained," and then backtracked to add, "But I wouldn't want it to be completely isolated. It wouldn't work all alone. The community must be integrated into the surrounding neighborhood."[117]

There were bus links to Queens, Manhattan, and other parts of the Bronx. These buses, however, were relatively infrequent, and in the case of the express bus to Manhattan, pricey. From 1964 onward, planners and later residents noted the need for a subway link to the rest of the city. Plans were floated for an extension of the No. 6 train, to make Co-op City the terminus of the yet-to-be-built Second Avenue Line, to add an Amtrak or MetroNorth station where those trains passed through, to construct a monorail, or even to use hydroplanes for commuters.[118] Residents universally wanted some sort of train line—both because it would enable them to leave the development for work or other reasons, and because being in a "two-fare zone" (i.e., having

FIGURE 12. Buses in Section One. Undated. Amalgamated Clothing Workers of America Records, Kheel Center, Cornell University.

to pay both for a bus to transfer to the subway and for the subway itself) made many Co-op City residents feel that they were second-class citizens. However, they were substantially less concerned with being connected to their immediate surroundings. An article on the transit dilemma in the *Co-op City Times* in 1969 spent more time discussing potential links between Co-op City with either Manhattan or with educational institutions such as the elite Bronx High School of Science and Lehman College than with the rest of the northeast Bronx.[119]

Walking to or from the development was difficult and unpleasant, because it meant crossing over or under a highway or large thoroughfare. In 1973 the Bronx Planning Commission proposed a highway overpass to connect Co-op City to its surrounding neighborhoods. At a hearing to discuss the proposal, "residents of all colors and nationalities" rejected it as "an affront to Co-op City and its residents" and a "blight on the community."[120] When rumors spread of plans for a low-income housing project to be built by NYCHA near Co-op City, the UHF responded carefully, confirming that yes, the Boston Secor Houses public housing project was near Co-op City, but that there were no plans for additional low-income housing in the immediate vicinity.[121]

Despite the reluctance of many Co-op City residents to be connected with their immediate surroundings, the neighborhood next to Co-op City was quite different from the West Bronx that many early Co-op City-ites had left. Baychester was home to fifty-five thousand residents—similar to the number that would live in Co-op City once it achieved full occupancy in 1972—two-thirds of whom were white and lower middle class. The remaining one-third was Black and generally recent arrivals in the neighborhood.[122] In other words, racially, Baychester and Co-op City were remarkably demographically similar. However, unlike Co-op City, Baychester was made up of single-family homes, and the white community tended to be Italian and Irish rather than Jewish. And while Baychester's minority families were generally homeowners like their white neighbors, they were looked on with suspicion by whites, who feared they would bring inner-city problems to this conservative, outer-borough neighborhood. Even more vigorously than Co-op City's residents fought the possibility of subsidized rental housing in the development, Baychester homeowners' associations fought the incursion of subsidized housing into their neighborhood.[123] The construction of Co-op City, with its majority population of liberal Jews who would constitute the largest Democratic bloc in New York State, made the northeast Bronx more rather than less liberal. Furthermore, while crime in the West Bronx had been rising over the later part of the 1960s, this was not true in the northeast Bronx neighborhoods that surrounded the new Co-op City development[124]

Yet this reality was rarely acknowledged by Co-op City's residents. According to one report in 1970, the Forty-Fifth Precinct that covered Co-op City and its surrounding neighborhood was the "quietest in the city."[125] But for the readers of Co-op City's two newspapers, the UHF-controlled *Co-op City Times* and the privately owned *City News*, Co-op City was situated in a roiling sea of crime, drugs, and disorder. Even minor crimes received front-page coverage. In 1970, the *City News*, for example, breathlessly reported a 105 percent increase in larcenies in one month in the Forty-Fifth Precinct, while noting in passing that there had not been a single homicide in the precinct over that time and failing to mention that the rise in crime may have had something to do with the thousands of new residents moving in.[126]

Co-op City's residents were keenly attuned to any sign of increased crime. The Co-op City Tenants Council released a statement in 1970 explaining that "a vast majority of us have come, or will be coming from areas, which were considered high crime areas. We can only count our blessings that thus far the same cannot be said about Co-op City. . . . But our continued good fortune cannot be guaranteed."[127] Even the slightest anxiety was blown out of proportion. In one instance, a woman complained that along one ramp,

FIGURE 13.   Outside of a building, 1969. Amalgamated Clothing Workers of America Records, Kheel Center, Cornell University.

there was "shrubbery and no police patrol," leading to people being harassed by "outsiders." She concluded, "We ran away from neighborhoods where we had to cope with this situation, came to Co-op City hoping to forget fears and live peacefully. We don't want this to be our way of life as we put a lot of money and work into furnishing our homes and don't want to have to run elsewhere."[128] This concern about crime was inflected by two anxieties that often bled into each other—one about youth, and the second about race.

The UHF publicly insisted that it was interested in creating a community of "thousands of people of all age groups from pre-school tots to senior citizens . . . [who] have enriched their lives by sharing their interests with others."[129] Nevertheless, it remained especially interested in appealing to families with young children. One ad stressed that the development was a "Young Family's World," while another announced "if you have children, you will love the wonderful new world of Co-op City."[130] The majority of apartments were designed with a family with young children in mind, and the UHF's plan for an Educational Park within Co-op City's borders was made specifically to attract families with school-age children.[131] The UHF worked with the city to design playgrounds, and recruited residents to help construct and clean up sandboxes.[132] This emphasis on providing homes and facilities for young families in Co-op City was also connected to the UHF vision of a cooperative future. Ostroff explained that in cooperative developments, "children will be educated for the purpose of being creative, to utilize leisure profitably, to enjoy life in a society based on abundance and cooperation rather than a system based on scarcity and competition."[133]

Despite this intent, Co-op City disproportionately attracted a very different age cohort: the elderly. The development's population skewed old, with 19 percent of the initial population over the age of sixty, a proportion that slightly exceeded that of the Bronx as a whole.[134] An early 1970s sociological study that examined Co-op City's status as a "Naturally Occurring Retirement Community" noted, "At any time, it is the elderly of Co-op City who appear to be omnipresent. It is predominantly this group which may be found sitting on benches, shopping, coming and going from various social centers, including clubs, churches and synagogues, and chatting among themselves—or just watching the passing parade."[135] The UHF was aware of the "excessive applications" from the elderly and hoped that the Educational Park might help reverse this trend.[136]

In fact, the UHF did manage to attract a good number of families with young children to Co-op City. But there were also many teenagers in the development. And for these teenagers, there was very little to do.[137] Younger children might enjoy playgrounds, young parents were preoccupied with raising their children, and the elderly seemed largely content with the out-size array of clubs and other organizations in the development, but there was little in Co-op City to engage teenagers. The UHF recognized the issue, offering a teen center for a brief time, and many of Co-op City's organizations had "youth" branches or offered youth activities.[138] Phillips particularly sought to bring teenagers and older residents together in discussion sessions, where he encouraged them to talk about issues of concern both in the development and the wider world, including everything from drugs to Vietnam.[139] These officially sanctioned activities failed to attract a very large audience. Instead, teenagers tended to congregate outside the buildings, often hanging out above the heating vents in the winter to stay warm.[140] Some older residents viewed these teenagers, talking loudly, smoking cigarettes, and listening to music, as "an irritant, a gesture of defiance."[141]

For many elderly residents of Co-op City, any use of public space by others was looked on with suspicion as a sign of the development's deterioration. A. Horowitz complained to the *Co-op City Times*, "This Tuesday, the first real summer day of the season, I was horrified to see the lovely view from our windows in Bldg. 9 transformed into an ordinary slum. Instead of sitting

FIGURE 14. Play structures in Section One. Undated. Amalgamated Clothing Workers of America Records, Kheel Center, Cornell University.

on the benches, women squatted on the grass, children romped, rolled and played all over this new grass. This was an instant slum."[142] In 1970, the *Co-op City Times* published an open forum asking whether residents should be allowed to sit in front of the buildings, and received almost entirely negative responses.[143] One respondent described the scene in the following terms:

> Now when the sun is shining some of my lovely neighbors come out, taking their beach chairs along, also a few cans of soda and some fruit. If the ice-cream man comes along they get ice cream and believe it or not, it looks like Coney Island in the olden days. I am asking the people who sit around these houses "Are you making a beachhead in front of your beautiful home? What will people who come to visit their friends and relatives say when they see all this? . . . I would like to see posters in places where people gather, telling them what to do and not to do, not only in English, but in Spanish, Italian and Jewish. Maybe that will keep our great community that is called Co-op City, a little better, a little nicer and more neat.[144]

In 1973, thirty-nine residents received summonses for playing ball on the grass, with the explanation that "too many of us who live here are ignorant about our roles in the community. We own that grass and all of us—mothers, fathers and younger cooperators should protect it. Too many of us have brought with us our tenant type of feeling. We understand what it is to be tenant, but this is a cooperative (we own the joint)."[145] The *Co-op City Times* tried to take a middle ground by educating readers as to the "Yesses and Noes of Grass and Shrubs," explaining that while "organized ball games, with a hard ball and bat, are not permitted on the lawn . . . an informal game of catch with a soft ball, will be permitted as long as bench sitters or passersby are not endangered."[146] Playing on the grass meant the destruction of the grass and was therefore a sign that one did not fully respect one's role as a caretaker of the environment of the cooperative. One teenager countered this criticism, writing to the *City News* to state that "people say the grass is for looking at. When grass is looked at—it serves no purpose at all. In the bad sections of the Bronx . . . they have much less grass but the people play ball, and enjoy themselves."[147] However, most simply ignored these admonishments. The conflicts between children and teenagers who wished to play, sit, or stand on the grass and older residents who wished to enjoy it from a distance did not abate.

The problems that many of Co-op City's senior citizens had with its youth were not limited to loitering and ball playing. Vandalism was also a major concern for many Co-op City residents of all ages, and this they blamed, almost universally, on the young. One Co-op City resident reported, "The youngsters are destroying the place, the vandalism is terrific."[148] Another suggested that parents of those children caught vandalizing property in Co-op City be responsible for paying damages.[149] For many residents, the sight of vandalism and graffiti was a tangible symbol that Co-op City was not an oasis free from social problems. In the words of Ernesto Christiano, a resident who wrote to the *Co-op City Times* in 1971, vandalism and graffiti were "'slum signs' that are gradually appearing in and about our beloved Co-op City."[150] The perhaps overweening response to the supposed degradation of their environment was a function of the combination of hopes and anxieties placed by its residents in this tenuous utopia. Each piece of graffiti, each incident where teenagers spoke a little too loudly, each can of soda that lay carelessly on the ground was a sign that their promised haven had been a disappointment. As one cooperator put it, "I love my apartment despite its creaking floors . . . I love the river that it faces, but I want it to be the Shangri-la that I dreamed of. I do hope that something will be done about the front of the house I live in. Let it not remain the blight that it is on our dream city—Co-op."[151]

Concerns about teenage defiance and crime could be exacerbated by racial anxieties, especially because the elderly of Co-op City were almost exclusively Jewish, while there was much more racial and ethnic diversity among younger people.[152] This was not always explicit in the stories that Co-op City residents traded about the behavior of youth in the cooperative. However, often it was only thinly disguised, as in this outlandish story one man told about an incident on a bus. "Two school girls got on . . . pushed to the back, pulled out cigarettes and lit them, and threw the empty pack at an elderly man [and] had the gall to say 'Enjoy Co-op City because in 3 years you'll be running again.'"[153] The role of race in concerns about neighborhood decline can also be seen in a story from Elba Cabrera about the afternoon her teenage son was playing the congas in his room. "One day, our neighbor . . . rang the bell and complained about the Conga . . . and then she added to that 'We thought we left it all behind.' She was referring to the fact that wherever she came from, there were Puerto Ricans . . . and they thought that moving to paradise that they weren't going to find people like us."[154]

Clearly, Ostroff had been correct when he stated that some of Co-op City's residents had not forgotten their old prejudices when they left their old neighborhoods. However, Co-op City was also not a tinderbox of racial resentments, ready to explode. This was made clear after an incident at a teen dance sponsored by the Black Caucus on March 7, 1970, which turned violent when a group of Black teenagers from the "Valley" neighborhood in

Baychester near Co-op City came in and started a fight. The UHF offered to increase security at future teen events, blaming the incident on "the evil of drugs, the evil of crime, and that granddaddy of evils, community apathy."[155] In a statement read at a public meeting about the incident, the Black Caucus said that they hoped "the melee on March 7 would not cause a schism in the community."[156] Indeed, it did not, in part because the Black Caucus sent spokesmen to talk to community meetings in both Co-op City and the "Valley" in an attempt to smooth relations, culminating in a "Afro-American culture night" held in Co-op City's Community Center that brought together both Co-op City residents and their neighbors.[157] The March 7 incident did not recur, and residents appeared to view the turmoil more as an issue of assuring adequate security and a problem of crime in the city as a whole.[158]

While it was certainly true that race was often the subtext of fears about neighborhood decline, it is also significant that it was rarely the text. Co-op City's Jewish residents complained far more about the problems of youth or the incursion of outsiders than they did about their Black or Puerto Rican neighbors. Furthermore, Co-op City's Black Caucus and Spanish-American Club were firmly part of the development's institutional life. For many of Co-op City's Jews, the presence of racial minorities simultaneously signaled their hopes and fears about Co-op City's potential. Many of them were accepting of, and indeed welcomed, a limited degree of diversity, which was part and parcel of their dreams for their new homes. However, the sight of Black and Latino faces could simultaneously spark potent fears of neighborhood degeneration. Nowhere was this tension more striking than with regard to the Co-op City Educational Park.

As previously discussed, the Educational Park was crucial to the UHF's plans for the development. It was also a significant draw that brought many cooperators to Co-op City in the first place. The president of the Educational Park Parents Association, Marcia Schneider, noted, "We the parents, moved to this area with the expectation that all of our children would now receive the very best education possible in New York City. . . . We were pioneers—pioneers in a new experimental community and pioneers in a new experimental educational facility."[159] This was as true for ethnic minorities in Co-op City as it was for its majority population. An open letter to Co-op City from "the Hispanic Community" explained, "Why did Latin-American families come to Co-op City? To find better homes and to seek a better education for their children. . . . Have they found what they were looking for? For most, the answer is a big 'Yes.'"[160] An article in the Co-op City Times explained that Black families selected Co-op City because "we want a good education for our children."[161]

Along with the UHF, the New York City Board of Education expressed the wish that the Educational Park would be racially integrated: "Co-op City was planned as an open community from the time it was no more than a concept in the minds of its founders. The community was to be integrated ethnically and culturally, open to all faiths and races. The Education Park was conceived in the same spirit, only more so."[162] As stated before, Co-op City's racial demographics in the 1970s roughly matched those of the city as a whole, and the fact that its schools would draw from that integrated community was a source of pride for residents. Furthermore, the fact that a number of students from the majority Black nearby Boston Secor Houses would be educated in Co-op City's schools was not controversial.[163] However, when a busing plan was released by city schools chancellor Harvey Scribner in 1971 that promised to send children from the surrounding, largely minority, districts to Co-op City, Co-op City would experience the worst racial crisis in its short history.

Originally the major controversies around education in Co-op City had little to do with integration at all. Instead they focused on the construction delays that meant that the Educational Park would not be finished when residents began to move into the development. IS (Intermediate School) 180 did not open until September 1971, nearly three years after the first residents had arrived in Co-op City. Until that point, students either attended schools in the surrounding neighborhood or in makeshift accommodations within the development itself.[164] The other schools in the development opened over the next two years, with Harry S. Truman High School, the last school to be completed in the Educational Park, opening in September 1973. Many Co-op City residents were initially able to put up with the delays and discomforts during these first few years because of their high hopes for what the Educational Park would become. However, they were in a less accommodating mood as months turned into years. When the district dragged its heels on appointing an administrator to oversee the entire Educational Park, the Committee for Quality Education (CQE), a parent group, which worked with a broad and racially diverse range of community organizations, protested, "By failing to make a commitment to early appointment of an administrator you are . . . telling us you favor division among the people because it is the vested interests of bureaucratic departments to prevent unity. You are paving the way to the educational and social chaos, prevalent throughout the school system, that are the inevitable results of a dream denied. We are prepared for battle. . . . We will use any means necessary to achieve the unity that will only come about [through] the Educational Park."[165] Co-op City's cooperators clung tenaciously to the belief that education, and the Educational

Park, would be the salvation of the fragile dream of social comity that had motivated the development. As New York as a whole struggled with deteriorating school infrastructure and rising violence among students, many believed that it was a "last chance [to provide] good quality education . . . in the City."[166] The city's foot-dragging awakened the sense of being misunderstood and unheard that would motivate so much resident activism in the development. The membership of the CQE saw themselves as underdogs, fighting a city that neither respected nor cared about them. "You have shown little respect for our Co-op City community," the CQE complained; "You have oozed platitudes but you have not shown you really care. You have treated Co-op City as a problem to be handled rather than as an obligation to fulfill."[167]

In April 1971, schools chancellor Harvey Scribner ordered that 750 students from neighboring Districts 12 and 8 would be bused into the Educational Park, starting when the park's first schools opened in the fall.[168] The UHF and the Board of Education had overestimated the share of young families that would move into the development, and as a result, all the schools had excess capacity.[169] Meanwhile, even more inflammatory rumors spread that nine hundred Co-op City children would be bused out at the same time.[170]

Co-op City was located in District 11, a district that was almost equally divided between white and nonwhite students.[171] In the early 1970s, District 11's leadership was made up mostly of Irish and Italians from the northeast Bronx neighborhoods that surrounded Co-op City, and these leaders were implacably opposed to busing.[172] When the news of the busing plan was released, Ed Marshall, UHF member and the only Black member of the Riverbay board, accused District 11 leadership of using "scare tactics" and stressed that Co-op City's residents should not allow District 11 to use them in their battles against busing. However, Marshall's claim that the "Central School Board did not specify that all of the 750 students will have to be bussed into the Education Park immediately" hardly served to placate many Co-op City parents.[173]

In pleading for calm, Marshall and the rest of the UHF were aware that schools had already proved to be the third rail of racial politics in New York and elsewhere in the United States. In 1968, growing tension between New York's increasingly vocal nonwhite populations and its powerful teachers' union, the United Federation of Teachers (UFT), came to a head in the Ocean Hill–Brownsville School District in Brooklyn. After the school board was awarded community control in this majority Black community, the district superintendent, Rhody McCoy, selected new principals from beyond the UFT-approved list of candidates and transferred out of the district nineteen teachers and administrators whom he considered unsupportive or ineffective. This angered the UFT, which protested what it saw as attacks on hard-won concessions on teacher pay, seniority, and the right to avoid transfer. This confrontation led to a series of three citywide teachers' strikes that paralyzed the Board of Education until November 1968.[174] This conflict between a majority Black school district and a teachers' union that was majority Jewish further exacerbated the racial and political atmosphere in New York City, pitting erstwhile progressive allies against each other. Jewish teachers used antisemitic incidents to claim the moral high ground, while Black residents viewed these teachers as part of the "unresponsive and racist power structure."[175] Co-op City's first residents, approximately 70 percent of whom were Jews and many of whom were teachers or other union members, arrived in the development a mere three weeks after the strike came to its bitter conclusion. According to historian Peter Eisenstadt, the teachers' strike destroyed the prospects of integrated education and an integrated community in the UHF's Rochdale Village.[176] The divisiveness of educational politics got its first major test in Co-op City when the Board of Ed's busing plan was released in the spring of 1971.

In the days after Scribner's plan was released, anonymous flyers circulated in Co-op City that attacked the children of Districts 8 and 12 as academically inferior and as discipline problems.[177] Shortly thereafter, a public meeting was held on April 12, in an atmosphere that one attendee later likened to a "lynch mob in the auditorium."[178] At the meeting, District 11 superintendent Carmella Nesi promised that every Co-op City child would get a seat at the Northeast Bronx Educational Park. She also promised to take legal measures against the required busing of out-of-district students.[179] Meanwhile, a spokesman for Republican state senator John D. Calandra read a statement from the senator calling the busing order "arrogant, ridiculous, and illegal," to roars of approval from the crowd.[180] Florence Colucci from the Northeast Bronx Committee for Neighborhood Schools, a pressure group that had earlier fought similar battles in nearby Pelham Bay and Throggs Neck, stated, "The disease of forced busing is now a cancer." She added that the battle over the Educational Park was merely a skirmish in a much larger war: "We must no longer allow the Board of Education to use our children as musical chairs or pawns in their efforts to by-pass the community in the educational process."[181]

Some of Co-op City's white residents shared this hostility toward busing. During the April meeting about the busing plan, audience members shouted racist slogans.[182] The CQE noted that the virulence of the debate was, in part, accounted for by racism: "We would delude ourselves if we supposed that objections to busing out of our children account for all the ugly emotionalism now in Co-op City. There is hatred and racism too."[183] Most of the assembled parents seemed particularly aggrieved by the suggestion that there might not be room for their children at the Educational Park. The activist and UFT administrator Arthur Taub insisted, "This is why we have all moved here, to have this Education Park for our children. We did not move here for our children to be bused out."[184] In a letter to the editor after the meeting, Joseph Laznow proclaimed that "the day that a Co-op City child is denied a seat in a school of the Northeast Bronx Educational Park because of overcrowding brought about by the influx of children from outside the local school district will mark the death of this community."[185]

However, for all the talk of Co-op City's splendid isolation, and for all the ways in which many of Co-op City's residents had come to the development looking to escape turmoil elsewhere in the Bronx, and for all the heated debate in the crowded auditorium, what Co-op City's residents mostly articulated was not an opposition to school integration or even busing. While District 11 officials and community leaders from outside the cooperative were unanimously opposed to busing of any kind, the leaders of major community groups in Co-op City at the meeting went out of their way to assert their support for busing *into* the Educational Park. Arthur Oshins, past chair of the CQE, stated that "there is no moral justification for not allowing outside kids to fill vacant seats here. The people have been told over and over that the school was for the Bronx."[186] The president of the Parents Association stated her support for busing, saying that "we must accept the responsibility of taking the initiative in pioneering the changes needed to rid us of some of our fears and prejudices. We need unity and understanding, and I implore all white and non-white parents to take bold steps to improve the education of our children."[187] Thomas Johnson, president of the Black Caucus, added that his group believed that "the park was going to be part of the New York City school system and that residents were going to have to face the fact that minority students were going to fill a large number of the seats in the Education Park."[188] George Schechter of the UHF added that his children had attended schools that were 90 percent nonwhite. As he concluded his statement, Nesi of District 11 cut him off. "Please George," she said, "that's enough."[189]

Many Co-op City parents also appeared to reject the suggestion by activists from elsewhere in District 11, such as Colucci, to see their issue as part of a larger struggle against forced integration. Rather, what upset Co-op City's parents was primarily the possibility that their students would not be able to take advantage of the benefits of an education in the Educational Park.

In this, Co-op City's white residents saw eye to eye with the leaders of minority groups in the development. Alfred Calderon of the Spanish-American Club stated that his group did not "go along with the proposal that out-of-district students be bussed in at all costs even to the exclusion of Co-op City children."[190] Johnson of the Black Caucus said he "hoped to see Co-op City students and Boston Secor students get priority in the Education Park."[191] Taub similarly emphasized that "every child in Co-op City and the Boston-Secor Houses must have a seat in this Education Park," not limiting the Park to Co-op City residents alone, who themselves already represented a more racially mixed population than many school districts in the city.[192] Despite the fact that they were overwhelming Black, the presence of Boston Secor students was not called into question in the busing controversy.

The position that was held by everyone who spoke, from the Spanish-American Club and the Black Caucus to the CQE to the Jewish community leader Taub, who had long been active in the UFT, appeared to be the same. It was okay for the Educational Park to accept other students, once Co-op City's students had been accommodated, but not okay for Co-op City students to be forced to attend school elsewhere. Busing may have torn apart communities from Boston to the Detroit suburbs, but in Co-op City, behind the heated rhetoric, it appeared to unify the community behind a shared opposition—not to busing or to integrated schools, but to the Board of Ed.[193] At the same time, the heated rhetoric was still there. It was all too easy for Co-op City's majority white parents to slip into racism when articulating what were generally more nuanced positions. Furthermore, in 1971, school integration was perhaps the most racially divisive issue in America. As much as Co-op City's parents may not have been comfortable seeing themselves allied with pressure groups that were much more aggressively anti-integration than they were, this was how their actions were going to be perceived. And it was this perception, rather than the actual intent of the parents, that had the potential to poison race relations in the community. Nevertheless, the legacy of the heated town hall meeting did not seem to linger long in the politics of the community or the memories of Co-op City's residents. It did not reappear in the pages of either the *Co-op City Times* or the *City News*. In 2006, the sociologist Judith Perez interviewed a number of Black residents and former residents of Co-op City. These residents were not shy about discussing racism in the development; however, none of them brought up the 1971 hearing.[194] If the hearing reflected preexisting and persistent tensions, it also did not appear to exacerbate them.

While the most explosive rumors during the busing controversy related to the possibility that Co-op City students could be bused to other districts, it does not appear that there ever was a plan to bus Co-op City students out of the development. Furthermore, a week after the April 1971 meeting, Chancellor Scribner issued an amended order stating that District 8 and 12 students were in fact designated for a variety of District 11 schools, not merely the Educational Park. He also sought to assure restive Co-op City residents that this was merely a continuation of a long-standing plan to bus District 12 students into District 11 and that "the Principals of District 11 state categorically that the pupils who have been bused into our schools performed in a manner comparable to that of children who reside in District 11."[195] District 11 appealed even this, more limited, busing order, and these appeals met a not-entirely unsympathetic audience at Board of Ed headquarters. Deputy Chancellor Irving Anker stated that he was concerned that "District 11 is one of the only districts in the Bronx that can maintain a fairly integrated system."[196] When new information came in June that the original figures regarding the Educational Park's capacity were overstated, Anker stated that he would not be in favor of busing out-of-district children into Co-op City at all.[197] Finally, in October 1971, Scribner officially rescinded the order to bus out-of-district children into District 11 altogether.[198] A year and a half later, District 11 educational officials realized that Truman High School would be significantly underutilized, based on the populations of Co-op City and Boston Secor alone. A new debate would ensue about how to properly fill the remaining seats. Race, and in particular the possibility of exceeding a "tipping point" in the percentage of minorities, would be an issue in this new debate. That debate, however, would proceed free of the rancor that accompanied the 1971 busing proposal—with the ultimate decision to admit students from the entire Bronx in a lottery system.[199]

During the planning process for Co-op City and in the years of its construction, critics repeatedly chided the UHF for the banality of its architectural and urban planning vision. To this day, even historians sympathetic to the UHF's social ambitions have criticized the cooperative's "banal" design, which "left buildings floating in poorly planned open spaces, distancing residents from surrounding streets and neighborhood life."[200] Nevertheless, it became clear that the towers and slabs that comprised Co-op City's thousands of apartments, and the open lawns and cul-de-sacs that were its public spaces, in no way hindered the development of a community. Whether it was children playing in the sandboxes, teenagers hanging out by the heating vents, or elderly people sitting in folding chairs in front of their high-rise towers, Co-op City's landscape was always populated by residents eager to enjoy its public spaces. Moreover, Co-op City's residents deeply cared about the space they occupied. However silly from today's perspective residents' fears might appear about things such as the effect too much playing might have on Co-op City's lawns, the fact was that Co-op City's residents really did care about those lawns. They also cared about the community that formed in this instant city.

Looking back at the development's initial period of occupancy, Don Phillips, Co-op City's community affairs director, reflected, "I often wonder if everyone was happy when Moses finally reached the promised land. I wonder if even today that promised land has lived up to the dreams and expectations of the people. Many good things obviously came out of it and a few bad things. But what the final outcome will be we may never know. I guess you can say the same for Co-op City."[201] This weary sense of equanimity was a fitting reflection on Co-op City's first years. Much of the initial, perhaps overblown, enthusiasm of the UHF and the development's first residents had waned. Nevertheless, Co-op City had become a community—one with all the tensions, dramas, and connections of any group of people, much less one of the size and complexity of Co-op City. When Phillips wrote that the final outcome was one "we may never know," he was thinking about the impossibility of predicting a distant future. However, this phrase also stands as a fitting epitaph to this first era of Co-op City's existence for a different

FIGURE 15. Co-op City Fair, Miss Hot Pants competition, 1972. Amalgamated Clothing Workers of America Records, Kheel Center, Cornell University.

reason. The first five years of Co-op City's existence featured ever-escalating financial pressures, which tested the sustainability of the development and the fortunes of its members. By 1974, these pressures dominated politics in the development, dwarfing the conflicts over race, class, and generation narrated in this chapter. We will never know the kind of community that might have developed in Co-op City had these financial pressures not existed, or if the state had had the means or willingness to ameliorate them.

CHAPTER 3

"We Remember Picket Lines"

Cooperator Militancy, 1970–1974

In 1937, during the depths of the Great Depression, Abraham Kazan issued a clarion call for cooperative housing to revolutionize social relations in American cities: "[Housing] can mold the social fabric. Cooperative housing, and only cooperative housing, can supply this great physical need, and, through it, greatly revise the relation of man to man in the big city. The social outlook and the very ethic and morale of our people can be transformed more effectively through such housing than through any other social agency, for no other institution touches so many facets of life as one's home and community."[1] Kazan argued that in a traditional tenant-landlord relationship, neither party had an authentic relationship to the other or to the home. Landlords viewed "the health, the comfort and the convenience of the occupants" as secondary to "the marketability of the product," while tenants were so alienated from their homes that they regarded them "only as temporary quarters."[2] For him, the solution to this disastrous state of affairs was to disentangle ownership from profit through the cooperative ownership of housing. A society based on cooperatives would promise "open vistas of social well-being combined with individual initiative that fascinate the imagination." To realize this vision, he called for a massive expansion of government credit to construct housing cooperatives. Loans to housing cooperatives, Kazan maintained, would unleash "the self-reliance and initiative of the individual citizen. . . . Through government

96

credit, a nation of cooperative homeowners promises a new era of stability based upon the wholesome foundation of self-help."[3]

Through the UHF, which he founded in 1951, Kazan created something very much like the cooperative landscape he sketched out in this article. Over the course of more than two decades, the UHF built tens of thousands of apartments for moderate-income New Yorkers. UHF cooperatives represented half of the affordable housing constructed in New York in the postwar period. True to Kazan's vision, these apartments were funded by government credit. New York State poured hundreds of millions of dollars into the UHF's coffers largely through low-cost mortgage loans as part of the Mitchell-Lama program. The UHF would build increasingly large projects—culminating in Co-op City's thirty-five towers and 236 town houses that housed over fifty thousand residents. By the 1970s, the UHF was both a major builder and power player in the firmament of New York power politics.

It was at this point, with the UHF's crowning development, that it all began to fall apart.

Co-op City, as both the final UHF project to be completed and by far the largest, was particularly hard hit by financial pressures. By the time construction was completed in 1972, total construction costs had gone from the $283.7 million estimated in 1965 to $422.7 million. Meanwhile, the amount of those costs financed by HFA bonds had ballooned from $235 million in 1965 to $390 million. Over that same period, the average interest rate on Co-op City's mortgage bonds went from 4 percent to 6.25 percent. Cooperators and the UHF alike appealed to the state government for assistance. Yet hemmed in by upstate legislators frustrated by what they saw as giveaways to lazy urbanites, and bankers wary of the potential for HFA default, officials were in no mood to help. The spigot of state funds was impossible to pry open. The UHF raised Co-op City's carrying charges in 1970 and again in 1971, 1973, and 1974. By the time they rose again in 1975, in a move that would prompt the rent strike discussed in the following chapter, they would be 250 percent of what residents had been promised when the development first opened for applications a decade earlier.

While the UHF was disappointed in the failure of the state to come to the aid of strapped cooperators, it preached the gospel of self-reliance and the responsibilities of ownership to Co-op City's residents. As Co-op City's financial situation faltered, the UHF insisted that cooperative responsibility meant that residents had to pay whatever was necessary to balance the books. "I am sure that each and every one of you joins in the hope that we can maintain fiscal solvency for the cooperative," Ostroff wrote in the pages of the *Co-op City Times*. "While we are all only too aware of the difficulties each and every one of our members is going through during this troubled economic period in our country, it does not lessen our responsibility to the cooperative as a whole."[4]

Yet to Co-op City's residents, calls for cooperative responsibility appeared the height of hypocrisy. They did not see themselves as in control of the "success or failure" of Co-op City; rather, as they saw it, control of the development lay with officials in Albany or with the UHF's management. As they repeated time and again in increasingly agitated meetings, residents were not the ones who had been responsible for the cost overruns that had created the development's current predicament. Indeed, although Co-op City residents each had a share of stock in the cooperative, their shares were Class B, or nonvoting, shares. Only the board of directors of Riverbay had Class A shares. The UHF controlled a voting majority on the Riverbay board, and so residents had little input in financial decisions as to how to operate the cooperative. As they saw it, Co-op City's residents were subject to UHF control, but they were also being told they needed to take responsibility for the cooperative's difficult financial situation. As one resident complained, "They tell us when they want us to be tenants and when they want us to be owners."[5] Like tenants, they lacked decision-making power. But as owners, they were expected to take financial responsibility for budget shortfalls, without even the protections offered by New York's rent control and stabilization laws that tenants could claim. In comparison to owning their own home or renting from a landlord, cooperative ownership appeared to be the worst of both worlds. Cooperative ownership may have been a dream to the UHF, but for residents of Co-op City in the 1970s, it had come to seem more like a nightmare.

Prior to Co-op City's inauguration, UHF leadership expressed their concern that people motivated by cheap rents might not demonstrate the community spirit that they hoped for. They needn't have worried. It was apparent from the first that this was a development full of joiners. Millie Vogel, who moved to Co-op City in 1971, explained that "when Co-op City opened, it drew all the people who lived on the Concourse, who were union-oriented, who belonged to things. When they came here, they brought their activism to the community."[6] The UHF saw Co-op City as the culmination of decades of dreams about the possibilities for activism to reshape the city. Its cooperators also saw Co-op City through the lens of a long history of activism. However, in their case, it was the struggle against carrying charge increases that would come to represent this continuity, and the new boss the cooperators had to fight was UHF management itself.

FIGURE 16. Children hold up an issue of the *Co-op City Times* with headlines concerning potential carrying charge increases, 1972. Amalgamated Clothing Workers of America Records, Kheel
Center, Cornell University.

The first rent strike in the new development was proposed not in response
to rent increases, but as a result of delays in providing air conditioning
and other services in June 1969, a mere six months after the first residents
arrived.[7] Within several months, angry parents began to organize around
the issue of education and ongoing delays in completing the Educational

Park.[8] Future Co-op City residents even picketed the UHF in 1970 in a futile attempt to change their delayed move-in date.[9] This was not merely a community of joiners and kvetchers; it was also a community of activists. The roots of this radicalism can be found in the same Lower East Side streets that birthed the UHF itself. The Jews who moved to Co-op City were at most a generation removed from those immigrant communities where labor activism flourished. Many of the men and women who lived in Co-op City were veterans of countless labor struggles, ranging from the prewar garment worker strikes to the 1960s' civil service and teachers' strikes. My family was fairly typical in this regard. Growing up, I did not have a single close family member who had *not* been a union member. Both of my grandmothers had worked as ILGWU seamstresses, my grandfather was a Teamster, my aunt was a teacher in the UFT, my uncle was a union plumber, and my parents met as NYC employees represented by District Council 37 (where my father was a union rep in the Welfare Department during the 1965 civil service strike). I still remember my grandparents' apartment in Building 23 filled with union tchotchkes ranging from ILGWU pens to International Brotherhood of Teamsters pins. Many residents in Co-op City had both similar families and similar tchotchkes.

By 1974, discussion of a rent strike began to take center stage in Co-op City discussions about the development's financial problems, but rent strikes were nothing new in New York City. The same immigrant Jews whose activism had fueled the growth of unions in New York City had also initiated the first American rent strike movement, aimed at protesting high costs and poor living conditions in crowded tenements.[10] Activist Jews, including Socialist Party members who sought to use tenant activism as the means to awaken New Yorkers to the need to fundamentally transform economic and social relations in the city, had been behind the citywide rent strike movement after World War I that ultimately led to the birth of rent control policies.[11] In the early 1960s, a renewed wave of rent strikes would come to be embraced by civil rights leaders and ordinary tenants fed up with the poor housing conditions in nonwhite neighborhoods. In Brooklyn, CORE (Congress of Racial Equality) led a rent strike movement in the early 1960s in Bedford-Stuyvesant. Like the Socialists involved in the post–World War I rent strikes, some leaders hoped that tenant organizing was a means toward "empower[ing] everyday people to take control of the politics in their own communities."[12] Similar groups were involved in movements in Harlem and other Black and Latino neighborhoods in the city. The older and newer generations of tenant activists had close ties to one another and to the labor movement to which so many Co-op City residents were at least tangentially connected.[13] The idea of tenant activism in general and the concept of a rent strike in particular were well familiar to the very people who now lived in Co-op City.

As Co-op City residents began to organize in earnest against rising carrying charges, they were aware not merely of this longer history of worker and tenant activism but also of the turmoil at Rochdale Village, where a resident tenants council had captured the majority of the development's board of directors and fired the UHF-appointed manager in the late 1960s.[14] With Rochdale as their explicit model, in January 1970 a Co-op City Tenants Council organized in response to the officially sponsored Advisory Council to protest against UHF paternalism and potential carrying charge increases. Harriet Colodney, the Tenants Council's first leader, who had also been involved in the threatened rent strike seven months earlier, referred to Ostroff as "Caesar."[15] Other members of the Tenants Council viewed the UHF as both patronizing and incompetent, denouncing its "high-handed attitude" and accusing it of acting in "a manner that smacks of authoritarianism."[16] Co-op City's resident directors of the Riverbay board accused the rest of the board of "treat[ing] us like children."[17] The name "Tenants Council" itself was a provocation—demonstrating that it refused to accept the UHF's insistence that there was a fundamental difference between the "landlord-tenant mentality" and cooperative living and management. Rather than seeking to leave tenancy behind for the cooperative promised land, Colodney and the Tenants Council defiantly insisted that Co-op City's residents were being treated exactly as they would be by unscrupulous landlords. Schechter from the UHF attended the Tenants Council's first organizational meeting. Once there, he dismissed the organization, stating that "your responsibility is not to get yourselves a Tenant Council. Your responsibility is to get yourselves a Co-op City."[18] From the perspective of the UHF, the residents of Co-op City still needed the guiding hand of the UHF leaders, who were experienced in building affordable housing, schooled in the relationship with city and state officials, and understood—and in many cases had personally experienced—the benefits of cooperative living. According to this perspective, too many cooperators still suffered from the "landlord syndrome" and failed to realize their responsibilities as co-owners. As one Co-op City resident who supported the UHF remarked in the spring of 1972, "In this crude, cold world our community could be a haven of harmony, good will and cooperation." Co-op City's economic problems were secondary to the issue of creating a cooperative community that was a "true bright monument for the late Abraham Kazan," who had died a few months earlier, in December 1971.[19]

The Tenants Council would fold within two years; however, this combination of mutual suspicions would only increase. A combination of condescension, combativeness, and defensiveness would mark much of the relationship between Co-op City's management and its residents over the next five and a half years. In and of itself, the fraught relationship between the UHF and Co-op City's residents was not fatal to the development, but it meant that they would have a hard time responding as a united front when financial pressures began to mount over the coming years.

Costs had already begun to spiral out of control during Co-op City's construction process. In 1969, the UHF was able to negotiate a raise of the development's tax exemption from 50 percent to 80 percent. However, this was not sufficient to avoid a major carrying charge increase. On July 1, 1970, a 15.1 percent carrying charge increase went into effect. After the increase, carrying charges would average over $28 per room. The UHF sought various means to limit further increases. In August 1970, the UHF speeded up construction on the remaining uncompleted buildings, explaining that this was made necessary by the financial strains on the development. Ostroff warned, "We could lose millions of dollars a year in carrying charges and interest charges if we don't get these buildings occupied rapidly."[20] Residents complained that maintenance suffered as a result, and it is also likely that the accelerated schedule impacted the quality of construction as well, with long-term effects for the cooperative. Moreover, the UHF began to charge differential carrying charges for apartments. Schechter explained that there was a premium for apartments with "good exposure, higher floor, favorable view, large foyer, a bathroom window, and extra closets."[21] Although it was not publicly announced, residents who moved in later paid higher carrying charges than those who first moved in. In 1971, the *City News* demonstrated that residents in Building 1 in Section One paid an average of $28.81 a room, while in Building 33 in Section Five they were charged $33.23 a room.[22] This disparity was even more galling because residents of Section Five, the final section occupied in the development, were more likely to be nonwhite.[23]

In early 1971, Ostroff announced the possibility of an additional 10 to 15 percent hike to carrying charges, blaming this on the need to employ 500 people as maintenance staff, rather than the originally planned 425. Ostroff claimed this was necessary because of the need to hire extra security personnel and locksmiths to combat "excessive vandalism" in the community.[24] Vandalism may have been a convenient scapegoat, but it was only part of the story. This became clear in July when Ostroff released a plan for a 35 percent rise in carrying charges spread out over three years. He apologized for any difficulties this hefty increase would cause for residents, but explained that it was made necessary by rising construction costs as the development neared completion.[25] Ostroff also worried that New York City's economic woes might lead the city to curtail "essential services," requiring the UHF to pick up the slack in its developments.[26]

Much of this rise in carrying charges can be traced to the rise in interest rates and project costs. In 1965, construction costs represented 91 percent of the total cost of Co-op City. By 1971, this had declined to 81 percent, owing to the rising cost of mortgage interest. In 1965, the HFA projected that Co-op City's mortgage bonds would earn an interest rate of 4 percent; however, they ultimately averaged a 6.25 percent interest rate. Meanwhile, the size of the mortgage itself ballooned by over $150 million over its 1965 estimate. By the time construction ended, Co-op City owed $390 million on its mortgage, and 40 to 50 percent of monthly resident carrying charges consisted solely of debt service.[27] Desperate to avoid increasing carrying charge rates, the UHF got the DHCR to agree to extend the initial occupancy period from March 1972 (when construction actually concluded) to December 1972. As Ostroff explained in a 1971 memo to the UHF board, "If the development stage were finished, it would be necessary to consider carrying charge increases. . . . However, since there is a commitment that the increase in carrying charges would only go into effect after the completion of the development stage, all of the operating losses incurred in the next year and a half are being capital-ized as development cost. . . . By this method, we are able to maintain the present carrying charge structure for another year and a half."[28] In other words, by extending the official construction period, the UHF was able to continue to take out loans to subsidize its operating costs for an additional nine months. Furthermore, so long as the UHF was in its construction phase, it was not responsible for paying back the principal on its mortgage. This was only a temporary fix. These loans would need to be paid back, and they only increased the debt burden on Co-op City's residents once the spigot was finally turned off at the end of 1972.[29]

On January 1, 1973, carrying charges went up an additional 20 percent.[30] Yet even this was insufficient. Co-op City was accruing an operating deficit that would reach $16,361,969 by March 31, 1975.[31] This was not merely a result of its ballooning mortgage. In 1973, a new problem began to make an impact. Because utility costs were not billed directly to residents but instead folded into monthly carrying charges, Co-op City and other UHF develop-ments were uniquely vulnerable to rising utility rates. The development used more than a million gallons of oil a month. As early as 1971, the price of the oil used to provide heat to the development had already risen 100 per-cent from the planning stages of Co-op City.[32] By the end of 1973, these costs began to reach devastating proportions, as the oil crisis caused by the OPEC oil embargo raised the price of heating oil. In December 1973, Ostroff

FIGURE 17.   Co-op City under construction, December 1970. AP photo / Jim Wells.

explained that heating costs had gone up from between four to five dollars a room to fifteen dollars a room, an increase of over 350 percent. Meanwhile, with the Co-op City power plant still not operational, the UHF was stuck paying Con Ed's skyrocketing electric rates.[33] UHF officials begged cooperators to restrict their use of heat and electricity. However, this was of limited effectiveness.[34] As 1973 turned to 1974, it was certain that carrying charges would rise again, as part of the originally planned 35 percent increase announced in 1971. But it was now unclear if this would even be enough to stanch the financial bleeding, fueling more intense anxieties among cooperators about ever-escalating costs with no end in sight.

As carrying costs rose, the UHF pleaded for calm from Co-op City's outraged residents and sought to impress on them that the economic issues afflicting Co-op City were due to forces beyond their control. Schechter told a reporter, "Do they think I'm responsible for these rent increases? Do they hold me responsible for the way the economy is going? I'm flattered if they think I have as much control over this country's economy as President Nixon. I had as much to do with the rent increases as the residents did."[35] Ostroff similarly announced to a packed auditorium of outraged residents, "I know that in spite of our national economic uncertainties, most of you will find Co-op City meeting a good portion of your hopes and aspirations.

This factor, economic stability, is a violently disturbing one. It is, however, the hard economic fact of life as it exists in the turbulent economy of the United States. This is a factor over which we in Co-op City have no control."[36] UHF leadership also stressed that cooperators had no choice but to honor their responsibilities as cooperative owners of the development.[37]

In private, UHF leaders were themselves increasingly distraught about rising costs in their developments. They worried that inflation meant not only their own fate, but that of the "entire democratic system" was increasingly precarious.[38] And they repeatedly agonized over the fact that "so-called middle income housing" was no longer affordable for ordinary families.[39] In 1972, the UHF canceled the Twin Pines project planned for Brooklyn because it would have been so expensive to construct that it would have been out of the reach of middle- and working-class New Yorkers.[40] For similar reasons it also scuttled a massive project in Jersey City that would have been partially financed by federal dollars.[41] However, canceling these projects left the UHF in a difficult position. The UHF had only been able to keep itself financially afloat because of the constant influx of construction funds from new projects. In May 1974, a CSI/UHF board meeting announced a deficit of $330,000 due to the absence of new construction money to fill its coffers. On the one hand, Ostroff insisted that the UHF could no longer responsibly build projects that its "basic membership could not afford."[42] But without construction money coming in, it could not subsidize Co-op City or its other projects as residents faced repeated carrying charge increases.

While the UHF may have found itself in a financially precarious situation it had never faced before, in response it turned to a strategy it had used time and again: lobbying the state legislature to give some assistance to Co-op City. It organized letter-writing campaigns to local, state, and federal officials.[43] In 1972, it arranged a caravan of senior citizens from Co-op City and other UHF developments to Albany to rally for a law to grant expanded tax abatement to senior citizen cooperators.[44] In 1973 and 1974 it supported state legislation that would have raised the income limits for large families, lowered Co-op City's mortgage interest rate, and increased the subsidies available to senior citizens.[45] Ostroff personally lobbied Governor Malcolm Wilson in 1974 to support relief for Co-op City and other Mitchell-Lama residents.[46] However, there were clear limits to UHF activism. The UHF had worked hand in hand with the state for two decades in order to construct tens of thousands of units of affordable housing; the idea that it would choose a path of complete opposition or default on its obligations was unthinkable. The UHF could only see the losses that might result from a strategy of confrontation. As Ostroff explained in a letter to the Riverbay board, "Consciously we could not and would not set in motion forces that could only lead to either a take-over by a State agency as mortgagee or absolute bankruptcy for the housing company." Furthermore, he argued, such a strategy could result in the forfeiture of the equity deposits that cooperators had had to pay when they moved in and "in effect, convert Co-op City into a public housing development."[47]

The UHF leadership saw themselves as stuck between an increasingly recalcitrant state and increasingly militant cooperators. They could understand the logic of state officials who were insisting on carrying charge increases to cover Co-op City's ballooning costs. In contrast, while they were sympathetic to the financial constraints experienced by many cooperators, they viewed the confrontational tactics embraced by many in Co-op City as an existential threat to their organization and to their mission to provide affordable housing. Ostroff described one lawsuit that was filed to halt a carrying charge as motivated by a desire to "destroy the reputation of the Foundation."[48] In an open letter to cooperators in June 1972, Edward Aronov, Co-op City's executive manager, explained that the UHF "want[s] to work closely with the Advisory Council to develop an overall set of goals, political and economic that can be fought for in the local legislature—State legislature—and perhaps even nationally so as to achieve the economic security that is so necessary for a viable community." However, he saw these economic problems as less important than the threat posed by cooperators themselves. "The only thing, in my estimation that can prevent Co-op City from becoming the outstanding example of [a cooperative] community in the United States is a downgrading and bad mouthing of the development by the cooperators."[49]

The state's commissioner of housing and community renewal, Charles J. Urstadt, was the state official most directly responsible for handling financial matters related to Co-op City. When Urstadt insisted on carrying charge increases, he framed these demands as the iron law of economic logic. In a 1971 open letter to a resident who complained about carrying charge increases, Urstadt emphasized that "the simple fact is that the dollars needed to operate the project and meet debt service have to add up. There is no manna from heaven falling to enhance the treasuries of non-profit cooperatives such as Co-op City."[50] Meanwhile, he sidestepped concerns about the UHF's fitness as managers by insisting that the state held itself aloof from such day-to-day matters. "We don't set rents. . . . Residents must understand that we are not the managers of Co-op City, and what we try to do is provide mortgage money. If we were to check every penny that management spent, then we might as well be the managers."[51] Urstadt made it clear that cooperators and the UHF should not look to the state to help bail out the development or prevent future carrying charge hikes.[52]

This is perhaps not surprising, considering the fact that by 1973, Co-op City was not the only Mitchell-Lama development in dire straits. In fact, Urstadt only had to look to New York City–backed Mitchell-Lama projects to see how bad the situation for the state might get. By 1971, fifty-one Mitchell-Lama projects backed by New York City loans were in arrears. The city had to cover these defaults. This problem was compounded by the fact that the city had floated bonds based not on the amount that developers could pay back, but rather based on the value of the real estate that was to be constructed. The city was responsible for over a billion dollars in loans, but it did not have billions of dollars of assets that it could sell to cover those loans, if (or increasingly when) these projects went into default. This was a major factor that contributed to New York City's growing financial crisis and near bankruptcy.[53] The main reason that the state had not fallen into a similar Mitchell-Lama crisis was that Urstadt was more willing to abide increases in rents and carrying charges than was his city counterpart.[54]

Few Co-op City residents understood the ins and outs of Mitchell-Lama financing. For them, the seemingly constant drumbeat of carrying charge increases took a financial and emotional toll. Living in Co-op City was a source of pride precisely because it represented residents' middle-class aspirations. As Betty Romoff put it, "We came to Co-op City to live in dignity. We came to Co-op City . . . to raise our children in good surroundings, with carrying charges as were promised for middle income families, allowing us the means to." However, rising costs threatened this vision. "People in Co-op City *do not* want 'Welfare'! They are hard working, dedicated people. Don't put people up against a wall and put a bullet through them!"[55]

Of course, just like middle-class homeowners elsewhere in America who relied on federally insured mortgages to afford their homes, Co-op City's residents were the recipients of government largesse. The development received a tax abatement from the city, and the HFA mortgage bonds that financed Co-op City's construction were backed by the state and thus were issued at interest rates far lower than would have been the case had Co-op City been constructed outside the Mitchell-Lama program.[56] Nevertheless, the self-perception of Co-op City-ites was that they were not in the same class as those who received direct assistance. "Other people think that a lot of welfare and subsidized families live at Co-op City. That's just not true. We all pay our own way."[57]

Co-op City residents may have been economically middle class, but they were often the first generation of their families to achieve this status.

Moreover, they often arrived in Co-op City either from neighborhoods that were rapidly becoming slums or from NYCHA projects themselves. Their grasp on a middle-class identity felt tenuous, a source of pride but also a source of anxiety.[58] Increasing costs raised both the possibility that residents could not afford to stay in the cooperative and the possibility that to do so might require the very reliance on the state that would threaten their identities as members of the middle class. Cooperators pleaded for the state and the UHF to recognize that "for us, Co-op City is the last outpost in New York City. If we get pushed out of here, we have to move elsewhere and we don't want to. Reducing this rent increase is a life or death struggle. If the people lose this fight and must continue to pay rent increases, they will have to move."[59]

As residents suffered the economic effects of the carrying charge increases, old rumors that Co-op City was prepared to accept welfare families resurfaced. When asked directly at one town hall meeting if this was the case, Ostroff replied defiantly, while punching at the air, "If anyone was on welfare when they applied and they had the down payment to move in, then they came in. I would be the last person to throw out a welfare family."[60] This was a shocking statement from Ostroff, who had been the most vocal proponent of denying welfare families a place in Co-op City during the initial application process in the late 1960s. At that point, Ostroff had rushed to assure potential residents that their neighborhood would be an exclusively cooperative community, one that would not admit people on public assistance. However, now faced with both financial pressures and cantankerous cooperators, Ostroff was no longer interested in accommodating the fears of these cooperators, and instead wanted both to assure the viability of the cooperative at all costs and to claim the moral high ground in his standoff with Co-op City's residents. Ostroff cast residents as "bigots" who feared admitting welfare families and cheats who were unwilling to shoulder their share of the burden of economic misery that afflicted the entire nation.[61] Faced with the economic and existential threat of financial ruin, the management of Co-op City and the cooperators that lived in it could not find common ground.

Some cooperators accepted the assurances of UHF leaders that they were doing all they could. Meyer Bernstein wrote, "Ways and Means must be found to stop the proposed increase. But it will not be done by a handful of Don Quixotes charging a windmill. Let's be realistic. Riverbay and UHF are against the rent raise even as you and I: and to accuse them of being responsible for it is inane. I think that we should join them in battling the real enemy. UHF is the wrong objective."[62] Lorraine Holtz agreed. "Our problems are not insurmountable, yet they cannot be swept away and ignored.

Only through positive action (not strikes or marches) such as meetings with our community leadership, can we succeed in making Co-op City problem free."[63]

Increasingly, however, the majority of residents saw the UHF as part of the same power structure that was imposing the cost increases in the first place. In part this was a problem of the UHF's own making. When, in 1971, UHF leadership initially heard about the need for a second increase in carrying charges, they did not immediately inform the Advisory Council. To many in the community who had just gotten over the 15 percent increase the previous year, this second one was a shock. Ostroff publicly apologized for this oversight, but the damage to public trust still lingered.[64] The UHF's credibility was weakened in other ways. A 1971 investigation sought to tie the UHF to a kickback scheme, whereby wealthy speculators with connections to Bronx politicians were able to get cheap leases in the development's shopping centers.[65] Revelations of construction problems also began to appear in the press.[66] Even if the shopping center investigation ultimately ended inconclusively, and even if the full extent of the construction issues was not yet known, all this press coverage contributed to a growing sense that the UHF was corrupt.[67]

Many critics intimated that the UHF was hiding graft behind its protestations of economic necessity. In their eyes, the UHF's claims that Co-op City residents needed to pay their fair share was actually a cover for a more nefarious conspiracy. According to Advisory Council member Michael Sicilian, the UHF was either incompetent or dishonest: "If Mr. Ostroff, with all his experience and know-how couldn't see the handwriting of spiraling inflation on the wall in the period of 1964–1971, then he is in worse shape than we are. No, I think it is more plausible that UHF and Community Services, once committed to sponsoring and developing Co-op City, had to attract clients with the hoax of moderate rentals. After all, once the families had established themselves in their 'Promised Land,' they would have little choice but to stay put and pay once the trap was sprung."[68] Another resident echoed Sicilian's logic: "Does Mr. Ostroff and company think he can completely pull the wool over the eyes of all people? . . . He and those who approved this outrageous [increase] feel they have the people of Co-op City by the throat! Their thoughts are 'Where can they go with all rents going for whatever is asked? They *must* pay and stay here. We have them trapped like a bunch of rats.'"[69] The image of rats recurred elsewhere in opposition to the UHF, such as in the words of the Tenants Council president, Leonard I. Hanks. "I liken Harold Ostroff to the Pied Piper of Hamlin, with this obvious exception. Whereas the Pied Piper drowned the rats to save the people,

Harold Ostroff is drowning the people to save the rats."[70] For some residents the UHF's refusal to take seriously concerns about affordability was a continuation of its generally paternalistic attitude toward the residents of UHF cooperatives. Sheila Silver, who became a building captain during the rent strike, recalled her mounting frustration: "They've treated us with contempt from the moment we moved in here. If anything ever went wrong, like once the a/c went off, and you'd walk into the office, very politely, to ask when is the air conditioning going back on, they'd say 'Whatsamatta. In the old neighborhood you had air conditioning? Here you can't live even one day without a/c?' I mean what kind of a way is that to talk to a cooperator?"[71]

Despite this rhetoric coming from Advisory Council members and other residents who protested rent increases, UHF leadership continued to believe that "the great silent majority" of Co-op City residents were still in their favor. Rather than addressing the concerns of the vocal dissenters, they believed that their "major job was to overcome the apathy which exists in the community."[72] Toward that end, in 1972, the UHF hired a public relations firm for an annual $48,000 fee and organized "Cooperators for Co-op City" to defend the reputation of the UHF.[73] Cooperators for Co-op City introduced itself as a group dedicated to providing a "constructive voice for the population of Co-op City" and counteracting the negative image created by those who "preach confrontation and distrust and who would divide the community."[74] But resident mistrust was too high for Cooperators for Co-op City to achieve its goals. Immediately after it was formed, opponents warned that its membership mostly consisted of UHF members "who obviously take us . . . for a flock of dupes."[75]

While no polls were taken, the mass support that the rent strike of 1975–76 would later enjoy points to the fact that the UHF's opponents were not merely the loudest voices—they were also in the majority. In 1971, the Advisory Council collected tens of thousands of dollars from cooperators to support activities aimed at achieving a rollback of the carrying charge increases.[76] In November 1971, it used $5,000 of this money to retain attorney Louis Nizer.[77] In April 1972, Nizer attended state hearings on the carrying charge increase, along with over four hundred Co-op City residents. They all walked out when they felt that their concerns had been unheard. Arthur Oshins, resident member of the Riverbay board, commented that he "was very proud of the community for . . . instinctively [knowing] that it was the proper thing to do (walk out). . . . The community realizes that a reduction in the increase won't come through persuasion of the people who imposed it in the first place."[78] In 1972, Nizer filed a $110 million lawsuit on behalf of residents against the UHF, Community Services, Riverbay, and New York State, alleging that the defendants misled Co-op City's potential cooperators about the cost of construction and then defrauded them by improperly allowing Community Services to pass excess costs on to cooperators.[79] Lobbying and legal actions were only part of the means that residents used to fight carrying charge increases. As tensions rose, cooperators increasingly turned to more aggressive tactics, including mass rallies attended by politicians such as Abraham Beame as he ran for mayor in 1973.[80] In an emotional speech to the Advisory Council, Sol Oratofsky of the Senior Citizens Club of Co-op City recommended militancy in response to carrying charge increases: "When it comes to action, come to the old timers. We remember picket lines; we've had our heads broken; and we're willing to do it again."[81]

In July 1974, Steering Committee III (SCIII) was formed by residents to fight further carrying charge increases.[82] SCIII consisted of representatives from the resident Advisory Council, resident directors of Riverbay, and building association leaders, as well as representatives from other civic organizations in the cooperative. From the outset, SCIII considered a "full carrying charge increase strike" as a response to further carrying charge increases and voted unanimously for a strike test-run in September. As one member stated, "The time for requests are over. We have got to have full community support for action. We have played by the rules—we went to Albany, we met with management, we were gentlemen and ladies—and still we face increased rents. Management has got to understand we are not fooling around."[83] SCIII boasted the support of local government officials, including City Councilman Stephen Kaufman and Assemblyman Alan Hochberg.[84]

The establishment of SCIII represented an escalation in Co-op City's three-sided standoff among the UHF, the HFA, and residents. Fearful of cooperator militancy, Ostroff suggested desperate measures, including delaying bills, withdrawing reserve funds, and employing accounting tricks with the hopes that the UHF could "squeeze out" every possible savings from Co-op City's budget and avoid a further increase until at least April of the following year. It was his hope that perhaps in the 1975 state legislative session, relief for Co-op City might be forthcoming. Yet this did little to win him the support of skeptical activists, who feared the possible consequences of spending down Co-op City's reserves.[85] Meanwhile, DHCR commissioner Lee Goodwin was equally unreceptive to Ostroff's plan, stating that Co-op City's carrying charges needed to rise not only to deal with its current $10 million deficit but also to cover long-range projections of future deficits. She floated the possibility of a 30 percent carrying charge hike.[86] Accounting gimmicks like the ones that Ostroff proposed were viewed as insufficient by both Goodwin and Co-op City's increasingly restive residents.

Avoiding explicit mention of a strike, Al Abrams, chair of both the Advisory Council and SCIII, wrote to Governor Wilson shortly after SCIII was founded to inform him that they would *"totally reject any future increases in rentals and will take all appropriate yet prudent preventative measures."*[87] Wilson repeated the state line, responding that "[DHCR] cannot responsibly bar a future carrying charge adjustment as the housing company has fixed obligations that must be met to protect the financial viability of the project and the equity investment made by the shareholders."[88] Abrams and Wilson were talking past each other. Abrams was concerned with the affordability of the complex for residents, while Wilson insisted that carrying charges needed to cover all the costs that Co-op City faced. In 1974, there was no way to do both at the same time: if Co-op City's costs were covered entirely by the carrying charges paid by residents, it would not be affordable for the majority of people who lived there. Co-op City and New York State were on a collision course.

To demonstrate their resolve to fight carrying charge increases, in September 1974, approximately 85 percent of residents turned over their carrying charge checks to SCIII. At noon on September 10, a caravan of residents wheeled over shopping carts containing plastic bags filled with rent checks to Riverbay headquarters in Shopping Center 2. From his wheelchair, an elderly resident "mustered the strength to turn over the first bag of checks" on the desk of Ed Aronov, Co-op City's executive manager. The entire spectacle was caught by reporters and photographers from New York's daily newspapers, including the *Daily News*, the *New York Post*, and the *New York Times*.[89] In a subsequent press conference, Abrams attacked Goodwin and Ostroff by name and declared, "We, cooperative residents of Co-op City, want the UHF and their fancy friends upstate to know—we don't give a hoot for the saleability of state housing bonds which are floated for super-profits for the few from the pockets of moderate income workers. We are fighting to maintain our homes."[90]

Ostroff wrote meekly to Governor Wilson to "investigate the possibilities of a state mortgage interest assistance loan program for Mitchell-Lama housing companies."[91] Wilson replied to Ostroff with vague promises of support if he won election later that year; however, he stressed again that he had no particular sympathy for Co-op City's plight. Instead, he asked for Ostroff's "cooperation in an even more broadly-based effort at the next Session to seek solutions to our overall housing problems which treat in an even-handed fashion the needs not only of the tenants living in publicly-assisted housing, but also the needs of owners and tenants in the private sector."[92] For her part, Commissioner Goodwin was unmoved. She repeated her conviction that she saw no alternative to a carrying charge increase and warned that a strike would lead to foreclosure and the takeover of Co-op City by the HFA on behalf of the banks that owned HFA bonds.[93] It was unclear what such a takeover might mean, but it was clear that Co-op City's residents could not expect relief from Wilson or his housing commissioner.

Co-op City residents placed their hopes in the upcoming gubernatorial election. After a visit to Co-op City in August 1974, Hugh Carey, then a candidate in the Democratic gubernatorial primary, released a statement that would come to haunt him: "I believe in this year of deceptions and cover-ups at the highest levels of government that we have had enough of politicians who break commitments to the people. I run for governor to honor the commitments we have made, not to break them. And I stand here to reaffirm my personal commitment to the thousands of people who live in Mitchell-Lama housing throughout the state." This promise led Co-op City residents to overwhelmingly support Carey in his successful bid to win the Democratic nomination.[94] In November's general election, 89 percent of Co-op City's voters cast their votes for Carey rather than Malcolm Wilson, the incumbent Republican governor—the highest percentage of any neighborhood in New York City.[95] The UHF and Co-op City residents were united in their hopes that Carey's election would provide them with long-awaited financial relief. However, they differed on what they would do if such relief was not forthcoming. Ostroff warned that this would mean "residents would have to accept the bitter pill of another rent increase to meet Co-op City's financial obligations." But Co-op City residents were not willing to accept this "bitter pill." Instead, Larry Sivak, SCIII member and Riverbay resident director, warned that "Co-op City has reached the point where if the state does not give us what we need in stable rentals, the majority of the people will say they are ready to break the law [by supporting a rent strike]."[96]

For the UHF, calls for a rent strike demonstrated that Co-op City residents were immature and ungrateful children. George Schechter, UHF vice president and a Riverbay director, wrote in an open letter, "Co-op City, as a community is only six years old, just as vulnerable and immature as any six-year-old seeking its own identity. . . . For those of us who designed and planned and labored to give it birth, it's quite proper to hold a sense of responsibility for its growth." The leaders of SCIII, he maintained "wish to lure this young community astray into lands of 'no-strings-attached.'" In contrast, he offered the "hard discipline" that Co-op City required.[97] For residents, however, the UHF was paternalistic and out of touch. Charles Parness, who was a member of SCIII and would later go on to be president of the River-bay board, wrote, "These gentlemen exhibited a remarkable insensitivity to the people of Co-op City. Do they think we can pay this increase? Do they think we will pay the increase? They are so out of touch with the residents, that they might as well be living on the moon."[98] In September 1974, Ostroff would tell the UHF board of directors that since "there will have to be additional increases in carrying charges to keep pace with increased costs due to inflation," he believed that "it is likely that there will be a rent strike at Co-op City sometime in the future."[99] Ostroff was correct. Less than a year later, a rent strike would be well under way, which would destroy the UHF while simultaneously representing the apotheosis of the community that it had helped create.

CHAPTER 4

"No Way, We Won't Pay"

The Rent Strike, 1975–1976

On the night of May 28, 1975, shortly before the Co-op City rent strike began, its leader, Charles Rosen, a young, bushy-haired, chain-smoking printer with a long history of involvement in left-wing politics, stood up before two thousand cheering cooperators at the Dreiser Loop Community Center. "We have been writing letters, demonstrating and cajoling for a year, and all we have to show for it is one empty promise. . . . We do not want this rent strike, but it was forced upon us." Further, he argued that Co-op City's struggle was not its alone; rather, if Co-op City succeeded in halting the relentless rise of carrying charges, it would be a "singular victory for all moderate-income developments across the state."[1] "This is war," Rosen declared. "We're not going to let those bloodsuckers do this to us anymore!"[2] Rosen's remarks were punctuated by cheers and concluded to a standing ovation. Rosen commanded the support not merely of the two thousand cooperators who had gathered to hear him speak, but also of an estimated 80 percent of the residents in Co-op City, along with all of the cooperative's local legislative representatives—Democratic and Republican. Three days later, Co-op City residents began the largest rent strike in American history. The strike would last thirteen long months. It would destroy the UHF, nearly lead the New York State Housing Finance Agency to default, and, finally, result in cooperator control of the nearly sixty-thousand-person development.

FIGURE 18. Charles Rosen speaking at the May 28, 1975, resident rally in the Dreiser Loop Community Center. Courtesy of the *New York Times*.

Co-op City residents were not the only New Yorkers to protest in 1975. The collapse of New York's social democratic model has been well told elsewhere and need not be rehearsed here.[3] But suffice it to say that the financial pressures created by inflation, rising interest rates, and rising rates of borrowing to fund New York's social programs would lead New York

City to the threshold of bankruptcy in 1975. New York's fiscal crisis was not confined to its largest city. In February, the state-run Urban Development Corporation (UDC), which had been established by Governor Rockefeller to both finance and construct affordable housing, received a state bailout to avoid bankruptcy and default. Meanwhile, the entire Mitchell-Lama program, including both the city and the state's separate initiatives, was in the midst of an existential crisis of its own. New Mitchell-Lama construction was suspended in 1974, and existing Mitchell-Lama developments struggled to make their mortgage payments. By 1975, 90 of 125 city-sponsored Mitchell-Lama projects were in arrears.[4] State-sponsored projects were in hardly better shape. A state comptroller's report found that of seventy-one housing companies in operation for the fiscal year that ended in March 1975, only eighteen had sufficient revenue to meet both debt service and operating reserve requirements.[5]

In New York City, bankers demanded massive cuts to social services as a condition for their continued investment in the loans the city required for its survival. In response, New Yorkers across the city protested the cuts to CUNY admissions, the closures of hospitals and libraries, and the pay cuts forced on city workers.[6] The rent strike in Co-op City was slightly different, as Co-op City residents faced off against New York State rather than New York City. Yet, by any measure, the Co-op City rent strike was one of the most successful of the protests that swept the city that year.

According to Rosen, the problems that Co-op City faced were not merely austerity and the end of state largesse that accompanied the crumbling of New York City's experiment in urban social democracy. Rather, he argued that the UHF model of public-private partnership was fatally flawed in the first place. Rosen was a veteran of leftist politics and a self-identified Maoist. He saw the UHF as "the same Social Democratic whores I've hated all my life."[7] By that he meant that the corruption and coziness to power that had fueled the UHF's rise reflected a model of public-private partnership that victimized ordinary citizens. As Kazan had once envisioned, the UHF had built cooperative housing for New Yorkers of moderate means by using hundreds of millions of dollars in financing in the form of low-interest HFA mortgages. However, while Kazan saw credit as a way to unleash individual initiative, Rosen argued that government credit was in fact a form of government control. The UHF was now responsible for paying the holders of HFA mortgage bonds, and as a result, Rosen would argue, UHF president "Ostroff's first responsibility is to the banks and the bond holders" rather than the men and women who lived in the developments he had built.[8] New York State financing had allowed the UHF to build thousands of apartments, but it was a deal with the devil, turning the UHF into an arm of the capitalist state that it had supposedly rejected. Not all participants in the rent strike used Rosen's Marxist vocabulary. However, his critique of the UHF resonated widely. As one resident leader decried, "The Harold Ostroffs have lived off the hard-earned money of working people for too long and the fraud is perpetuated by his organization and powerful friends in Albany."[9] In Rosen's analysis, the financial crisis of the mid-1970s revealed the precariousness of the UHF's position and, indeed, the very complex of unions, state and municipal programs, and private entities that had guaranteed New York's welfare edifice. The problem, in other words, went beyond inflation and the other economic strains that had broken the social democratic model of urban liberalism, to the very idea that finance capital should or could be used to help working people.

Yet if Rosen critiqued the financial model and probity of the UHF, he had more in common with the UHF than its leaders might have suspected. Indeed, in an irony that the UHF could not possibly have appreciated, the rent strike was seen by many residents as a model of cooperation. As Rosen said, 'I would suggest that the ultimate in cooperation is the manner in which the vast majority of our residents are working together to save our homes."[10] Or as another member of SCIII put it, "They don't understand that it's all of us, that we are organized to go on replacing each other forever, that this strike has changed our lives and that nothing will make us give up."[11] Furthermore, the strikers' key demand was cooperator control. Just as Kazan had once called for the self-reliance of cooperators, the strikers believed that Co-op City's economic problems were the result of corruption and mismanagement, and they argued that they could run the cooperative better themselves. Rather than offering an indictment of the idea of a cooperative, they celebrated the rent strike as a means to attain a "true cooperative."[12] In ways that neither side would recognize, the Co-op City rent strikers were the heirs of the UHF just as much as they were its opponents.

In January 1975, Charles (Charlie) Rosen became the leader of SCIII.[13] The rent strike might well have happened without Rosen—residents had been talking about a potential rent strike for years before Rosen assumed a leadership role in resident politics—but by the force of his personality, the attention he paid to organizing, and the nature of his critique, he put his indelible stamp on it. When Rosen assumed control of SCIII at the age of thirty-one, he was a generation younger than many of the leaders of Co-op City politics.

He was the son of immigrant Jews who had become Communist activists during the Depression. Rosen was a true believer, who visited the Soviet Union and met with Khrushchev.[14] In the early 1960s, he had switched his affiliation to the Maoist Progressive Labor Party and met his future wife, Lynn, at a Progressive Labor Party meeting. Taking a step back from activism, Rosen became a union printer, working at the *New York Post*, and in 1970 he and Lynn moved to Co-op City because they, like so many other residents, wanted "stable rents and a decent, integrated environment in which to raise their children." Once in Co-op City, Rosen did not avoid politics for long and soon became the chairman of the Building 22 Association.[15]

Rosen brought his experience and perspective from years of left-wing organizing to his new role as leader of SCIII. The New York Jews who made up most of Co-op City's population were generally undeterred by his political views, which were—if somewhat more colorful than most— certainly not as far removed from the mainstream as they might have been in many other places in America at the time. Larry Dolnick, a former resident director of Riverbay and member of SCIII, described his attitude toward Rosen's politics: "One day I went up to Charlie's apartment and saw all these books by Mao and Lenin and it scared me, but we talked it out and it was okay. As long as he didn't try to change me or impose his politics on Co-op City, I didn't care."[16] In a letter to the editor of the *Co-op City Times*, Marge and Steve Glusker rejected what they saw as a "red-baiting" campaign against Rosen, insisting that "Mr. Rosen has a perfect right to his political beliefs and his community will not allow a 'McCarthy' type attack to succeed here."[17] "Everybody knew he was very out of the mainstream in his political beliefs," Eliot Engel, who later would go on to represent Co-op City first in Albany and later in Washington, recalled. "We all knew he was sympathetic to the Chinese and Soviets, and maybe that was part of his allure to some people."[18] According to SCIII leader and trade union organizer Nathalia Lange, "when [Rosen] proved his leadership ability, they accepted his politics. I don't know, maybe people accept Maoists more readily than Stalinists nowadays."[19] Even if they might not have themselves identified as socialists, the Jews of Co-op City were little more than a generation removed from the Lower East Side streets where socialist rhetoric was common and many residents continued to "read the radical press regularly, if not religiously" and participated in organizations like the Arbeter Ring and Jewish Socialist Varband with roots in that culture.[20] For decades, socialist organizers in the Jewish community had complained that Jews would mouth socialist phrases but did not act unless an issue affected their personal livelihood.[21] For many residents of Co-op City, including the largely Jewish leadership of SCIII, the seemingly incessant rise in carrying charges was just such an issue.

Rosen was charismatic and drew people to his vision of a "powerful organization led by residents to represent residents" that would combat what he saw as a dangerous alliance of the state, the UHF, and the banks that was oppressing Co-op City and middle-class men and women across America. Benjamin Cirlin recalled, "One night he came in with a 30-page memo showing how we could win a rent strike. It seemed so unbelievable. I never thought it could be carried out, but he had the whole thing there. Months later, I looked back at the memo and he had been right. I wondered where he had learned to do such a thing."[22] Cirlin was a bus driver for handicapped children, who had considered himself apolitical before the rent strike. Like many residents, Cirlin and his wife, Norma, had moved to Co-op City because its low rents, integrated community, and new apartments seemed to them the ideal place to start a family. Cirlin got an apartment in Building 24 and got involved in the building association because of his concerns about vandalism and quickly became the association president. However, it was Rosen who led him to become a fervent believer in the potential of a rent strike.[23]

Rosen's Marxism was central to his understanding of why the rent strike had to happen and how it would be won. As Rosen saw it, the UHF leaders were "right wing socialists" who had become arrogant and complacent.[24] However, he was also clear that they were not the real enemy. Rather, the real enemy was the nexus of government and financial power represented by the HFA. The reason why Co-op City faced carrying charge increase after carrying charge increase was that the state government cared more about satisfying its bondholders than its citizens. Furthermore, in a bit of dialectical reasoning out of the Marxist playbook, it was precisely the HFA's fealty to its bondholders that would allow Co-op City residents to triumph. Cirlin later explained Rosen's analysis:

New York State could not exist unless it sold bonds. That's the way you stay in business. That's the way cities stay in business. They sell bonds, bonds they use for road construction, for colleges, for hospitals, for university, for everything. That's the way they do everything in New York State, by selling bonds. HFA was literally, if you picture a table, they were one leg of that table. What happened is these bonds weren't sold to ordinary people, they were sold to stock companies, corporations. . . . The State was going to default under payment of interest on those bonds. That was the basic reason that they really gave in. Because we had the money. They could put us in jail, they could close our accounts, but you're not getting the [carrying charge money].[25]

Unity was key to Rosen's strategy for victory. "Mr. Ostroff may believe that a lobbyist and polite conversation at breakfasts gets desperate people money, but that is not my view. Only organized action is going to bring our plight to the front pages of the press and to the TV screens. Only political pressure and embarrassment will force the legislature."[26] At one town hall, he emphasized that "the people who built this place consider us animals. When they built this zoo, it never dawned upon them that the animals might organize."[27] While difficult to achieve, unity would result in Co-op City's salvation: "Steering Committee III to Stabilize Rents in Co-op City continues and relies on each cooperator family to save our homes. We are firmly convinced that the support will be forthcoming. . . . Co-op City will win!"[28]

Almost immediately on becoming SCIII chair, Rosen began to organize, personally going door to door to prepare his neighbors for a potentially long and costly strike.[29] According to Lange, Co-op City's vertical architecture proved particularly fortuitous for organizing. "Whatever you would otherwise think about Co-op City, it was always a good place to organize people. Everyone needed to pass through the lobbies twice a day."[30] Rosen and SCIII also organized the existing network of building associations and assigned a building captain to each building, laying the groundwork for the massive effort that would be activated when the rent strike finally began in June.[31] Throughout the winter and spring of 1975, Rosen and SCIII leaders met personally with representatives from the UHF and state officials in the hopes of securing help for Co-op City's dire financial situation.[32]

For its entire history, the UHF had been able to use construction funds for new projects to pay operating costs at existing developments. In Co-op City, the construction period had been kept open for an artificially long time so that Co-op City could avoid beginning to pay back its mortgage and continue to receive additional funds, which it used to cover ongoing costs. However, the construction period was finally over, and with no new UHF construction planned anywhere, in March 1975 Co-op City's manager Edward Aronov laid out the plain facts: "For the first time since the development opened, there is no longer any excess construction funds which can be counted on to offset a portion of our budget deficit. The various rollovers that were available as budgetary and administrative tools have all been used. Payments have not been made to operating escrow fund and operating reserves and in fact, the sources for operating expenses have all been but exhausted."[33]

In a bid to increase the pressure on Albany to offer relief in the hopes of avoiding a carrying charge increase, on March 16, 1975, SCIII narrowly approved a June 1 deadline for a rent strike if there was no movement by that date. In doing so, SCIII was supported both by the district's Democratic assemblyman Alan Hochberg and the Republican state senator John Calandra. Indeed, Hochberg and Calandra sniped at each other over their relative degree of support for a Mitchell-Lama relief bill. Neither wished to be outdone in the eyes of the cooperators who made up such a large portion of their respective districts. In the meantime, SCIII began to collect three dollars per apartment to fund their efforts and a potential strike.[34]

Co-op City residents and UHF representatives reached out repeatedly to Governor Carey in the hopes that he would more aggressively push legislative action to alleviate Co-op City's debt burden, culminating in a caravan of buses that brought thousands of cooperators to Albany to personally press their case. In particular, they lobbied for a bill to lower the interest rate on Co-op City's mortgage.[35] Carey had promised to support such a bill when he was running for governor, and as a result he had won the support of a majority of Co-op City residents in both the primary and general elections. In 1975, 70 percent of Co-op City's budget consisted of mortgage payments, taxes, and supervisory and administrative fees, and only 30 percent was spent on services and equipment for the cooperative itself. Therefore, a reduction in Co-op City's interest rate on its mortgage bonds would have had a dramatic impact on its monthly obligations.[36] True to his word, Carey sent a draft mortgage subsidy bill to the Assembly.[37]

SCIII and other Co-op City community leaders testified alongside UHF members in April 1975 before the state Assembly's Mitchell-Lama Subcommittee to explain why they should pass the bill.[38] However, Carey never aggressively lobbied for his own bill, in part because he knew how much upstate and suburban voters and their representatives resented the benefits already afforded to Mitchell-Lama residents. On April 16, the Mitchell-Lama Subcommittee in the Assembly decided to table the bill after Speaker Stanley Steingut told the panel's chair that the bill faced certain defeat on the floor of the Assembly.[39] With any hope of state relief now gone, Riverbay officially approved a proposal by Ostroff to increase carrying charges by 25 percent, to begin on July 1 and retroactive to April. This would raise average per-room carrying charges from $42.77 to $53.46.[40] This was an amount almost 250 percent higher than what carrying charges had been when Co-op City was initially approved ten years earlier. A New York

State audit conducted in 1976 found that this level would have meant that 26 percent of non-retired residents and a whopping 92 percent of retired residents would have paid more than 25 percent of their income for carrying charges, the measure the state used at the time to calculate housing affordability.[41]

Riverbay's five resident directors unanimously voted against the increase and then resigned in a joint letter so that they could "free themselves to engage in militant action including a rent strike."[42] In a survey, *City News* found that 80 percent of residents voiced full support for a rent strike.[43] At the start of May, SCIII collected carrying charge checks from residents and delivered them as a show of strength and as a test run for a full-scale rent strike the following month. This time, instead of bringing them to the UHF-appointed executive manager, they dumped them at the door of Governor Carey's New York City office. In a letter to Carey, Rosen begged, "The people in this community are desperate. In the midst of terrible economic times the one item which we felt had some stability in our lives was our rent. . . . I hope that you understand this extreme effort which this community of over 15,000 families is making to save itself. Their hopes are pinned to legal, moral and political commitments which have been given them and they are utilizing every method to achieve a successful conclusion."[44] Carey responded with vague promises to pass a Mitchell-Lama relief bill at some point in the future, but made no firm commitment.[45]

Ostroff made one final attempt to appeal to Co-op City residents with what he saw as economic sanity. "There are those who say we are not militant enough but we urge you not to follow a course which may see the operation succeed but the patient die. There are actions proposed which could seriously endanger our tenuous economic situation."[46] Yet Rosen saw Ostroff as doing nothing more than fear-mongering: the "first salvo in a campaign to strike fear in the hearts and minds of residents to break the back of protest actions."[47] Meanwhile, many residents were less interested in whether or not the UHF or SCIII had the right analysis of Co-op City's plight but rather in their own economic circumstances. Bernice Kornreich explained to a reporter that she did not know how her family would afford a carrying charge increase: "We have four small children and I can't go back to work full-time to help supplement my husband's income. It leaves us in a bind. I mean, we don't go out, so of course this is not a luxury we can cut out, eating, clothes, doctors? They have got us through the wall already, why are they actually trying to draw blood from a stone."[48]

On the evening of May 18, SCIII voted to approve a June 1 rent strike.[49] In a prepared statement, SCIII insisted that the strike was necessary because the state had refused to take action to halt the multiple carrying charge increases the community had faced in the previous four years and was also mandating the additional increase that would come due on July 1. Altogether, in the decade between when Co-op City was initially proposed in 1965 and the rent strike in 1975, carrying charges had increased 250 percent. SCIII insisted that the strike was against the state, not Riverbay. In fact, "We would desire that those who run Riverbay join the community in this fight for survival but are ready to work without them as we have these many months. There may be risks to a June Strike Against Any Rent Increase. But we must pit the so-called risks against the reality of what a $14.25 per room monthly rent increase will do."[50]

The strike was on.

When the rent strike began, residents were instructed to make out their check, with the full amount of their monthly carrying charges, to "Steering Committee III Inc., Escrow" and then give it to an authorized SCIII representative in their building or town house cluster.[51] The organizing structure that Rosen had worked out over the previous months was now put into effect. In addition to Rosen, there was a ten-person strike steering committee, which consisted of nine white Jewish men and Esther Smith, an African American woman. Aside from one retired furrier on the committee and Rosen, who took a leave of absence from his printing job, the rest of the committee continued to work throughout the strike. Their jobs were typical of the working- and middle-class jobs that characterized Co-op City's residents. There was a shoe salesman, a bus driver, an electrician, an accountant, and so on. Cirlin had the youngest child, Gail, who was less than four months old

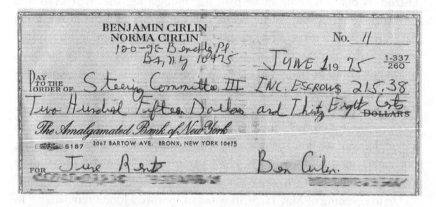

FIGURE 19. Check to Steering Committee III. Courtesy of Ben Cirlin.

when the rent strike began, but many of the rent strike leadership, including Rosen, had young children.

It was up to this group to run the largest rent strike in American history. Floor representatives in each building reported to a building captain, who in turn reported to area marshals. To communicate with residents, every day, SCIII wrote, printed, and distributed a newsletter to all 15,372 apartments. There were six mimeograph machines, which were kept hidden in a room in Building 24 and which ran constantly—day and night—printing newsletters and other communications.[52] There were backups for every leadership position, in case someone was arrested, and ten extra mimeographs hidden inside and outside Co-op City in case equipment was seized. One SCIII member drove around the cooperative conveying messages from the steering committee by megaphone. SCIII also held several meetings each week, all of which were open to cooperators. It administered a twenty-four-hour hotline so that residents could reach an SCIII leader at any time of the day or night and opened four service centers in building lobbies to answer questions about the strike. Over one thousand representatives manned collection tables in building lobbies from 7 to 9 p.m. for the first two weeks of each month. Altogether over two thousand of the approximately sixty thousand residents of the cooperative were involved in the administration of the strike.[53] Banners and flags flew from terraces and hung in windows emblazoned with the slogans "No Way, We Won't Pay" and "Co-op City on Strike!"[54] Upward of 80 percent of residents supported the strike by writing checks to SCIII rather than to Riverbay.[55]

On June 2, the day after the strike began, the UHF members who sat on Riverbay's board resigned, relinquishing control over Co-op City to the state's Department of Housing and Community Renewal (DHCR). The resigning UHF members released a mournful statement insisting that "we are not enemies in the fight to preserve lower monthly [charges] . . . and we refuse to be cast in that position. Nor are we willing to go to court to commence action against the Co-op City residents. Our position has, therefore, become impossible."[56] As a final irony, in the last moments before the rent strike, both the UHF and SCIII had insisted that, despite years of open warfare over carrying charge increases, the UHF was not the enemy of Co-op City's residents.

Privately, the UHF was less conciliatory. One member of the UHF board said that the problems in Co-op City stemmed "from the fact that so many of the people came from rent controlled apartments and, therefore, deeply resented any increases in carrying charges." Others placed the blame on Co-op City's size. One commented that it was "too big to function as a cooperative," while another stated that the size of Co-op City meant that politicians kowtowed to their wishes, undermining the true "interests of the cooperative." The UHF lawyer Robert Szold went even further, praising Commissioner Lee Goodwin for her refusal to negotiate with the rent strikers, stating that "her actions could only have a salutary effect in the community."[57]

For years, the UHF leadership had found itself torn between the cooperators, whose plight they sympathized with, and state politicians, whose logic they understood. Now in the final reckoning, they chastised Co-op City's residents for their ingratitude and lack of cooperative values. In contrast, the UHF did not see the state's refusal to provide mortgage assistance as a similar betrayal. Ostroff defended the 25 percent carrying charge increase that had triggered the strike, insisting that it was necessary "to maintain the fiscal stability of Co-op City." Ostroff further stated that the failure of the bill in the state Assembly to provide mortgage assistance was understandable, given the recent default of the UDC and the growing fiscal crisis in New York City.[58] Ultimately, just as Co-op City's residents had suspected, the UHF was more sympathetic to the state's financial plight than theirs.

As the strike began, Rosen, in a fiery speech to an overflow crowd at the Dreiser Loop Community Center, attacked the UHF, accusing Ostroff of hypocrisy. For all his professed sympathy with the middle-income residents of Co-op City, Rosen noted, "Ostroff's first responsibility is to the banks and the bond holders." Rosen vowed that Ostroff would be forced to walk on the streets "in sunglasses and disguise. . . . I want to drive him [out] like you drive a cockroach." Ostroff was not the only target of Rosen's ire. He referred to Jacob Potofsky, a UHF director and former president of the Amalgamated Clothing Workers Union, as an aristocrat of labor. Responding to the fear that services might be cut off to punish Co-op City for failing to pay carrying charges, he charged that "we will rip [Potofsky] from his throne of Amalgamated if he makes a resident walk up three flights of stairs."[59] Rosen concluded his remarks to a standing ovation.[60]

Yet for all the anger Rosen directed toward Ostroff and his colleagues, he took time at the town hall to emphasize that their primary antagonist was not the UHF but the State of New York. The SCIII saw the rent strike as a pressure tactic and planned to aim that pressure squarely at the HFA's creditors. "All these people understand is pressure, especially pressure in their pocketbooks," Rosen said. Rosen and the SCIII planned advertisements in the *Wall Street Journal* targeted at bondholders: "Beware—Co-op City residents are reneging on your profits." Even if Governor Carey wanted to ignore the rent strikers themselves, Rosen predicted that he would "jump for a call from David Rockefeller," the chair of Chase Manhattan Bank, as soon as he heard that the HFA might not be able to pay back its bonds.[61]

Rosen correctly recognized that the rent strike was a disaster for the HFA: "They could foreclose on the mortgage, but if they did, they would destroy the solvency of HFA bonds. And whom would they sell Co-op City to? Who would buy it? The state doesn't want it and private realtors don't want it. And who would live here? The rich won't move back from Westchester to live here, so the only people who would take up the cooperative are those on total assistance and that would cost the government far more to support."[62] Co-op City's $390 million mortgage represented over a third of HFA's entire portfolio of $1.135 billion in bonds.[63] Paul Belica, the executive director of the HFA, tried to project confidence by publicly stating that foreclosure would not endanger the HFA's ability to pay back its bonds.[64] However, in internal memos, HFA officials recognized that it would struggle to find buyers for bonds for new construction. Even larger problems loomed. Every month, the HFA needed to pay off bonds that it had issued previously as they came due. Ordinarily, it used carrying charge and rental income from Mitchell-Lama projects to cover some of this expense and then issued new bonds to cover the rest. However, without Co-op City's millions of dollars of monthly carrying charge income, the HFA would need to issue much larger bonds to cover its shortfall. Co-op City's rent strike was a financial danger, but it also represented a hit to HFA credibility. After all, with the largest of its financed projects in receivership, the HFA could no longer claim that its bonds were a safe bet.[65] What if it could find no buyers for its bonds? As designed in 1960, HFA bonds were "moral obligation" bonds. This meant that the state was not legally obligated to pay HFA bondholders; it merely had a "moral obligation" to do so. Would New York State bail out HFA bondholders? Would it allow the HFA to default?

These were not idle questions. Just as the HFA struggled with Co-op City's default, the state-backed Urban Development Corporation was in the process of its own collapse. Building on the success of the HFA, Rockefeller had created the UDC in 1968. Unlike the HFA, the UDC was no mere lender. Rather it raised moral obligation bonds that it then used itself for urban development. By 1970, over forty-five thousand units of UDC housing were either planned or already under construction.[66] However, because of a combination of factors, including a 1973 moratorium on federal housing spending and the departure of Rockefeller from the governor's mansion to serve in the federal government, the UDC was soon in serious trouble. In February 1975, the UDC went into default on $135 million in bond notes.[67] Meanwhile, an even larger entity was facing bankruptcy: New York City itself. After several months in which the city had struggled to find anyone willing to buy its municipal bonds, in May 1975 Mayor Beame, Governor Carey, and several representatives of New York City's large banks traveled to Washington, hat in hand, to beg Treasury Secretary William Simon and President Gerald Ford for short-term federal loan guarantees to enable the city to have enough money to avoid default. Simon and Ford turned them down.[68]

Instead, Simon and Ford demanded austerity. Working along with the leaders of New York's largest banks and as a condition of advancing loans to allow the city to pay its bills, Governor Carey set up the Municipal Assistance Corporation (MAC) in May to guarantee and then sell bonds. In order to assure bondholders that MAC bonds were creditworthy, "Big MAC" was independent of mayoral control. Its board—consisting of business leaders and bankers—were now effectively in control of municipal spending. They demanded that New York slash the number of municipal workers, drastically reduce spending on social programs, and raise transit and other fees. Felix Rohatyn, banker and MAC chair, stated that "'an overkill' was required if for no other reason than that of 'shock impact.'"[69] New York's credit was so low and the rest of the nation's distrust of it so high that only devastating cuts would do. As Simon testified several months later, any aid to New York City would have to be on terms "so punitive, the overall experience made so painful, that no city, no political subdivision would ever be tempted to go down the same road."[70]

While attempting to solve the crisis in New York City, Carey now faced a similar crisis on the state's own books. This was not a situation where the HFA could reduce its spending, so austerity, as proposed for New York City, was not an option in quite the same way. However, this was a no less perilous revenue crisis. As a memo written by one of Carey's aides stated, the stakes of the rent strike could not have been higher for New York State. An unsuccessful conclusion to the rent strike could mean either the default of the HFA, foreclosure and eviction of tens of thousands of cooperators, and the possibility that residents in other Mitchell-Lama projects might refuse to pay their rent increases.[71] Faced with this situation, DHCR commissioner Goodwin chose a strategy of confrontation. Goodwin threw blame for the rent strike on SCIII, accusing them of trying "to coerce the state into granting financial relief by threatening the continued viability of the largest middle-income cooperative in the nation and in placing the cooperators' rights to continued occupancy in jeopardy."[72] On June 3, she warned that the state "had neither the funds nor the authority to maintain services."[73] SCIII tried to get her to guarantee that services such as electricity and water would be maintained. She refused to respond.[74]

Abraham Bernstein, Co-op City's state senator, sent a series of desperate telegrams to Governor Carey, begging him to intervene. "Continuation of Co-op City Strike must have catastrophic results," Bernstein pleaded. "Commissioner Goodwin stubbornly refuses to meet with [SCIII]. Her arbitrary attitude precludes her from acting with objectivity. Respectfully request that you assume leadership and take control."[75] Carey refused Bernstein's entreaties and those of others, including Rosen himself.[76] Instead, he struck a posture of public neutrality, avoiding all but the most banal statements about his desire to find "a prudent solution" to the rent strike and refusing all calls to meet with SCIII or its political representatives.[77] In doing so, he was following DHCR's instructions to refuse to endow the rent strike with legitimacy by entering into public negotiations with its leaders.[78]

The DHCR filed suit in Bronx Supreme Court to force an end to the strike and require the turnover to the state of all the checks that SCIII had collected. On June 17, 1975, Justice Joseph Brust issued an injunction ordering SCIII to comply with the state's demands.[79] After SCIII ignored the injunction, on August 4, 1975, the HFA initiated formal foreclosure proceedings against the cooperative. Meanwhile, Robert Infantino, the state representative appointed to run Riverbay, informed residents that foreclosure meant the forfeiture of the equity payments that residents had made when they initially moved in. He also told them that the HFA had requested a court-appointed receiver who would "take all necessary action to collect carrying charges."[80] The HFA's formal foreclosure complaint named all 11,500-plus families who were in default, which was interpreted as a threat to rent strike participants.[81]

Because the state had seized checks from the first month of the rent strike after the Bronx Supreme Court had declared the strike illegal, thereafter SCIII leaders refused to deposit checks in an escrow account for fear that the state would once again seize them, destroying their leverage and ability to continue the rent strike. For precisely that reason, the state focused its efforts on finding these hidden checks. Attempts to find the withheld carrying charge checks could reach comical proportions. At one point, Rosen joked that he would deliver them to Carey's summer home on Staten Island. The state immediately alerted the Coast Guard to seize any boat moving in that direction, a measure that, unsurprisingly, proved fruitless.[82] Yet state sanctions could also be deadly serious. In early October, twenty-two members of the strike leadership went on trial for contempt for ignoring the State Supreme Court's order to stop rent strike activities and turn over the money that they had collected. Leaders were threatened with jail time for refusing to turn over the money.[83] The spouses of SCIII leaders were also subpoenaed and threatened with jail unless they testified. The state backed off, realizing that jailing the mothers of young children would be a public relations disaster.[84] In December, SCIII was fined $250,000, with an additional $25,000 charged to each of the members of the strike leadership. A further $5,000 was charged to SCIII, and $1,000 to each strike leader for each day that the strikers failed to turn over the carrying charge checks they had collected.[85] When SCIII leaders refused to pay the fines, their bank accounts were seized.[86]

Finding SCIII leadership unwilling to bend, the state tried other means to intimidate rebellious cooperators. After backing off of eviction threats in August, Goodwin once again raised the specter of mass eviction three months later.[87] She also threatened cuts to services: "Unless the Court . . . require the defendants to pay over the withheld monies immediately, the health, safety and well-being of thousands of residents of Co-op City, including many elderly persons, will be imperiled, since Riverbay will no longer be able to pay for vital services."[88] In January, Goodwin announced layoffs of nearly half of Co-op City's staff, leading to drastic cuts in maintenance, landscaping, and security. She also ordered the reduction of hot water, heat, and electricity to the bare minimum required by law.[89] That same month, officials burst into Co-op City lobbies, escorted by city police, and took pictures of the residents involved in collecting checks in an effort to intimidate them.[90]

Throughout the thirteen months of the strike, the rent strikers remained defiant. Unbowed by the threat of eviction, Rosen announced at a rally, "We'll defend our homes—what will they do, bring a platoon of police or the National Guard?" With a keen awareness of the strength in bargaining from weakness, Rosen referenced the large number of the elderly living in Co-op City, stating, "Who would dare to evict 12,500 retired people?"[91] Louise Freeman, another resident, told one reporter, "If they want to evict us, they'll have to get the marshal for the 384 families that live in this building. They can't just put hundreds of people on the street."[92] When the state printed booklets with the names of residents who faced eviction for supporting the strike, residents referred to the booklets as an "Honor Roll." One resident even asked, "If there is no money, where did they get the dollars to print those booklets?"[93] When the wives of SCIII leaders ignored fines, they wrote a joint statement: "We are furious that the government has forced us to make this decision even as they have threatened our lives rather than deal with the issues in the Co-op City rent strike. We will not be intimidated and will not permit the heavy hand of corrupt politicians to destroy us."[94] After SCIII was levied with fines, a resident stated, "Doesn't the state realize we are people and not robots? When we say 'no way, we won't pay,' we mean it."[95] Cirlin added, "I had to decide whether I was constantly going to go through life being threatened and giving up. I have to look at myself in the mirror every morning."[96]

Supporters of the strike believed that the state was simply out of touch with the suffering of the middle-class people who lived in Co-op City. "I'm not going to pay a rent increase," one resident stated. "One can stretch a rubber band so far until it breaks. How can they expect us to pay more? I am furious at the State for treating us as numbers and not as human beings."[97] Referring to the judges who issued hundreds of thousands of dollars of fines to SCIII in December 1975, Sadie Hirschfeld told a reporter, "What do these judges know? They make their big salaries and are not aware of the sacrifices we have to make."[98] Meanwhile, residents charged officials with betrayal. "Remember Guv, when you were here in Co-op City before election, you promised us reforms in the M-L [Mitchell-Lama] area? Where are they? Are you one of the do-gooders only before election?"[99] Another resident wrote to Carey, "I don't understand why we in Co-op City have to pay more and more in rent each month because you in Albany can't afford to help us out when you splurge on yourself continuously."[100] Residents insisted that their actions were the result of desperation. As Rosen wrote to the *New York Times*, "Mitchell-Lama tenants pass an economic means test each year. If we make enough to pay market-value rents, we are legally required to pay a premium on our rent. It is interesting to note that if Co-op City tenants could pay the latest increase they would have been legally ineligible to move here in the first place."[101]

When Rosen and other strike leaders went on trial for contempt in October 1975, thousands of Co-op City residents stood in front of the courthouse the first day. They chanted the strike slogan, "No way. We won't pay," and hanged Governor Carey in effigy.[102] Every day of the trial, residents packed the courtroom and protested outside. Cirlin's wife, Norma, took their infant daughter to court with a sign on her stroller, "Don't put my daddy Ben Cirlin in jail."[103] When the state threatened to cut off electricity, SCIII paid Con Ed directly from the checks it had collected.[104] When services were cut, buildings organized volunteer cleaning and security patrols.[105] Co-op City residents repeatedly protested at the governor's New York City offices. After one such protest, Erika Teutsch, Carey's New York City office director, wrote

FIGURE 20. Demonstration outside the Bronx County Courthouse, 1975. Courtesy of the Bronx County Historical Society Research Library.

that "75–100 people [were] roaming around the tenth floor at the New York office, pretty much holding us hostage in the office for some six hours."[106] As Rosen said in a rousing speech to a town hall meeting packed with cooperators, "We have men and women . . . 2,000 volunteers that cannot be defeated. Not a governor, not a yo-yo judge, smart judge or a dopey judge, nobody can defeat the power of an organized force. We are not only right, we are strong. When you are right and strong and disciplined, it may take you time, but you will win!"[107]

Rosen became a celebrity in Co-op City. A reporter described his entrance into a room filled with residents: "Suddenly, hundreds of these people were on their feet shouting, applauding, raising their fists in the power sign, their eyes shining behind their union-discount glasses."[108] "Old women come up to him with tears in their eyes to say 'Every night I pray for you, nothing should happen to you.' . . . Housewives in the bakery turn apologetically to him and say 'I'm sorry Charlie, I wasn't at the meeting last night, I'll be there Wednesday.'"[109] One resident recalled, "He was our messiah. I don't know how he can get to sleep at night with all the facts and figures in his head." "He was just in a different league than the rest of us," Cirlin remembered admiringly.[110] One resident wrote excitedly to Rosen, "I have a masters degree in community organization, but am learning more from you than I did at Fordham!"[111]

Rosen's brash self-assurance and hyperbolic eloquence made the "Lenin of the North Bronx," as an article in the *Village Voice* described him, an irresistible subject for the reporters who now flocked to Co-op City to cover the strike. When speaking with them, Rosen cultivated his image as someone who gave voice to the frustration of thousands of residents who felt themselves to be underdogs facing the mighty fist of the UHF and now of the entire State of New York. "They treat us like garbage," Rosen told one reporter. "Rabble. You should see them at those uptown meetings, you wouldn't believe the way they talk to us. But me, I don't take that shit from anyone. . . . I leaned across that negotiating table and I said; 'My mother raised me to believe I was a prince of Israel. Who the fuck do you think you're talking to?'" As part of a political tactic to emphasize the unity of the community, Rosen stressed that it was merely his outspokenness that had made him a leader: "It isn't me, it's all of us . . . it's everyone in this damned community. What's more it's not even just us here in Co-op City. It's everyone in Mitchell-Lama housing we're fighting for. Me, I've got a big mouth and I'm not afraid of Lee Goodwin or the judge so I've become a symbol of the struggle."[112]

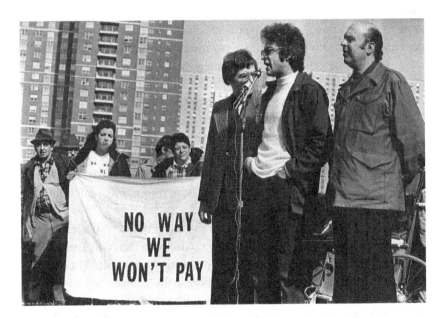

FIGURE 21. Charles Rosen speaking at a rally on the Co-op City Greenway. Courtesy of the *New York Times*.

State officials made it clear in public statements that they had no patience for Co-op City's residents. Goodwin accused the residents of demanding "massive subsidies" and special treatment. In a statement that ignored the fact that so many Co-op City residents were themselves public employees, she told the *New York Post* that "considering the state of the State's budget and the city's budget, you know we're in a difficult period when we're laying off teachers and policemen. There are horrible things we just have to do right now across the board."[113] Anonymous DHCR staffers accused Co-op City residents of refusing to recognize reality: "The Steering Committee thinks the Riverbay Corp. runs on thin air."[114] Paul Belica of the HFA referred to the rent strike as "a very selfish idea" that "is killing it for everyone else in the state."[115] Roger Starr, leader of the New York City Housing and Development Administration, wrote an open letter to Rosen: "You may be having a marvelous time in your role as revolutionary martyr, preparing yourself for a few Spartan days in the civil clink, but it really is time that you started to think seriously about the hardships that your stellar performance will inflict on your fellow cooperators. . . . Your present heroics will be remembered only as the pretentious posturing of one who has sacrificed his colleagues to his own taste of the spotlight."[116] These sorts of statements were reprinted gleefully in the Co-op City newspapers, as yet more evidence that Rosen and the other rent strikers were underdogs who would ultimately triumph over those who patronized them.

In a letter to the *City News*, Yetta Weinstein, a resident of Building 15, responded to the idea that strikers were irresponsible dilettantes. Weinstein listed the promises that Carey and others had made to prevent carrying charge increases and the fact that they had never been realized: "We in Co-op City have been lied to, treated with contempt and in an undignified manner by our politicians and bureaucrats. We do recognize that the bond holders are entitled to a fair return on their investment and that we also receive certain tax abatements. This does not alter the fact that 14,000 of the 15,372 families who live in Co-op City joined together, not as rebellious tenants, but as responsible citizens who want to live in a safe community with stabilized rents."[117]

For many residents, the rent strike was a defining moment, one that could lead to a political awakening. According to SCIII leader Nathalia Lange, "For the first time, the strike created a feeling of community here. There was a sense of solidarity. The people had something to do. Their lives suddenly had a meaning."[118] One resident excitedly told a film crew from the 1977 documentary *On the Line*, "I never thought I'd be active in something as great as this."[119] In the same documentary, Cirlin described how participating in the rent strike had changed his views: "Banks are not concerned about people. They see bricks, they see buildings, they see money. When I look at this place, I see people, I see children, senior citizens. . . . I'm now considered a radical because I'm fighting the system. I guess I am. . . . I see a moderate-income community being destroyed by people who don't give a damn about us."[120] Resident Gerry Rosenstrauch wrote to the *City News*, "If what we are doing is considered [to be] a socialist revolution, so be it. The people who put up Co-op City . . . had their own socialist revolution in the '30s when they unionized the City of New York."[121] Yet support for the rent strike also crossed conventional political lines. The president of the local Hutchinson Republican Club responded to accusations that the strike was controlled by Communists: "This smear is totally without foundation. I am part of SCIII and I personally resent the insinuation. Far from being a Communist, I am president of the Hutchinson Republican Club."[122]

There was a minority of residents—estimates ranged from 15 to 20 percent—who rejected the rent strike. In some cases, they supported the goals but opposed the tactics of the strikers. Supporters of the UHF organized a group called "Common Sense," which accepted the state's logic that carrying charge increases were inevitable; however, the group never numbered more than thirty members.[123] Other opponents to the rent strike had more idiosyncratic reasons. Michael Agovino remembers his mother's justification for not supporting the strike, which echoed the resentment at elite condescension that so many rent strikers articulated but aimed it in a different direction: "Better to let the rent go up and keep the better people here." Reading a pro-strike article in the *Village Voice*, she scoffed, "Oh please, what nonsense. . . . That's liberal propaganda they're spouting. If it's so great why don't these liberal newspaper editors move here. They wouldn't move here in a million years. Who are they kidding."[124] There were a few isolated instances of violence against those who opposed the strike, but for the most part, abstainers kept their heads down and were ignored by the majority who supported SCIII.[125]

The rent strike led to an earthquake in local politics, which had long been dominated by the Democratic machine. The first casualty was City Council representative Stephen Kaufman. In public, Kaufman acted as if he supported the strikers. However, when the state published its booklet of cooperators who were in default, his name did not appear on the list. After an investigation by the local *City News*, it was discovered that Kaufman was playing both sides—paying his carrying charges to the state and also writing a monthly check for SCIII to hold in escrow. Kaufman originally claimed that his double payment was "inadvertent," but when it was revealed that he had done this monthly, Kaufman was caught in yet another lie. His credibility with local residents was destroyed.[126]

Kaufman was not the only political figure to fall as a result of the rent strike. The local Democratic club was taken over by Rosen allies (including Eliot Engel, who would later become a congressman representing the northeast Bronx).[127] Assemblyman Alan Hochberg, another machine politician, approached Rosen and offered him a truce: if Rosen agreed not to challenge him for his Assembly seat, Hochberg would offer Rosen a "no show" job and financial support for future political activity. At the behest of Special State Prosecutor Joe Hynes, Rosen wore a wire to a meeting with Hochberg and got these offers on tape. Hochberg was subsequently tried and convicted of corruption.[128]

The rent strikers saw themselves as part of a long history of tenant activism in New York. Throughout the twentieth century, New Yorkers had engaged in tenant activism to demand better living conditions and lower rents.[129] Indeed, the cooperative movement and the UHF were born of the tenant activism of an earlier era. In the 1960s and 1970s, tenant activists fought urban renewal and negligent and prejudiced slumlords, often in conjunction with radical groups like the Black Panthers and the Students for a Democratic Society.[130] Most directly, Co-op City was consciously following the example of Rochdale Village, which had a short-lived rent strike in 1974.[131] SCIII directly reached out to Mitchell-Lama groups, as well as broader tenant organizations.[132] In January 1976, representatives of twelve tenant organizations, including the Mitchell-Lama Council, the Chelsea Coalition on Housing, and the West Side Tenants Union, urged Carey to negotiate a solution to the rent strike. Arthur Camins, the chairman of the Ad Hoc Mitchell-Lama Action Coalition, warned, "The government's attempt to crush the Co-op City strike . . . will not intimidate other Mitchell-Lama tenants from continuing to organize against crippling rent increases. On the contrary, it will accelerate rent strikes."[133] Often, representatives from other Mitchell-Lama developments attended Co-op City protests.[134] In February 1976, the Citywide Tenants United, a coalition of fourteen tenants' rights groups, brought tenants in twenty-eight buses from across New York City to a rally on the Co-op City Greenway.[135] Jane Benedict of the Metropolitan Council on Housing gave a fiery speech insisting on the broader implications of what was going on in Co-op City: "Tenants are saying you pushed us this far and you're not going to push us any further. . . . We are in a period in which the people are being cut down and the fight has not really begun!"[136] Michael McKee of the New York Tenants Council stated, "I salute Co-op City. You are leading the fight for all of us." Elva Torres of the Cooper Square Development Committee narrated an allegory to explain how Co-op City's struggle had revealed callousness and hypocrisy of government:

> The government is like a man with a beautiful suit. But his underwear is full of holes. People saw only his beautiful suit and they thought, he must be very powerful so they did whatever he said. But after some time they began to stand up to the man. Then one day they went to him and took off his shirt, his belt and his pants. They discovered his underwear full of holes. The people found out he was all ass. I like to think that at Cooper Square we have taken off the man's belt and that at Co-op City you have taken off the pants.

The crowd erupted in wild applause.[137]

Tenants' rights groups were only part of the many groups fighting against the austerity politics that was beginning to demand cuts to social services across New York City. Teachers and students at Hostos Community College in the South Bronx protested after massive budget cuts threatened layoffs or even potential closure of the campus, collecting signatures on petitions, blocking traffic, and ultimately organizing a sit-in in May. After three thousand sanitation workers were laid off in June, ten thousand other sanitation workers walked off their jobs in a wildcat strike that left garbage rotting on the streets. After policemen were laid off to conform with the austerity demands of the MAC, five hundred of them blocked the Brooklyn Bridge, letting air out of tires of motorists who sought to cross and threatening both motorists and their fellow policemen who tried to stop them. New Yorkers protested the closures of hospitals and fire stations; they railed against hikes in public transit fares and CUNY tuition. Much as the bankers who had assumed control of the city recognized that austerity was as much about the symbolic value of destroying New York City–style urban liberalism as it was a response to the specifics of the fiscal crisis, so, too, those who protested against it saw their actions as an attempt to strike back at the bankers who sought to profit off others' misfortune.[138]

The Co-op City rent strike was not directed at the MAC or the mayor, but its antagonists were the very same banks who seemed to control the city's fortunes. Here too, for some observers, what was at stake in the strike was whether or not New York would be a city for the middle class. Brooklyn assemblyman Frank Barbaro wrote, "Middle income people who have bought co-ops have often made sacrifices in contemplation of a stable rent situation. To say to those people 'The joke's on you . . . you've got to bear the burden of astronomical rent hikes' is unconscionable. In fact, it's a prime example of why people don't trust government anymore."[139] Representative Bella Abzug, an activist leader in Manhattan, then preparing to run for statewide office, spoke to the Co-op City Independent Democrats Club and declared that the rent strike was "a necessary fight to save Co-op City. . . . If you are forced out of New York by impossibly high carrying charges, our entire city will be the loser. We have to keep the middle class in New York."[140] On the theme of government trustworthiness, Fred Harris, a former populist Oklahoma US senator, president of the Democratic National Committee, and then presidential candidate, wrote about the strike in 1975, "The Co-op City rent strike is symptomatic of the unholy alliance of concentrated economic power and indifferent governmental authority that has led to the long night of the American soul which is shaking the very roof of our democracy."[141] Cesar Chavez sent a telegram to SCIII expressing solidarity with the rent strikers: "Your brothers and sisters of the United Farm Workers stand beside you. We stand beside you till your strike is won. Co-op City is part of a larger confrontation between working people and established political and economic systems."[142]

Yet despite their bravado and despite their supporters, many rent strikers were scared. They feared that the rent strike might not halt the rise in their carrying charges. They feared the loss of their equity deposits. They feared eviction. They feared jail. They feared the toll that months of reduced services were having on the community. Co-op City's residents wanted the strike to end.

As the rent strike dragged on, the possibility of default of the state Housing Finance Agency that had been recognized in June became a very real threat. In August 1975, the HFA had to pay a 10.8 percent interest rate to find buyers for its tens of millions of dollars in bonds, more than twice what it had paid the previous winter.[143] On September 3, the HFA warned Carey that "the markets appear to be closed to our notes." In order to reduce the amount of bonds it would need to sell, the HFA was forced for the first time to raid its reserve fund, as well as take from monies earmarked for the state university construction fund and the state university system itself.[144] Desperate to avoid default, Goodwin begged SCIII in vain to halt strike activities for a month so that the HFA could sell new bonds to cover the $68 million in notes that were coming due.[145] As HFA executive director Paul Belica explained, the problem was not merely the Co-op City rent strike, but the saturation of the bond markets owing to the simultaneous debt crises at the UDC and in New York City. "It began with the UDC crisis and then came the city, with the Municipal Assistance Corporation moving into the market for huge amounts. That drowned out the potential for everyone else. The market is drying up and we're living from day to day."[146]

As Belica suggested, the fiscal crises of the UDC, the HFA, and New York City were hopelessly entangled. In September, Belica noted that Governor Carey was so consumed with New York City's ongoing woes that there was little time or attention to figure out a solution to the HFA crisis.[147] In fact, a month later, New York City—still in the thick of its financial crisis—was actually called to bail out the HFA. In October, New York City was expected to transfer $20 million to New York State. However, because the state could not directly transfer that money to HFA without a special legislative session, it requested that the city instead buy $20 million in HFA bonds so that HFA could meet its debt obligations. SCIII saw this as an opening to put pressure on the HFA and New York State.[148] As the city's Board of Estimate met to consider the extraordinary measure of purchasing the HFA bonds, a crowd of Co-op City residents filled the chamber. Rosen urged them, "Do not become a party to passing along $20 million to the bankers of the State of New York without wresting something in return for the people of the City of New York."[149] On October 10, the Board of Estimate refused to use the $20 million to buy HFA bonds. Bronx borough president Robert Abrams insisted that Carey instead agree to "good faith negotiations" with the rent strikers. He was joined in this stance by enough allies to deny the measure the three-quarters majority it needed to pass. After the vote, Rosen exulted outside the chambers, "We did it! We had to blackmail [public officials] to get them to listen to us!"[150] However, Rosen's moment of triumph was short-lived. The city counsel's office ruled that rather than the previously mandated three-quarters majority, the transfer required only a majority vote, and three days later, by a slim twelve-to-ten majority, the New York City Board of Estimate voted to authorize the city to instead use those funds to buy HFA bonds, ignoring the Co-op City residents who crowded the chamber pleading with the city not to let Co-op City be used "as a conduit to save the banks."[151] Deputy Mayor Stanley Friedman explained that the board's hands were tied—if they did not transfer state funds to the HFA, New York City would not have been able to count on the state to support it in its still ongoing financial crisis.[152]

Nevertheless, the Board of Estimate's action only bought the HFA a few weeks of respite. As Rosen had predicted, every month that the rent strike dragged on, the amount of bonds that the HFA needed to sell increased, and every month it got harder for the HFA to sell those bonds, because the lengthening strike only made the HFA's prospects look riskier.[153] In November, the HFA's reserve fund dipped more than $10 million below its statutorily mandated limit, while the HFA also faced $130 million in maturing notes that would require a new bond issue to cover.[154] However, by this point, the HFA, locked out of the credit markets, could find no one to buy its bonds at any price. Governor Carey requested an emergency $576 million loan from the Federal Reserve to address the problems at the HFA and several other troubled agencies but was turned down because of concerns about "the Co-op City situation." Instead, he was forced to raid a variety of special funds, get the assurance of construction unions to use their welfare funds to buy HFA bonds, and finally use state treasury funds to cover the remaining $80 million in maturing bonds.[155] Even as President Ford announced an emergency package of aid to New York City that averted its bankruptcy in November 1975, the HFA's troubles continued.[156] In December, Carey was forced to liquidate half the assets of the State Insurance Fund to redeem $200 million in maturing notes at the HFA and two other ailing state agencies.[157] A month later, the HFA was barely able to cobble together $176 million from a combination of sources, including the State Insurance Fund, the State Treasury, and the State Teachers' Retirement System, to cover maturing notes.[158] Clearly, this was not a sustainable situation, especially since in a few months the problem was about to get a lot worse, as the first of the high-interest, one-year notes that had accompanied the start of the Co-op City rent strike would come due. Finally, in March 1976, Carey was able to put together a $2.6 billion rescue package, consisting of long-term bonds, purchased by both state pension funds and private banks, which put the HFA on somewhat more solid ground.[159] Officials heralded a new era of partnership between the state and banks. As one high-ranking aide to Carey put it, "The banks and the state know they don't always have the same interests. But what's different from a year ago is that they have co-opted each other."[160]

Throughout the crisis, as officials scrambled save HFA from default, HFA officials and others continued to insist that Co-op City's rising carrying charges were simply a matter of fiscal responsibility. As one *New York Times* editorial put it, "Residents have insisted that the state—meaning state taxpayers—should absorb increased fuel and maintenance costs that other New Yorkers must pay out of their own pockets. That is an unconscionable demand, especially in view of the precarious fiscal condition of state and city, whose attempts to regain financial credibility have been compromised by the cooperators' intransigence."[161] However, Rosen and local politicians challenged this logic and repeatedly sought to tie state aid for Co-op City and other Mitchell-Lama developments to the frequent HFA bailouts.[162] "There can be no relief for bankers," Rosen told a packed town hall meeting, "if there is no relief for communities."[163] Early in the rent strike, Rosen compared the hard line the state was taking with Co-op City's residents with its bailout of the UDC.[164] "We contend people are more important than banks. . . . We have already had four increases. If the state can find $80-million for UDC, which has no people, why can't it find $10-million for Co-op City? The State assumed the responsibility of guaranteeing this would remain a moderate-income community. And now the state abrogates that responsibility."[165] In this quote, Rosen turned the language or responsibility against the state. Rather than residents owing a responsibility to pay their mortgage, he argued that the state owed a responsibility to New Yorkers. Rosen further maintained that the language of fiscal responsibility was a cover for the deliberate choice to privilege banks and bondholders over residents. Bondholders had taken a risk in backing the UDC and HFA; why was New York State more beholden to their concerns than the needs of its citizens?

Although the March 1976 deal gave the HFA some breathing room, state negotiators knew that both bondholders and HUD negotiators considering insuring HFA mortgages wanted an end to the turmoil in Co-op City before they would be willing to touch HFA bonds.[166] From the beginning, SCIII had sought to negotiate a deal with the state that would forestall carrying charge increases as well as give them a larger say in the management of the cooperative. In September 1975 they had released a twenty-two-point plan that they believed could make the cooperative solvent without the need for carrying charge increases.[167] As the state's tactics escalated to fines, subpoenas, and threats to withhold necessary services, Goodwin's representatives met regularly with SCIII but refused to consider any of SCIII's proposals, instead threatening even more draconian carrying charge hikes or suggesting cuts to security and utility services as cost-cutting measures. Occasionally, they made even more absurd suggestions, such as asking Co-op City residents to organize fund-raisers to raise millions of dollars to replace the HFA's lost carrying charge income. Rosen and SCIII dismissed such proposals as "bull," and for months both sides appeared locked into their respective positions.[168]

Publicly, Carey formed a united front with Goodwin's hard-line tactics, refusing to meet directly with the strikers.[169] However, behind closed doors, his advisers complained about Goodwin's lack of flexibility.[170] One adviser expressed concern about the fact that Co-op City's residents saw Carey as personally responsible for their plight and stated that Carey needed to do something "'little people' oriented" because "too much of the public seems to think of the Governor in terms of Big MAC and Big Banks, etc."[171] They entertained a number of ideas to offer some financial relief to Co-op City, including using federal Section 8 funding to subsidize Mitchell-Lama projects or revitalizing the dormant mortgage subsidy bill. However, these were all discussed in secret. As one aide explained about a proposal to cap rents at a certain percentage of income, "It would be wonderful if we could promise the tenants that no one shall pay more than 20 percent–25 percent of their income for rent. But until we get [more information], we will have no idea what the cost of a program like that would be. It would be disastrous for the governor to again make a promise that he couldn't keep."[172] Carey's advisers also scrambled to come up with a comprehensive housing plan that would resolve problems not merely at Co-op City but with other Mitchell-Lama projects, as well as public housing.[173] Finally, they sought in vain to find someone besides the "militant elements" in SCIII that they could talk with.[174]

Jim Introne, Carey's director of state operations, recommended that Carey appoint someone to negotiate with SCIII outside of the stalled talks that Goodwin's office had been conducting.[175] In December 1975, Carey followed up on Introne's suggestion and asked Rosen to begin "fact-finding" discussions with Mario Cuomo.[176] Cuomo was an ambitious Democratic politician from Queens who was serving as New York secretary of state when Carey tapped him to talk to Rosen.[177] While the fact that Rosen and Cuomo were in discussions was revealed several weeks after they began talking, both men kept the substance of their discussions close to the vest.[178] In February, the two men reached a memorandum of understanding. However, the agreement did not end the strike, as neither Carey nor Goodwin was willing to accept Cuomo's plan, because it did not include a provision for an immediate carrying charge increase.[179] Instead, the strike continued to drag on.

On May 10, 1976, the need for a rent strike settlement suddenly obtained a new urgency when the Bronx County Superior Court approved an HFA foreclosure of Co-op City. Belica, HFA's executive director, immediately announced his intention to sell Co-op City. Residents would lose their equity investments and could potentially face eviction.[180] However, although foreclosure appeared to be a victory for the HFA, it was actually the last thing the HFA really wanted. After all, who would want to buy Co-op City, a

development with an uncertain future and restive residents? As Rosen recognized, "[The foreclosure ruling is] obviously a disaster for the state and
the Housing Finance Agency; it is an albatross around your administrative
necks."[181] An anonymous state official echoed Rosen's logic, stating that
the timing of the foreclosure decision "could not have been worse." The
state was involved in negotiations with the US Department of Housing
and Urban Development to insure HFA mortgages, a condition of March's
$2.6 billion bailout. A foreclosure at HFA's largest development would make
HUD even warier.[182]

The possibility of imminent foreclosure increased the pressure on both
sides to make a deal. Cuomo publicly released the outlines of the plan that
he and Rosen had agreed to back in February. SCIII would immediately hand
over the carrying charges it had been holding. There would be no foreclosure and no immediate carrying charge increase. Instead, residents would
be given six months to run the cooperative on their own and prove that
they could do it for cheaper than the UHF, thus avoiding the increase that
had been proposed over a year earlier. Meanwhile, the state would appoint
a Mitchell-Lama Task Force that would investigate potential solutions to
the financial issues at Co-op City and other developments in the troubled
program.[183]

Cuomo's plan immediately ran into a firestorm of criticism. A *Wall Street
Journal* editorial castigated the strikers for their arrogance. "No one seriously
thinks the rent strikers can avert a rent increase by their superior management." It warned further that "this compromise could also collapse the
shaky foundations of New York's housing programs and possibly put the
coup de grace to New York City's plans for recovery."[184] An organization of
private landlords and developers of Mitchell-Lama projects cautioned the
governor that "there is no doubt in the minds of any of our members but
that a capitulation to the Co-op City rent strikers will have the immediate
effect of creating a snowball which will result in rent strikes in every Mitchell-
Lama building now in occupancy. The consequences of the foregoing are
horrendous to contemplate, but at the very least, will result in a further
eroding of New York's credibility in the financial marketplace."[185] A Carey
administration official involved in the ongoing negotiations about the HFA
bailout similarly warned that "if Co-op City residents were permitted to
escape from their maintenance-charge increases, the state would not be able
to resell its other mortgages—even with Federal insurance—at the price for
which it had been hoping."[186] Cuomo responded that residents would not
agree to higher carrying charges unless they could control the cooperative

and satisfy for themselves that higher carrying charges were, in fact, necessary. "Our proposal," Cuomo said, "is a device to get things back to normal again. . . . I believe we can make an arrangement that will satisfy the bankers, the Federal Government and the people of Co-op City."[187] On June 29, Carey and SCIII agreed to the plan. Shortly thereafter, Goodwin tendered her resignation in protest.[188]

SCIII claimed victory, holding a huge rally on the Greenway in the center of Co-op City. The journalists Paul DuBrul and Jack Newfield described the scene: "The weather was ominous. As huge banks of black, rain-laden clouds blotted out the rays of a sinking summer sun, thousands of people, many of them elderly couples trundling aluminum beach chairs, emerged from the red brick towers . . . and made their way to [the Greenway]. As they filed along the dirt paths that had been worn in the grass, they glanced at the lowering clouds. . . . 'Don't worry, Charlie won't let it rain—not tonight.'"[189] Rosen gave a fiery speech and then paused for a moment before shouting into the microphone to the thousands assembled before him: "We beat the bastards!"[190]

On that day, it appeared that they had. The HFA had been brought to its knees. Goodwin, the hated commissioner of housing, had resigned. The UHF had been effectively destroyed, never again to take on another housing project. There was no immediate carrying charge increase, and Rosen was now the leader of the cooperative, tasked with a six-month grace period to find enough money to keep one from occurring. SCIII-backed candidates had swept the governing Democratic machine out of power. Hailing the rent strike, Bienvenida Quintana, a resident in Building 15, said, "At least it gives our community an opportunity to find out by itself if the increases [the state] asked for were legitimate. And since Co-op City is to be operated and run by cooperators, it will be a true cooperative."[191] Esther Smith, SCIII leader and future president of Riverbay, stated that she believed the settlement would allow Co-op City to realize its promise: "The people of Co-op City came here with certain hopes. I think we are all finally going to see that kind of community."[192]

A week later, SCIII handed over the checks it had held for so many months. After carrying charge income had been seized from SCIII bank accounts during the first month of the rent strike, SCIII had refrained from depositing the checks it collected in later months and instead held them in a series of undisclosed locations. Thereafter, the state's court efforts were largely devoted to getting Rosen and others to either turn over the checks or give up their location to the court. Rosen and others pleaded the Fifth

Amendment to avoid disclosing the information, risking jail time.[193] After all, if the state discovered the checks and cashed them, this would do away with the only leverage that SCIII had and effectively end the strike. So where were the checks?

Throughout the strike, SCIII couriers had delivered garbage bags full of checks each month to Cirlin's apartment in Building 24. SCIII then had couriers deliver both the bags filled with the real checks but also dummy bags filled with old newspapers to places where they could be packed in boxes. Each box was labeled. However, not every box had real checks in it. Only Rosen knew where all the real checks were, so that if any other strike leaders were called to trial, they could honestly say that they did not know where the money was. The boxes of (real and fake) checks were stashed with friends and sympathizers both inside and outside Co-op City. Boxes were stored under beds and behind secret doors. In many cases, the people who had boxes didn't even know what they were storing. A couple moved to New Jersey and took the boxes they had been given with them without ever opening them or knowing what was inside.[194] On the day when it was finally time to deliver the checks, Rosen took television crews on a tour of some of the hiding places they had used. Then Cirlin drove a rental truck filled with hundreds of boxes of collected checks to the Bronx County Courthouse.[195] A bucket brigade consisting of sixty-five Co-op City residents passed boxes of checks hand to hand into the courthouse, up the elevator, down the hallway, all the way to the judge's desk.[196]

During and immediately after the rent strike, observers saw it as a harbinger of a new relationship between the state and its citizens. Fearful about the consequences of cooperator control, the *Wall Street Journal* was apoplectic. Co-op City residents needed to face the full consequences of their defiance immediately, according to the *Journal*, up to and including the loss of their homes: "If the state wants to regain its financial credibility, it will have, to put it brutally, to make an example of the Co-op City rent strikers. . . . The state may find . . . that the rent strike will collapse after the first tenants lose their apartments. But in any case, it will be more humane to throw people out into the June sunshine than into the December snow."[197] This vision of a state devoid of credibility and a citizenry run amok, which struck terror into the heart of the *Wall Street Journal*, was celebrated by others. Vivian Gornick introduced the drama of the rent strike to readers of the *Village Voice* by writing, "What is happening in Co-op City is what happens when the resigned become resistant, the scattered become organized, the meek become militant. And that—whatever your political sympathies—is a human spectacle on the grand scale."[198] In a rare moment of agreement, the *Village Voice* and the *Wall Street Journal* shared the sense that Co-op City's rent strike victory and the achievement of tenant control was the first step in a new political order in New York.

They were wrong.

Rosen had anticipated that the HFA's need to satisfy its bondholders would be the leverage that would ultimately bring the state to the negotiating table. This was why in June 1975 he had proposed ads in the *Wall Street Journal* targeted to HFA bondholders, and two months later led the fight against the city Board of Estimate's bailout of the HFA. It was why Rosen sought to try to tie bailouts of HFA bondholders to additional funding for the residents of Mitchell-Lama housing, where construction had been financed by those bonds. However, what Rosen and the rest of SCIII had failed to take into consideration was the fact that the bondholders continued to have leverage beyond the end of the rent strike. As a condition for investing state pension resources in HFA bonds, Arthur Levitt, the state's comptroller, insisted on an end to moral obligation financing, meaning that the governor would have much less leeway in future debt issues. Moral obligation bonds had underwritten billions of dollars of social spending, including affordable housing, colleges (including much of the SUNY system), and hospitals. Now that era was over, and the state government would face much stricter debt limits. Further, the participation of lenders in the March 1976 rescue package was also contingent on the willingness of the federal government's Department of Housing and Urban Development to insure HFA-backed mortgage bonds. HUD set a condition that carrying charges and rents at projects that it guaranteed had to cover the costs of debt service and management of the cooperatives.[199] The instability of HFA financing had forced the state to bargain with SCIII, but it also limited the concessions that it was willing or able to make.

Tellingly, while the Cuomo plan allowed cooperators to take control of Co-op City, it was not offering any additional state subsidy or a renegotiation of the mortgage. Chastened by near default by both the HFA and the nation's largest city, limited by their inability to issue new moral obligation bonds, and emboldened by a new urban governance philosophy that celebrated austerity, state officials would offer little in the way of financial assistance to Co-op City's middle-class residents.

During the rent strike, Rosen and others had articulated a critique of the cooperative ownership model. As owners, they were asked to bear the burden of keeping the cooperative solvent, facing the prospect of repeated carrying charge increases, while at the same time they had little ability to affect the management of the cooperative. Where they erred was in believing that the cooperator control that residents had achieved during the rent strike would change that equation. The cooperative's new masters would struggle to contain costs just as their predecessors had. They would also face new challenges, stemming from Co-op City's crumbling infrastructure and rising levels of white flight. Having accepted the responsibility of ownership, they could no longer use Co-op City's indebtedness as leverage to force the state to make concessions. Instead, debt would turn out to be a much more powerful master for Co-op City's residents than the UHF had ever been.

CHAPTER 5

"We Inherited a Mess!"

After the Rent Strike, 1977–1981

With cooperator control established and a temporary settlement in place, Steering Committee III turned toward the future. Part of the deal that Rosen and Cuomo had negotiated was a requirement to put Co-op City's finances on a solid footing. And so SCIII turned immediately to the task of figuring out cost-cutting measures. Rosen scoffed at the need for expertise, arguing that cooperators could do what the United Housing Foundation and the New York State Division of Housing and Community Renewal could not. "Did you ever meet any of those dopes that run big corporations? The only difference between them and us is that they got a chance to do it and we didn't."[1] He explained: "We have a big body of experience among the tenants and we call on it. . . . Take the thermal unit. There was this little old retired guy with a Yiddish-Russian accent who kept walking around the plant asking questions. They got sick of seeing him and finally one day they threw him a copy of the specs. Turned out he was a retired engineer and he worked out a plan to turn the plant into a generating plant. He showed it to me, and that's what we are working on now."[2] SCIII member Ben Cirlin, a bus driver with no engineering or building management experience, was assigned the problem of the broken laundry machines in building basements. After some research, he decided on the machines that he wanted and selected a private contractor that would guarantee a minimum payment of $520,000 per year to operate the machines that could be found in the basement of each apartment building.[3]

The confidence of Rosen and Steering Committee III was well-earned. After all, they had led a thirteen-month strike, faced down courts, sanctions, and fines, wrested control of the development from the UHF, nearly triggered a bankruptcy of the HFA, and forced the state to accept their terms. If they could do this, was it wrong to bet that they could earn a similar victory over financial exigencies?

As Rosen and other cooperators would soon find, the achievement of cooperator control was a pyrrhic victory. The financial bind that Co-op City found itself in had not gone away. The only difference was that now the cooperators were in charge of finding a solution. Rosen's successors would find the challenges of running a cooperative the size of Co-op City just as daunting as did the UHF. Desperate to stabilize their own credit situations, neither the city nor the state was in any mood or position to offer relief to strapped residents of a "troubled" housing development. Finally, as the scope of Co-op City's construction defects continued to emerge in the years after the rent strike settlement was announced, the development's economic troubles would mount.

At the same time that Co-op City's leadership sought to stabilize the finances of the cooperative, the community in the development itself evolved in the post–rent strike era. Perhaps the most tangible sign of this evolution was the mounting challenge of white flight, which accelerated dramatically in the late 1970s. To some degree, the exodus of white residents was intimately connected with the financial turmoil of the development. However, in many cases, it was motivated less by the reality of rising carrying charges, which largely remained within the means of the young families who were most likely to leave, and more by an anxiety about greater increases to come. It was the specter of uncertainty, something that neither state officials nor Riverbay did much to combat, rather than economic realities that motivated people to leave. Co-op City's white residents had always balanced two contradictory beliefs—the desire to live in a racially integrated community and fears that nonwhite neighbors were a harbinger of crime. As the optimism of Co-op City's early years faded amid seemingly endless carrying charge increases, and as Co-op City became increasingly less white, that balance tipped toward fear, and white flight became a self-reinforcing process.

The agreement that concluded the rent strike in July 1976 was only a temporary solution. As SCIII and the State of New York approached the negotiations to draft a final settlement, they were both interested in making Co-op City financially solvent. SCIII, now in charge of the Riverbay Corporation that governed Co-op City, wished to safeguard its control of the development and avoid undue financial pressure on residents. The state was interested in maintaining the stability of its nearly $400 million mortgage.

The memorandum of understanding that ended the strike gave control of Co-op City to cooperators and allowed them six months to negotiate a final settlement and find cost savings to avoid a carrying charge increase. As SCIII assumed control of Riverbay, the group was confident that it could find these savings. "We have an enormous body of knowledge in this community, and we should be willing to share our knowledge," one SCIII member explained. After all, they had often repeated that Co-op City's ever escalating carrying charges were a function of UHF corruption and mismanagement. Rosen imagined a community that would operate differently, based on the creativity and cooperative spirit of its residents:

> The figures from the Co-op City budget don't add up. If viewed from the traditional vantage point it will be impossible to understand SCIII's rationale. . . . The one item the traditionalists do not put into the program is the creative talent of the people. . . . But we who come from the garment shops and the printing plants, from the taxicabs and the offices, from the school rooms and the hospitals, from painting and plumbing and electrifying and fixing and carpentering and buying and selling and cooking and cleaning—we know different. No one ever asked us if it could be done better faster or cheaper. . . . Our greatest natural resources, our minds, experiences and talent have always been disregarded by the "professionals." . . . When we talk about unleashing the talents of cooperators it means getting people to volunteer their services and setting up a procedure to do so efficiently. . . . A willingness to share your ideas is a tremendous contribution.[4]

More concretely, the SCIII-led Riverbay board developed a proposal to the Carter administration's Energy Research Development Administration (ERDA) to retrofit the power plant to use methane gas from the Pelham dump to meet Co-op City's electrical needs and serve as a demonstration project for future power plants.[5] They investigated the possibility of lowering the interest rates on Co-op City's debt and looked for new, more profitable tenants for commercial spaces. And more than anything else, they tried to get out from under the service agreements that Riverbay had signed with Community Services Incorporated when it had been under UHF control.

Meanwhile, since maintenance had visibly suffered during the rent strike owing to the state's refusal to fund anything but essential services, cleaning up vandalism was a top priority. As one letter to the editor of *City News* complained, "Broken window glass, broken hall glass, graffiti: you name it and you will see it in Co-op City." SCIII estimated that it could cost up to $2 million to undo the vandalism that had occurred during the rent strike, and here too, they called on the community to take responsibility for the physical state of the place they called home.[6]

It proved difficult to turn the community solidarity that had held throughout the thirteen difficult months of the rent strike toward new goals. New York State and, in particular, the HFA and DHCR had presented Co-op City with concrete villains throughout those long months. But in the case of vandalism, the enemies were one's own neighbors, and solving the problem led to recriminations within the community itself. In a typical statement, Rosalind Rosenberg explained her frustration to a reporter: "I wash my hallway and I'm the only person on my floor who does it. It's not right for the same people to do it all the time. There has to be more cooperation."[7] Co-op City's financial problems were even more intractable. ERDA rejected Co-op City's proposal for the powerplant. The maintenance workers employed by Riverbay threatened a strike and won a contract that included wage benefits that were over 10 percent higher than for similar agreements elsewhere in the Bronx and Manhattan. Other cost-cutting measures proved to yield less in savings than SCIII had hoped for. Plans to increase revenues—including a forty-two-lane bowling alley and lounge, a sports center in a garage, and "a dining and catering facility on the roof of Garage 7 or 8"—also went nowhere.[8]

Meanwhile, SCIII struggled as it realized the magnitude of the task of managing a cooperative of Co-op City's size, complexity, and financial constraints. During the rent strike, SCIII had collected rent checks but did not deposit them because of fears that the state would seize monies in an escrow account, given that multiple court orders had deemed the strike illegal. As a result, residents had spent thirteen months without actually having payments deducted from their accounts. Some residents found that this offered an irresistible temptation to spend all or part of this money. When the Steering Committee agreed to turn over its collected checks to the state, thousands of private dramas ensued as families scrambled to cover money that may have been long gone. Over a thousand families received eviction notices.[9] Even several "well-known community leaders" struggled to pay the money they owed.[10] This was, to say the least, not an auspicious start to post–rent strike life in the cooperative.

In January 1977, the state agreed to extend the period for residents to find a solution to their economic problems. That same month, Rosen announced that he would step down as Riverbay president. He explained his reasoning in an open letter published in the *Co-op City Times*:

> It would be, in my estimate, incorrect to continue in the role of "leader," Co-op City does not need any "first among equals.". . . There must be a return to normalcy with each opinion having equal weight and each person given an equal chance to develop their leadership potential. I have no desire to be another UHF hoodlum-type and I am fearful that if there is no break at this point, while we have some breathing space, then there will always be a built-in excuse for maintaining my position and institutionalizing my role.[11]

Instead, Rosen suggested that he stay on as a consultant to train new members of Riverbay and also interact with government officials, whom he had come to know well during the rent strike. The DHCR agreed to hire him at a salary of $800 a week, nearly three times what he had earned as a union printer.[12] Rosen's offer triggered unease among some residents of Co-op City. One anonymous former rent strike building captain printed an open letter titled "What Price Glory, Charlie?" and posted copies in lobbies across Co-op City. "Charlie, if you deserve this high price for your salary, then why not us? We're tired of collecting rents, arguing with our wives or husbands and missing personal time to help in this rent strike. You expect us to continue to back you while you laugh at us? No, Charlie!"[13] Other critics were more measured, stating that they believed that Rosen was due compensation for his work for Co-op City but chafing at the high figure. "The money he is going to get is a little outrageous," one resident told a reporter, "He had a job making $300 before, if he was going to get $500 a week I would say okay, but $800 is far too much money."[14] Whether or not it was fair to expect a consultant with Rosen's degree of organizing experience to be paid little more than a union printer, the controversy over his compensation revealed the extent to which the elation of the rent strike victory had dissipated.

By the spring of 1977, Joel Dannenberg, a member of SCIII and a Riverbay board member, found himself on the defensive, trying to justify progress that had been made since the rent strike ended. "Progress has been slow. Sometimes the slowness has been frustrating, not only to the average resident but to each member of the board," Dannenberg conceded. Furthermore, "[Riverbay] has been subjected to criticism of varying degrees, some of it extremely hostile. There are many persons who would criticize us no matter how well we performed. They are, and always will be, the enemies of this community." Nevertheless, Dannenberg insisted that there was reason for optimism. A contract had been signed with an outside firm to restore and manage the laundry rooms; they had secured a contract with the unions; they were "in the initial stages of establishing a youth program"; they hoped to bring in cable television and full-service health care facilities, and more.[15] Dannenberg's list of plans and accomplishments demonstrated the vast difference between a militant challenge to the power brokers of the state and the mundane work of half-measures and negotiations that constituted the tasks of governance.

Just how much had changed became clear three months later, in July 1977, when a final settlement to the rent strike was announced with the backing of SCIII leadership and put to a vote from the entire community.[16] The settlement was a compromise. It called for an increase of $8.56 a room, or 20 percent, in carrying charges, effective August 1, 1977, through October 31, 1979. Residents would also need to provide a fifty-dollar-a-room "equity overcall"—in other words fifty dollars a room in equity from each household in addition to the down payment they had provided when they first moved into the development. Riverbay also pledged to restart its dormant income verification program to make sure that residents who made above the Mitchell-Lama income restrictions paid the required surcharge. On the side of New York State, Governor Carey agreed to appoint a task force to recommend comprehensive legislation to solve issues at Mitchell-Lama projects more generally. The HFA agreed to discontinue foreclosure proceedings against Co-op City and give up on all charges against residents who participated in the rent strike. Furthermore, as it was already clear that "unusual and extraordinary" repairs would be necessary to Co-op City's physical plant, in what would become a bone of contention in the ensuing years, the HFA agreed that Riverbay would be allowed to utilize its carrying charge income to correct construction defects rather than make mortgage payments to the state. Finally, Riverbay, the corporation in charge of managing Co-op City, would now be under full resident control.[17]

SCIII's negotiating team threw their support behind the settlement. In a stormy community meeting, some residents complained that a 20 percent increase in carrying charges and a fifty-dollar-a-room equity overcall was a disappointing end to a rent strike with the slogan "no way, we won't pay." One man charged that SCIII "had a lot of nerve to ask for an additional $50 per room for the equity."[18] SCIII leadership replied that they had no alternative but to accept the agreement. Rosen said, "We've been on strike for three years. If the alternative is perpetual strike, then vote that way. But recognize that that is not a rational option."[19] In the end, 74 percent of Co-op City's residents voted for the rent strike settlement.[20]

While the end to Co-op City's rent strike was being negotiated, Carey had already appointed the developer Richard Ravitch to make recommendations regarding the entire Mitchell-Lama program.[21] Ravitch had been brought in by Carey to run the troubled Urban Development Corporation in 1975, and now, two years later, he was asked to write a report on Co-op City and the Mitchell-Lama program as a whole. Ravitch's report was only one of a series of audits performed by both the state and the city on Mitchell-Lama, and his 1977 report would become the one with the most lasting impact. Ravitch considered a number of strategies to make Co-op City solvent, including cutting costs, making money through commercial leases, and trying to start Co-op City's dormant power plant so that the development could avoid its massive payments to Con Edison.[22] In his report, Ravitch concluded that such measures were insufficient to reduce Co-op City's yearly budget deficit, which was variously estimated in 1976 as ranging from $10 million to $12.7 million: "There is no realistic prospect of reducing expenses or increasing non-residential revenues at Co-op City in amounts sufficient to have a significant impact on the basic problem of the present insufficiency of residential revenues. In this respect, it should be noted that, because of the size of Co-op City, a $1,000,000 savings in expenses or increase in non-residential revenues translates into only a $.14 per room per month reduction of the burden that must be met from residential rentals if financial self-sufficiency is to be achieved."[23] Needless to say, a new laundry room contract or the assistance of retired engineers in restarting the HVAC plant would not be enough.

Once it became clear that the financial solvency of Co-op City could not be achieved by cutting costs, commercial leases, or a plan to more fully utilize the power plant, the interests of cooperators and the state diverged. Co-op City's leadership wanted to save money in order to make the development affordable for residents; but as Ravitch explained, the state needed to view Co-op City "from its vantage point as a mortgage banker."[24] What was at issue here was a fundamental difference between the goal of the Mitchell-Lama program and the reality of the financial situation the program found itself in in the 1970s. When Mitchell-Lama had been designed in 1955, the idea behind it was that by offering low-cost mortgages and loan guarantees to developers with the promise that these developers would not raise costs beyond certain levels, enough developers could be enticed to build middle-class housing so as to solve the problem of affordable housing in New York.

What the program did not include was any provision for subsidies to either landlords or tenants after the completion of construction. By the mid-1970s, it had become clear that Mitchell-Lama was not financially viable without such subsidies. It was also clear that neither the state nor the city was willing to offer them.

In a letter to Governor Carey accompanying his report in early 1977, Ravitch summarized the state's position:

> The overall financial difficulties and tenant unrest in the Mitchell-Lama program is a direct result of the inherent inconsistency between the essential financial and social concepts that underlay the establishment of the program, i.e. the conflict between the financial concept of economic self-sufficiency and the social concept of limiting initial occupancy to tenants whose income bore a fixed ratio relationship to rent, a limitation which circumscribed the tenants' ability to pay rent increases. This dilemma was not realized at the time the program was established and the statutory framework governing rent increase has proved to be inadequate to reconcile the competing objectives.[25]

At the same time, Ravitch's solution to this problem was caught on the horns of the same dilemma. He advocated that rents be gradually increased at Mitchell-Lama developments until they reached what he termed the "economic rent," or the amount needed in order for projects to meet both mortgage debt service and operating expenses. However, Ravitch was well aware that a large number of residents would be unable to afford this higher number. Therefore, his plan mandated that no tenants would be required to pay more than 25 percent of their annual income. Yet this lower increase would be insufficient to balance Co-op City's budget. The state comptroller estimated that if rents rose even 25 percent from their pre-rent strike values, half of Co-op City residents would have been paying more than a quarter of their income to Riverbay, the standard the comptroller's office used to measure affordability. To try to solve this dilemma, Ravitch insisted that while established residents would continue to pay a lower amount, all new residents would have to certify that their income was high enough to be able to afford Co-op City's "economic rent." He argued further that should the apartment be able to fetch an even higher price on the open market (the so-called "market rental" price), then it should be rented for that higher amount. Ravitch made it clear that Mitchell-Lama-mandated maximum income limits should be increased or eliminated altogether. Instead, by arguing that new residents would have to be able to afford Co-op City's "economic rent," Ravitch was effectively arguing that Mitchell-Lama would have a minimum income threshold for new residents. Rather than seeing this as potentially pricing out middle-class families, in Ravitch's mind, wealthier new residents would "offset the shortfalls created by the limits on the rent paid by poorer tenants."[26] Co-op City would go from being an affordable housing program for a middle-class clientele to a mixed-income development, with a gradually increasing percentage of higher-income residents who could afford Co-op City's economic rent.

Ravitch's proposal was enthusiastically embraced by Carey and the state budget director.[27] Its appeal lay in the fact that it offered a way to preserve the Mitchell-Lama guarantee of affordable housing to existing residents while not costing the state a dime in additional money. However, it was also a plan with several key shortcomings: what would happen if new residents lost their jobs or saw their income dip beneath the 25 percent threshold? What happened if Co-op City's economic rent level changed? Would a Co-op City that was substantially more expensive for new arrivals still be attractive enough to potential residents? What would it mean for the cooperative to have two classes of residents—one of which was subsidizing the other? How would the state even begin to administer this complex system, in which prices depended on a bewildering variety of factors, including the time of initial residence, current income, and family size? Indeed, at this very moment, the DHCR had fallen far behind in the comparably simpler task of checking whether families qualified for rental surcharges based on their earning above the Mitchell-Lama cutoff. The Ravitch plan would have been both impossible to administer and would, ultimately, have led to the end of the Mitchell-Lama program altogether as tenants moved out and were replaced by those paying economic or market rental prices. Perhaps for those reasons, it was never enacted in its entirety, even though the concept of an "economic rent" would remain a mainstay of HFA and DHCR thinking well into the 1980s.

While Ravitch's plan sought to recruit new cooperators who could pay an economic rent, other plans to rescue the Mitchell-Lama program focused on finding higher-income families already living in Mitchell-Lama developments and forcing them to pay surcharges. In theory, Mitchell-Lama residents were responsible for undergoing a regular income verification process. If they were found to earn an amount that was above the maximum income threshold for eligibility (set at six to seven times the apartment rent or carrying charge), they had to pay an additional monthly amount up to 50 percent of the rent or carrying charge paid by other residents. A 1977 investigation by Arthur Levitt, the New York State comptroller, found that the income verification process was rarely carried out and urged that it be restarted.[28] The "free rider" who lived in Mitchell-Lama housing while not being truly needy appeared often in government reports in the mid-1970s on the Mitchell-Lama program's precarious financial status.[29] Frank Kristoff, the housing economics director of the Urban Development Corporation, estimated that 15 percent to 20 percent of Mitchell-Lama residents were over-income and dodging the required surcharges, and "thus we have the spectacle of about $30 million of subsidy going to middle income tenants . . . many of whom are cheating on surcharge obligations that could substantially reduce debt service charges."[30] If Kristoff's analysis was correct, the problem of Mitchell-Lama affordability could potentially be solved merely by making existing residents pay their required surcharges. However, it was unclear just how accurate this estimate was.

In 1978, after a stepped-up verification process was put into place, 1,576 families, or about 10 percent of Co-op City's residents, were subject to a surcharge based on a disparity between their tax returns and the income they claimed on their income affidavits submitted to Riverbay. However, of this number, few were eligible for the maximum surcharge of 50 percent.[31] Levitt admitted that income verification was a drop in the bucket as far as Co-op City's indebtedness was concerned. After castigating the laxness of DHCR officials in supervising the income verification process, he conceded that the amount of surcharges that had not been accurately levied was under $100,000 a year, an "insignificant" amount compared to Co-op City's obligations.[32]

Rather than a realistic means of solving Mitchell-Lama's financial woes, the focus on income verification reflected the suspicion that the residents of Co-op City and other Mitchell-Lama developments were taking advantage of the system. A *New York Times* editorial that advocated for income verification across Mitchell-Lama developments contended that "all [Mitchell-Lama residents] benefit from large tax exemptions and government subsidies. Further subsidy obviously should go only to those in genuine need."[33] Accusations of financial turpitude were a way to avoid the reality that economic rent was a mirage—if Co-op City required residents to pay an economic rent, then it would no longer be affordable to the middle class. As Levitt recognized, there simply were not enough "free riders" to make a dent in the Mitchell-Lama program's indebtedness. And yet, even if the "free rider" myth could easily be disproven, the state was increasingly reluctant to provide Mitchell-Lama projects with the additional funding to make them viable for middle-income residents.

Riverbay's leadership begged for the state to take into consideration the fact that Co-op City's costs included factors that were beyond their control and that had been misrepresented to them. "For the most part, the unfairness we speak of here is neither the fault of anyone presently in office, nor of Co-op City residents."[34] In making this argument, they had the support of a 1978 audit by Levitt, which analyzed UHF costs and DHCR oversight and found serious problems with both. Moreover, neither the UHF nor the DHCR had ever been up-front with residents and prospective residents about the fact that significantly higher carrying charges would be necessary to pay for construction costs. Given this set of circumstances, Riverbay argued, how could Co-op City residents be asked to take responsibility for errors committed by the UHF and New York State? Errors, they added, that they had been unaware of when they had bought into the development. "The HFA argument [that cooperators were responsible for cost overruns as owners of Co-op City] begs the real question—How many of these cooperators would have signed up if the real cost was made known to them?"[35]

Indeed, Levitt's 1978 audit was damning. He noted how, in a series of five increases between the signing of the original construction contract and the completion of the project, costs ballooned (see appendix, table 1).[36] Some of these revisions were due to changes in design—for example, adding the town houses cost money, as did substituting open spaces for apartments on the first floors of the buildings.[37] However, Levitt found that other increases were a result of poor planning. An additional $5.4 million was needed simply because CSI had not adequately understood or accounted for Co-op City's marshy soil.[38] Moreover, from the very beginning the DHCR had grievously failed in its oversight function. The DHCR never analyzed costs in a detailed way, even though its preliminary analysis indicated that they would be far higher than the budgeted amounts provided by CSI.[39] Indeed, Levitt found that "no evidence existed that DHCR made a concerted effort to effectively supervise the general contractor."[40] Finally, the DHCR had misrepresented the state's responsibility, implying to other state officials that the risk of cost overruns lay with the UHF/CSI, when in fact the contract mandated that increased costs would be subsumed within the mortgage, and thus were ultimately New York State's responsibility.[41]

Levitt's report was a scathing indictment of DHCR oversight. But precisely because of these oversight failures, it was impossible to say to what degree the ballooning costs were a function of unavoidable inflation, to what degree they reflected corruption, and to what degree they were a result of incompetence. At the very least, the fact that almost the entirety of both the state and city Mitchell-Lama programs found themselves in a similar position points to the fact that the UHF was at least not disproportionately corrupt or ill-administered.

By 1978, the UHF was out of the picture. As a result, costs would have to be paid in one of three ways—Co-op City's cooperators could be forced to pay higher carrying charges, New York State could offer direct subsidies to the cooperative, or Co-op City could be allowed to add further debt to its already massive HFA mortgage. Levitt made it clear that cost estimates, and hence carrying charge estimates, were based on "unreliable and preliminary construction plans," and that cooperators had been misled as a result.[42] But with the bills coming due, and with the cooperators assuming responsibility for the mortgage under the terms of the rent strike settlement agreement, someone was going to have to pay.

This was bad enough, but the situation was made significantly worse by another factor that became increasingly apparent: construction defects. As residents of Co-op City watched railings crumble and sidewalks sink, they could not help but be aware that there were at least some problems with how Co-op City had been built. In building after building, issues came to light. Cirlin described entering Building 11 shortly after Steering Committee III assumed control to see that "the electrical line was in such bad shape that we had to bring in these commercial fans to keep the generators cool so the building wouldn't lose its power!"[43] A 1977 investigation at Truman High School revealed huge gaps in the ceiling tiles, exposed electrical wires, and plumbing that had never been completed.[44] Residents complained about gas lines that sank into poorly prepared landfill, sidewalks that cracked and buckled, slanted town house terraces, and ever more issues.[45] The HFA retained Perkins + Will, an architecture and engineering firm, to determine the extent of the problems. In June 1978, the firm released a damning report, which laid the blame squarely on issues with Co-op City's initial construction.[46] "Oh my God!" Cirlin later recalled. "We inherited a mess! A mess! And none of us, we never ran a corporation!"[47]

Unfortunately, most of the companies that had constructed Co-op City had long since shuttered their doors. As Cirlin explained, the harsh reality facing Riverbay's new cooperator-controlled board was that "there was no one to sue."[48] According to the Statement of Understanding that ended Co-op City's rent strike, Co-op City was allowed to deduct construction costs from its mortgage payments to the HFA.[49] However, according to a later state investigation of the Co-op City repair program, "Riverbay, the Division of Housing and HFA had not agreed on what was and was not a construction deficiency."[50] Once the monumental scale of the necessary repairs began to become clear, HFA officials balked at the idea that they were on the hook for untold millions of dollars of damages.[51]

After all, not only was Riverbay deducting millions of dollars a year for repairs, but it was increasingly possible that the cost of construction repairs could outstrip the mortgage payment altogether. Less than a year and a half after the final rent strike settlement was agreed to in mid-1977, the HFA sued Co-op City for failure to pay its full mortgage obligations.[52] Struggling to pay its mortgage and also afford construction repairs, Co-op City also failed to pay city taxes, leading Mayor Koch to threaten foreclosure in 1979.[53] A mere two years after the conclusion of the rent strike, in June 1979, Governor Carey decided that the state would directly pay for Co-op City's repairs. He authorized the construction of a state-funded Emergency Repair Program (ERP) to be administered by the HFA.[54] To explain why the state took this on, budget director Mark Lawton recalled how Co-op City's rent strike had "contributed materially to the credit market access problems experienced by the state and its public benefit corporations in 1975–6." As a result, he argued, the state was fearful that if the HFA continued to use bonds to fund Co-op City's construction defect repairs, problems in Co-op City could create "future credit market difficulties." Therefore, the state had no choice but to directly fund Co-op City's construction repairs.[55] Without the potential room for maneuver allowed by HFA's debt financing structure, however, this decision put the state's resources under even more strain.

Fearing that Co-op City's ongoing financial problems and the state's increasing burden of construction repair costs would lead to yet higher carrying charges for residents, and wishing to avoid such a situation, Co-op City residents and their elected representatives hoped to get public opinion on the side of the cooperators. They sought to do this by arguing loudly that they had been duped—swindled by unrealistically low carrying charges and unscrupulous contractors.[56] Co-op City's residents also complained in vain that higher rents might drive younger people to move away or force people who could not pay to suffer.[57] Abraham Bernstein, the state senator representing Co-op City in Albany, expressed his concern that plans like the Ravitch plan might increase divisiveness in the community, with younger people resenting the elderly who were more likely to receive subsidies.[58] But Riverbay and others rarely made a larger case about the importance of either subsidized housing or the cooperative model.

One of the few people to articulate the importance of affordable housing was Ronald Shiffman, a professor at the Pratt Institute and longtime activist and expert in community development. The task force convened by Governor Carey as part of the rent strike settlement consisted of seven members, two of whom were appointed by SCIII: Shiffman and the muckraking journalist Paul DuBrul.[59] The task force's recommendations, released in early 1978, largely focused on the solvency of the program in terms reminiscent of the Ravitch report. In his dissent to the report's recommendations, Shiffman complained that "social considerations and substantive long term solutions to the Mitchell-Lama housing problem became secondary to 'short-term economic solutions.'"[60] Noting that the Mitchell-Lama financial problems were a result of mismanagement, inflation, and other causes beyond the responsibility of tenants, Shiffman insisted that "the cost of the [DHCR]'s failure to properly regulate and protect the tenancy and prospective tenancy of Mitchell-Lama housing is being passed on to the victims and tenants of that housing, rather than to the population of the state as a whole."[61] Instead, Shiffman argued for a more comprehensive solution to return Mitchell-Lama to its original plan of providing housing to people of moderate means. The centerpiece of this plan was a mortgage stabilization program that would rely on either an extension of the terms of Mitchell-Lama mortgages or federal financing to reduce mortgage payments to an amount that would keep carrying costs in a range that would allow the program to serve the middle class.[62] The SCIII's other appointed member of the task force, DuBrul, was the only person to sign on to Shiffman's dissent.

Shiffman's was a moral argument, one that was often countered by the claim that owning a piece of a cooperative, like any kind of property ownership, came with some risk, and it was the responsibility of the cooperators to pay the necessary costs. Letters to Governor Carey and the *New York Times* repeatedly depicted Co-op City's residents as freeloaders, seeking to take advantage of the state for their own benefit. One letter received by Carey complained, "No one said to us forget your problems, like you are now doing at Coop City and other Mitchell-Lama Housing Cooperatives. . . . I am dismayed and disheartened by the actions of public officials who are permitting the citizens of New York to ignore and even laugh at their responsibilities."[63] Stanley Egelberg wrote to the *New York Times* to describe Co-op City's residents as "tax delinquents" whose "whims" were catered to by weak-willed politicians greedy for their votes.[64] Roger Starr, the executive director of the Citizens Housing and Planning Council, stated that "the issue, as we see it, is that Mitchell-Lama projects have to carry their own weight. . . . As managers they [residents] must live up to the responsibility for assuring the building produces sufficient income to pay costs. That is the issue at Co-op City."[65]

Co-op City's elected representatives responded to these attacks. Eliot Engel, Co-op City's new assemblyman, wrote in a letter to the editor of the

New York Times, "I am tired of the implications that people living in Mitchell-Lama housing are somehow wealthy and are getting a free ride and can afford to pay more and more. The fact is that these are the last vestiges of middle and lower-middle income people living in the city."[66] Bernstein similarly wrote to Carey. However, it was clear that these arguments held little sway with the governor. In response to Bernstein, Carey expressed his exasperation that Co-op City's residents were "naïve and unrealistic" in their belief that the legislature would do anything to help them when "average home-owners" had experienced "relentless" inflation with only limited relief.[67] Furthermore, it was easy for the state to plead poverty. With nearly every Mitchell-Lama development in similar shape, with the HFA still teetering on the edge of insolvency, and with New York City just starting to emerge from its own devastating fiscal crisis, the state seemed just as unlikely as the cooperators to pay for Co-op City's problems.

Moreover, if only Shiffman and a few others were willing to articulate a defense of state assistance to create affordable housing, there were fewer either within Co-op City or beyond its borders who defended or explained the importance of cooperative ownership as an alternative to the single-family home. This was not altogether surprising. Despite some efforts on the part of the UHF, the majority of Co-op City's residents had neither known nor cared much about cooperative housing. They were interested in living in Co-op City largely because it offered good, affordable apartments in what promised to be a safe neighborhood. In letter after letter to the governor or other outside organizations, Co-op City residents and their leadership expressed the fact that they had been deceived into buying into a poorly con-structed development with artificially and unsustainably low costs, but rarely mentioned either that affordable housing was necessary for the city, or the idea that cooperative housing offered an important alternative to individual mortgages. Residents of Co-op City had many reasons to have been suspi-cious of and ultimately to destroy the UHF, but in these days, they missed the full-throated defense of affordable housing and cooperative values that the UHF had provided.

In a small but telling sign, from the late 1970s onward, Co-op City resi-dents referred to their monthly payments as "rent." In the days of UHF con-trol, residents often used the (correct) nomenclature of "carrying charges," reflecting the fact that they were not paying rent to a landlord, but rather making payments on a mortgage and paying for operating expenses. While residents in those days sometimes referred to "rent," they usually did so as a political gesture. Their choice to describe themselves as "tenants," their monthly payments as "rent," and ultimately the strike as a "rent strike" was a conscious one, to highlight the fact that they were not owners in the true sense of the word. As Arthur Taub, one of the Riverbay directors who was a Co-op City resident, stated on the eve of the rent strike, "It is very nice to think of tenants as their own landlords when you're teaching a course on the cooperative movement in school. But the word 'tenants' far better describes the status of local residents in the scheme of things."[68] As a result of the rent strike, residents had achieved control of the cooperative. However, their description of their monthly obligations as "rent" made it clear that they did not necessarily see it this way. Cooperative nomenclature and ideology faded quickly from the memory of cooperators.

By stressing the perfidious behavior of the state and the UHF, Co-op City residents argued that they deserved state subsidy and support because they were a special case. The argument then became about how truly unique or deserving Co-op City residents were, rather than a referendum on the importance of affordable housing in an unequal city or the value of alternative models of providing that housing. Moreover, whether this was intended or not, the rhetoric of deception and fraud divided the tenants into two groups—those who moved in during the initial occupancy period and had not known what they had gotten themselves into, and those who arrived later, who had only themselves to blame for choosing to live in a "troubled" development. It should also be mentioned that the split between first occupants and later arrivals mapped, albeit not perfectly, onto a racial divide between whites and others.

Although the residents of Co-op City bitterly resented New York State officials and others who insisted that they pay an "economic rent," in some ways the logic of both sides was not so different after all. On each side of the divide, economics and morality were deeply connected. Co-op City residents argued that they had been lied to and thus were due economic recompense. Critics argued that those residents had a moral responsibility to discharge their financial obligations. This connection between morality and debt service was not unique to the debate over Co-op City but rather part and parcel of a wider revolution in political economy that convulsed the West in the 1970s: the triumph of neoliberalism. At its most extreme, neoliberalism could be an alibi for a libertarian approach that advocated a complete abandonment of any government role for the state in the provision of social services. However, more often in the 1970s and 1980s, neoliberal ideas reflected a preference for "market-based" solutions to social problems, including the creation of enterprise zones to encourage business investment, the denationalization and deregulation of key industries, and the sale of public goods to private citizens.[69] It was a truism of neoliberal housing policy that homeownership was both a moral good and a basic desire of all humans and that government officials should do all that they could to promote it.[70]

In New York, such ideas became ascendant in the aftermath of New York City's near bankruptcy in 1975.[71] New York's austerity program inaugurated under the auspices of the MAC was not merely motivated by a desire to punish the city's profligacy but also by the belief that the state's role was to unleash private enterprise and thus encourage the growth of an economy where a rising tide would lift all boats both economically and morally. In 1977, Edward Koch was elected as New York City's first post-fiscal-crisis mayor. According to his biographer, Jonathan Soffer, Koch sought to "give priority to the interests of revenue providers, not service consumers, and appealed for people with capital—a category that in 1977 mostly meant white people—to come to New York to rehabilitate and rebuild the city's housing stock, create jobs, and make it economically viable again."[72] Or, in Koch's words, in previous administrations "the thrust of city policy was to make this a town where business and economy were of less importance than the welfare syndrome," while he intended to do the opposite.[73] To revitalize New York, the city's government should be the servant of the monied and creative classes, rather than acting to ameliorate the crushing weight of their power.

In his inaugural mayoral address, Koch called on Americans to join "the urban pioneers of this generation. . . . There are homes to be rehabilitated and maintained, schools to be reclaimed and preserved, neighborhoods to be freed from the oppression of crime and the stranglehold of unemployment."[74] The "urban pioneers" Koch was referring to comprised the neighborhood movement that had flowered in New York over the previous decade. This movement began as a revolt against the vision of the urban renewal era. "Rather than renewal, neighborhood groups talked of preservation: preserving old buildings, preserving ethnic identity, preserving authentic communities. . . . Angry white ethnics, urban hipster pioneers, and excited white-collar townhouse renovators all turned nostalgically to the deindustrialized landscape as a refuge. . . . African American activists similarly evoked images of a black community."[75] As much as the neighborhood movement hearkened to a lost community, it also heralded the power of the individual, celebrating "do-it-yourself" voluntarism. Inspired by this new neighborhood-oriented urban vision, the 1973 experimental "homesteader" programs, including that of New York City, were designed to attract new residents to the urban core, then strained by serious abandonment and vacancy problems. It allowed residents and newcomers to buy city-owned or abandoned properties for extremely low prices (often mere dollars) and provided funds to renovate them. According to Suleiman Osman, the neighborhood movement did not necessarily represent a rightward evolution of urban policy but rather "a shift inward."[76] Indeed, homesteader programs had enthusiasts across the political spectrum. By 1980, both Republican and Democratic party platforms embraced urban homesteading.[77] As the Koch administration and other municipal leaders cast about for a way to revitalize a troubled city, they were attracted by a movement whose urban vision "dovetailed seamlessly with a new corporate skepticism about government bureaucracy and fiscal waste."[78] Furthermore, the neighborhood movement's promotion of homeownership as part of their "pro-accountability" stance echoed, if inadvertently, the political and moral economy of New York's new elite.[79]

The Koch administration pursued a number of projects based on a fundamental belief that homeownership was central to revitalizing both neighborhoods and the city as a whole. In 1978, his first year of office, Koch announced the Tenant Interim Lease Program, in which tenants in city-owned buildings could form cooperatives to manage their buildings that had been abandoned by landlords and then purchase their apartments for a mere several hundred dollars apiece.[80] Shortly thereafter, the Koch administration began putting abandoned apartments up for private auction. In the South Bronx, the Koch administration sought to foster homeownership under the theory that the overabundance of rental properties had caused the area's decline and that homeowners would take better care of their homes and their neighborhoods.[81] Nor was this solely driven by the Koch administration's priorities. As the political winds shifted toward homeownership as a means to revitalizing struggling neighborhoods, working-class activists in the 1970s and 1980s in New York and elsewhere sought to lay claim to these programs as a means of improving their fortunes.[82]

It is hard to imagine a place more at odds with this vision of individual responsibility tied to individual homeownership than Co-op City, a massive, government-financed, cooperative development. And yet, its logic was inescapable. Co-op City's residents and its critics argued about who was responsible for paying its mortgage, but no one denied that the mortgage must be paid. Even Co-op City's most vociferous defenders did not claim that a mortgage was not a binding obligation—merely that the corruption of the UHF and the lax oversight of New York State meant that in this case—and this case only—it should not hold. With the terms defined in this way, it was not surprising that the state's negotiators had the upper hand. After all, the UHF/CSI and its subcontractors no longer existed, so it was hard to place financial responsibility on their shoulders. Moreover, while state oversight had been lax, was that really worth forcing the state—or rather New York's taxpayers—to foot the bill of a $400 million (and counting) mortgage and untold millions more in construction defect repair costs?

In 1978, CERL—the Committee to Elect Responsible Leadership—was formed in Co-op City. Despite the fact that it was led by Charles Parness, who had formerly been a member of SCIII, CERL members denounced what they perceived as SCIII's unnecessarily confrontational style. CERL vowed to "end the rent strike mentality of those in power, and the use of constant confrontation as a community policy."[83] In March 1979, CERL-backed candidates swept local elections, becoming a majority on Riverbay's board.[84] Several months later, they faced their first test when in November 1979, Carey announced a plan for carrying charge increases of 69 percent. This increase was based on Ravitch's approach, which called for Mitchell-Lama residents to pay an "economic rent" sufficient to cover the development's costs without state subsidy. Carey's spokeswoman explained that a 40 percent increase would be necessary even if mortgage and tax arrears were not included. However, since such arrears existed, even higher increases were necessary. In announcing these carrying charge hikes, Carey put himself on the side of New York taxpayers fed up with the state's leniency toward Co-op City: "The people of Co-op City can't pay abnormally low rents and expect other people to pay for them."[85]

Co-op City residents were shocked. Mere months earlier, Carey had backed legislation that had called for carrying charge increases of only 12 percent, phased in over three years.[86] This 12 percent figure was roughly in line with the increases that the New York City Rent Guidelines Board issued in 1980 for rent-stabilized units, ranging from 11 percent to 17 percent for apartments that, like Co-op City, provided heat at no charge to tenants.[87] The 69 percent figure that Carey was now asking for was of a different magnitude entirely. Co-op City's newspapers predicted the ruin of the community if Carey's new proposal carried the day: "Only a fool cannot see that Co-op City families cannot pay more than $86 million of accumulated debt; our families cannot see their rents doubled and tripled; and the community will not last long if there is a massive exodus of middle income families."[88] Parness wrote an angry letter to Robert Steves, head of the HFA, decrying Carey for betraying promises he had made to residents of Co-op City and accusing the state of being "bereft of any proposal for a constructive solution."[89] Immediately, Co-op City's grassroots activists were reengaged.

On January 21, 1980, some fourteen hundred people jammed Lerner Auditorium in the Dreiser Community Center to listen to community leaders blame state mismanagement for Co-op City's economic troubles. Riverbay president Parness insisted that Co-op City "had always carried our fair share and we want the State to know that we won't pay twice for the incompetency, the defects and the cost overruns the State permitted."[90] Further, Parness charged that since this amount did not include additional fuel costs, full repair costs, or city tax arrears, the true increases might be far higher.[91] Under a state government that did not wish to subsidize affordable middle-class housing, Co-op City's potential obligations were limitless. Other speakers lamented the loss of Co-op City's initial promise. As one resident put it,

> When the community was first built, it represented to most of us the fulfillment of a dream unsurpassed. But hardly had the ink dried on the preliminary papers before vultures began to make their plans. There were those who saw in the existence of this unborn infant an opportunity for profits undescribable. . . . And they call us freeloaders. What we see is the result of absolutely unconscionable greed. They call this free enterprise, but this, my friend is nothing more nor less than greed—take what you can from the weakest, like a wolf that attacks the deer that runs slowest.[92]

But if Co-op City residents were united in their anger at Carey's proposal, what was to be done? Some called for a new rent strike, arguing that Co-op City had fought the state and won before and would do so again.[93] One resident told a reporter, "I am sick and tired of getting kicked around by Gov. Carey. . . . I can't afford to pay the rent increase the state now wants. I am willing to pay a little more, but there could be a rent strike if they [the state] insist on a large increase. Co-op City was built for the man in the middle, who is now being wiped out."[94] However, such calls never received much traction. After all, people could see that the victory they had achieved in the rent strike several years earlier had not been as transformative as they had hoped. In a 1979 survey in the *City News*, only 20 percent of people believed that Co-op City was a "better place to live because of the rent strike," while 42 percent believed it had gotten worse.[95] Less than three years after the final strike settlement, they were once again fighting major carrying charge increases. The desire to fight back had not abated, nor had the residents' engagement, which once again led thousands of them to turn out to meetings to decry the state's latest perfidy. But now that residents were in charge, they no longer had the UHF to rail against. SCIII member Joel Dannenberg explained the bind that residents now found themselves in were they to call for a renewed rent strike: "This time we will not be withholding the State's money because we use now virtually all the mortgage money for our own purposes. About two-thirds goes for operating expenses and the rest for construction defects repairs. Withholding monies will result in cuts in services and possibly stoppage of construction repair work."[96]

Instead, the newly formed Coordinating Council of Committees and the Council of Community Organizations organized protests at Carey's Manhattan office and the office of Citibank, which was the trustee for Co-op City's bondholders. Demonstrators turned over to the HFA petitions with over ten thousand signatures, asking that carrying charge increases be limited to 12 percent and that the state hold to its original pledge to pay for construction repairs.[97] Yet rallies, petitions, or angry letters were hardly the kind of things to strike fear in the hearts of officials in Albany.

Even as residents protested, CERL took a more conciliatory line. Parness quickly abandoned the combative posture he had taken early in the crisis and instead asked meekly for the "12% figure to be accepted" by the state. Parness bowed to the state's logic, explaining to cooperators that such a figure was "'politically unachievable.' . . . The members of the legislature must answer to their constituents and they feel they can no longer be in a position to vote for funds to limit the increase in Co-op City to twelve percent."[98] Parness accepted the idea of an "economic rent" that would make Co-op City sustainable without continued state investment; he merely hoped for slower increases that would give residents time to adjust.[99] In March 1980, four months after the increases had been proposed by the HFA, a CERL-headed Riverbay reached an agreement with the state. In this "workout" settlement, there would be an immediate 20 percent increase in carrying charges as of April 1980 and lasting until July 1982. In August 1982, there would be another increase of 16 percent, and then a further 16 percent increase in August 1984, a cumulative increase of over 60 percent.[100] Additionally, in July 1986, an unspecified final increase would raise carrying charges to an economic rent level.[101] As part of this settlement, the state agreed to lend Co-op City money for its operating expenses that exceeded its receipts. However, the agreement also mandated that Co-op City would need to begin paying back these loans in 1986. Some $40 million in already incurred debts to the city and state would be pushed back to the conclusion of Co-op City's mortgage in 2006.[102] Parness sought to put the best possible spin on the agreement, arguing that it meant that residents could expect six years of relative stability. "With rapidly rising inflation, with fuel cost increases escalating, these 16 percent increases will be less than what anyone would pay under rent control or rent stabilization during these periods."[103] Few residents found this an acceptable compromise. SCIII's new leader, Frank Tolopko, called it a "sellout . . . that amounts to a five year eviction notice." However, even he did not call for a rent strike, explaining that a strike against a resident board of directors was "meaningless."[104] Ultimately, by a vote of 57 percent to 43 percent, Co-op City's residents approved the plan.[105] Afterward, Governor Carey issued a press release stating that the vote "is a signal to the financial community that the residents are willing to meet their responsibilities and protect their community."[106]

With the Greenway no longer filled with protesters, most people encountered the ongoing political drama in the development through the pages of the *Co-op City Times* and *City News*. Co-op City's two political blocks—SCIII and CERL—constantly railed against each other in the pages of Co-op City's two newspapers—"Charles Rosen makes up facts like a child losing an argument,"[107] "CERL, Parness-Engel & Co. sabotaged the settlement, ripped the community apart,"[108] and on and on. Others attacked both sides: "Has all this fighting between Steering Committee III and 'CERL' provided our community with capable people who can begin to give leadership that will help solve our problems? Let's face it—they haven't. Their divisiveness has only caused our community to go downhill."[109]

All this political activity and outrage seemed both exhausting and unproductive. For all of the drama of the rent strike, it had not halted the march of carrying charge increases. Co-op City's more accommodating stance during the workout negotiations had similarly realized little benefit. The thousands of cooperators who filled the Greenway and meeting halls to protest carrying charge increases bemoaned their fate but seemed to have little impact on negotiations. In the early 1970s, both the state and (especially) the UHF had genuinely feared the protests that culminated in the rent strike. In its aftermath, the protests had not abated, but both Co-op City's leadership and their negotiating partners in Albany no longer saw them as an existential threat.

For those with the means to leave, there seemed little to recommend either in the collective virtues that the UHF had promoted or in the collective actions taken by Co-op City's residents during the rent strike. Yet, in the recollections of the many Co-op City residents who left during this period, neither finances nor politics are mentioned. While some residents referenced personal issues—a new job, the desire to own a home, health concerns, and so on—many explained their moves as a result of rising crime.

One former resident later recalled, "Sadly by the early 80s Co-op was changing. A so called less desirable element started moving in as well as others coming from the nearby projects. . . . Crime did go up and it was not as safe as it had been 10–15 years earlier. . . . It just was not a nice place to live any more. The so called Co-op security was a warm fuzzy idea but they were powerless and a joke and wouldn't stop Grandma Moses from robbing a bank. . . . Sad situation all around."[110] Another wrote, "We were leaving our building one day and a savage was urinating against the wall. . . . Besides . . . I knew I wanted to get out of the city before we had kids."[111] Residents who left often cited the elevators and stairwells as particular sources of fear. "I had a young son at the time and children were being attacked in the elevator coming home from school. Women were also being attacked. It was time to move."[112] Some former residents stressed that they were responding to an increase in crime in the city as a whole, not something specific to Co-op City. "I was mugged in the lobby of Building 7 in 1979. . . . The entire city, and many cities, we're [sic] getting rough then."[113]

Crime did rise in the late 1970s and early 1980s across New York City. In 1980, violent crime in New York City was nearly 50 percent higher than it had been a decade earlier.[114] Nevertheless, Co-op City remained a relatively safe community.[115] In 1979, Co-op City's security chief, Philip Sussman, sought to assuage residents: "We are one of the best—if not the safest—communities in the City. . . . I fully understand that if I tell you crime is increasing everywhere, except here, and you or your loved ones are the victim of a crime, it becomes poor consolation for you." Indeed, he argued that from his perspective, neither vandalism nor serious crimes rose to the level that he had expected. Instead, "responding to nuisances, ball playing, and noise complaints are the most time consuming and greatest single manpower drain that is exhausting our availability."[116] The statistics published by Co-op City's newspapers appeared to bear him out, such as a 25 percent drop in major crimes from 1976 to 1977, or a nearly 18 percent drop in Co-op City's crime rate from 1980 to 1981.[117]

Yet regardless of the statistics, many residents believed that crime in Co-op City was high and rising fast. Residents fearfully traded stories and ignored attempts at reassurance.[118] Some claimed that crime statistics could not be believed because "there was also a lot of stuff that happened in Co-op that wasn't reported to the police. . . . Co-op security was all crooked. . . . Half of those Co-op security guards had criminal records. And that was a fact."[119] One resident who moved out in 1980 explained her sense that "slowly gradually, it got progressively worse, where everyone we knew had someone who was getting hurt, beat up, mugged, knocked off a bike, so many. . . . I know several people who were raped in Co-op City. . . . In the elevators, my friends would get their jewelry ripped off. So many. One person got gang raped on the Greenway."[120] After Michael Agovino's mother had her car stolen in 1980, their neighbor Ravi commented, "What do you expect from this place? They're stealing cars every day here. Co-op is like the highest or second-highest hotbed of stolen cars in the city. They even steal them from the garages. It's becoming a big ghetto. We all have to get out of here."[121] Agovino also described the spread of increasingly fantastical rumors: "We heard other things. Our neighbor Ricardo told my mother that he heard that someone was scaling the sides of the buildings in Co-op City and breaking into apartments. When she told me, I said, 'That's crazy, impossible, some kind of urban legend.' 'I believe it,' she said. 'I don't put it past anyone.' . . . What was Rumor . . . and what was real?"[122] The responses by Co-op City's security department only seemed to exacerbate the very panic they sought to assuage. In response to the murder of an elderly woman in her apartment, the chief of security urged residents to "get to know your neighbors. Our hi-rise buildings have an average of 400 families. Find someone you can place your trust in, *especially* if you live alone." He advised that residents not ride public transportation alone, be wary of strangers on elevators, carry a whistle in case they were accosted, and keep their doors locked at all times. Co-op City's Security Department wanted to make it clear that "WE CANNOT DO IT ALONE!!!"[123] Security's ineffectual exhortations to parents, such as "explain to your children not to damage the lobby [or elevator] . . . there are a few [who] mark up the elevators with filthy words," only served to raise the ire of residents without decreasing either vandalism or fear.[124]

Meanwhile, CERL's successful 1979 campaign to take over the board focused in part on vandalism and crime, arguing that SCIII's mismanagement of these issues was representative of its general failures. Eva Pellman, who would later serve as Riverbay president, wrote in her candidate statement, "Security must receive high priority. . . . Vandalism prevention is nonexistent. We pay tens of thousands of dollars to repair the destruction of vandalism every year and nothing to prevent it. . . . My program is to get security off their seats and on their feet, inside buildings where vandalism and crime happen."[125] Another candidate began her proposed cooperators' "Bill of Rights" with "the right to live in decent housing without crime or vandalism"[126]

Sociologist Jonathan Rieder wrote of the middle-class neighborhood of Canarsie in South Brooklyn, "The basic fact of life for [them] was the precariousness of their hold on middle class status, the recency of their arrival in that exalted position and the intense fear that it might be taken from them."[127] This was true in Co-op City as well. And just as in Canarsie, anxieties about crime were inextricably connected to anxieties about race. From the moment that Co-op City's residents moved in, they were hyper-vigilant for any sign that their new neighborhood would deteriorate. Any piece of graffiti, any piece of litter on the ground, and, certainly, any black or brown face had the potential to cause residents to revisit their experiences in the West Bronx or what had happened in other formerly Jewish enclaves across the city.[128] In the early 1970s, these fears had been matched with hope about the new community in Co-op City and with a sense of familiarity—everyone had moved in at about the same time, and many had gotten to know each other as a result. The Co-op City of the early 1970s was an optimistic place, filled with young families of all racial backgrounds eager to make a fresh start. By the latter part of that decade, economic strains, political turmoil, and crumbling infrastructure combined to dim this optimism, providing less of a counterweight to preexisting anxieties about race and crime. It was also in this period that Co-op City was in the process of becoming significantly less white.

In the 1970 census, taken when only a small portion of Co-op City had been occupied, census statistics indicate that Co-op City was roughly 85 percent white, with the remaining population largely made up of Blacks and Hispanics.[129] By the time Co-op City was fully occupied in 1972, the percentage of white residents was closer to 70 percent. By 1980, census statistics show that Co-op City was only 60 percent white (see appendix, figure 25). While whites still made up the majority of residents, the trend was clear. At the conclusion of the rent strike, the wait list of families hoping for an apartment to become available was nearly 90 percent Black and Latino.[130] On August 18, 1976, the Riverbay board passed Resolution 131, a set of policies designed to prioritize families on the wait list. After internal transfers, relatives of Co-op City families would have priority; after them, priority would be given to families who could get recommendations from existing tenants.[131] After receiving a number of whistleblower complaints, the Urban League initiated a formal complaint to the State Division of Housing against Co-op City's "discriminatory practices" against Blacks on its waiting list. Citing the recent Justice Department suit against Trump Village in Brooklyn for bias against Black applicants, the Urban League decried what it believed was an attempt to preserve Co-op City's 70 percent white/30 percent Black racial balance with the potential result that "virtually no Blacks could apply."[132] While there was no evidence of such a 70/30 percent quota system, and the idea that "virtually no Blacks could apply" was something of an exaggeration, the Urban League's complaint was not entirely off base; after all, a policy that favored family members and people who knew existing cooperators was likely to perpetuate Co-op City's existing racial demographics at the expense of the majority of families on the waiting list.

Rosen, then newly serving as Riverbay president, was apoplectic in his response to these charges: "This scoundrel [from the Urban League] must be stopped. The issue of racism is too important to be left to irresponsible people from prestigious organizations who sully the work so many Americans have been involved in attempting to democratize our society. To pit black against white in a vain struggle to get newspaper headlines is counterproductive to the cause of civil rights and criminal in terms of our attempt to save Co-op City."[133] Co-op City's Black representatives on the Riverbay board distanced themselves from the complaint, without necessarily denying the truth of the allegations, and Resolution 131 was quietly shelved.[134] It would most likely not have worked in any event. Given Co-op City's need to fill vacant apartments, and given the overwhelmingly nonwhite nature of its wait list, even such a policy could do little to alter the fact that Co-op City was increasingly populated by Black and Latino families.

If the color of Co-op City's new residents was different, little else about them was. The census indicated that the income of Co-op City residents remained nearly at the median for residents of New York City (see appendix, figure 27). Furthermore, just as many of Co-op City's first residents had moved to the cooperative to escape crime in their former neighborhoods, this was generally the case for its arrivals a decade later.[135] In fact, given that most of Co-op City's new residents were young families, and given that Levitt's audit had demonstrated that senior citizen residents were more likely to have trouble affording to live in Co-op City, it is likely that Co-op City's new Black and Latino families were among the wealthier residents of the cooperative.[136] The financial and social status of Co-op City's arrivals had not changed. Their color, however, had. Many residents took the darker skin of their new neighbors as a sign that Co-op City's incipient decline—always a potent fear—was now a reality.

Complaints about rising crime and newcomers were not confined to white residents. One Black former resident explained that by the late 1970s, "[Co-op City] started getting kind of rough and violent."[137] A Black woman wrote to the *City News* that "there is a rumor going around that welfare people are moving in by the numbers. I invested my hard-earned savings to live in a decent and comfortable place. . . . I hope that this does not exist. Some people call it racism, I do not agree on this point. . . . I do not prefer welfare people, be they white or black. Welfare people are unreliable and irresponsible. . . . I am not compelled to live here[;] under such conditions, how can I?"[138] The *City News* published a second letter a week later from another Black woman, Della Brown, who echoed these points. "I am also Black and I never lived in a place like Co-op City. I enjoy living here very much. We get along with everybody. I am also against welfare residents. They have no responsibility. . . . May I say it is also for the good for Black people to resist welfare clients. They have no idea how this place can become a slum city."[139] Just like their white neighbors, these women were fearful of crime and connected it to new residents of the cooperative.

Nevertheless, racist assumptions about blackness and crime were present in Co-op City just as they were pervasive in America as a whole. White residents were more likely to see crime and racial change as linked. For them, their own recent experiences in the West Bronx contributed to their belief that Black newcomers were a sign of rising crime and neighborhood deterioration. While earlier in the decade this attitude had been counterbalanced by excitement about the fresh start that Co-op City represented, the pessimism of the late 1970s proved fertile ground for already existing prejudices to flourish.

People who stayed in Co-op City were generally more willing to discuss the role of race in decisions to move out of the community. In a Facebook thread among a group of former residents, one Black former resident wrote, "Crime was never really an issue in Co-op City. White people saw more and more Blacks and Latinos moving in and . . . FLED."[140] A Jewish resident looking back on these years echoed this charge: "I still think people moved out for ethnic reasons alone. They wanted to be with people who look like them and they wanted their children to have boyfriends and girlfriends who looked like them."[141]

Generally, when Jewish former residents who had moved out during this period explained their reasoning, they took pains to explain that their departures were unrelated to race—that they were less concerned Co-op City was becoming a majority-minority community than they were by the fact that it was becoming more dangerous. For example, one former resident insisted that since Blacks were also the victims of the rise of crime, her departure was not about race: "I left by 1980. . . . A little black child six years old had his hand sliced open at the school and another boy about 12 was raped in the building. Seeing this made me move[,] not because it was getting dark."[142] This was similar to Rieder's experience talking to Canarsie Jews, whose racial "resentment contained more conditionals, elaborate apologetics, and wordy defensiveness" than their Catholic neighbors expressed.[143] Yet for all their denials and conditional statements, Co-op City's departing residents ignored statistics and other evidence of Co-op City's relative safety. Indeed, the very insistence that Co-op City was crime-ridden may have been, for some, a way to explain that leaving was not motivated by racial anxieties but rather due to the fact that the cooperative had become too violent for them to remain.

Anxieties about crime and anxieties about race operated in a self-reinforcing and self-justifying loop.

Anxieties about crime and race often focused on Section Five, or as one former resident wrote, "Co-op City has generated its most drama from Section Five."[144] Section Five was the final section built and was separated from the rest of the development by a stretch of road. Section Five had a reputation from the beginning as a place that was both less white and less safe than the rest of Co-op City, with some referring to it as "Lil Harlem."[145] Another resident recalled, "Section Five was the place Domino's Pizza didn't deliver to because their delivery men had been robbed in the lobbies too often!"[146] While there are no statistics that can confirm Section Five was more dangerous than the rest of Co-op City, there was some truth to the sense that Section Five was more Black than the rest of the development. In 1980, census statistics indicate that 51 percent of Section Five's residents identified as white, less than the 60 percent for the cooperative as a whole. There were constant rumors that Co-op City had directed Blacks to Section Five so that the rest of the development would be white.[147] I could find no evidence that this was the case, and Section Five's greater Black population could be explained without reference to a specific conspiracy. Since the percentage of nonwhite applicants to live in Co-op City rose over time, later-constructed sections would tend to have a larger nonwhite population than those that were occupied earlier. As the final section constructed, Section Five had the largest Black population. Nevertheless, the idea that Section Five's greater Black population was a result of a deliberate UHF policy to create residential segregation in a supposedly integrated community was a durable myth.

In light of the association of Section Five with Black residents and criminality, the Black Caucus committed to holding several meetings a year to focus specifically on Section Five's image problem. In 1977, Section Five residents started a PR campaign to change the image of the area. The campaign largely focused on calls for residents to participate in cleanup campaigns and enforce community standards. Building 30 chairman James Parker said that "if I'm afraid to go down the hall to speak to my neighbor, that's the sign of a broken floor. We must tell our neighbors not to hang their clothes on terraces and not to litter our hallways."[148] The fears and prejudices focused on Section Five were a microcosm of a broader fear held by many residents—that Co-op City was not, in fact, as separate from the Bronx as many of its residents had hoped. The specter of the slums had never been far from the minds of Co-op City's residents, many of whom, regardless of their own racial background, had moved from NYCHA housing projects or neighborhoods that they saw as in decline. In the late 1970s, these slums seemed closer than ever. According to the group dedicated to improving Section Five's image, "Section Five has been much maligned by downgrading, constant adverse references to 'slumland' and 'badmouth' connotations that our area is one to avoid."[149] One former Co-op City resident noted, "We tried to stay away from Section Five. We had no reason to go there. We had supermarkets by us, schools by us. The only reason to venture out to Section Five was to visit someone. We had no reason to go."[150]

Apart from the social impact of move-outs and racial change, which will be discussed further in the next chapter, Co-op City was financially particularly ill-equipped to deal with vacancies. The development needed as many carrying charge payments from residents as possible to be able to make its gargantuan mortgage payments. Every apartment that stood empty meant less money that could be used to pay Co-op City's mortgage or construction defects. There was little margin for error. According to Riverbay, even the 5 percent vacancy rate in 1978 was a "serious problem given our current situation."[151] Mayor Koch referred to Co-op City's vacancies as "like cancer. You need to excise it before it spreads further. You need to take whatever steps to make the patient well."[152]

Under both SCIII and CERL leadership, Riverbay sought to fill vacancies and keep even more residents from leaving. Riverbay board member Cecil Atkins said that "one of our most immediate goals must be to mount an all-out effort to attract young families to Co-op City. The task shouldn't be difficult either. Co-op City has many sought-after amenities: we have some of the finest schools in the City of New York; we have many wide open spaces and safe play areas."[153] Riverbay tried multiple avenues to entice residents to apply. Playground equipment was upgraded with an eye toward attracting "new families looking for homes."[154] Riverbay also set up three furnished model apartments on the thirty-first floor of Building 35 in Section Five, for prospective residents to tour.[155] The Model Apartment Program opened with great fanfare in the late summer of 1978. Indeed, it appeared to have an immediate effect. The *Co-op City Times* reported that applications rose by a whopping 1,400 percent in the program's first three months.[156] Article after article crowed that not only were applications soaring, but that new applicants were precisely the "young families and newlyweds" that the UHF had originally hoped to attract and that Co-op City needed so desperately to fill its surplus of larger apartments.[157] Yet all this positive publicity proved to be a mirage, and less than a year later, Riverbay closed the Model Apartment Program and deemed it a failure.[158]

Booster campaigns sought to attract potential residents. As one article in the *Co-op City Times* in 1977 proclaimed, "Co-op City's Got It—Let's Flaunt It!"[159] Co-op City's 1978 fair had the theme "Co-op City—a Wonderful Place to Live."[160] Another ad, with the tag line "Co-op City, where we can all afford to live with pride," explained that "in other communities, people stopped caring and neighborhoods withered and died. But here in Co-op City, the spirit is alive and continues to grow. Because here, people continue to care. Just look around you."[161] According to these ads, Co-op City was home to a unique community, which stood in proud opposition to the degradation of the rest of the borough.

The reality was otherwise. Community leaders bemoaned that Co-op City's political squabbles had led to it developing a bad reputation, arguing that residents needed to tone down their rhetoric in order to avoid damaging the development in the eyes of potential residents. Joel Dannenberg, Riverbay's vice president, said that "I am optimistic that we can sell apartments because Co-op City is a desirable community." However, he cautioned that potential buyers were wary "because the turmoil hasn't ceased in Co-op City."[162] Indeed, Co-op City had become such a symbol of a "community of turmoil—a community of problems" that in 1981, CERL president Charles Parness considered a name change from "Co-op City" to "Riverbay" as a way to "enhance its attractiveness."[163] Some residents agreed with this suggestion: "I am tired of people looking at me horrified when I tell them I live in Co-op City. We have had so many things bad printed about us that people think it's an awful place to live. . . . You never know, if you change the name, people may start moving in again. Riverbay may be the start of a whole new community."[164] But on the whole, residents responded negatively, asserting their preference for Co-op City. Abraham Schenck, a frequent commenter in the pages of the *Co-op City Times*, expressed skepticism: "To change the name is the easy way, but if the besmirchers will continue in the same old manner, prospective tenants will say, 'Riverbay? Oh you mean what used to be called 'Co-op City'? It won't work I'm afraid."[165] Another resident, Henry Mahler, explained his reasons for preferring Co-op City:

> Last week I found myself on the Jerome Avenue train. . . . As I was gazing out of the window, I was shocked at the sight of row after row of burned out buildings with black holes. . . . When I returned home to a beautiful and light apartment, I gratefully paid homage to Co-op City, a name that represents and brings forth the image of a community of people of different races, colors, religions, living in peace and harmony; a community of so many social, religious, political, cultural

organizations, medical groups, outdoor concerns, fairs, art exhibitions, newspapers, a wonderful library and so on.[166]

Tellingly, as Mahler defended Co-op City, he noted three things: its diversity, its plethora of community institutions, and its separation from the rest of the Bronx. Mahler was silent on the cooperative values from which Co-op City had received its name.

Co-op City's name did not change. Instead, in 1979, Riverbay tried a new advertising campaign designed to counteract the "bad rap" that had become associated with the development.[167] The new campaign was titled "Co-op City. A Nice Place to Live." In some ways, this ad campaign was similar to the UHF's marketing materials a decade earlier. As had been the case then, ads emphasized the natural setting of Co-op City's towers, its "rolling acres of trees," and its waterfront location. It also stressed Co-op City's affordability in "an era of changing neighborhoods and skyrocketing housing costs."[168] Moreover, like the UHF's promotional materials a decade earlier, ads of the late 1970s and early 1980s drew attention to the development's spacious apartments and excellent schools. And yet the differences were even more striking. One brochure, titled "City Living the Way It Used to Be," gave a clue to how much had changed. The UHF had been relentlessly oriented toward the future, rejecting nostalgia for the architecture of the past. However, Co-op City's new marketing team asked readers to "come and discover for yourself why the dream of city living the way it used to be is still a reality in Co-op City."[169] Co-op City would offer its residents a "forgotten dimension to family living."[170] There was a certain irony to this rhetoric. "Co-op City. A Nice Place to Live" echoed the nostalgic urban vision of Jane Jacobs's idealized "urban village," precisely the urban perspective that the UHF had fought so hard against. Needless to say, a ten-year-old high-rise development made up of thirty-five tower buildings arranged in superblocks was an odd fit for this urban romance.

Up until the end of the rent strike, Co-op City had been an aspirational symbol. In its early days, under the UHF, it was a symbol of the promise of cooperative living. During the rent strike, it was a symbol of the power of the people in an era of tenant activism across New York City and beyond. Now, as the force of financial exigency crushed the utopian hopes invested in cooperator control, Co-op City became a symbol of something else: failure. The corruption of the UHF, the insufficient oversight of the DHCR, the inability of tenants to limit carrying charge increases—there was no end to the ways that Co-op City came to represent disappointment.

Co-op City's financial problems stemmed from the fact that it had been paid for with a mortgage that had ballooned from $235 million in 1965 to nearly $400 million a decade later. The fact that payment was deferred throughout the construction period, which only ended in 1972, meant that it was easy for both the state and the UHF to avoid the full impact of the costs that piled up over the construction period. And the fantastic sums involved almost made the money feel unreal. This is not to say that the UHF was not concerned with the cost of the development; but its concern was primarily with what that cost would mean for carrying charges, not with the overall size of the mortgage. They, and later the cooperators, once they assumed control of the development, fought hard to keep carrying costs as low as possible. As a result, obligations were often deferred in an attempt to balance the books in the immediate term while not placing an undue burden on residents. It was also undeniably true that graft and corruption contributed to cost overruns during the construction period. Furthermore, the cooperators who assumed control as members of SCIII or CERL were not professional property managers. It is certain that they made mistakes as well.

However, to lay blame for Co-op City's financial hardship on the UHF, and later the cooperators, is to miss the bigger picture. The UHF and the residents of Co-op City were beholden to the state by the terms of the mortgage. They negotiated for better options or lower costs, but short of a rent strike, they had little ability to force the state to bend. Meanwhile, as both sides discovered over the course of the rent strike, the state was almost equally beholden to Co-op City, because of both its size and the size of its mortgage. The two were caught in a relationship that neither could leave. This had been true since the project had been proposed in 1965. However, the power balance had shifted once cooperators assumed control. Riverbay's board of directors now were keenly aware of their responsibility as owners of the cooperative and saw fewer options available to them than they had when the UHF was in charge. When faced with another series of carrying charge increases in 1980, Riverbay's new resident directors rejected future mass actions, such as a renewed rent strike. Co-op City's economic fate would be determined by negotiation, and cooperators would face growing intransigence on the part of the state and its negotiators, who did not see affordable middle-class rental or cooperative housing as worth spending precious dollars to support.

At the same time, the development itself began to change as the first wave of cooperators began to leave. Co-op City's new residents were much more likely to be Black or Latino than the families they replaced. The Co-op City of the late 1970s was not the isolated, majority Jewish utopia of a decade earlier. In a 1978 interview, Esther Smith, Riverbay's first Black president, explained her hope for the future: "If rents were stabilized, peace and unity came to the community, and all of our construction problems were taken care of, this would be the greatest reward I could receive."[171] The UHF had hoped to use Co-op City as the nucleus for a broader social transformation. A decade after Co-op City's first residents moved in, Smith's dreams were more prosaic—peace and financial stability. And yet, even they would prove elusive in the decade to come.

CHAPTER 6

"Co-op City *Is* the Bronx"

A Middle-Class Community, 1982–1993

In 1988, the *Co-op City Times* published a supplement to honor the cooperative's twentieth anniversary. It began with an elaborate description of Co-op City's massive scale: "If you wanted to construct a solid earthen tower that was 12'x12' at the base and stretched 178 miles into space, you would first need some 5,000,000 cubic yards of dirt, or an amount equivalent to the hydraulic fill used to prepare that 300 acre area which would one day be called Co-op City."[1] After rehearsing the now familiar tales of Co-op City's first pioneers and the construction site they moved into, the newspaper struck a defiant tone as it exalted Co-op City's residents in the face of naysayers: "As the critics harped about aesthetics and population density, cooperators could only smile quietly to themselves. After all, they are the ones who enjoyed spacious, affordable, and cheerfully sunlight [*sic*] homes; they are the ones who knew when a shriek echoed across the Greenway that it came from playful children and not some terrified citizen beset by thugs."[2] Equally important was what the anniversary issue did not celebrate. The UHF barely rated a mention. There was no explanation of the history of cooperatives or cooperative values, and little more than a cursory discussion of the rent strike. Twenty years since its first residents moved in, Co-op City's ideological origins had been forgotten.

Even at this moment of celebration in 1988, Co-op City's turmoil in the late 1980s was impossible to ignore. Al Shapiro, Riverbay president, noted that some critics believed "the 'spark' has gone out of Co-op City." "Many folks are at a loss to describe just how things are different. Some say it's the intrusion of politics . . . for some it's the physical deterioration and ever-present construction . . . others look to the hardships the state has caused." Even Shapiro, for his part, could not help but admit that he sensed "a certain loss of community innocence," though he sought to chalk this up to the natural maturing process any community goes through. His fellow director, Tony Illis, was blunter. Pointing to Co-op City's ongoing strife with New York State, ongoing issues with construction defects, and its upcoming carrying charge increase, Illis noted that "there are still rough waters to sail" as Co-op City looked to its future.[3]

Aside from its monumental scale, the Co-op City of 1988 barely resembled the neighborhood that the development's first residents had encountered two decades earlier. The buildings that they had seen rise from the ground were now covered by scaffolding, part of an ever-growing number of projects designed to address the construction defects that had been discovered in the intervening decades. Rather than a majority-Jewish development, Co-op City in the late 1980s was more than half Black and Latino, the latter mostly Puerto Rican but with a growing Dominican population (see appendix, figure 25). Across this period, community leaders continued to express the belief in Co-op City's integrated community that their predecessors had heralded in earlier decades. Calls to celebrate "the premise of Co-op City—friendly people of all kinds living together," as one Black Riverbay director put it, reflected a deeply held belief in the importance and viability of integration, but they do not tell the full story.[4] It was also during this period that crime, always a concern among Co-op City residents, went from a worry to an obsession. The panic expressed by Co-op City's residents about crime reflected a real rise in crime in the 1980s in both the community itself and in the city as a whole; however, it was also a reflection of anxieties about the ability of the neighborhood to avoid becoming a slum as its white population fell. Co-op City residents had always occupied the hazy space between the lower-middle and working class; many of them experienced their hold on middle-class identity as fragile. Residents of all races called for an increased police presence in the community as a means to defend its tenuous position as a middle-class neighborhood.

Co-op City's original, largely white and Jewish, residents continued to move out as the 1980s progressed. Their departure was less precipitous than the exodus from the West Bronx that had first populated the cooperative; however, by 1990, census statistics indicate that Co-op City's population was nearly equally white and Black (40 percent each), with an additional 18 percent identifying as Hispanic and a tiny percentage that did not fit into any of those categories (see appendix, figure 25). This transition mirrored that of New York as a whole. In 1990, the census found that New York City was 43 percent white non-Hispanic, 28 percent Black, 24 percent Hispanic, and 7 percent Asian.[5] Just as in 1970, Co-op City's racial demographics were a rough approximation of that of the city, albeit with a somewhat higher Black population and lower percentages in other categories.[6] When Co-op City's Orthodox synagogue scaled back in 1989 for lack of congregants, giving up space and laying off employees, its rabbi explained that it had been the victim of "the three M's: mortality, move-outs and Miami Beach."[7] As this quote suggests, Co-op City had always been vulnerable to demographic transition because of the age of its residents. From the time Co-op City opened, its elderly population was always more white and Jewish than the rest of the development. Many of those who were already elderly in the 1960s died or moved closer to family or friends in the ensuing decades. Racially inflected fears about crime led some white people to leave Co-op City. The desire to own a home was also a factor. Although the UHF had seen Co-op City as a place that people would stay in forever, many residents viewed it as a transitional space. These residents had moved to Co-op City to escape the projects or the slums and then ten or fifteen years later moved on to buy a house. What caused Co-op City to become less white was not so much that white people moved out but that so few white people moved in.

Although Co-op City had hosted Jewish cultural events since its founding, in 1979 it hosted a Black Heritage Festival for the first time.[8] By the late 1980s, February had become a monthlong celebration of Black History Month, and Truman High School began to offer a course on African American history.[9] The racial composition of Co-op City's leadership also changed. Already in 1978, Esther Smith, who had previously been the only Black and female member of SCIII, became Co-op City's first Black Riverbay president. As the 1980s wore on, increasing numbers of Blacks and Latinos were elected to Riverbay's board of directors. However, official celebrations and official leadership posts were far from the only cultural markers of Co-op City's growing Black population. Co-op City's new residents in the 1970s and 1980s were most likely to be Black or Latino, and young families were the most likely to move to Co-op City. As a result of these two trends, the ethnicity of young people shifted earlier and more quickly than the population of the development as a whole. By the late 1980s, young people were mostly Black or Latino, while older adults were mostly white.

FIGURE 22.   Young and old gather outside Building 4, 1980s. Photograph by Gregory Myers.

Greg Myers, a Black former resident, recalled, "It was the late seventies
going into the early eighties. That's when you started seeing a change. . . .
In the early days a lot of Jewish kids would be at the paddleball courts and
handball courts . . . but as the decade progressed, I didn't see many of the
Jewish kids. I would see a lot of Puerto Rican kids and Black kids hanging out."[10] During these years, according to Robin Nurse, "Co-op City was
becoming known for rappers coming and giving street parties. It seemed
like every Saturday afternoon on the basketball courts, there was a party.
Grandmaster Flash was there, Run-D.M.C. All of those guys came through.
It was packed."[11] Historian and former resident Frank Guridy recalled that
"literally after school, people would come out, put that cardboard box on
the floor, and then people would just dance. It was just extraordinary."[12] In a
memoir that begins with his childhood in Co-op City, Miles Marshall Lewis
quotes his friend John Reed's recollection of what he wore to his eighth
grade prom at IS 181 in 1984: "White Lees with the permanent crease, white
Chams de Baron shirt, white on white Adidas with white fat laces, white
band gloves, a long white scarf that hung over my neck like Tyson wore his
heavyweight belts, a white Kangol hat with Section Five's five popular letters
ironed on the front: F.R.E.S.H. Also, a name buckle with JAY and a medallion
and chain.[13] Lewis described the prom "ending with a breaking battle in our
cafeteria; John won and walked off with Liticia Padilla a/k/a Bunny Tee,

FIGURE 23.   The Fascinating Four MCs rap group, 1985. Photograph by Gregory Myers.

one of the finest girls in eighth grade. He was what you might call a ghetto celebrity, one of the neighborhood superstars."[14] By the 1980s, Black cultural references dominated among young people regardless of their own racial background. Agovino recalled his pride at being "as fluent as any white boy in Co-op City—the lyrics of Melle Mel and Afrika Bambaataa easily came to my lips."[15]

As more Black and Latino residents came to Co-op City, residents of all colors no longer perceived the neighborhood as separate from the borough it resided in. In his memoir, Lewis does not describe moving to Co-op City in the mid-1970s as an escape from the Bronx. Rather, he saw his home in Co-op City as a vital and authentic part of the Bronx, and in particular its Black cultural heritage:

> I came of age eight miles from the Sparkle at 1590 Jerome Avenue where Grand Wizard Theodore cut up "Johnny the Fox Meets Jimmy the Weed" by Thin Lizzy, thereby inventing the scratch technique, three miles from the Big 3 Barbershop where my uncle's homeboy cut hair with his pops (the shop's owner) and Slick Rick would come in for an occasional fade, two miles from where Slick Rick actually lives on Baychester Avenue, six miles from the hospitals Woody Allen and Louis Farrakhan were born in . . . five miles from the Mount Saint

Michael's Academy that Sean Combs attended, some railroad tracks and a greenway away from the 6 train at Pelham Bay Park which I frequently rode into Manhattan (Jennifer Lopez would hop on five stops later at Castle Hill Avenue), buildings away from where Kurtis Blow and hiphop historian Davey D and Queen Latifah and Tigger of BET's *Rap City* and Jarobi White from A Tribe Called Quest all lived in Co-op City, directly across from the tenement building of Born Unique Allah, one of the Fresh 3 MCs who recorded "Fresh."[16]

As Lewis explained, "Co-op City *is* the Bronx."[17]

Lewis was not the only person to see Co-op City this way. A 1986 documentary on New York hip-hop titled "Big Fun in the Big Town" was partially set at Truman High School in Co-op City. When one Black student was asked how she learned to rap, she responded that she "learned rap from the streets." A white music teacher further explained that "this was the Bronx, the hotbed of rap. It started here, this is where it's still growing. . . . In this part of the city, people can't afford music lessons." For both this student and her teacher, Co-op City was a part of the Bronx, its musical culture and its economic struggles, not an exception or escape.[18] Agovino describes the 1980s as a time when "more and more of the Co-op City originals began to flee and the place became more—not sinister, not darker—just more and more like the rest of the Bronx."[19] As another former resident, Toni Mendez, put it jokingly, "Now it's really the Bronx, right? You can't get away from the crazy."[20]

The schools were ground zero for Co-op City's changing demographics. By the mid-1980s, even though 40 percent of the development's residents were white, less than 20 percent of the students at Co-op City schools were.[21] By the end of the decade, Truman High School was 71 percent Black, 20 percent Hispanic, and less than 7 percent white.[22] While a decade earlier, Co-op City parents had feared that their children might be bused to surrounding districts, by the late 1970s, School Board member Bruce Irushalmi recalled that "the Pelham Parkway kids, who at that time were largely white, didn't necessarily want to come to Co-op City because they saw that was changing. So, the paradigm shift is from 'don't bring them in' to 'I don't want to go there with them.'"[23]

As they became a minority, some white students began to perceive the schools as racially tense. One white former resident recalled how in the early 1980s there would be fights between Black and white teenagers, and other students of all races would gather and chant racially charged chants while they watched their classmates fight.[24] Janice Hoetz Goldstein later remembered, "There were random and targeted physical attacks on white students by angry black students in the hallways and on the stairways. Racial tension was high in many public schools throughout the Bronx. Coop City was not immune to this newer phenomenon in our schools. Co-op City was no longer the safe haven that so many families hoped for."[25] In 1992, a ninth-grade Truman student was arrested after he and a group of friends attacked two light-skinned Latinas while saying, "We're messing with the white bitches."[26] As I will discuss later in this chapter, nonwhite students also experienced Truman as dangerous; however, for them, this danger was not understood through a racial lens.

Although there were racist attacks on Blacks elsewhere in the northeast Bronx, this was generally not the case in Co-op City.[27] Instead, for Black residents, racial and generational tensions often intermingled—older whites castigating Black teens for playing loud music, or assuming that they were criminals—or in the more subtle but no less hurtful terms of social ostracism.[28] Black residents also complained of institutional discrimination. In 1982, Shirley Saunders, a Black woman who was then newly elected to Riverbay's board, began an investigation into racial discrimination in Co-op City's hiring practices.[29] Nearly a decade later, and after years of serving on Riverbay, Saunders charged Co-op City authorities with a long-standing pattern of racial discrimination, culminating in the fact that a visit from Mayor David Dinkins, New York's first Black mayor, was ignored by the *Co-op City Times*.[30] Other Black political figures occasionally hinted at a racist conspiracy that could even explain why Co-op City's carrying charges had risen so much, namely as an attempt "to attract better quality families— that is, white."[31] While this rumor was relatively easy to disprove—after all, a majority white Co-op City had fought tooth and nail against carrying charge increases, including waging a thirteen-month rent strike—other rumors had greater staying power. For instance, Black political figures regularly repeated the rumor that Section Five had been reserved for Blacks, even though here, too, there was little evidence to confirm the truth of such a charge. In 1990, a controversy was unleashed when Riverbay chose to lease space to the white owner of a bingo parlor instead of the rapidly growing Black Community Protestant Church. Rev. Calvin Owens charged that "Riverbay has leased properties to religious organizations whose congregations are predominantly white at more favorable rental rates than it has to congregations whose members are predominately black or Latino."[32] The racial nature of this controversy was less clear cut than it might have appeared, however, as the opposition to the church was spearheaded by Ron Ceasar, who was himself Black and stated that he preferred that the space be occupied by the bingo parlor because it was a revenue-generating business.[33] Perhaps for this reason, Owens dropped his bias suit against Riverbay shortly after he filed it.[34]

The biggest controversy in Co-op City's transition from a majority white and Jewish community to one that was majority Black happened in 1987. By the mid-1980s, the wait list to apply for an apartment in the cooperative was nearly entirely Black and Latino. In 1987, the Riverbay board decided to spend $250,000 on an advertising campaign to recruit more whites to apply for apartments in an attempt to "reach a more balanced pool of potential buyers" and maintain Co-op City's status as an integrated development. Eva Pellman, the white board president, explained that this was something that Black residents themselves wanted: "The point is, unless you keep this an integrated community, the blacks themselves will start moving out. . . . They did not move in wanting this to be an all-black and Hispanic community. They wanted it because it was integrated." Tony Illis, one of four Black Riverbay board members, vehemently opposed Pellman's logic: "It bothers me that when it first opened and this place was 90 percent white, I never heard of anyone on the board saying 'Gee, what can we do to attract more minorities?'" In the 1960s, the UHF and many of Co-op City's original Jewish residents balked at proactive attempts to achieve a higher Black and Latino population through changing some of the apartments to rentals or using racial quotas. At the same time, the UHF was open to using advertisements to increase Co-op City's visibility in the Black and Spanish-speaking press. In essence, the marketing plan was a continuation of this logic—Riverbay was not suggesting a racial quota system or a change to the structure of the cooperative, but a marketing plan aimed at attracting a new pool of applicants. At the same time, as Illis suggested, the UHF's marketing to nonwhite families was often begrudging at best and not accompanied by anything like the $250,000 budget that was now being proposed.

Illis was the only Black Riverbay board member who rejected the plan. The remaining three Black board members told a reporter they "strongly supported" the plan to market to white families. "That's always been the premise of Co-op City—friendly people of all kinds living together," Wilana Lerner, a Black board member and longtime resident, said in support of Pellman's proposal. In November 1987, the *New York Times* published a front-page article about the plan to market Co-op City to white families to achieve racial balance. It quoted several Black residents who gave more cynical motives to support the plan. One Black resident, Sharon Brown, said, "You'll have less crime, from my experience and with some white people around you'll have cleaner buildings as far as graffiti is concerned, and less in-and-out, in-and-out of the buildings all day long." Chris Ballantine, a Truman student, added, "I'm black. I'm realistic. It's going to turn into the projects if all the whites leave."[35]

The *New York Times* article about the marketing plan ignited an immediate firestorm of controversy. Riverbay directors of all racial backgrounds who had initially supported the plan backtracked. In a letter to the *Co-op City Times*, Shirley Saunders vented her frustration at the *New York Times* for publicizing the plan, even if she did not dispute the accuracy of the article.[36] Gladys Luciano, the sole Hispanic director on the Riverbay board, also did not deny the plan's existence, even if she insisted that there was never a "racial *quota*" under discussion.[37] Even white directors distanced themselves. "I realize that a lot of people were confused and hurt by that article," Caroline Sozio wrote. "I, for one, want decent hard-working people to move into Co-op City. I don't care what color they are."[38]

Co-op City's Black residents especially chafed at the suggestion—whether it was made by other Black residents, their white neighbors, the author of the *New York Times* article, or the existence of the plan itself—that Co-op City's transition to a majority Black community was both a harbinger and cause of its decline. Co-op City residents of all races had always feared the possibility that their neighborhood would decline. To feel accused that they were the cause of this was bitterly hurtful. Robert Durham spoke at a packed community meeting to discuss the article: "Just because the community is black doesn't mean it will necessarily aspire to be a slum."[39] Another resident chimed in that Pellman's strategy had backfired because "when whites read about the high number of blacks, they won't want to move here."[40] Black Riverbay director Saunders wrote, "[The article] shed some light on people's perception of acceptable integration. Some families in Co-op City feel intimidated about living in a community which is predominantly black and latino, while had or have no trouble at all living in a community which is integrated, but majority white. . . . The color of a person(s) skin does not secure basic services in a development or a community. People of concern who are dedicated to community service will."[41]

Residents accused Pellman of injecting racism into the community and generally ignored the fact that both Black Riverbay board members and Black Co-op City residents had expressed their support for the plan before it was publicized in the *Times*. A letter to the editor of the *Co-op City Times* that Harriet Jeffries, a Black woman and Co-op City Council president, co-wrote with her husband stated,

Eva Pellman's quoted statement that Blacks and Hispanics will move out of the community if more residents of their own ethnic persuasion move in has the distinct implication that cooperators from these two ethnic groups had not and will not contribute to the viability of this community and further implies that we are fearful of living with one another. . . . Our repugnance and dismay cannot be adequately expressed at this time. . . . Certainly, we the cooperators have endeavored to promote an auspicious relationship among the residents of Co-op City, which transcends the insular psychosis of ethnic biography.[42]

Rather than blaming Pellman specifically, others castigated the article itself, accusing the New York Times of racism for publishing it. Ignoring the fact that the article quoted not only Pellman but several Black residents and Riverbay board members, Laurie Shlafmitz, a white resident and member of the Co-op City Council, wrote that the "article makes the assumption that communities where minorities predominate somehow deserve inferior [services]." Furthermore, she wrote, "lily-white" communities in New York City are "not attacked by the New York Times for their racial imbalance." Saunders, who had voted for the plan as a member of the Riverbay board, wrote, "I thought that contents of [the Times] article was extremely insensitive (at best) to the black, latino and other majority members of our community. Blacks and other ethnic groups in our community appear to be under verbal siege."[43] In other words, the problem was not racism within Co-op City but rather the New York Times article itself.

Rather than promoting racial balance as an explicit goal, residents of all races argued that Co-op City would be best served by race-neutral policies to improve the community's amenities. Rod Saunders, the husband of Shirley Saunders and the president of the African American Association of Co-op City, released a statement that "the preservation of the racial diversity in our community will best be achieved when the commitment to excellence in our general services, quality of education, and overall community development, is aggressively addressed."[44] Riverbay director Illis wrote, "The article went on to say that only 20 percent of White students attend the six public schools. However, if our schools graduated 90 percent of the students to colleges, we would not need a marketing group because the decent middle-class people would be knocking down our doors to enter to live here."[45] A white resident agreed: "While it is true that the ethnic structure of our community has changed, the attempt to alter this with a racial policy is repugnant. . . . The community that can boast diverse social, cultural, recreational and educational organizations is one that can grow and prosper. However, when the organizations are not interrelated with each other our social fabric deteriorates."[46] A multiethnic group of community leaders cosigned a public letter: "The marketing plan . . . is an insult to us all. . . . No juggling of ethnic composition will take the place of correcting chronic defects in maintenance, delivery of services, attitudes towards cooperators, and fulfillment of State obligations here."[47]

As the controversy spread and the marketing plan was overwhelmingly rejected by community leaders of all races, Pellman issued a public apology. "Like most people I am not particularly well trained in the fine art of being interviewed by the media and this is what led to the misunderstanding. My description of our marketing program was understood by some to mean that people of one ethnic background are a more valuable asset to our community than are people of other ethnic backgrounds. This is not true. This is not what I believe."[48] The marketing plan was first postponed and then scrapped entirely. Several months later, Pellman decided that she would not seek another term on the Riverbay board.[49]

Criticisms of the marketing plan tended to emphasize the fact that Co-op City was a harmonious multiracial community that needed to be defended against Pellman's divisiveness. This was not entirely wishful thinking, as residents repeatedly affirmed that racial tensions in Co-op City remained less potent than elsewhere in the city. While Shirley Saunders was clearly willing to call out the racism of some cooperators, she also spoke repeatedly of Co-op City's relative racial comity:

> I personally take pride in the fact that I can live in a community that is racially integrated and that I enjoy relationships with many who are of different religious faiths and whose color is different from mine. . . . I am not trying to give a false view that we have a "Utopia" in Co-op City but we must admit that when a problem does arise, we have vehicles of communication within our community network whereby we can all sit down at the same table to enable us to resolve problems.[50]

Saunders's view was echoed by other residents. One longtime Jewish resident said in 1988, "We're all working class. We all have the same type of jobs. We all want the same things. Almost every family has [racially] mixed friends."[51] In 1982, Pat Campbell, who was Black and moved into Co-op City in 1977, similarly told a reporter that she appreciated "the idea of so many different types of people, every race, creed, and color."[52] Among young people, there were some homogeneously Black friend groups, particularly among students who went through high school in Co-op City. However, many friend groups were mixed. I and other white people of my generation recall being teased for being white and being told not to go to certain areas "as a white girl," but it was impossible to be a white teenager in Co-op City in the 1980s and 1990s and not have friends who were Black or Latino. In part this relative racial harmony was due to the fact that Co-op City was spared the collisions between new middle-class white homeowners and the working-class renters they displaced, which happened elsewhere in New York. In Co-op City, everyone—regardless of race—was of roughly the same class status. Racial tensions existed in Co-op City to be sure, but they remained relatively uncomplicated by differences in income or social class.

Racial incidents elsewhere also had only a muted resonance in the faraway precincts of the North Bronx. The 1986 murder of Michael Griffith in Howard Beach and the 1992 riots that followed the acquittal of white police officers in the beating of Rodney King each led to antiracism discussion groups and rallies in Co-op City rather than violence.[53] After Black teenager Yusuf Hawkins was killed by a mob of Italian teenagers in Bensonhurst in 1989, there were protests elsewhere in the city. In Co-op City, the Hawkins murder inspired an open letter on the front page of the *Co-op City Times* cosigned by the entire Riverbay Board of Directors, calling for other neighborhoods to learn from Co-op City:

> We at Co-op City, having achieved 20 years of growth and successful racial harmony, respecting and celebrating our cultural differences, join the rest of the decent and fair-minded citizens of New York in deploring this tragic shooting and untimely death. Co-op City has always been and will continue to be an integrated community believing in the American ideal of an equal and open society where all persons, regardless of race, religion or national origin can work, live and play wherever their abilities and dreams take them.[54]

The insistence that Co-op City was a racially harmonious community was one continuity across the first two decades of the development's existence, uttered equally vehemently by Jewish leaders of the mostly Jewish cooperative in the late 1960s and by Black leaders of an increasingly nonwhite community in the late 1980s. However, the Riverbay directors' celebration of the community's achievement of an "equal and open society" was just as much an expression of their hopes for Co-op City as an expression of reality. For just as Co-op City celebrated its integrated community, it was also in the throes of a panic about crime that was rife with racist assumptions and anxieties.

For the first two decades of its existence, Co-op City had largely been an oasis from the rise in crime elsewhere in New York City. While crime rates never reached the levels they did in some parts of the city, by the late 1980s, Co-op City was no longer as exceptionally safe as it once had been. Crime really did increase in these years in Co-op City, just as the crime wave in New York as a whole crested in this period. However, Co-op City was still not a particularly dangerous community, certainly compared to many other neighborhoods in New York. The reason that crime became the dominant political and social issue in Co-op City in the late 1980s and early 1990s was that the reality of crime was compounded by its role as a symbol of demographic change and decline. The 1987 marketing plan controversy put a spotlight on Co-op City's demographic transition and also brought to the surface fears that associated the fact that the neighborhood was becoming less white with its potential to become "the projects." Co-op City's panic about crime followed shortly after the marketing plan controversy came to light.

From its inception, Co-op City had been defined by a certain paradox. On the one hand, residents celebrated the community's racial integration; but on the other, racially inflected fears about crime and neighborhood decline were also part of the community, from its first days. Neither of these things changed as Co-op City became a majority nonwhite community. Indeed, while Co-op City experienced racial transition in these years, the basic anxiety that neighborhood deterioration was an ever-present threat, together with the (usually unspoken) assumption that such deterioration was caused by the growth of the neighborhood's Black population, was an unfortunate continuity. Calls for a greater police presence were the flip side of celebrations of racial harmony in Co-op City; both were motivated by the anxiety that a Black Co-op City would become a slum and a belief that this fate could only be avoided by the hard work of residents to maintain the neighborhood's character as an integrated, middle-class community.

These fears were compounded by the fragile nature of the community's middle-class identity.[55] Sociologist Mary Pattillo studied a middle-class Black neighborhood on the South Side of Chicago and found that the very tenuousness of the neighborhood's literal and metaphorical location between white middle class and poorer Black neighborhoods led to a certain defensive mentality. "Unlike most whites, middle-class black families must contend with the crime, dilapidated housing and social disorder in the deteriorating poor neighborhoods that continue to grow in their direction. Residents attempt to fortify their neighborhoods against this encroachment."[56] For Patillo, this liminal status between middle-class whites and poor Blacks was the defining characteristics of what it meant to be a Black middle-class neighborhood. Patillo contrasts the experience of Blacks in the middle class with that of "most whites"; by that definition, the white people in Co-op City were not "most whites." The white people who lived in Co-op City were of the working and lower middle class, little more secure in their middle-class status than their Black neighbors. Furthermore, as "ethnic whites," only a generation at best removed from the time that they had been excluded from mainstream white identity, their racial status was insecure as well.

While Co-op City's anxieties about crime were inescapably connected with racism, fears about crime and calls for vigorous efforts to combat it were not limited to white residents.[57] This did not make Co-op City unique. As historian Reiko Hillyer writes, "Fear of crime was neither the monopoly of the white middle class nor merely a construction of politicians. . . . The concerns and strategies of communities of color—indeed, more likely to be the *victims* of crime—often overlapped with those of conservatives."[58] The law scholar James Foreman Jr. has written about the Black enthusiasm for tough-on-crime measures in these years as a function of the fears produced by the crack epidemic, which was particularly vicious in poor Black urban neighborhoods across America. Many Black community leaders and ordinary citizens saw a greater police presence and punitive anticrime and antidrug measures as the only way to protect their communities from a scourge that the president of the Prince George's County, Maryland, NAACP chapter called "the worst thing to hit us since slavery."[59]

Complaints about crime were nothing new for Co-op City. Mere months after moving into the development in 1968, Co-op City residents were already worried about rising crime, vandalism, and disorder. In the late 1970s and early 1980s, such complaints often referenced the rent strike as a turning point. Residents later in the 1980s began to associate crime with the arrival of Bay Plaza, Co-op City's outdoor mall, which first opened in 1988. In each case, residents contrasted the peace of some earlier time with the more dangerous neighborhood Co-op City had become.[60] And yet, if there was one constant, it was the fact that Co-op City residents often believed that crime had only recently gotten worse. In 1974, residents bemoaned the "increasing crime rate."[61] In 1979, a survey found that 68 percent of residents believed that Co-op City had gotten worse since they had moved in.[62] In 1985, a woman stated that recently "I am scared stiff in both the building and the elevator."[63] In part this was a function of the reason most Co-op City residents decided to move to the development. As the previous chapters have discussed, from the time that Co-op City was founded, the majority of residents moved to Co-op City because they had seen their previous neighborhoods becoming more dangerous. They experienced their new homes as vulnerable and were hyper-alert to signs of deterioration in this new environment.[64]

Concerns about crime accelerated in the late 1980s. In the aftermath of a 1989 incident in which a gunman opened fire with an automatic weapon on a group of older teenagers hanging out in front of Building 20 in Section Four, a twenty-one-year-old woman told a reporter that "everyone is talking about moving. You realize you're vulnerable. I used to feel safe knowing these kids were always out when I came home at night."[65] "Crime has really increased in the last six months," one man told a reporter in 1990; "there have been two homicides in the last five days."[66] By 1988, the weekly crime blotter in the *Co-op City Times* reported at least one crime each issue, mostly petty crimes—muggings, purse-snatching, fights that escalated too quickly. Within a few years, the list of crimes was much longer and regularly featured guns. The *City News* had always included sensationalized reports on Co-op City's criminal activities. However, by the late 1980s, each week seemed to bring new horrors. "Murders which were unusual in past years have become alarmingly not unusual; muggings have become frequent; and the sale of drugs commonplace," one typical editorial read in 1988. "The increase in crime is apparent to most residents, for when a person says he feels like a prisoner in his apartment, the fear of crime is real."[67] At a 1992 meeting to discuss crime, one woman stated, "In *City News*, we read all these things. It's very scary."[68] As late as 1985, a *City News* survey showed that 50 percent of residents felt safe in Co-op City; by 1992, that number had dropped to 15 percent.[69]

Statistical evidence confirms that Co-op City had become more dangerous. Co-op City accounted for 56 percent of the population of the Forty-Fifth Precinct.[70] In 1990, there were 4,727 major crimes reported in the precinct. Its two neighboring precincts, the Forty-Ninth and Forty-Seventh, had 6,295 and 7,097 respectively.[71] In other words, in 1990, the Forty-Fifth Precinct's crime rate was still lower than those of its neighbors. However, the difference was no longer as striking as it had been in the 1970s, when the Forty-Fifth Precinct had been one of the quietest in the city.[72] Furthermore, many residents insisted that Forty-Fifth Precinct statistics did not necessarily provide a full picture, because much of Co-op City's crime either went unreported or was reported only to Co-op City security. "As far as statistics, you're talking about what is reported," a young woman told an official of the Forty-Fifth Precinct at a packed community meeting after a young man was shot and killed in 1992. "That covers only about half. What about the people who are shot and don't report it, because they don't think anything is done?"[73] At the same time, the NYPD resisted calls for more police in Co-op City by stating that it allocated police officers to the neighborhoods that needed them more. In 1992, Captain Gertrude LaForgia of the Forty-Fifth Precinct reiterated that despite residents' fear of crime, it was not, in fact, "rampant" in Co-op City: "there were 43 burglaries in six months in Co-op City. Some precincts get 43 in one day."[74] Co-op City's crime rate had gotten worse, but it was still a comparatively safe part of the borough.

Such reassurances were cold comfort to Co-op City residents, who developed mental maps of the safe and unsafe areas in the cooperative. Basement laundry rooms were one source of fear. Every building had laundry rooms in its basement. For the chevron and triple-core buildings, which connected two or three high-rises respectively, there was one laundry room for the entire building, and it was reached by walking through a series of tunnels. While the basement laundry rooms had been a source of pride when Co-op City was first built, by the 1980s they had come to signify danger. One former resident described his memory of the laundry rooms: "I look back on that and I can't believe how creepy that was. There is no way. I would send the laundry out or drive to a Laundromat. Or I would go down there with a bike helmet and run. It's so dark, it's so confined, no one's ever going to know you're down there. It's a dungeon!"[75] Other residents discussed the stairwells or elevators as particularly dangerous. Agovino described in his memoir what the staircases were like: "All the graffiti, the smashed fluorescent bulbs, two, three floors at a time, of complete darkness, the ominous footsteps of someone walking down or up, it was always hard to tell."[76]

Many residents saw Truman High School as the epicenter of violence in the cooperative. Years later, one woman recalled when she was a student in the mid-1980s: "There were kids fighting, cutting class, smoking weed in the stairs, so people got robbed."[77] Another former resident described fighting off a potential mugger in 1981 behind the school.[78] Another recalled having her necklace stolen by a fellow student in the mid-1980s.[79] Crime at Truman escalated markedly during the early 1990s, going from petty crime to more dangerous gunplay.[80] After a series of incidents in 1990 where students were badly injured on school grounds as a result of what was suspected to be gang activity, four hundred parents attended a meeting with Truman's principal and Co-op City's security's director to discuss security efforts, including attempts to create "safe corridors for students when they go home."[81] Nevertheless, incidents continued. One former resident spoke of leaving the school after her freshman year in 1992, in the course of which one student pulled a gun on her during math class and another jumped her after school. She recalled that "dealing with anything on Truman's property was always a fight."[82] A drama teacher would later explain that he had to cancel a production of *West Side Story* in 1993 because "kids who I chose as Sharks and Jets got into their parts so well that they actually were fighting each other! I mean, really, fighting!"[83] By 1995, the number of violent incidents at Truman was the fourth-highest of all Bronx high schools.[84]

Co-op City's Educational Park had been built by the UHF, who hoped and believed that the development would be largely populated by young families.

However, from the very beginning, Truman had significant excess capacity. As a result, Truman always educated some nonresident students, many of whom came from the Baychester neighborhood known as "the Valley," which lay on the other side of a pedestrian bridge that crossed the I-95 freeway and terminated at Truman. Conflict between "the Valley" and Co-op City residents had long been a problem.[85] However, while the conflicts in the 1970s were often sparked by racial tension, that was not an issue in the 1980s and 1990s, when both groups of teens were overwhelmingly Black. In fact, it was unclear why the rivalry got so bad.[86] But regardless of the reason, fights between kids from the Valley and from Co-op City became increasingly deadly by the end of the 1980s. Although neither the "Valley Boys" nor the "Section Five Boys" were organized gangs, parents complained of the fact that "kids come to school and have to decide between joining one gang or another."[87] In 1988, two Co-op City residents were shot by three young men from the Valley. Over the next few years, at least four more teenagers were killed as a result of the same conflict.[88]

Truman fought its deteriorating image by instituting an honors track, but according to school board member and Co-op City resident Bruce Irushalmi, "Honors programs were code words for segregation. They were not honors academically, they were just segregated programs [for non-Black students]."[89] In 1988, Truman added a grab bag of programs, including a Business Institute, a Fashion Institute, a Math and Science House, and a Sports Academy.[90] However, in part because these programs were not viewed as actually offering academic rigor, and in part owing to the very dynamics that led to their existence in the first place, they did not succeed in arresting Truman's perceived decline. After several thousand dollars' worth of materials were stolen or destroyed in 1982, the Educational Park instituted a twenty-four-hour closed-circuit video system.[91] Ten years later, in 1992, metal detectors and X-ray machines were installed at Truman's entrances. "It's a necessary evil given society today," Truman's principal explained wearily.[92] The school board also moved the district school safety office to Truman, in the hopes that a greater police presence would fight crime and increase the sense of safety among students. This, too, appeared to have had little effect. "By the eighties," Irushalmi recalled, "I think there was a significant flight from Truman. . . . It's a self-fulfilling prophecy. If kids that are performing well are afraid and leave, they're replaced by kids who are not performing as well. And someone says, 'See? It's not performing as well!'"[93]

The intermediate and elementary schools in Co-op City were not isolated from the turmoil at Truman. In 1984, 77 percent of IS 181 and 71 percent of IS 180 students were reading at or above grade level, making them the eighteenth and twenty-seventh highest-scoring intermediate or junior high schools in the entire city.[94] Four years later, 70 percent of IS 181 and 51 percent of IS 180 students were able to achieve grade-level results.[95] By 1991, PS 153 students ranked 182nd out of 621 elementary schools on citywide standardized reading tests.[96] While these schools still far outpaced the city's worst-performing schools, a Co-op City education no longer ranked among the best in the city, as it had when the development first opened. Meanwhile, violence began to spread to lower grades. I went to IS 181 in the late 1980s, and I remember seeing multiple fights, sometimes with fists and sometimes with knives, outside the school. My sister had older friends escort her home from IS 180 in the early 1990s because of fears of violence. Former resident Toni Mendez recalled multiple fights with classmates in IS 180 in these years as well.[97] Ben Cirlin, the former rent strike leader, described how he decided to leave in 1986: "Because at that point, the schools really got bad. They were starting to get bad. My daughter came home one day [from IS 180] . . . there was a knife fight. I'll never forget, when she came home, she had a little blood on her shirt. I looked at her and I said, 'I love this place, but there's no way I'm going to let my kid be in that kind of situation.'"[98]

For white families, in particular, eighth-grade graduation was a common time to make the choice to leave Co-op City.[99] However, many parents of all races who stayed in Co-op City tried to avoid sending their kids to Truman. Beyond violence, students complained of apathy and a lack of quality education. The simplest path to leaving lay in getting into one of New York's elite magnet schools. Bronx Science was a short bus ride away. Stuyvesant, Brooklyn Tech, and Hunter College High School were farther afield. However, few students could pass the selective admission exams for those schools.[100] Artistic and musical students had the option of LaGuardia High School.[101] This, too, featured a highly competitive admissions process. A few excellent Black and Latino students were able to attend elite private schools for free through the Oliver Scholars program.[102] For other students, avoiding Truman required more creativity, or money. When Agovino didn't get into Bronx Science, his parents paid private school tuition to send him to New Rochelle Academy in Westchester.[103] Agovino describes his Black friend Calvin transferring from Truman after one year. "It's horrible," Calvin told Agovino's mother shortly before he transferred from Truman to Mount Saint Michael, a nearby Catholic school that many Co-op City students attended.[104] Another friend, Ahmad, went to a private school in Connecticut.[105] Many students went to nearby Catholic schools, including Cardinal Spellman or Mount Saint Michael Academy, which were often cheaper than other private schools. It was also possible to game the system of public school admissions. One of my sisters went to Townsend Harris High School, an excellent public school in Queens, which required not only that you have a good middle school transcript but that you list it first on the New York City high school application. Other students applied to nearby Lehman or Columbus High School. My mother helped my sister's friend fill out the application to a charter school when she tried to leave Truman after her first year.

Some residents of Co-op City blamed Co-op City's problems on outsiders. David Burke, the president of Co-op City's Black Forum, described how he felt when he saw crack vials in Co-op City. "To just walk outside my home and see that made me feel rejected. It wasn't something I was accustomed to seeing. I felt threatened. It tells me someone is invading my community, my lovely, lovely community, and I don't like it."[106] Others spoke of Riverbay allowing group homes and foster homes to relocate to Co-op City.[107] Nearby short-stay motels that acted as "magnets for prostitution and crime" were also blamed.[108] For some residents, the construction of Bay Plaza was a turning point.[109] A common reason residents offered to explain the rise in crime at the development had to do with the fact that Co-op City began to allow people with Section 8 housing assistance to move in. However, Section 8 was nothing new for the cooperative. So long as someone could pay the equity deposit, Co-op City had accepted recipients with Section 8 since the program began in 1974.[110] Others blamed the prevalence of illegal sublets. It is impossible to tell whether or not the number of sublets increased in these years.[111] However, in 2004, Riverbay president Al Shapiro admitted, "Let's face it, it's common knowledge that many people illegally sublet their homes in Co-op City."[112]

In reality, Co-op City's rising crime rate was largely related to factors beyond the development itself. Starting in the mid-1980s, crack was the engine of a crime wave that engulfed New York and other parts of America.[113] At the height of the crack epidemic in New York in 1988, there were 1,896 murders in the city, a single-year record.[114] Co-op City was not at the center of the drug trade in the Bronx; but it was not immune from it either. Co-op City's convenient location right off I-95 and the Hutchinson Parkway made it an ideal drug-trafficking spot. After visiting with a Co-op City youth group, Kids Against Crack, in 1986, Representative Mario Biaggi stated that there were dealers "operating with impunity" in Co-op City and warned that it was in danger of being "enveloped" by the crack problem.[115] Several weeks after Biaggi's visit, an article in the *City News* breathlessly reported two teenagers' discovery of crack vials in the staircase of their Section Five apartment building. "I didn't think this happened in our building. You hear about this happening in Manhattan," one of the teens told a reporter.[116] Less than a year later, a combined NYPD and Co-op security operation disrupted a "real life French Connection" crack operation run out of a Section One apartment.[117] That same year, local community and political figures held an antidrug "Crack Attack" rally.[118] Over the next few years, many antidrug presentations and community meetings followed.[119]

By the late 1980s, crack detritus had become an everyday part of Co-op City's environment. David Burke told a reporter from the *New York Times* about a walk he took with his five-year old-son, who noticed crack vials on the ground. "'I stopped counting at 32.'"[120] A resident named V. McDowell wrote to the *Daily News* to complain about drugs: "I live in Co-op City and have seen more pushers and junkies than I ever saw in the so-called ghettos. Why? The parents don't give a damn. The police (45th Precinct) and the Co-op Security Officers try—oh! How they try—but it is a losing battle."[121] At a 1990 antidrug workshop, one participant remarked "My son is 8 years old. He knows who the drug dealers are. . . . You see them on the corners. They're picked up and back in two days."[122] Co-op City put signs up in its playgrounds warning children to stay out of the sandboxes for fear they would find syringes or crack vials. This was not an idle fear. I worked at an after-school program in the early 1990s and remember kids regularly finding crack vials in the sandbox. At Goose Bay Nursery School in Section Five, a similar situation existed. "Teachers equipped with pails, shovels and gloves, clean a play area of condoms, crack vials, hypodermic needles and defecation before their children can come out to play." One teacher explained that "sometimes the kids fill [crack vials] with sand and call them 'sand shakers.'"[123]

Again, the fear of crime and drugs that Co-op City experienced in these years was not unique. Rev. Calvin Butts III, who led an influential congregation in Harlem in the 1980s, explained that "on the ground sales people peddling [drugs] were in the community. And many community people were arguing with the Cuomos and others to 'lock 'em up,' 'kill them.' *I was standing right there*. People were saying this to the officials and anyone who would listen."[124] In Washington Heights, community groups similarly called on the police to aggressively combat drugs and crime.[125] Across the borough from Co-op City, in the northwest Bronx, fear of crime and drugs was a unifying factor, bringing together a multiracial alliance that demanded a punitive response toward both crack dealers and their clients.[126]

Just as in these poorer neighborhoods, Co-op City's middle-class residents begged for greater protection from crime.[127] Often residents connected their calls for greater police patrols to their belief that lessening Co-op City's crime rate was crucial to keeping the neighborhood from becoming a slum.

"Yes, there are those who do care about this beautiful community. However, there are those diehards who believe that our community will [be] or is heading for a ghetto," Riverbay director Illis wrote. "You visit the sand pits and you'll find crack vials and hypodermic needles. . . . Now we have to resort to arming [Co-op security] because of an increase of break-ins, armed robberies, the drug heads that we allow to live here and raise havoc."[128] In another article decrying the rising crime in Co-op City, Illis concluded, "Most of us are here because the old neighborhoods started to go down: drugs and robberies. Co-op City was a safe place for you and your family. Get involved. Join an organization. Enough said."[129] Assemblyman Eliot Engel, who lived in Section Four, explained his support for an increased police presence in the community by stating that the city should "not allow a community of 50,000 to degenerate into a high-rise, drug-infested slum."[130]

Like Engel, residents began to call for a greater police presence, as well as other security measures, including cameras in the laundry rooms, locks on stairwell doors, bulletproof security kiosks to allow security officers to maintain a constant presence across the cooperative, and (most controversially) the arming of all Co-op City security officers.[131] In regular community meetings, often spurred by one incident or another, residents begged for more police. Al Shapiro, later to become Riverbay president, announced at one meeting in 1987, "People are afraid to go out at night. We need more cops for a while to show the hoods that the streets do not belong to them."[132] Elected officials echoed their concerns. "You're angry and frustrated and justifiably so," Councilor June Eisland told a room filled with cooperators. "I'm not shy. I'm not a shrinking violet and I will yell so voices in Co-op City will be heard."[133] Residents regularly called for more NYPD patrols.[134] "We are not getting our fair share of police protection," Shapiro told a group of cooperators. "We should not allow Co-op City to become a locked-door community afraid to venture out at night."[135] One of the most vocal leaders to decry rising crime was Iris Herskowitz Baez, a Jewish woman who had married a Puerto Rican man. "You must take back the streets from the drug dealers and throw them out of Co-op City. You must let them know that you will not let them destroy this beautiful community. Co-op City residents will not give in to pushers by becoming prisoners in their homes," she said after a young man was murdered in 1988.[136] Baez was able to translate her prominence as an anticrime activist to become a local power broker who would go on to hold positions in Riverbay and the local Democratic Party.[137]

Calls for an increased police presence crossed racial lines. Local Black politicians were as vociferous as their white counterparts in articulating their fears of crime and demanding police protection.[138] At a June 1988 City Hall protest to demand police protection shortly after the drive-by shooting of Kevin Carter, a college student in Section Five, Illis stated, "Our first and foremost objective is to increase police visibility in Co-op City. It's been two and a half years in the making where our streets are slowly being taken over by these people. Now it's not only local drug dealers but people coming in from the outside. The next thing you know there are going to be territorial disputes."[139] After the 1992 murder of Gary Gonzalez in Section Five, Riverbay director Harriet Jeffries spoke at an impassioned community meeting: "How many children must flee school at recess to protect life and limb, how many of your seniors must be robbed . . . how many of our children must dodge bullets; how many of our children must die before we become human beings." As she concluded, the audience of six hundred cooperators chanted "Give us more cops!"[140] At a rally later that summer to demand a greater NYPD presence in Co-op City, Richard Thompson from Building 12 said, "Make no mistake. We like cops. We want cops. In fact, we want more cops."[141] Shirley Saunders wrote that "we should see a constant patrolling of officers around our buildings; after all, that's one of the services that we are paying for in our carrying charges. We, as cooperators, need the security of knowing that there will be an officer within hollering distance."[142] When the city decided to locate the headquarters of the Bronx antidrug Tactical Narcotics Team in Co-op City, Black and Latino board members were among the loudest voices congratulating them. "Co-op City will have in its midst a larger police department presence than the entire 45th Precinct," Michael Pabon celebrated. "That's nothing to sneeze at and I hope the drug dealers and users will sit up and take notice."[143]

In addition to calling for more police protection, some Co-op City residents began to take matters into their own hands. The Guardian Angels, a New York-based vigilante group, twice gave talks to hundreds of residents and even offered to "map out a campaign" to fight crime in Co-op City but never established a formal presence in the community.[144] In 1988, Baez began "Operation Safety," a group of volunteers who gathered information to report to the police regarding crime and drug activity in the cooperative.[145] Some teenagers began to carry weapons. Agovino describes his friends all getting weapons in the 1980s for protection. Calvin got a knife: "[He] had a job at Waldbaum's, the big supermarket on the edge of Co-op City. He worked late, and had to walk home. He needed protection. You kept hearing stories about muggings." Another friend got a gun: "Don't worry, I ain't gonna use it . . . it's just for protection."[146] Riverbay director Saunders described parents needing to act as "vigilantes" to protect their children.[147] After the murder of Gary Gonzalez in 1992, Ruben Garcia called for residents to be proactive in fighting violence: "I agree that we must insist on receiving a fair and equitable portion of our city's police budget and manpower. However, unless we the shareholders take a personal and aggressive stand, there will be no change. It's time to take to the streets! . . . Other communities throughout the nation have said 'enough is enough' and taken back their block and/or neighborhood. It can be done here."[148] Delia Polite of Building 31A echoed Garcia's call: "I've shed too many tears, let's talk about what we're going to do. The police should have been there. Do we have to take it in our own hands?"[149]

Some residents advocated teen programs to reduce violence. In 1990, Roger Dunson, a social worker and resident of Section Five, began a "Stop the Violence Teen Club," which aimed to resolve "seething conflict" between boys in the Valley and those in Co-op City.[150] He and others called for a greater emphasis on youth programming run out of the Educational Park, noting that the lack of things to do for teenagers contributed to the violence in Co-op City. Teenage boredom was a perennial problem in the development, but for the first time in the 1990s, it could have deadly consequences. Steve Lieb, the director of the Educational Park, was sympathetic to these concerns. "The young people we're talking about are at an age where, even if they are good kids, they can get into trouble if they don't have anything to do." However, he insisted that the problem was an economic one. Government cutbacks, including both citywide austerity programs dating from the 1970s and the "Regan era legacy of decreased federal spending" meant that the Educational Park was left with a shoestring budget, and "we don't address a problem until it gets really out of hand."[151]

Through it all, Co-op City security and NYPD officials continued to insist that Co-op City was still relatively safe. At a 1988 meeting attended by over one hundred anxious residents, Riverbay security chief Ken Jones explained, "We have burglaries, assaults, selling and buying of narcotics here, but these crimes are not peculiar to Co-op City."[152] In 1989, the NYPD placed a tactical narcotics team (TNT) in the Bronx, which aimed to disrupt drug trafficking through saturating problem areas with undercover police. The Bronx team's headquarters were in Co-op City, in part because of a lobbying effort by Co-op City politicians.[153] Yet just because the TNT was headquartered in Co-op City did not mean that it patrolled there. In its first year of operation, the TNT was responsible for 10,700 arrests, a mere 8 of which were in Co-op City.[154] "There is a public perception that crime is running out of control," Jones's successor Gerald Tuomey said in 1992. "It happens every time a community is hit with a particularly brutal or senseless crime."[155] Tuomey insisted that there was little the police could do. He said, "We could probably do a sweep of the entire complex and come up with 700 guns. And five days later 700 more would come up from South Carolina."[156] Despite Tuomey's skepticism, he also took measures to fight crime—hiring new plainclothes officers, doubling the number of patrols, and beginning a program of random building sweeps throughout the development, all of which contributed to a 50 percent drop in crime in 1993.[157]

Two decades after it had been constructed, there were few utopians left in Co-op City. Instead, Co-op City's residents were hard-bitten realists. Describing Co-op City in 1995, Gretchen Hazell, the newly elected president of Riverbay, said, "We're fighting to keep it a stable community. . . . We're a city within a city, and all cities have problems."[158] Co-op City did have problems—its crime rate had risen, its schools had declined, its politics remained as fractious as ever, and it continued to struggle with the crumbling infrastructure that was its birthright. Yet as Hazell hints, the Co-op City of this era was not a dystopian landscape, but rather an ordinary—albeit huge—middle-class neighborhood.

CHAPTER 7

"The Biggest Housing Bargain in Town"
Achieving Financial Stability, 1981–1993

Co-op City's fortunes were always connected to those of New York City as a whole, but the relationship was never straightforward. In its first years, Co-op City thrived as an escape from New York's woes. Its cooperative ownership structure offered an appealing alternative to both owning and renting in a city with declining property values and neglectful landlords. Meanwhile, Co-op City's distance from the center of New York was a selling point for residents who feared what they saw as an increasingly dangerous city. In the mid-1970s, physical distance from the city center provided no protection from the fiscal crisis that engulfed the city and state. New York's and Co-op City's economic woes were inextricably connected. In the 1980s, Co-op City began to experience new strains, not despite New York's financial recovery, but rather because of it, culminating in a vacancy crisis in the early 1990s. At the same time, New York's increased financial stability and retreat from neoliberal austerity in this period contributed to a less contentious relationship between Co-op City and both New York State and New York City.

As Co-op City's residents and leadership dealt with the complexities of racial transition, their relationship with the state and the city would enter a period of comparative stability. Even though carrying charges in 1988 were $82.94 per room per month, or almost twice what they had been at the time of the 1975 rent strike and four times what they had been when Co-op City had first been proposed, there would be no rent strike, and resident participation in elections and other political activities would gradually decline. Meanwhile, in these years as New York City became increasingly unaffordable, policy makers began to retreat from the austerity panic of the late 1970s and came to a growing appreciation of Co-op City's role as a site of affordable housing. As Co-op City faced infrastructural and financial challenges, including a vacancy crisis in the early 1990s that threatened the very survival of the cooperative, Riverbay found the state a more willing partner than it had been in the past. While not devoid of conflict, Co-op City's negotiations with the state in this period were significantly less acrimonious than previous standoffs. By Co-op City's twenty-fifth anniversary, it had finally achieved the stability of resident carrying charges that had long been so elusive.

When Mario Cuomo assumed the governorship of New York State in 1983, there were significant grounds for optimism in Co-op City. After all, Cuomo had been the lead mediator in the rent strike settlement several years earlier. In his successful gubernatorial campaign and in later dealings with Riverbay and individual residents, Cuomo did not hesitate to remind people of this fact.[1] As a result, when he became governor, Cuomo was the object of many personal requests for assistance from Riverbay board members and ordinary residents alike.[2] Yet although Cuomo occasionally reassured letter writers that he was "personally monitoring" the goings-on in the development, there is little evidence that he actually took a personal interest in Co-op City.[3] While Cuomo proclaimed his affection for the residents of the gargantuan housing complex come election time, he otherwise sought to keep it at arm's length, declining to even appear at Co-op City's fifteen-year anniversary celebration in December 1983 or its twenty-year anniversary in 1988.[4] Cuomo may not have arrived in Albany with any intent to put Co-op City's troubled relationship with New York State on a new footing; however, by the end of his time in office, Co-op City and the state would manage to establish a substantially more conciliatory relationship, one that would come at a time when Co-op City needed the state more than ever. Over the course of the 1980s, hostility to Co-op City and resentment toward its enormous debt burden was gradually balanced by an increased sense of pragmatism and state recognition of Co-op City's value as a relatively stable and affordable community.

The state and city's pragmatic approach to Co-op City comes as a surprise when viewed from the perspective of the growing historical literature on the 1980s as the heyday of neoliberalism in New York. Scholars who study New York in this period have examined the tax incentives to private developers, the hostility toward unions, and the rise of privatized approaches to security, all of which served as harbingers of a shift in the city to emphasize market-based solutions to social problems.[5] There is perhaps no clearer way in which the priorities of both Cuomo and Mayor Koch aligned with this approach than in the domain of housing. In this sense, both were well within the mainstream of American policy opinion in the 1980s, when programs to encourage homeownership among low-income and nonwhite Americans enjoyed bipartisan support across the United States. As historian Nancy Kwak writes, "By the 1980s and '90s, low-income homeownership had become the favored policy of all politicians, whether Democrat or Republican. Homeownership constituted a laudable, uncontroversial goal that showcased concern with poverty and racial inequalities while still endorsing government-backed 'private' housing over any openly public provision."[6] National funding for such programs continued to grow over the decade, even as other forms of housing assistance shrank.[7]

Koch and Cuomo saw homeownership as key to New York's future and pursued policies to encourage it. Koch was partial to programs that encouraged homeownership, believing that "by privatizing future maintenance costs, homeownership programs created less of an obligation for the city than did city-owned rental units."[8] Koch also offered hundreds of thousands of dollars in tax abatements to encourage condo conversions and the construction of market-rate apartments.[9] Cuomo was similarly enthusiastic. In 1983, he personally directed William Eimicke, commissioner of the DHCR, to find $5 million in pilot funds, taken from other housing programs, to help fund a statewide program based on New York City's homesteading program.[10] In 1985, under Eimicke's leadership, Cuomo enacted a major expansion of homeownership programs for middle- and lower-income New Yorkers, including a $25 million Affordable Housing Ownership Program and a $25 million Low-Income Housing Trust Fund Program. Under Cuomo's leadership, the SONYMA (State of New York Mortgage Agency) Affordable Housing Program, which assisted first-time home buyers with financing, expanded from approximately $50 million to $400 million per year.[11] These plans were enabled by new bond issues, to the tune of $1 billion for HFA and $1.25 billion for SONYMA.[12]

Yet this does not tell the full story. Cuomo described himself as a "progressive pragmatist" and contrasted his approach to using government to provide a social safety net with the "cruelty" of President Ronald Reagan's America.[13] "We believe," he announced in a speech on the floor of the Democratic National Convention in 1984, "in *only* the government we need, but we insist on *all* the government we need . . . a government strong enough to use the words 'love' and 'compassion' and smart enough to convert our noblest aspirations into practical realities."[14] As Cuomo explained it, rather than an ideologue bent on market solutions to social needs, he was a pragmatist who would pursue different approaches, both market-based and not market-based. In his time in office, Cuomo's actual progressive accomplishments reflected this philosophy, generally tweaking existing programs to make them more generous rather than inventing new ones out of whole cloth—measures like sponsoring only the second increase in Supplemental Security Income in the program's history and the creation of an Infrastructure Trust Fund.[15]

Cuomo's pragmatism also manifested itself in his administration's policies toward Mitchell-Lama. According to the Mitchell-Lama law, after twenty years, owners of Mitchell-Lama buildings could pay off their mortgages, leave the program, and thereby circumvent Mitchell-Lama limits on rents/carrying charges and profits. In some cases, privatization meant that rental or limited-equity cooperatives became market-rate rentals. In other cases, privatization meant that residents were given the right to purchase their apartments at lower rates.[16] Starting in the late 1980s, a few developments began to privatize, enticed by the potential windfalls on offer in New York's improving real estate market.[17] Converting rental buildings into condos or (non-limited equity) cooperatives had been a key strategy of the Koch administration to deal with the New York real estate crisis.[18] Although Co-op City was not legally eligible to privatize until the 1990s, in 1984, the Cuomo administration briefly considered allowing Co-op City residents to sell their apartments at market rates in order to provide an infusion of cash for the development.[19]

When Mitchell-Lama privatization began to become a bigger issue in New York with the rebound of the real estate market in the mid-to-late 1980s, the Cuomo administration increasingly sought to stabilize the Mitchell-Lama program rather than encourage its demise. In a 1988 statement to the congressional House Ways and Means Committee, Eimicke explained that even though New York State was pursuing other housing programs, he viewed Mitchell-Lama privatization as something that needed to be reined in: "Yet for all our affordable programming, we have lost more than 3,000 units of affordable housing through 'buyouts.' How can we justify spending millions of dollars to produce housing when our existing affordable housing stock is slipping away faster than it can be replaced."[20] In 1986, Eimicke announced that even if developers privatized their Mitchell-Lama buildings, they would still be subject to rent stabilization in order to keep residents from being forced out.[21] A year later, after broader measures to protect Mitchell-Lama residents were stymied by Republican state legislators, Cuomo passed an emergency bill to slow the process of privatization by forcing landlords to hold public hearings prior to privatization and undergo increased state scrutiny even after leaving the program.[22] In 1989, a New York State law gave local governments the power to make Mitchell-Lama tax exemptions permanent, extending the thirty-year sunset clause in the original law.[23] As Eimicke explained, he and Cuomo did not see Mitchell-Lama in opposition to programs for homeownership, but rather viewed new programs and old as each playing a part in the effort to assure a supply of affordable housing. "There were people who said, 'haven't we done enough, isn't it now time for the market to work.' And so I think the people on the advocacy side would make the argument, 'Yes, we're working with Co-op City to make sure it is sustained and survives, and we're also focused on other programs.'"[24] In the 1970s, Democratic New York state officials saw Mitchell-Lama as a boondoggle that represented the ills of urban liberalism. Ten years later, they actively worked to shore it up.

New York State's retreat from austerity politics and increasingly accommodationist attitude toward Mitchell-Lama and Co-op City developed gradually over the course of the 1980s and early 1990s and was not just a function of ideology but also a result of the state's generally improved financial situation in the late 1980s. In an interview, Eimicke described the state's perspective: "In the broader context, both the city and therefore the state, we're digging out of the financial crisis, so we're hardly back, right. But we were better. There wasn't this [sense that] we don't have money, we can't do anything, we can't pay anything, we don't have access to the markets. . . . So we were not in a crisis . . . and so there was less of this, 'if we don't go to war, we're going to get screwed.'. . . It was more, 'let's deal responsibly.'"[25]

When Cuomo assumed the governorship in 1983, Co-op City was embroiled in conflict with New York State regarding the ever-growing amount of money needed to cover construction defects. As discussed in the previous chapter, the rent strike settlement in 1977 had included a provision by which the state promised to provide for repairs. In June 1978, the HFA released a study it had commissioned from the architectural and engineering firm Perkins + Will. The study found significant construction defects and concluded that these defects were the cause of the rapid deterioration of Co-op City's physical condition.[26] In 1979, Governor Carey instituted the Emergency Repair Program, in which the state (rather than HFA bondholders) would assume direct responsibility for the costs incurred by correcting Co-op City's construction problems. With the dawning realization that Co-op City would require repairs well into the future, the 1980 "workout" agreement had authorized the establishment of a Permanent Repair Program, administered jointly by the HFA, the DHCR, and Riverbay, to supersede the emergency fund.[27] Overall, 80 percent of construction defects were judged to be the responsibility of the state, and 20 percent were the responsibility of Riverbay. For each specific construction issue, Riverbay and the state were assigned a specific degree of responsibility and were required to fund repairs accordingly.[28] Despite the fact that almost $25 million had already been spent in repairs, additional issues were uncovered shortly after this agreement was made, including the need to replace Co-op City's entire plumbing system. These would require at least a further $100 million in estimated repair costs, with no clear sense that even this amount would be sufficient to fix Co-op City's faulty infrastructure.[29]

In 1983, New York State's Commission of Investigations released a report into the problems with the Co-op City repair program, which revealed that much of the money that had already been spent had been lost to incompetence, corruption, and fraud.[30] Meanwhile, the report also found that since 1981, barely any work had taken place at all.[31] When the repair program began in 1979, the Division of Housing's priority had been to limit state expenditures. It required Riverbay to go through an extensive review process of every stage of each individual project to determine whether work was clearly related to an original construction deficiency before releasing money.[32] Yet despite these supposed checks in the system, as the 1983 investigation report detailed in exhaustive and colorful detail, the entire repair program was rife with corruption.

Almost $20 million in repair contracts between September 1979 and March 1981 were signed without a competitive bidding process.[33] EBASCO was Riverbay's construction management company. When an EBASCO employee complained that City-Wide Plumbing's $10 million contract should have been competitively bid, Co-op City's executive manager, George Steiner, put him off by stating that owing to "all the problems at the time, it was not prudent to competitively bid jobs."[34] When the state investigation subsequently sought to obtain City-Wide's records from this period, it was informed that they had been destroyed in a flood.[35] Meanwhile, Steiner's twenty-four bank accounts (including one located in Grand Cayman, Bahamas) showed deposits far out of proportion with his official $52,000 annual salary.[36] Steiner was arrested and ultimately convicted in federal court of extorting more than $350,000 in kickbacks.[37] There were similar issues with other contracts. Rey Caulking was awarded a $2.6 million contract through a noncompetitive process despite no previous experience performing brick and masonry repairs. The company subsequently laundered $700,000 in profits through shell companies.[38] A-PRO, another contractor that received a noncompetitive bid, was owned and operated by members of Co-op City security.[39] George DeMeo, Riverbay's senior inspector, received thousands of dollars in bribes between October 1979 and his imprisonment in July 1981 for illegal gun trafficking.[40] Riverbay, EBASCO, and state employees received gifts of turkeys, cheese platters, perfume, liquor, Yankees tickets, and gift certificates of up to $600 from contractors.[41] Altogether, state auditors deemed that of nearly $11 million in labor costs billed to the repair program, $2.2 million was unjustified.[42] When the Permanent Repair Program went into effect in October 1981, it sought to institute better procedures and oversight through the coordination of DHCR, HFA, and Riverbay. This led to repairs grinding to a halt. By January 1983, repairs to only three of Co-op City's thirty-five high-rises were complete.[43]

Faced with this undisputed and spectacular evidence of corruption and mismanagement, Riverbay board president Charles Parness tried to divert blame, explaining that Riverbay could not be expected to have conducted an adequate review: "It is inherent in the limited income requirements for occupancy of Co-op City that, by and large, the elected directors are not likely to be people with tremendous experience or sophistication in running large corporations. . . . I believe we had every right to rely on the knowledge and expertise of the Division of Housing."[44] At the same time that Parness claimed that the residents on the Riverbay board could not be held responsible for the corruption that occurred on their watch, he also bristled at the interference of state officials: "The bureaucrats have got to stop second-guessing the architects and engineers they hired to do a job."[45] Parness was clearly desperate to avoid having to take responsibility for the scandal, yet as had been the case with the construction of Co-op City a mere decade earlier, he was not wrong that the problems with the repair programs were simultaneously failures of state oversight. Furthermore, the HFA and the DHCR had proven themselves incapable of working together on the repair program owing to their constant infighting and failure to keep watch over the contracting or construction process.[46] The 1983 investigation into the repair program concluded with a vain hope that Riverbay, the HFA, and the DHCR would demonstrate an "ability [to resolve] their differences," but even at the time, this seemed a remote possibility at best.[47] A subsequent audit found that on average, jobs took four times longer to complete than their contractual deadlines and that infighting, mismanagement, and corruption continued to be problems.[48] In 1986, Parness and CERL lost control of the Co-op City board, in part owing to Parness's seeming toleration of corruption. Their opponents compared him and his wife, Sandra (also involved in Co-op City politics), to the Marcoses and Duvaliers, petty tyrants who had used their control to enrich themselves personally in the Philippines and Haiti respectively, and were both overthrown in 1986.[49]

While Co-op City and New York State continued their seemingly endless wrangling over the repair program, they also began negotiations for a carrying charge increase schedule to supersede the 1980 workout agreement, which was due to expire in 1986. Co-op City and New York State appeared poised for conflict here as well. As part of the 1980 workout deal, in 1986, Co-op City's carrying charges were supposed to be raised to an "economic rent" level, in which the charges would cover all of the development's costs, including mortgage payments, ongoing management, and construction repairs. The 1980 workout agreement also assumed that construction repairs would be largely complete by that date.[50] Both of these assumptions proved to be wildly optimistic. In 1984, state officials estimated that an economic rent level for Co-op City would be $142 per month per room, which would necessitate a 71 percent increase in resident carrying charges.[51] Beyond this amount, Co-op City also owed millions to HFA in delinquent mortgage payments, as well as millions to the City of New York in unpaid real estate taxes and utility charges, which could collectively drive Co-op City's economic rent level even higher.[52] Robert Harris, executive director of the HFA, conceded that to set Co-op City's carrying charges at the level of an "economic rent" would mean that the rent/income ratio would have to be much higher than at other Mitchell-Lama developments.[53]

In order to escape this dilemma, Harris considered exotic schemes, such as the sale of Co-op City, or a wholesale overhaul of the cooperative's ownership structure. He admitted, however, that both were unlikely or impossible. Consequently, Harris recognized that he had two options: push for Co-op City to pay an economic rent in 1986, as originally foreseen by the 1980 workout deal, which would mean that it would cease to be affordable to its residents, or preserve the development's affordability, which would require ongoing state subsidy.[54] Rather than giving up on Co-op City's affordability, when state officials began to articulate their negotiating position for the 1986 workout deal, they abandoned the concept of an economic rent, at least for the short term. Instead, going into the 1986 negotiations, the goal of state negotiators was more modest—merely to "decreas[e] Riverbay's dependence upon the State," but with no insistence that this dependence be eliminated entirely.[55] As repair costs mounted, officials also hoped to place a dollar cap on the state's liability for repairs to Co-op City's infrastructure, which by then had already risen to over $127 million.[56] Finally, they wished to resolve both the problem of Co-op City's municipal tax arrears and several ongoing lawsuits, some of which dated back to the early 1970s and continued to drag on long past the UHF's bankruptcy.[57] To be clear, although New York State officials had abandoned the idea of Co-op City paying an "economic rent," they were also not interested in doing anything to help Co-op City escape or renegotiate some of its debt. Harris was clear that bondholder concerns meant that debt forgiveness for Co-op City was off the table.[58] Instead, state negotiators were seeking a middle ground. In the late 1970s, Co-op City residents and their leadership had retreated from the confrontational stance that had led to the rent strike. Now, a few years later, the state, too, had realized that it needed to find an accommodation with its largest Mitchell-Lama development.

As state officials compiled wish lists for the upcoming negotiations, they realized that their leverage was extremely limited. In a 1985 memo, the state's lead negotiator explained that in its initial offer, "Co-op City will have the obligation to implement any future carrying charge necessary to cover its obligations [for debt service]." To which Eimicke responded in a handwritten note, "Yes, but what happens if debt svs is paid last? What punitive action does the State have?"[59] Eimicke was correct—short of foreclosure, there was nothing that the state could do to punish Co-op City if it failed to meet its debt obligations.

For a number of reasons, Co-op City had leverage in Albany that other affordable housing developments simply could not command. First, Co-op City's size meant that it had its own advocates in Albany, and so residents had the ability to politicize their concerns—the funding of the construction repair program, the pace of carrying charge increases, and so on—where elsewhere residents did not have nearly this degree of influence. Eimicke later recalled, "The bottom line for Co-op City was it was so large . . . [people in government asked] how could you be so stupid? You've created a congressional district where everyone in the district has the same housing interest. And so they have a huge amount of leverage." According to Eimicke, Co-op City's financial and infrastructural issues were not extraordinary, but rather, what was unique was the development's ability to get the state to pay attention: "In any construction project, you will have construction defects, you will have things that weren't done according to plan, you'll have contractors who don't perform, and whereas normally these would be handled by private citizens and private companies, through the courts or through negotiations, but [because of the size of Co-op City] you didn't go to the court first, you went to the government." This was not merely a function of Co-op City's size but also its contentious past. Although New York City and New York State's economic health had significantly rebounded from the crisis years of the 1970s, the memory of the rent strike continued to haunt government officials. "You didn't have to be Albert Einstein," Eimicke said, "to figure out that it was important that this be handled in a way that didn't lead to a large, public escalating threat."[60]

If state negotiators recognized the limits of their ability to enforce the state's wishes in negotiations with Co-op City, Parness at Riverbay came to a similar conclusion about Co-op City's limited leverage against the state. Parness explained his reasoning: "Many years ago, we had a rent strike. We won the battle, but we too had a great number of casualties—the people who moved out, many never to return to Co-op City. Vacancies rose by more than 700 families. That was our Pyrrhic victory. Another rent strike, even if we won it, would totally destroy this community."[61] Ten years after the conclusion of the rent strike, Co-op City and New York State could not escape each other.

The Memo of Settlement signed by Riverbay and the State of New York in January 1986 reflected this reality. In addition to the 14.75 percent rise in carrying charges due to take effect on July 1, 1986, there would be a further 14.75 percent rise in 1988 and a 13 percent rise in 1990.[62] Residents who moved into Co-op City after July 1, 1986, would also pay an additional 10 percent in carrying charges above what cooperators paid who had lived in Co-op City prior to that date.[63] Meanwhile, state obligations to the repair program would be capped at $145.5 million, and Co-op City would agree to drop all remaining pending lawsuits against the state.[64] Riverbay accepted a cap on state funding to the repair program that was quite a bit lower than Co-op City's initial demands of $350 million.[65] While the late-1980s carrying charge increases were still resented by cooperators, the state had acquiesced to a significantly lower figure for carrying charge increases than what its original calculations of "economic rent" had mandated. The state was now willing to accept that Co-op City's deficit, and hence its mortgage, would continue to climb as a result, a retreat from the austerity politics of the late 1970s.

In an open letter to cooperators urging them to approve this settlement, Eimicke stated that he saw it as a "fair deal" for cooperators and in effect threatened them that if they rejected it, DHCR would be "required to obtain 'economic rent' through a mandated increase estimated at 70 percent on July 1, 1986."[66] In other words, Eimicke was now using "economic rent" as a threat to try to get Co-op City residents to accept this deal, rather than seeing it as an actual policy goal. Parness also lobbied for Co-op City residents to approve the plan, releasing a statement that he was "pleased with achieving a very satisfactory agreement with the State of New York that ensures the future of our community."[67] Initially, the vote of residents on whether to approve the plan Parness had negotiated with the state passed by 6,107 to 4,483.[68] However, in a spurt of the irascibility that Co-op residents were now famous for, they subsequently forced a return to the bargaining table. In May, a newly elected slate of Riverbay directors sent a telegram to Cuomo accusing Eimicke of "unwarranted and blatant intrusion into the internal affairs of Co-op City."[69] After some further negotiation with the DHCR, a compromise plan, in which Co-op City's carrying charges rose by only 10.5 percent in the first year, passed.[70]

Five years later, New York State and Co-op City went back to the negotiating table to revise the 1986 workout agreement, largely to deal with the fact that the original cap on state construction liabilities was woefully inadequate as more and more construction defects were discovered.[71] The 1991 workout deal represented a further softening of the state's position in its negotiations with Co-op City. The state agreed to contribute $106 million to a "superfund" to pay for repairs, and Riverbay took control of the construction repair program with more limited state input.[72] "This agreement will culminate five years of hard work. I believe it will inject a new lifeblood into a community that has endured insurmountable hardship from leaking pipes to site settlement to construction defects and government inefficiency," Riverbay board director Ron Caesar exulted. "This deal . . . gives us the ability to be masters of our own destiny," director Harriet Jeffries added. "When we become the master of our own destiny, we also assume responsibility. The Board of Directors must be willing and ready to make the fiscal policy decisions that are necessary to make this agreement successful."[73] A year later, the board was forced to ask for another 5 percent carrying charge increase to cover unfunded repair costs.[74] Nevertheless, unlike the increases of the 1970s or even 1980s, this new increase was accepted with little pushback. Co-op City residents and state officials had reached a weary equanimity. After the 1992 carrying charge increase, carrying charges increased only an additional 4.77 percent over the next ten years. Today, Co-op City residents pay approximately 80 percent more than they did in 1992, not quite keeping pace with inflation and considerably less than the rise in both market-rate rents and market-rate home prices over the same period in New York.[75]

The 1986 and 1991 workout agreements marked a new era of pragmatism in the relationship between Co-op City and New York State. This could not have come at a more welcome time, as Co-op City experienced a series of infrastructural and financial challenges that would culminate in a severe vacancy problem in the early 1990s—as much an existential crisis for the development as the rent strike years had been nearly two decades earlier.

There were several factors that contributed to Co-op City's vacancy crisis. One of them had to do with the particular contours of New York City's recovery after the financial crisis. As the city emerged from the crisis, tax incentives encouraged the construction of office buildings in Manhattan, where municipal money poured into redevelopment of areas like Times Square. As the economic and cultural gravity shifted ever more to the city center, gentrifiers sought "authentic" communities in the abandoned factories of Tribeca and the decaying brownstones of Park Slope.[76] Susan and Norman Fainstein describe how southern Manhattan changed in these years: "By the 1980s, the social and functional heterogeneity of southern Manhattan was noticeably reduced. . . . An uncounted number of factories had disappeared or had been converted to other uses, and large expanses of proletarian tenements had been replaced by expensive apartment towers. Chic restaurants occupied abandoned factory showrooms. The fabric of the central business district had changed: many strands of its previous industrial woof had been exchanged for the golden threads of late capitalism."[77] Areas of the city with newly attractive real estate but poor residents gazed uneasily at the ways that their neighborhoods were transformed by the arrival of new residents and new money.[78]

In both location and appearance, Co-op City had nothing in common with these zones of gentrification. The UHF had advertised Co-op City as a quasi-suburban space, with its own "park-like environment within the city."[79] Many of Co-op City's initial residents appreciated its physical and cultural distance from the rest of New York, especially as the city struggled in the dark days of fiscal and social crisis. However, as New York began to rebound, it did so in a way that left many of its outer-borough neighborhoods behind. Since its inception, Co-op City had been assailed by charges that it lacked the kind of authenticity that would be appropriate for building a true community. Now, these charges took on an additional sting, for it was precisely this sense of authenticity—whether it was found in the exposed brick of abandoned factories or the restored gleam of Victorian hardwood—that seemed to motivate real estate decisions, both for individual families deciding where to live and for policy makers deciding which programs, areas, and developments to support. In this regard, Co-op City was similar to much of New York's outer boroughs, which aside from a swath of gentrification in so-called "Brownstone Brooklyn," did not experience much of a rebound in the 1980s. This also matched a national trend. Housing values in inner-ring suburbs—the functional equivalent of these outer-borough neighborhoods—in American cities generally fell in the period between 1970 and 2000 in comparison with both newer suburban areas and inner cities.[80] American cities in these years were poised between the centrifugal forces of suburbanization and expansion, and the centripetal force of gentrification. Urban geographers observed that beginning in the 1980s, inner-ring suburbs "are being left behind, literally and metaphorically. The continued outward suburban expansion is coupled with the simultaneous decline of older suburbs located near the central city."[81] This was not merely a question of location, but also one of race. The loss of cachet of inner-ring suburbs was dialectically related to their growing minority populations. This was true of Co-op City in much the same way it was in Wayne, Michigan, or Ferguson, Missouri.[82]

Co-op City, of course, could not change its location on the outskirts of the Bronx, and for now it could not improve its transit connections to the rest of New York. However, in 1988, a new shopping mall opened in Co-op City—Bay Plaza—which was designed to attract shoppers from not only Co-op City but also its surrounding neighborhoods. This outdoor shopping mall adjoining the development was the first new retail space constructed at Co-op City since its inception.[83] Developed by Prestige Properties, Bay Plaza offered 270,000 square feet of retail space in addition to office space and a ten-screen multiplex.[84] Right off I-95, it offered a commercial link between Co-op City and the rest of New York. The construction of Bay Plaza brought the ambivalence that Co-op City residents felt toward the rest of the Bronx to a head. In a community starved for amenities, the proposal for a large outdoor mall filled with chain stores and restaurants seemed to many like a dream come true. It offered the possibility of entertainment, employment, and shopping opportunities for a community with limited access to any of these. As one resident wrote in a letter to the *Co-op City Times,* "If the truth be known . . . Co-op City is a boring place in which to live. Shopping and entertainment are limited, transportation is expensive and time consuming . . . there is a dearth of culture here; and practically no employment opportunities in the immediate vicinity."[85] Another resident enthused, "I like the idea because it will give us something new to do in our community. We will have a chance to go shopping in a new place and see something different."[86] I was among the swarm of teens and tweens who flocked to the opening of Bay Plaza's first tenant, a hardware store. Few of us had any interest in construction but just enjoyed the fact that there was something new to do in Co-op City. Meanwhile, other residents were less sanguine about this new commercial development, fearing that the mall would act as a magnet for crime and traffic, once and for all ending Co-op City's splendid isolation. Even before Bay Plaza opened, David Cooke, president of the Co-op City Chamber of Commerce, sounded the alarm: "Not to sound self-serving, and as a merchant you run that risk, but this center will mean tremendous traffic, increased pollution and no question about a higher crime rate."[87] Riverbay director Shirley Saunders echoed Cooke: "What might be the impact of approximately 43 stores and 24 offices upon the commercial rental spaces here in the Co-op City Community[?] . . . [Security] will have the added burden to protect our residents against any individual or groups of undesirables once off the premises of Bay Plaza. . . . We feel this complex could possibly do enough harm to destroy our community."[88] Another resident despaired, "Even if the new shopping area has sufficient security, will they prevent the countless number of individuals from entering our buildings and grounds? As we see it, this would not possibly be controlled."[89]

While the construction of Bay Plaza improved Co-op City's commercial offerings, the community continued to struggle throughout the decade with the infrastructure challenges that had been its birthright, further contributing to its problems attracting new residents. In a series of articles in 1990 charting the history of Co-op City's ongoing construction defect crisis, former rent-strike leader Charles Rosen wrote,

> The *Co-op City Times* regularly carries banner headlines about "this sinking" and "that sinking" and the "fear that there will be no hot water or heat for Section 5 in a few weeks." On a walking tour through Co-op City, one cannot but be impressed with construction machinery and materials strewn over the greenway. Dying, uprooted plants are stored behind link fencing. . . . Heavy equipment, like moles, are in a constant state of digging craters; 12-foot high green periscopes set willy-nilly throughout the project, spew boiling steam as if sending smoke signals from below: yellow barriers block residents from walking traditional routes home.[90]

Construction defects, however, while a constant problem, were not the cause of all Co-op City's infrastructure problems. Riverbay director Illis wrote, "Anyone will move out if they have to continue to live in filthy buildings, be handled by impolite employees and supervised by non-community oriented management . . . [see] filthy floors, walls, etc. That is what will drive people away."[91] At a community forum, resident Rodney Beckford stated that "the perception of the quality of life is very important to a community. There is a smell of urine in the elevators. I don't know who is doing it, but I don't like it. This is the kind of thing that matters when people talk about what kind of place this is."[92] In 1993, Riverbay's new president, Iris Baez, referred to Co-op City as "the world's largest pigsty."[93]

As if Co-op City's crumbling infrastructure was not enough, scandals, ranging from a major web of embezzlements and kickbacks related to the state-sponsored infrastructure repair program, to smaller-scale pilfering of community funds or the awarding of apartments and jobs to friends and colleagues, often dominated both local news and politics, even if they had little impact on the day-to-day life of most cooperators.[94] Co-op City also continued to be as politically fractious as ever. While none of the protests of the 1980s approached the scope of the rent strike, residents continued to fight to keep affordable carrying charges, to increase police protection, to fight against the placement of a homeless shelter nearby, against racism, against the transport of nuclear waste on I-95 that ran alongside much of the development, and even against a spate of mysterious stains that ruined clothing after the purchase of new washing machines.[95] While some residents clearly appreciated Co-op City's "fighting spirit," others found it wearying. "I only want to state the people in our community are sick of all these fights that come from all these politicos. What we are interested in is bread, milk, kasha and good health," Sam Fenster, a longtime resident, wrote in a 1987 letter to the editor of the *Co-op City Times*.[96]

Even as protests dwindled and participation in local elections began to decline in the early 1990s, political infighting remained as caustic as ever. Riverbay board members often castigated one another for contributing to Co-op City's problems with their contentiousness. Discussing the vacancy problem in 1993, director Larry Barnard called out his fellow directors for their attitudes: "Much of our vacancy problem is due to economic conditions, which unfortunately is a national problem. However, much of our problems have been self-induced in that many [leaders] tend to downgrade Co-op City."[97] In a 1988 article titled "Let's Restore Our Good Name," Michael Rosenberg upbraided his fellow directors for "the fear, intimidation and bullying of staff members and cooperators."[98] In 1991, Barbara Jones attacked Illis: "The solution to our problems is not to consistently paint a picture of doom, but to try and solve the problems. . . . A shareholder, after reading one of Mr. Illis's doom and gloom viewpoints, said to me: Mr. Illis frightens me. I am thinking about moving out of Co-op City. I tried to reassure her that Co-op City still has so much to offer and not to let one cynical person drive her from Co-op City."[99]

For all these reasons, Co-op City's vacancy problem that had developed after the rent strike worsened during the following decade and became a full-blown crisis during the recession of the early 1990s.[100] In an attempt to fill apartments, in 1991 Co-op City received approval from the DHCR for a plan to settle 250 Soviet Jews in the cooperative as part of a wider plan to offer subsidized loans to cover the equity charges for immigrants who had sponsoring organizations.[101] However, even this was not enough to stop the growing number of vacancies. By 1993, fifteen hundred apartments in Co-op City stood empty—approximately 10 percent of the development.[102] For a community reliant on the income from resident carrying charges, Co-op City's vacancy problem was an existential crisis, no less serious than that caused by rising carrying charges two decades earlier.

For some observers, the vacancy problem was a result of the limits that the cooperative ownership structure placed on who could move into the development. In order to move into Co-op City, applicants had to buy into the cooperative by paying an equity deposit of several thousand dollars per room.[103] The equity deposit had been an important part of cooperative living—it meant that residents had an ownership stake and investment in the cooperative from the time they moved in—and the UHF had bitterly fought attempts by the city to eliminate it in order to open up the development to a wider range of New Yorkers. During the 1960s and 1970s, many residents did not mind the fact that they did not own their individual apartments. As real estate prices remained flat or even declined in many New York City neighborhoods, living in Co-op City was a way to avoid both the hassles and financial risks of ownership. Meanwhile, they appreciated the fact that the equity deposit limited the pool of potential residents to those who could afford to pay thousands of dollars to secure an apartment. But as real estate in the city rebounded, greater numbers of middle-class people chose to buy their own house or apartment rather than live in a cooperative, particularly one with Co-op City's reputation for financial and infrastructure problems.[104] Iris Baez, who became Riverbay president in 1993, explained, "If someone has to pay nearly $3,000 a room, most people who can afford that will go for a private house."[105]

By the new century, rising prices would put homeownership out of reach for all but the wealthiest New Yorkers. The popularity of Mitchell-Lama limited-equity cooperatives would rise in response.[106] But in the 1980s and 1990s, Co-op City was caught in a period where homeownership had become more popular among middle-income New Yorkers, while the city was still affordable enough to make owning a house or an apartment a real possibility for people in the middle class. The affordability and desirability of homeownership in the city and its surrounding suburbs led to direct competition with Co-op City and other limited-equity cooperatives.[107] In 1990, the average New York City home still cost less than $200,000. The homes in the city's suburbs that many former Co-op City residents favored were similarly priced.[108] In the early 1990s, the average equity deposit required for a family to move in to Co-op City was approximately $14,000. As Myron Holtz, deputy commissioner of the DHCR, explained, "Families with $14,000 prefer to use it as a down payment towards a house. It's a struggle for Co-op City."[109]

Building on the flexibility it displayed in the 1986 and 1991 workout negotiations, the state adopted a conciliatory approach that ultimately solved the vacancy crisis. In 1992, Riverbay and the state DHCR slashed the per-room equity deposit from $2,800 to $1,750. Furthermore, the state arranged for low-cost loans to new residents to finance up to 100 percent of their equity deposits. In doing so, it tacitly admitted that Co-op City was competing for renters and not for people who could otherwise choose to own a home. At the same time, Co-op City began to advertise aggressively for new residents. "Tired of paying rent to a landlord you can never see or talk to?" one ad announced. "It's time to join the thousands of families who are their own landlords at Co-op City."[110] Another ad bragged that "the world's largest housing cooperative, is also quite literally the biggest housing bargain in town."[111] For those who purchased three-bedroom units, Co-op City offered a credit for the first month's carrying charges, as well as a $389.70 "Housewarming Gift Certificate" toward the purchase of a refrigerator. By 1995, Co-op City had arrested the rise of vacancies, with only 579 vacant apartments, the lowest number in a decade.[112] During the period of Co-op City's construction and initial occupancy, city officials had criticized the equity deposit for making the cooperative out of reach for many families who could otherwise afford its monthly payments. The UHF vigorously defended the deposits as essential for giving residents a financial stake in the community. Now, under the pressure of financial exigency and with the UHF a distant memory, Riverbay and the state worked together to make the equity deposit both much smaller and completely financeable, simultaneously opening up Co-op City to a wider range of residents and largely abandoning a key component of the UHF's limited-equity cooperative model.

When Co-op City celebrated its twenty-fifth anniversary in 1993 amid carrying charge increases and an ever-growing list of necessary construction defect repairs, it was hard to judge this experiment in urban living a success. And indeed, Co-op City's tumultuous story of infrastructure woes, corruption, and financial turmoil continued beyond the period covered by this book. In 1995, Co-op City's internecine political feuds reached a climax as three different Riverbay presidents served in a four-month period and five top administrators were fired by the board. Subsequent investigations found endemic corruption and mismanagement. Co-op City brought in a professional property management firm, Marion Scott Real Estate, for the first time in 1999. It, too, however, would later be fired and investigated for corruption.[113]

Yet, in retrospect, even if Co-op City continued to face financial challenges and management turmoil in the ensuing decades, the 1991 workout agreement appeared to be a turning point for the affordability of the development. Carrying charges between 1991 and 2020 rose a cumulative 80 percent, barely keeping pace with inflation. In 2020, the monthly carrying charge for a small one-bedroom apartment in Co-op City was $675 a month, and $1,475 a month for a large three-bedroom apartment.[114] This is at a time that New York City has become increasingly unaffordable, with median Manhattan apartment prices reaching $1 million in 2015 and average monthly rents for a one-bedroom apartment well above $3,000.[115] Recognizing a good deal when they see it, Co-op City residents rejected privatization in the early 2000s, choosing instead to remain a housing cooperative.[116] At Co-op City's fiftieth anniversary celebration in December 2018, a parade of politicians lauded the development as a successful, stable, and diverse neighborhood of affordable homes. Mayor Bill De Blasio congratulated Co-op City as a "vibrant and inclusive complex" and a "vital ally in my administration's efforts to expand access to affordable housing." Bronx borough president Rubén Diaz Jr. described it as "one of the city's true gems."[117]

The seeds of this success can be found in the fact that over the course of the 1980s, New York State and Riverbay began to collaborate rather than remain locked in seemingly intransigent and insolvable conflict. The 1986 and 1991 workout deals and the state's 1993 response to Co-op City's vacancy crisis all reflected this more collaborative relationship between Co-op City and the DHCR. In part, this was due to the retreat of state officials from an insistence on austerity and neoliberal orthodoxy. As the economic fortunes of New York State and New York City began to improve, and as the rise in real estate prices and the appeal of privatization threatened the supply of affordable housing, New York officials began to take a less parsimonious stance toward Co-op City, which enabled the relative stability in carrying charges that has marked Co-op City ever since that time. However, this was not merely a result of shifting fortunes in the state's financial situation or governing philosophy. Rather, the accommodation with New York State that Co-op City achieved over the course of this decade was a result of the activism that residents had engaged in since the development was founded. It may have taken a quarter of a century of struggle, but Co-op City's residents forced the state to negotiate with them, and in the end, they got what they wanted: "the best deal in New York City."[118]

Epilogue
Freedomland Today

Co-op City only exists because the Freedomland amusement park failed. It was in the wake of that failure that the United Housing Foundation was able to purchase the land on which the cooperative now sits. From its very first days, Co-op City's story has always been one of pragmatic reinvention. The hopes that residents, the UHF, New York State, and New York City invested in Co-op City were not based on magical thinking. Rather, Co-op City was and is built on the idea that the everyday actions of residents, working in common purpose, would ultimately forge a durable and secure community, one that has survived decades longer than the "fantasy world" of Freedomland U.S.A. that it replaced.[1] Or as Fred Clarke, one of Co-op City's pioneers, said on the occasion of Co-op City's fiftieth anniversary: "Here we are, a half century, fifty years later, and Co-op City is still standing. This milestone squashes all rumors of our impermanence. We have not sunk into the marsh once home to Freedomland. We're still standing and we're still strong."[2]

This combination of realism and optimism was built into the very brick and mortar of Co-op City's buildings. Even as they cracked and buckled owing to shoddy construction, these thirty-five towers (and 236 town houses) have served as the home of hundreds of thousands of New Yorkers over the past half century. The UHF was an organization whose leaders retained at their core a belief in the power of cooperative housing to create livable buildings and communities for ordinary people. In the pages of this book, I have been quite critical of the UHF for its coziness to power and its proximity to corruption, but these were not the reasons that Co-op City suffered economic challenges; those causes lie more with the broader economic and political crises of the 1960s and 1970s, which engulfed not merely New York but arguably the entire world.[3] While the UHF failed to protect residents from carrying charge increases in the 1970s, this stemmed from the fact that the UHF viewed state officials as partners, after several decades of working hand-in-hand to provide tens of thousands of units of affordable housing for New Yorkers. The UHF's leadership were slow to recognize that economic crisis had shifted the political winds in Albany and elsewhere toward a kind of austerity politics that made such collaboration significantly less possible. The rent strikers recognized the need for a more confrontational stance, and Co-op City residents led by Charles Rosen were adept at maneuvering to ultimately gain control of the cooperative. However, like many revolutionary movements, they struggled when confronted with the mundane realities of governance.

When the rent strike failed to stop carrying charge increases altogether, many residents concluded that it was a failure. However, I would argue that this was a misreading of both the peril that Co-op City and indeed the entire Mitchell-Lama program faced in the 1970s, as well as what the rent strike in particular and resident activism in general had achieved. Once the UHF was removed from the picture, Co-op City's resident board had to negotiate directly with the state. Burned by the collapse of the debt finance model that funded Co-op City along with many of the city and the state's other social programs, officials in Albany saw their responsibility to taxpayers and HFA bondholders as equally if not more important than their responsibility to keep Co-op City affordable. The refusal of New York State to restructure Co-op City's debt, or to invest any but the most immediately necessary funds to address the development's construction delays, poured cold water on the transformational ambitions that had defined Co-op City in its first decade. This was in no small measure responsible for the bitter disappointment felt by many supporters of the rent strike.

Yet by the mid-1980s, state officials retreated from the austerity panic of the previous decade and came to recognize the importance of Co-op City and places like it as housing prices began the inexorable rise that led to the unaffordable city that we know today. The pendulum then swung back toward greater state munificence, such as the willingness to renegotiate the 1986 workout plan, the relatively generous terms of the 1991 workout plan, and the 1993 program to allow new residents to finance their equity payments. Co-op City's residents drove a hard bargain to maintain carrying charges as low as possible both during and after the rent strike. This bought them the time to benefit from this shift in state priorities. While I am reluctant to speak in counterfactuals, a world without militant Co-op City residents and where there had never been a rent strike might well have been a world where Mitchell-Lama housing in general met a much earlier and more ignoble end.

Co-op City's story shows that the supposed transition between the urban liberal era to the neoliberal era was neither simple nor inevitable. Co-op City residents' insistence that they were owed an affordable place to live may have been perplexing and infuriating to outside observers, who bemoaned such a lack of realism. But it represented the persistence of an approach to urban governance that privileged the rights of citizens above other concerns. And it worked. Co-op City remained a "good deal," as resident after resident told me, because of the vigilance of its cooperators and the fear they inspired in Albany. As Governor Mario Cuomo's housing director, Bill Eimicke, later recalled in a conversation, the memory of the rent strike meant that "there was always, from my perspective, an extra incentive to see you could keep that situation under control."[4] Furthermore, Co-op City's sheer size, its most obvious characteristic, gave it a clout that made the voices of residents impossible to ignore. Co-op City is not merely a gargantuan oddity to be gawked at by travelers on I-95. Rather, because Co-op City is so large, it has always had political clout in Albany that no other Mitchell-Lama development could command.

If the story of Co-op City forces us to complicate any simple account of a neoliberal takeover in New York, it also forces us to complicate the history of race in the city. From the time it was founded, Co-op City residents have been castigated as fearful white racists who abandoned the Grand Concourse and were ultimately responsible for the collapse of much of the Bronx in the 1960s and 1970s. Such a narrative has always been oversimplified. In part this is because the racial demographics of Co-op City when it was fully occupied in 1972 were not very different from those of the city as a whole. Regardless of their own race or ethnicity, the working-class and middle-class residents of Co-op City moved there for very similar reasons—the perceived decline of their old neighborhoods. While this declensionist narrative was inflected by race, it was not solely defined by it. Furthermore, the attempts to create a multiracial community in Co-op City were largely genuine on all sides, if never simple or unfraught. It is easy to decry the hypocrisy of white Jews, who paid lip service to integration while being fearful of their Black neighbors. This is something I have certainly done in the pages of this book. But the enthusiasm—among residents of all races—for living in a multiracial community was both real and enduring. It helped Co-op City weather the kind of controversies that led to considerably more bitter conflicts elsewhere in New York and beyond.

I do not want to paint too rosy of a picture here. Many of Co-op City's white residents long balanced two opposing impulses: a desire to live in a multiracial community and become friends with their Black neighbors, and fears that the presence of Black residents was a harbinger of decline and rising crime. With the loss of optimism that accompanied the post-rent strike period, for many, the balance between welcoming and fearing their Black neighbors tipped toward fear. Why did Co-op City's white residents understand Co-op City's infrastructure woes and financial insecurity in terms of racist anxieties about crime? It is perhaps facile to say that one of the stories that this book tracks is how Co-op City's Jews "became white" and in the process decided to abandon the integrationist project that lay at the development's heart. After all, Co-op City's Jews were always simultaneously aware of their whiteness and their Jewishness. However, it is worth noting that when Co-op City was an overwhelmingly Jewish place in the early 1970s, a general Jewish belief in color-blindness—fraught as it often was—took center stage. Yet once Co-op City's racial demographics started to change in the mid-1970s, that changed as well. Not all at once, and not for everyone. For many residents, anxieties about Blackness and crime existed simultaneously—and unstably—with a belief in an "integrated melting pot." The history of Co-op City's first decades may provide as good a case study as any in both the potential and limits of Jewish racial liberalism.

Perhaps what is more interesting is what happened in Co-op City as white flight subsided. By the late 1980s, Co-op City was a majority Black community, with a significant Latino minority and a smaller and shrinking white population. One of the ways that residents responded to Co-op City's demographic transition was with panic that it would lead to rising crime and the neighborhood becoming a slum. Crime did rise in this period, but not nearly as much as the omnipresent rumors about it might lead one to suspect. Rather, the panic about crime in this period can be seen as reflective of anxieties about whether Co-op City could continue to be a safe middle-class neighborhood despite becoming a majority Black community. In my research, I expected to see that white Co-op City residents panicked about crime more than their nonwhite neighbors. This was not what I found. Anxieties about crime crossed racial lines, as did calls for a greater police presence. The second way that Co-op City residents responded to the neighborhood's demographic transition was with celebrations of its multiracial community. Such calls to celebrate Co-op City's inclusivity may ring hollow or appear as a cynical cover for racism, as professions of color-blindness in America so often are. However, it is noteworthy that Co-op City did not descend to the level of racial conflict that affected other outer-borough neighborhoods. This is in no small measure due to the deeply felt belief among residents of all races that Co-op City's multiracial identity was something valuable and worth defending. This belief has persisted to the present day. A commemorative brochure for Co-op City's fiftieth anniversary featured ad after ad by resident groups and organizations celebrating the cooperative's "unity in a multicultural community."[5] A community group recently explained their mission to be a "community of more than just neighbors, but as one family of many cultures."[6] Such statements could easily have been uttered by Co-op City's first residents fifty years earlier, and the stable quality of this discourse across Co-op City's racial transition is noteworthy, even if its limits must also be acknowledged.

In an election-year contest that received national attention, in 2020, Jamaal Bowman, an outspoken progressive, scored a striking victory, by a resounding margin, in his primary against Eliot Engel, who had represented Co-op City for decades.[7] To some outside observers, Engel's defeat marked a kind of racial and generational changing of the guard.[8] That analysis, however, belies the ways in which Bowman represents a continuity with Co-op City's past. As his many Jewish supporters could attest, Bowman succeeded in crafting an interracial coalition and built his campaign on a language of shared struggle across racial divides.[9] In an interview shortly after his victory, he explained, "So I'm Black in America. . . . But in addition to that, I'm also human. And as a human, we all have similar experiences—not the same but similar. . . . You know, we all have our experiences of collective trauma and pain and oppression, and we've all had our experiences of fighting through that and uplifting ourselves and one another. And what we've tried to capture in this campaign is not just our collective struggle but our collective humanity."[10] Bowman represents a continuity with Co-op City's past in a second sense. In a discussion with me in late summer 2020, Bowman reflected on the fighting spirit of Co-op City residents and their insistence on the importance of an urban liberalism long thought to be past its expiration date:

> Working-class, law-abiding, taxpaying people should be able to live with dignity and age gracefully. There's a sense that Co-op City is still fighting to maintain itself as a space for that. It captures the working-class

energy of New York City, New York State, and the entire country that continues to be beaten down by an economic and social system that is becoming more and more oppressive and unresponsive to the needs of the people. . . . So when people were saying it's time for a change, that's what they were communicating.[11]

It is not hard to see how Bowman reflects a progressive universalism that has always been a part of Co-op City's DNA. In his vision of greater public investment in social democracy, including a Green New Deal, Medicare for all, and expanded funding for affordable housing, it is possible to imagine a way in which Co-op City would represent the vanguard of a better America rather than its past.

It is easy to walk through Co-op City today and see the ways in which it remains much as it always has been. As much as ongoing construction defects have cost Riverbay and the state, Co-op City's housing towers, town houses, shopping centers, and garages are still standing. The views from the upper floors are still just as good. There is still no direct subway line from Co-op City to Manhattan, and the rumors about an extension of the new Second Avenue line or the addition of a Metro North stop continue, just as they did in the 1960s when Co-op City was first planned. After Co-op City was refinanced in 2014, Wells Fargo came to hold the $621.5 million, thirty-five-year mortgage, which was guaranteed by HUD.[12] In 2016, Riverbay hired Douglas Elliman Property Management to run the day-to-day operations of the cooperative.[13] Co-op City residents today are much less likely to protest to protect the affordability of the development—a 2019 DHCR hearing on carrying charge increases attracted a mere fourteen residents, a far cry from the thousands who once packed the Dreiser Community Center or the Greenway.[14] This is perhaps because Co-op City's affordability no longer seems to be so much in danger. Voting in local elections has also declined. Riverbay board election deadlines are regularly extended so that the mandated election quorum can be reached. Nevertheless, residents still do show up for causes that matter to them. In June 2019, six hundred residents turned out for a rally to protest proposed cuts to Co-op City's bus service.[15] In June 2020, Black Lives Matter protests brought a multiracial crowd of cooperators to a rally organized by two sisters and lifelong Co-op City residents Pearl and Emerald Fletcher. Pearl explained their motivation: "I want to show that we, the Co-op City community, can peacefully protest, and we can use our voices for good. . . . There's a revolution going on and it's going to bring the change that our ancestors have been forever fighting for."[16] For all that Co-op City has changed, it remains a community of survivors—and fighters—on the literal and figurative margins of New York.

The fears that Co-op City could not survive as a middle-class neighborhood once it lost its original majority white population turned out to be unfounded. Co-op City remains a diverse place, even if its racial balance has changed considerably since the late 1960s. As of the 2010 census, Co-op City was 60 percent Black, 28 percent Hispanic, and only 10 percent white.[17] Just as in 1970 or 1990, in the 2010 census, Co-op City residents still earned the median income for residents of New York City (see appendix, figure 27). The omnipresent repair work to fix construction defects has largely abated, and the development is full of well-maintained landscaping. The panic about crime of the late 1980s and early 1990s has also subsided. Crime in Co-op City began to decline later in the 1990s and continued its decline in the years that followed. The 2019 murder rate in the Forty-Fifth Precinct was 82 percent less than that of 1990, with other categories of major crime showing

FIGURE 24. The author's childhood apartment on Adler Place, 2021. Photograph by Gabrielle Sammartino.

similar declines, similar to the falloff in crime across New York City.[18] Co-op City's schools may no longer rank among the best in the city, as they were in the 1970s; however, test scores put the elementary and middle schools at roughly average for the state as a whole.[19] As was always the case, Co-op City still has a large population of elderly residents; according to one accounting, 47 percent of Co-op City's residents are over sixty-two years old.[20] My mother is now among them. She still lives on Adler Place, in the same town house she moved into in November 1976. My father lived there with her until his death in December 2020 at the age of eighty-six.

The period this book covers concludes roughly when I left for college. More than a quarter of a century later, when my sisters and I visit, the apartment I grew up in is once again filled with the sounds of children playing. We take our kids to the same pizza parlor, the same playgrounds, and the same Greenway that we once spent hours in ourselves. My mother has new toys for the grandkids, the pizza parlor has new owners, the playgrounds have new equipment, and the Greenway is no longer the construction site it was for much of my childhood. Like all neighborhoods, Co-op City has and will continue to evolve. I have written a story about Co-op City's first twenty-five years, and I eagerly await what will be written about the next twenty-five, just possibly by a young resident, now leaving New York for the first time to go to college herself.

APPENDIX

Co-op City schedule of project: Development cost estimates, 1965–1971

COST CATEGORY	ORIGINAL CONTRACT 6/18/1965	MODIFICATION #1 3/13/1967	MODIFICATION #2 1/22/1968	MODIFICATION #3 3/29/1968	MODIFICATION #4 9/15/1969	MODIFICATION #5 5/1/1971	TOTAL INCREASE (DECREASE)
Land acquisition	$16,113,450	$16,018,982	$16,018,982	$16,018,982	$16,018,982	$16,018,982	($94,468)
Construction costs	258,507,750	267,830,750	268,080,750	269,980750	310,500,000	340,500,000	81,992,250
Professional services	3,650,000	3,850,000	3,850,000	3,870,000	5,900,000	5,910,000	2,260,000
Selling & renting expenses	450,000	500,000	500,000	500,000	600,000	600,000	150,000
Carrying & finance charges	12,300,800	12,835,000	12,302,000	12,302,000	31,113,000	94,125,000	81,824,200
Surplus from pre-occupancy operations	(10,000,000)	(10,000,000)	(10,000,000)	(10,000,000)	(4,600,000)	(38,950,000)	(28,950,000)
Contingency	2,00,000	2,000,000	2,000,000	1,000,000	1,000,000	2,000,000	
Working capital	673,550	768,468	1,051,468	1,031,468	2,167,718	2,495,718	1,822,168
Total development costs	$283,695,550	$293,803,200	$293,803,200	$293,803,200	$362,699,700	$422,699,700	$139,004,150

Source: Reproduced from Arthur Levitt, *The New York State Mitchell-Lama Program Supervision of Development Costs of Co-op City by the Division of Housing and Community Renewal,* Audit Report NY-AUTH-18-78, December 29, 1978, 37.

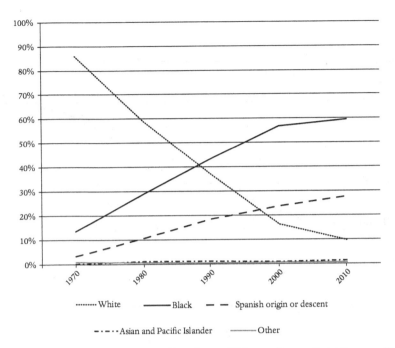

FIGURE 25. Co-op City racial demographics. *Source:* US Census Bureau, Racial Demographics for the Co-op City Census Tracts, 1970–2010. Prepared by Social Explorer. Chart compiled by Michael Kennedy, May 7, 2018. *Note:* The data for 1970 reflect only the portion of the development that had been occupied as of that date, largely in Sections One and Two. See chapter 2 for a discussion of the racial demography of Co-op City once Co-op City was fully occupied, in 1972.

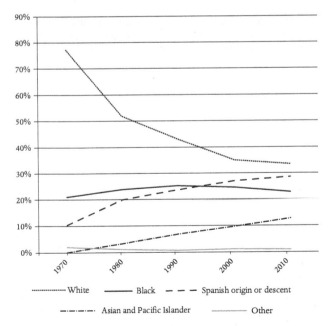

FIGURE 26. New York City racial demographics. *Source:* US Census Bureau, Racial Demographics for New York City, 1970–2010. Prepared by Social Explorer. Chart compiled by Michael Kennedy, May 7, 2018.

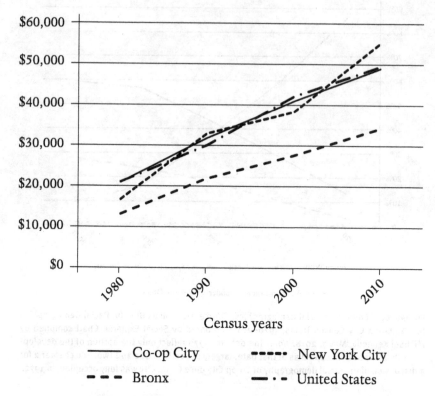

FIGURE 27. Median family incomes, 1980–2010 (2010 five-year estimate). *Source:* US Census Bureau, Median Family Income, 1980–2010. Data prepared by Social Explorer. Chart compiled by Michael Kennedy, May 7, 2018. *Note:* The census began to record median family income in 1980.

Notes

Newspapers frequently cited in the notes have been identified by the following abbreviations:

CCT   *Co-op City Times*
CN   *City News*
DN   *Daily News*
NYT   *New York Times*

Preface

1. Ada Louise Huxtable, "Co-op City's Grounds: After 3 Years, a Success," *New York Times* (hereafter cited as *NYT*), October 26, 1971, 43.

2. Ian Frazier, "Utopia: The Bronx," *New Yorker*, June 26, 2006.

3. Richard Meislin, "Carey Proposes Mitchell-Lama Rent Rises Up to 20%," *NYT*, May 2, 1980, B3.

4. "We're the Light of Con-Ed's Life," *Co-op City Times* (hereafter cited as *CCT*), February 27, 1988, 3.

5. Alan Feuer, "Haven for Workers in Bronx Evolves for Their Retirement," *NYT*, August 5, 2002, A1.

6. Quote is from Daniel Doctoroff, *Greater Than Ever: New York's Big Comeback* (New York: PublicAffairs, 2017), xi.

7. Huxtable, "Co-op City's Grounds."

8. Judson Hand, "Co-op City: A Town with a Thousand Stories," *Daily News* (hereafter cited as *DN*), September 7, 1971.

9. Harold Ostroff, "Welcome to Your New Home! A Message from the President of Riverbay Corporation," *Co-op City Living: A Guide for Members*, n.d., 2.

10. Annemarie Sammartino, "Mass Housing, Late Modernism and the Forging of Community in New York City and East Berlin, 1965–1989," *American Historical Review* 121, no. 2 (2016): 492–521.

11. With a few exceptions, the literature on neighborhoods like Co-op City is nostalgic in content and tone. Peter Eisenstadt, *Rochdale Village: Robert Moses, 6,000 Families, and New York City's Great Experiment in Integrated Housing* (Ithaca, NY: Cornell University Press, 2010), and Jeffrey Gurock, *Parkchester: A Bronx Tale of Race and Ethnicity* (New York: NYU Press, 2019), are two excellent books by former residents that are exceptions that prove the rule in this regard. For more nostalgic accounts see Corinne Demas, *Eleven Stories High: Growing Up in Stuyvesant Town, 1948–1968* (Albany: SUNY Press, 2000), and the 2015 documentary *Pomonok Dreams*, dir. Terry Katz.

Introduction

1. Kimberly Phillips-Fein, *Fear City: New York's Fiscal Crisis and the Rise of Austerity Politics* (New York: Metropolitan Books, 2017), 270–71.

2. Peter Grad, "Blackout '77: We Saw the Ugly and the Good," *CCT*, July 16, 1977, 26.

3. Beame speech in "New York Blackout II," 1977 Year in Review, UPI, December 1977, https://www.upi.com/Archives/Audio/Events-of-1977/New-York-Blackout-II/.

4. Tom Wicker, "A Prophecy Fulfilled," *NYT*, July 17, 1977, 143.

5. James Goodman, *Blackout* (New York: Farrar, Straus and Giroux, 2003), 224.

6. For more on both the blackout and the summer of 1977 see Goodman, *Blackout*; Jonathan Mahler, *Ladies and Gentlemen, The Bronx Is Burning: 1977, Baseball, Politics, and the Battle for the Soul of a City* (New York: Picador, 2006); and, of course, the Spike Lee film *Summer of Sam* (1999).

7. Grad, "Blackout '77."

8. Marc Bosyk post to "Co-op City Web" Facebook group, May 16, 2012. Co-op City had been built with its own power plant, but as I discuss in chapter 2, a series of construction issues meant that it was not operational at this time.

9. Larry Dolnick, "Riverbay President Reports on Blackout," *CCT*, July 16, 1977, 3.

10. Debby Prisco post to "Co-op City Web" Facebook group, June 16, 2011.

11. Grad, "Blackout '77."

12. Bosyk Facebook post.

13. Greg Myers, conversation with the author, September 3, 2020.

14. Moshe Friedman post to "Co-op City Web" Facebook group, June 17, 2011.

15. Dolnick, "Riverbay President Reports on Blackout."

16. Joshua B. Freeman, *Working-Class New York: Life and Labor since World War II* (New York: New Press, 2000), 124.

17. "Tower Buildings High and Mighty," *CCT*, July 1967, 1.

18. *United Housing Foundation: Twenty Years of Accomplishment* (New York: United Housing Foundation, 1971), 21.

19. Sibyl Moholy-Nagy, "Response to Venturi-Brown," *Progressive Architecture*, April 1970, 8.

20. Campbell Gibson and Kay Young, "Historical Census Statistics on Population Totals by Race and Hispanic Origin, 1970 to 1990, for Large Cities and Other Urban Places in the United States," US Census, Population Division, Working Paper No. 76 (February 2005), table 33: New York—Race and Hispanic Origin for Selected Large Cities and Other Places: Earliest Census to 1990, https://www.census.gov/population/www/documentation/twps0076/NYtab.pdf, accessed July 29, 2020.

21. "Carrying charges" refers to the combination of maintenance fees and mortgage payments that made up the monthly payment of Co-op City residents. Many residents referred to their carrying charges as "rent," especially by the late 1970s. In the manuscript, I use the term "carrying charge" primarily; however, where residents use the term "rent," I have not corrected them.

22. "74% Vote 'Yes' to OK Pact," *CCT*, July 23, 1977, 1.

23. Lizabeth Cohen, *A Consumers' Republic: The Politics of Mass Consumption in Postwar America* (New York: Vintage Books, 2003), 22.

24. Hillman quoted in Peter Eisenstadt, *Rochdale Village: Robert Moses, 6,000 Families, and New York City's Great Experiment in Integrated Housing* (Ithaca, NY: Cornell University Press, 2010), 27.

25. Daniel Rodgers, *Atlantic Crossings: Social Politics in a Progressive Age* (Princeton, NJ: Princeton University Press, 1998), 463. In Europe developers received direct subsidies, but the New York model provided tax exemptions instead.

26. Richard Plunz, *A History of Housing in New York City* (New York: Columbia University Press, 1990), 168.

27. Plunz, 165.

28. Eisenstadt, *Rochdale Village*, 26–27.

29. Matthew Lasner, *High Life: Condo Living in the Suburban Century* (New Haven, CT: Yale University Press, 2012), 118–19.

30. Gail Radford, *Modern Housing for America: Policy Struggles in the New Deal Era* (Chicago: University of Chicago Press, 1996), 177.

31. For three different perspectives on Stuyvesant Town see Martha Biondi, *To Stand and Fight: The Struggle for Civil Rights in Postwar New York* (Cambridge, MA: Harvard University Press, 2003), chap. 6; Joel Schwartz, *The New York Approach: Robert Moses, Urban Liberals, and the Redevelopment of the Inner City* (Columbus: Ohio State University Press, 1993), chap. 4; and Samuel Zipp, *Manhattan Projects: The Rise and Fall of Urban Renewal in Cold War New York* (New York: Oxford University Press, 2010), chaps. 2 and 3.

32. Mason B. Williams, *City of Ambition: FDR, La Guardia, and the Making of Modern New York* (New York: W. W. Norton, 2013).

33. Freeman, *Working-Class New York*, 105.

34. Freeman, 4.

35. Schwartz, *New York Approach*, 136–37.

36. *United Housing Foundation: Twenty Years of Accomplishment*, 2.

37. Hilary Botein, "'Solid Evidence of Union's Present Status': Unions and Housing in Postwar New York" (PhD diss., Columbia University, 2005), 72.

38. *United Housing Foundation: Twenty Years of Accomplishment*, 11.

39. *United Housing Foundation: Twenty Years of Accomplishment*, 13. Other developments include the East River Houses in Manhattan completed in 1956 (with four buildings and 1,672 apartments) and the Amalgamated Warbasse homes near Brighton Beach in Brooklyn, completed in 1965 (with five buildings and 2,585 apartments).

40. On the history of Rochdale, from the perspective of a former resident and with a view to its embeddedness in New York history, see Eisenstadt, *Rochdale Village*.

41. Botein, "Solid Evidence," 76.

42. Freeman, *Working-Class New York*; Daniel T. Rodgers, *Atlantic Crossings: Social Politics in a Progressive Age* (Cambridge, MA: Belknap Press of Harvard University Press, 2000).

43. Freeman, *Working-Class New York*, 67–68.

44. Although the National Housing Act of 1949 established the Cooperative Housing Division at the FHA and had a new program, Section 213, which enabled federal mortgage insurance for limited equity cooperatives, this was substantially less generous than the direct granting of mortgages offered by New York Mitchell-Lama. Lasner, *High Life*, 138. More generally, see Lasner for an excellent critique of

the suburban/urban model to represent the full spectrum of American living situations in the postwar era.

45. Plunz, *Housing in New York City*, 274.

46. Plunz, 274.

47. Nicholas Bloom, *Public Housing That Worked: New York in the Twentieth Century* (Philadelphia: University of Pennsylvania Press, 2008). The literature on failed public housing ventures in America is vast. Chicago provides an important and well-studied counterexample to New York's relative success story. See Arnold Hirsch, *Making the Second Ghetto: Race and Housing in Chicago, 1940–1960* (New York: Cambridge University Press, 1983); John F. Bauman, Roger Biles, and Kristin M. Szylvian, *From Tenements to the Taylor Homes: In Search of an Urban Housing Policy in Twentieth-Century America* (University Park: Penn State University Press, 2000); Bradford Hunt, *Blueprint for Disaster: The Unraveling of Chicago Public Housing* (Chicago: University of Chicago Press, 2009).

48. "History of Rent Regulation in New York State, 1943–1993," New York Division of Housing and Community Renewal, http://www.tenant.net/Oversight/50yrRentReg/history.html.

49. The vast majority of limited-equity cooperatives were in New York City. On the broader spectrum of working-class and middle-income cooperatives in New York see Lasner, *High Life*, chap. 3.

50. Prior to 1955, Moses used State Redevelopment Companies Law monies. This act had been passed to provide monies to insurance companies, especially Metropolitan Life, for the construction of middle-income housing during World War II. Botein, "Solid Evidence," 5.

51. *New York State Laws of 1955*, 307. For more on New York State's financing of urban middle-class housing see Hilary Botein, "New York State Housing Policy in Postwar New York: The Enduring Rockefeller Legacy," *Journal of Urban History* 35, no. 6 (2009): 833–52.

52. Plunz, *Housing in New York City*, 281–82.

53. Botein, "Solid Evidence," 7. In the case of cooperatives, this referred to their carrying charges, which consisted of a combination of the mortgage payments for the development and its ongoing maintenance and operating expenses.

54. Nelson Rockefeller quoted in Samuel Bleeker, *The Politics of Architecture: A Perspective on Nelson A. Rockefeller* (New York: Rutledge, 1981), 113.

55. Botein, "New York State Housing Policy," 838.

56. Botein, 837.

57. Botein, "Solid Evidence," 140.

58. Bleeker, *Politics of Architecture*, 113–14. For more on the funding mechanisms behind the HFA see Committee on Housing and Urban Development, "Development of State Housing Finance Agencies," *Real Property, Probate and Trust Journal* 9, no. 4 (1974): 471–91.

59. Botein, "Solid Evidence," 159.

60. Robert Caro, *Power Broker: Robert Moses and the Fall of New York* (New York: Vintage, 1974) remains the definitive work on this "master planner." Moses's reputation has recently undergone something of a renaissance. See Hilary Ballon and Kenneth T. Jackson, eds., *Robert Moses and the Modern City: The Transformation of New York* (New York: W. W. Norton, 2007). A not nearly comprehensive list of Moses's

projects includes the Throgs Neck, Verrazzano-Narrows, Whitestone, and Triborough Bridges, the Brooklyn-Queens Expressway, the Cross Bronx Expressway, the Belt Parkway, the Henry Hudson Parkway, and the Laurelton Parkway, Shea Stadium, Lincoln Center, Jones Beach, the Brooklyn Battery Tunnel, and the UN Headquarters, as well as scores of local parks and pools.

61. Zipp, *Manhattan Projects.*

62. Plunz, *Housing in New York City,* 281. Moses's affinity for housing towers was such that in 1956, all of the seventeen projects proposed by his Mayor's Committee on Slum Clearance used the "towers in a park" model.

63. A wide literature in the past decade examines these developments. For an international overview see Florian Urban, *Tower and Slab: Histories of Global Mass Housing* (New York: Routledge, 2012). On the utopian expectations that sociologists and urban planners placed on the now-notorious French suburbs see Kenny Cupers, *The Social Project: Housing Postwar France* (Minneapolis: University of Minnesota Press, 2014) and Nicole Rudolph, *At Home in Postwar France: Modern Mass Housing and the Right to Comfort* (New York: Berghahn, 2015). On the popularity of such housing in the Eastern Bloc see Stephen Harris, *Communism on Tomorrow Street: Mass Housing and Everyday Life after Stalin* (Baltimore: Johns Hopkins University Press, 2013); Virág Molnár, *Building the State: Architecture, Politics, and State Formation in Post-war Central Europe* (New York: Routledge, 2013); Julia Maxim, *The Socialist Life of Modern Architecture: Bucharest, 1947–1865* (New York: Routledge, 2018); Eli Rubin, *Amnesiopolis: Modernity, Space, and Memory in East Germany* (Oxford: Oxford University Press, 2016). On the adaptability of modernist housing developers in the 1960s and 1970s see Annemarie Sammartino, "Mass Housing, Late Modernism, and the Forging of Community in New York City and East Berlin, 1965–1989," *American Historical Review* 121, no. 2 (2016): 492–521.

64. Francesca Russello Ammon, *Bulldozer: Demolition and Clearance of the Postwar Landscape* (New Haven, CT: Yale University Press, 2017).

65. Schwartz, *New York Approach,* 1.

66. Abraham Kazan, *ILGWU Cooperative Village: A Dream Come True* (New York: United Housing Foundation, 1959), 1.

67. *United Housing Foundation: Twenty Years of Accomplishment,* 23.

68. Harold Ostroff, "The Impact of Housing Cooperatives in Urban Areas. Speech from the National Association of Housing Cooperatives, February 19, 1966," *Co-op Contact,* Spring 1966, 19.

69. Ostroff, 20.

70. Ostroff, 19.

71. "Statement of Harold Ostroff, Executive Vice President United Housing Foundation, before the National Commission on Urban Problems," September 7, 1967, 7, as cited in Adam Tanaka, "Private Projects, Public Ambitions: Large-Scale, Middle-Income Housing in New York City" (PhD diss., Harvard University, 2019), 146.

72. *United Housing Foundation: Twenty Years of Accomplishment,* 21.

73. See Samuel Zipp, "The Roots and Routes of Urban Renewal," *Journal of Urban History* 39, no. 3 (2012): 366–91.

74. Caro, *Power Broker.*

75. See Ballon and Jackson, *Robert Moses and the Modern City.*

76. Evelyn Gonzalez, *The Bronx* (New York: Columbia University Press, 2004); Jill Jonnes, *We're Still Here: The Rise, Fall, and Resurrection of the South Bronx* (New York: Atlantic, 1986).

77. Roberta Gold, *When Tenants Claimed the City: The Struggle for Citizenship in New York Housing* (Urbana-Champaign: University of Illinois Press, 2014), 239–41.

78. Phillips-Fein, *Fear City*, 269.

79. Lasner, *High Life*, 157–58.

80. Freeman, *Working-Class New York*, 119–23.

81. Jane Jacobs, *The Life and Death of Great American Cities* (New York: Vintage, 1961); Caro, *Power Broker*; Anthony Flint, *Wrestling with Moses: How Jane Jacobs Took On New York's Master Builder and Transformed the American City* (New York: Random House, 2009); Roberta Brandes Gratz, *The Battle for Gotham: New York in the Shadow of Robert Moses and Jane Jacobs* (New York: Nation Books, 2010); Christopher Klemek, *The Transatlantic Collapse of Urban Renewal: Postwar Urbanism from New York to Berlin* (Chicago: Chicago University Press, 2011).

82. Klemek, *Transatlantic Collapse*, 112.

83. Klemek, 119 and passim.

84. Eisenstadt, *Rochdale Village*, 125.

85. Jacobs quoted in Eisenstadt, 129.

86. Schechter quoted in Robert Venturi and Denise Scott Brown, "Co-op City: Learning to Like It," *Progressive Architecture* 51, no. 2 (1970): 69–70.

87. *Yale Daily News* quoted in Brian Goldstein, "Planning's End? Urban Renewal in New Haven, the Yale School of Art and Architecture, and the Fall of the New Deal Spatial Order," *Journal of Urban History* 37, no. 3 (2011): 408.

88. Suleiman Osman, *The Invention of Brownstone Brooklyn: Gentrification and the Search for Authenticity in Postwar New York* (New York: Oxford University Press, 2011), 176.

89. Samuel Zipp and Michael Carriere, "Introduction: Thinking Through Urban Renewal," *Journal of Urban History* 39, no. 3 (2013): 360.

90. Wendell E. Pritchett, "Which Urban Crisis? Regionalism, Race, and Urban Policy, 1960–1974," *Journal of Urban History* 34, no. 2 (January 2008): 272.

91. Pritchett.

92. William E. Simon, *A Time for Truth*, quoted in Phillips-Fein, *Fear City*, 279.

93. Alice O'Connor, "The Privatized City: The Manhattan Institute, the Urban Crisis, and the Conservative Counterrevolution in New York," *Journal of Urban History* 34, no. 2 (2008): 336.

94. On the particular New York origins of this movement see O'Connor, "Privatized City," 333–53. For a more detailed discussion of the overlap between Jacobs's thinking and that of figures on the right see Peter Laurence, *Becoming Jane Jacobs* (Philadelphia: University of Pennsylvania Press, 2016), 289–305.

95. Benjamin Holtzman, *The Long Crisis: New York City and the Path to Neoliberalism* (New York: Oxford University Press, 2021); Suleiman Osman, "The Decade of the Neighborhood," in *Rightward Bound: Making America Conservative in the 1970s*, ed. Bruce Schulman and Julian Zelizer (Cambridge, MA: Harvard University Press, 2008), 106–27.

96. Judith Stein, *Pivotal Decade: How the United States Traded Factories for Finance in the Seventies* (New Haven, CT: Yale University Press, 2011); Jefferson Cowie, *Stayin'*

Alive: The 1970s and the Last Days of the Working Class (New York: New Press, 2012); Bruce Schulman, *The Seventies: The Great Shift in American Culture, Society, and Politics* (New York: Da Capo, 2002); Thomas Borstelmann, *The 1970s: A New Global History from Civil Rights to Economic Inequality* (Princeton, NJ: Princeton University Press, 2013); Robert Self, *All in the Family: The Realignment of American Democracy since the 1960s* (New York: Hill & Wang, 2013); Kevin Kruse and Julian Zelizer, *Fault Lines: A History of the United States since 1974* (New York: W. W. Norton, 2019).

97. Borstelmann, *1970s*, 3–4.

98. David Harvey, *A Brief History of Neoliberalism* (New York: Oxford University Press, 2005), 2.

99. Jason Hackworth, *The Neoliberal City: Government, Ideology, and Development in American Urbanism* (Ithaca, NY: Cornell University Press, 2006).

100. Holtzman, *Long Crisis*; Osman, *Invention of Brownstone Brooklyn*; Brian Goldstein, *The Roots of Urban Renaissance: Gentrification and the Struggle over Harlem* (Cambridge, MA: Harvard University Press, 2017); Aaron Shkuda, *The Lofts of Soho: Gentrification, Art, and Industry in New York, 1950–1980* (Chicago: University of Chicago Press, 2016); Derek Hyra, *The New Urban Renewal: The Transformation of Harlem and Bronzeville* (Chicago: University of Chicago Press, 2008). See also the work of sociologists and geographers including Neil Smith, *The New Urban Frontier: Gentrification and the Revanchist City* (New York: Routledge, 1996); Sharon Zukin, *Naked City: The Death and Life of Authentic Urban Places* (New York: Oxford University Press, 2010); and Lance Freeman, *There Goes the 'Hood: Views of Gentrification from the Ground Up* (Philadelphia: University of Pennsylvania Press, 2006).

101. Heather Lewis, *New York City Public Schools from Brownsville to Bloomberg: Community Control and Its Legacy* (New York: Teachers College Press, 2013); J. Phillip Thompson III, *Double Trouble: Black Mayors, Black Communities, and the Call for a Deep Democracy* (New York: Oxford University Press, 2006).

102. Matthew Delmont, *Why Busing Failed: Race, Media, and the National Resistance to School Desegregation* (Berkeley: University of California Press, 2016); J. Anthony Lukas, *Common Ground: A Turbulent Decade in the Lives of Three American Families* (New York: Vintage, 1986); Thomas Sugrue, *Sweet Land of Liberty: The Forgotten Struggle for Civil Rights in the North* (New York: Random House, 2009); Jason Sokol, *All Eyes Are Upon Us: Race and Politics from Boston to Brooklyn* (New York: Basic Books, 2014); Brian Purnell, Jeanne Theoharis, and Komozi Woodward, eds., *The Strange Careers of the Jim Crow North* (New York: NYU Press, 2019).

103. Jonathan Riedler, *Canarsie: The Jews and Italians of Brooklyn against Liberalism* (Cambridge, MA: Harvard University Press, 1987); Thomas Sugrue, *The Origins of the Urban Crisis: Race and Inequality in Postwar Detroit* (Princeton, NJ: Princeton University Press, 1998).

104. Elizabeth Hinton, *From the War on Poverty to the War on Crime: The Making of Mass Incarceration in America* (Cambridge, MA: Harvard University Press, 2016), statistic from p. 30, quote from p. 3. See also Michelle Alexander, *The New Jim Crow: Mass Incarceration in the Age of Colorblindness* (Cambridge, MA: Harvard University Press, 2010); James Forman Jr., *Locking Up Our Own: Crime and Punishment in Black America* (New York: Farrar, Strauss and Giroux, 2017); Doris Marie Provine, *Unequal under Law: Race in the War on Drugs* (Chicago: University of Chicago Press, 2007); Heather Ann Thompson, "Why Mass Incarceration Matters: Rethinking Crisis,

Decline, and Transformation in Postwar American History," *Journal of American History* 97 (December 2010): 703–34.

105. Sonia Song-Ha Lee, *Building a Latino Civil Rights Movement: Puerto Ricans, African Americans, and the Pursuit of Racial Justice in New York City* (Chapel Hill: University of North Carolina Press, 2014); Robert Self, *American Babylon: Race and the Struggle for Postwar Oakland* (Princeton, NJ: Princeton University Press, 2003); Donna Murch, *Living for the City: Migration, Education, and the Rise of the Black Panther Party in Oakland, California* (Chapel Hill: University of North Carolina Press, 2010); Matthew Countryman, *Up South: Civil Rights and Black Power in Philadelphia* (Philadelphia: University of Pennsylvania Press, 2006); Peniel E. Joseph, ed., *Neighborhood Rebels: Black Power and the Local Level* (New York: Palgrave Macmillan, 2010).

106. Gonzalez, *Bronx*, 116.

107. Gold, *When Tenants Claimed the City*, 239.

108. Freeman, *Working-Class New York*, 119.

109. Phillips-Fein, *Fear City*; Hackworth, *Neoliberal City*; John Mollenkopf and Manuel Castells, eds., *Dual City: Restructuring New York* (New York: Russell Sage, 2002); Susan S. Fainstein, *The City Builders: Property Development in New York and London, 1980–2000* (Oxford: Blackwell, 2001). For those interested in other work that complicates this narrative see Holtzman, *Long Crisis*; Nancy Kwak, *A World of Homeowners: American Power and the Politics of Housing Aid* (Chicago: University of Chicago Press, 2015); and Amy Offner, *Sorting Out the Mixed Economy: The Rise and Fall of Welfare and Development States in the Americas* (Princeton, NJ: Princeton University Press, 2019), which each argue that "neoliberal" aspects of US policy have deep roots in the earlier postwar period. See also Lizabeth Cohen, *Saving America's Cities: Ed Logue and the Struggle to Renew Urban America in a Suburban Age* (New York: Macmillan, 2019), which uses the career of Edward J. Logue to present a nuanced portrait of the evolution of attempts to address America's urban crisis across the supposed neoliberal divide.

110. Riedler, *Canarsie*; Joseph, *Neighborhood Rebels*.

111. Michael Dawson and Megan Ming Francis, "Black Politics and the Neoliberal Racial Order," *Public Culture* 28 (178): 23–62; Eduardo Bonilla-Silva, *Racism without Racists: Color-Blind Racism and the Persistence of Racial Inequality in America* (Lanham, MD: Rowman & Litttlefield, 2014); Charles Gallagher, "Color-Blind Privilege: The Social and Political Functions of Erasing the Color Line in Post Race America," *Race, Gender and Class* 10, no. 4 (2003): 22–37.

112. See Phillips-Fein, *Fear City*.

1. "The World's Greatest Housing Cooperative"

1. Edith Evans Asbury, "Ground Broken for Bronx Co-ops," *NYT*, May 15, 1966, 70.

2. "Rockefeller Addresses 2,000 at Co-op City Ground-Breaking," *Cooperator*, June 1966.

3. Lyndon Johnson to Potofsky, telegram, n.d., collection 6129, box 6, Kheel Center for Labor-Management Documentation & Archives, Cornell University (hereafter cited as Kheel Center).

4. "Co-op City," *NYT*, May 14, 1966.

5. "Remarks of Robert Moses Chairman of the Triborough Bridge and Tunnel Authority at the Groundbreaking of Co-op City, Bronx, New York, Saturday Morning, May 14, 1966," p. 1, http://issuu.com/makingroom/docs/robert_moses_at_groundbreaking_of_co-op_city?e=3465461/2879068, accessed January 4, 2016.

6. "Remarks of Robert Moses," 4.

7. Ralph Lippman, interview in *Crossroads*, 1986, 48.

8. OPU CPC to R. K. Bernstein, J. C. Smith, and M. Isler, "Freedomland Housing Development," October 19, 1964, CPC Goldstone, Subject Files, box 11, Municipal Archives, City of New York (hereafter cited as NYCMA).

9. There was a high temperature of fifty-five degrees, according to Weather Underground, Historical Weather, http://www.wunderground.com/history/airport/KLGA/1966/5/14/DailyHistory.html, accessed January 4, 2016.

10. Thomas W. Ennis, "15,500 Apartment Co-op to Rise in the Bronx," *NYT*, February 10, 1965; "Major Crime Up 52% in Subways; 9% Citywide," *NYT*, February 10, 1965.

11. John McNamara, "History of the Land That Becomes Co-op," written for Dollar Savings Bank, 1969, 1. The name of the Native American people in this region is contested. Historians originally referred to them as the Sinawoy, but more recently some have instead insisted that Weckquaeskeek is the proper term. For more on this controversy see Historic Pelham, http://historicpelham.blogspot.com/2014/01/there-were-no-native-americans-known-as.html.

12. Anthony Piccolo, "Anne Hutchinson: Puritan Rebel and Westchester Pioneer," *NYT*, October 7, 1990, WC33.

13. McNamara, "History of the Land."

14. Paul Nash, "Fantasia Bronxiana: Freedomland and Co-op City," *New York History*, 2001, 264. See also Molly Rosner, "Freedomland," Gotham Center for New York City History, February 1, 2017, https://www.gothamcenter.org/blog/freedomland.

15. Nash, "Fantasia Bronxiana," 266.

16. William Zeckendorf, with Edward McCreary, *Zeckendorf: The Autobiography of the Man Who Played a Real-Life Game of Monopoly and Won the Largest Real Estate Empire in History* (New York: Holt, Rinehart & Winston, 1970), 292.

17. UHF board meeting minutes, June 23, 1964, collection 6129, box 17, Kheel Center.

18. Cynthia Curran, "Administration of Subsidized Housing in New York State—Co-op City: A Case of the Largest Subsidized Cooperative Housing Development in the Nation" (PhD diss., New York University, 1978), 53.

19. Thomas W. Ennis, "Huge Bronx Co-op a Staggering Job," *NYT*, February 14, 1965, R1.

20. UHF board meeting, June 23, 1964, collection 6129, box 17, Kheel Center.

21. Curran, "Administration," 53.

22. Ostroff to UHF board, January 28, 1965, collection 6129, box 17, Kheel Center.

23. Jessor, "Comments on the Author's Text," *Progressive Architecture*, February 1970, 72.

24. Ennis, "Huge Bronx Co-op a Staggering Job."

25. Thomas W. Ennis, "15,500 Apartment Co-op to Rise in the Bronx," *NYT*, February 10, 1965. While this may have been true in 1965, several larger developments

in the Soviet Union and elsewhere had been constructed by the time Co-op City was completed in 1972.

26. Szold, Brandwen, etc., Lawyers for Riverbay, to NYC Board of Estimate, February 3, 1965, CPC Goldstone, box 11, NYCMA.

27. Ostroff to UHF board, January 28, 1965, collection 6129, box 17, Kheel Center.

28. Asbury, "Ground Broken for Bronx Co-ops."

29. Special meeting of the UHF board, September 17, 1965, collection 6129, box 17, Kheel Center.

30. J. Chanin, CPC Division of Public Improvements, Project Summary, August 17, 1964, CPC Goldstone, box 11, NYCMA.

31. Operational Planning Unit to R. K. Bernstein, J. C. Smith, M. Isler, October 19, 1964, CPC Goldstone, box 11, NYCMA.

32. Minutes of UHF board meeting, October 3, 1967, 3, collection 6129, box 17, Kheel Center.

33. "Remarks of Robert Moses," 3.

34. "Freedomland Housing Development (plan dated 11/16/64)," Charles Smith to Edward Friedman, November 24, 1964, CPC Goldstone, box 11, NYCMA. Emphasis in original.

35. William E. Farrell, "Architects Score Co-op City Design: Project Is Called Negation of 'Great Society' Ideals," NYT, February 20, 1965.

36. Steven V. Roberts, "Planners Accept Bronx Co-op City," NYT, May 13, 1965.

37. Giorgio Cavaglieri statement to the CPC, April 28, 1965, CPC Goldstone, box 11, NYCMA.

38. April 28, 1965, handwritten meeting notes, CPC Goldstone, box 11, NYCMA.

39. Ostroff statement to the CPC, April 28, 1965, CPC Goldstone, box 11, NYCMA.

40. "Please Tell Us," Co-op Contact, Winter 1966, 3.

41. Jessor quoted in Peter Eisenstadt, Rochdale Village: Robert Moses, 6,000 Families, and New York City's Great Experiment in Integrated Housing (Ithaca, NY: Cornell University Press, 2010), 127.

42. Ostroff quoted in Eisenstadt, Rochdale Village, 128.

43. William Farrell, "In Co-op City, the 'Pioneers' are Genial," NYT, November 9, 1969, R10.

44. Don Phillips, "It's Getting Close to That Time!," CCT, May 1968, 2.

45. Giorgio Cavaglieri statement, June 2, 1965, CPC Goldstone, box 11, NYCMA.

46. "Second Statement of the AIA to the CPC," June 2, 1965, CPC Goldstone, box 11, NYCMA.

47. See also Alison Isenberg, Downtown America: A History of the Place and the People Who Made It (Chicago: University of Chicago Press, 2005) on the long-standing idea of American small towns anchored by their downtowns.

48. Ostroff statement to the CPC, April 28, 1965, CPC Goldstone, box 11, NYCMA.

49. On Kazan versus Jacobs see Eisenstadt, Rochdale Village, 129.

50. Jane Jacobs, The Death and Life of Great American Cities (New York: Vintage, 1961), 50–51.

51. Harold Ostroff, "Even in the Center of the City They Can Be Individuals . . . ," Cooperative Housing, Spring 1966, 13.

52. Jacob Potofsky, Oral History Interview, August 4, 1970, 29–30, box 6, Roosevelt University Labor Oral History Project, Chicago.

53. "Building Cooperative Communities: New York's United Housing Foundation," *Lawyer's Title News*, June 1968, 9.

54. "A Cooperative from the Ground Up: That's What the United Housing Foundation Is Building in New York City," *Cooperative Housing*, Summer 1965, 11.

55. "People Often Ask," *CCT*, April 1967, 2.

56. Ostroff statement to the CPC, April 28, 1965, CPC Goldstone, box 11, NYCMA.

57. "A New Look at Townhouse Cooperatives," *Cooperative Housing*, Summer 1965, 12.

58. Richard Bernstein, "Freedomland. Preliminary Draft," November 13, 1964, 2, CPC Goldstone, box 11, NYCMA.

59. Operational Planning Unit, "Freedomland Housing Development," October 19, 1964, CPC Goldstone, box 11, NYCMA.

60. "Rent Subsidies Don't Apply to Co-op City, Commissioner Says in Letter to Mrs. Schiff," *CCT*, April 1967, 3.

61. CPC, Approval, May 12, 1965, CPC Goldstone, box 11, NYCMA.

62. CPC Approval, May 12, 1965, CPC Goldstone, box 11, NYCMA.

63. Letter from Ostroff to the UHF board, September 28, 1967, collection 6129, box 17, Kheel Center. The Amalgamated Bank was owned by the Amalgamated Clothing Workers Union and had close ties to the cooperative movement, including sponsoring the Amalgamated Cooperatives where Kazan got his start.

64. "14,700 Applications Made for Baychester Co-op Suites," *NYT*, March 21, 1965, R12.

65. "First Co-op City Applicants Selecting Their Apartments," *Co-operator*, April 1966, 3. If people made more than this they were allowed to move in but were subject to surcharges of up to 50 percent of the ordinary carrying charge rate.

66. "Visiting Applicants Office a Pleasant Experience, Notes Co-op Reporter," *CCT*, October 1967, 1.

67. Report of the Meeting of City Agencies and Other to Co-ordinate Programs, September 29, 1967, Co-op City files, Bronx County Historical Society.

68. Community Services Inc., meeting minutes, March 21, 1968, collection 6129, box 5, Kheel Center.

69. Vincent Cannato, *The Ungovernable City: John Lindsay and His Struggle to Save New York* (New York: Basic Books, 2001).

70. On Lindsay and race see Clarence Taylor, "Race, Rights, Empowerment," in *Summer in the City: John Lindsay, New York, and the American Dream*, ed. Joseph Viteritti (Baltimore: Johns Hopkins University Press, 2014), 61–80.

71. Paul Goldberger, "A Design Conscious Mayor: The Physical City," in Viteritti, *Summer in the City*, 139–62.

72. Ostroff CPC Statement, April 28, 1965, CPC Goldstone, box 11, NYCMA.

73. "Freedomland: Preliminary Cost-Benefit Analysis," November 24, 1964, CPC Goldstone, box 11, NYCMA.

74. Samuel Bleecker, *The Politics of Architecture: A Perspective on Nelson A. Rockefeller* (New York: Routledge, 1983), 112.

75. *CCT*, December 10, 1988, 2.

76. Roger Starr statement to CPC public hearing, April 28, 1965, CPC Goldstone, box 11, NYCMA.

77. CPC Approval, May 12, 1965, CPC Goldstone, box 11, NYCMA.

78. Robert Sweet (executive assistant to the mayor) to William Ballard, March 23, 1966, CPC Goldstone, box 11, NYCMA.

79. Evelyn Gonzalez, *The Bronx* (New York: Columbia University Press, 2004), 116.

80. Deborah Dash Moore, *At Home in America: Second Generation New York Jews* (New York: Columbia University Press, 1981), 76.

81. Constance Rosenblum, *Boulevard of Dreams: Heady Times, Heartbreak, and Hope along the Grand Concourse in the Bronx* (New York: NYU Press, 2009), 8. In 1957, approximately two-thirds of the Concourse neighborhood residents identified as Jewish. Jeffrey Gurock, *Jews in Gotham: New York Jews in a Changing City, 1920–2010* (New York: NYU Press, 2012), 120.

82. Moore, *At Home in America*, 61.

83. Isa Kapp quoted in Eli Lederhendler, *New York Jews and the Decline of Urban Ethnicity, 1950–1970* (Syracuse, NY: Syracuse University Press, 2001), 16.

84. Alfred Kazin, *Walker in the City* (New York: Harcourt, 1951), 12.

85. Rosenblum, *Boulevard of Dreams*, 92.

86. Gornick quoted in Gurock, *Jews in Gotham*, 111.

87. Gurock, 110.

88. Constance Rosenblum, *Boulevard of Dreams*, 168.

89. Moore, *At Home in America*, 76.

90. Rosenblum, *Boulevard of Dreams*, 181. See also Gonzalez, *Bronx*, chap. 7.

91. Rosenblum, *Boulevard of Dreams*, 177.

92. Jill Jonnes, *We're Still Here* (New York: Atlantic, 1986), 275.

93. Rosenblum, *Boulevard of Dreams*, 178.

94. Jonnes, *We're Still Here*, 273.

95. See Wendell Pritchett, *Brownsville Brooklyn: Blacks, Jews, and the Changing Face of the Ghetto* (Chicago: Chicago University Press, 2002).

96. Michael Greenberg and Thomas Boswell, "Neighborhood Deterioration as a Factor in Intraurban Migration: A Case Study in New York City," *Professional Geographer* 24, no. 1 (1972): 13.

97. Sachs Quality ad, *Daily News* (hereafter cited as *DN*), April 13, 1969, 63.

98. Roberta Brandes Gratz, *The Living City: How America's Cities Are Being Revitalized by Thinking Big in a Small Way* (New York: Wiley, 1994), 100.

99. This was the conclusion reached by a HUD study of the effect of Co-op City on the Bronx conducted by Lindon, Mields and Coston Inc. in 1972. Kenneth H. Brook, "A Defensive Community and Its Elderly Population" (PhD diss., New York University, 1974), 103.

100. Ben Schumann to Gus Tyler, ILGWU, n.d., collection 6129, box 6, Kheel Center.

101. Brook, "Defensive Community," 66.

102. UHF 1965 Annual Report, 7. While this was the 1965 Annual Report, it cited the May 14, 1966, groundbreaking, meaning it was written at least after that date.

103. Greenberg and Boswell, "Neighborhood Deterioration," 14.

104. Brook, "Defensive Community," 190. Spelling from original transcription.

105. Kitty Braun to Ostroff, n.d., collection 6129, box 6, Kheel Center.

106. Greenberg and Boswell, "Neighborhood Deterioration," 11.

107. Brook, "Defensive Community," 65. Brook does not provide a date for this study.

108. Greenberg and Boswell, "Neighborhood Deterioration," 14.

109. Rabinow Report from March 22, 1966, office visit, CPC Goldstone, box 11, NYCMA.

110. Robert Sweet to William Ballard, March 23, 1966, CPC Goldstone, box 11, NYCMA.

111. Steven V. Roberts, "Project for 6,000 Families Approved for Canarsie Site," NYT, June 28, 1967, 1.

112. Steven V. Roberts, "Grand Concourse: Hub of Bronx Is Undergoing Ethnic Changes," NYT, July 21, 1966, 39.

113. Sweet to Ballard, March 23, 1966, CPC Goldstone, box 11, NYCMA.

114. Roberts, "Grand Concourse," 39.

115. "Rockefeller Addresses 2,000 at Co-op City Groundbreaking," Cooperator, June 1966, 1.

116. Herman Badillo, "Opening Co-op City," New York Magazine, April 11, 1988, 63. On the association of cooperatives with Jews see also Matthew Lasner, High Life: Condo Living in the Suburban Century (New Haven, CT: Yale University Press, 2012), 97–98.

117. Harold Ostroff to board of UHF, September 29, 1966, collection 6129, box 17, Kheel Center.

118. Eisenstadt, Rochdale Village, 79.

119. Moon quoted in Eisenstadt, 80.

120. "Finns—Bohemians—Jews," Cooperator, April 1967, 4.

121. Lasner, High Life, 98.

122. Eisenstadt, Rochdale Village, 12.

123. For this entire, fascinating story see Eisenstadt, Rochdale Village.

124. Kazan quoted in Eisenstadt, 130–31.

125. Asbury, "Ground Broken for Bronx Co-ops."

126. Ostroff to Riverbay board, August 24, 1972, collection 6129, box 14, Kheel Center.

127. "First Co-op City Residents Selecting Their Apartments," Cooperator, April 1966, 3.

128. Julius Kaufman, letter to the editor, CCT, February 14, 1970, 2.

129. "Visiting Applications Office," CCT, October 1967, 1.

130. Harold Ostroff to board of UHF, September 29, 1966, collection 6129, box 17, Kheel Center.

131. Eden Ross Lipson to R. H. Nolte, May 19, 1969, http://www.icwa.org/wp-content/uploads/2015/10/ERL-19.pdf.

132. Steven V. Roberts, "Co-op City Blend of Races Sought," NYT, April 30, 1967, 31; Laura Vandes (Co-op NAACP president), letter to the editor, CCT, December 5, 1987, 6.

133. John Saul, "Co-op City: Regional Planning and Community Development," unpublished manuscript, 85.

134. Joseph Fried, "Debate Still Swirls around Co-op City," NYT, March 17, 1968, R6.

135. Sameth quoted in Saul, "Co-op City," 84.

136. Harold Ostroff, "What Is the Role of Management in Housing Cooperatives?," *Cooperative Housing*, Fall–Winter 1965, 16.

137. Roberts, ""Co-op City Blend."

138. Thomas W. Ennis, "Huge Bronx Co-op a Staggering Job," *NYT*, February 14, 1965, R1.

139. "Q&A," *CCT*, May 1968, 3.

140. "Applications Office," *CCT*, October 1967, 3.

141. I have been unable to ascertain how many families actually took advantage of these loans. In interviews and conversations with former residents I have not had a single family admit to having taken them.

142. Brian Purnell, Jeanne Theoharis, and Komozi Woodard, eds., *The Strange Careers of the Jim Crow North* (New York: NYU Press, 2019).

143. Roberts, "Co-op City Blend."

144. Saul, "Co-op City," 84. This quote comes from Lindsay's civil rights commissioner William Booth at an August 10, 1966, meeting to discuss Co-op City's impact on the Bronx.

145. Roberts, "Co-op City Blend."

146. James Patterson, *Brown v. Board of Education: A Civil Rights Milestone and Its Troubled Legacy* (New York: Oxford University Press, 2002).

147. Jerald Podair, *The Strike That Changed New York* (New Haven, CT: Yale University Press, 2002), 22. See also David Rogers, *110 Livingston Street: Politics and Bureaucracy in the New York City Schools* (New York: Columbia University Press, 1968), 15–35; Matthew Delmont, *Why Busing Failed: Race, Media, and the National Resistance to School Desegregation* (Berkeley: University of California Press, 2016), 23–53.

148. Eisenstadt, *Rochdale Village*, chap. 9.

149. Conde Corp., "A Report on the Education Park," 13, Board of Ed, series 385, box 9, NYCMA.

150. Conde Corp., "Report on the Education Park," 15.

151. See the letters collected in Board of Ed, series 385, box 9, NYCMA.

152. Ostroff to CSI board, June 17, 1968, collection 6129, box 5, Kheel Center; "Co-op City Lesson," *NYT*, September 21, 1968, 32.

153. Leonard Buder, "First Unit in 'Educational Park' System to Open Monday," *NYT*, September 11, 1971, 29.

154. Co-op City Policy Statement, *CCT*, April 24, 1971.

155. August Gold (School Planning and Research Division) to Adrian Blumenfeld, Program of Requirements—Northeast Bronx Educational Park, February 24, 1967, Board of Ed, series 385, box 9, NYCMA.

156. Board of Education informal meeting minutes, February 22, 1967, p. 2, Board of Ed, series 1011, NYCMA.

157. Brochure from the Board of Education about educational parks, untitled draft, December 1966, Board of Ed, series 385, box 9, NYCMA.

158. Board of Education informal meeting minutes, December 20, 1966, p. 1, Board of Ed, series 1011, NYCMA.

159. Co-op City ad in *NYT*, October 2, 1966.

160. Co-op City Policy Statement, *CCT*, April 24, 1971, 4.

161. Report of telephone conversation between William Ballard and William Booth, May 16, 1966, CPC Goldstone, box 11, NYCMA.

162. Ostroff to Board of Directors of Community Services, June 17, 1968, collection 6129, box 5, Kheel Center.

163. Ostroff to Ellicott, City Planning Division, June 5, 1968, collection 6129, box 5, Kheel Center.

164. Ostroff to Board of Directors of Community Services, June 17, 1968, collection 6129, box 5, Kheel Center.

165. Ostroff to Board of Directors of Community Services, June 17, 1968, collection 6129, box 5, Kheel Center.

166. Ostroff to Board of Directors of Community Services, September 16, 1968, collection 6129, box 5, Kheel Center.

167. Ostroff to Board of Directors of Community Services, September 18, 1969, collection 6129, box 5, Kheel Center.

168. Ostroff to Board of Directors of Community Services, September 18, 1969, collection 6129, box 5, Kheel Center.

169. Ostroff to CPC, December 7, 1968, Division of the Budget—Office of Rudy Rudko, RG 16569–92, box 5, New York State Archives, Albany (hereafter referred to as NYS Archives).

170. Curran, "Administration," 92–93.

171. Curran, 93.

172. Jack Newfield and Paul DuBrul, "How 50,000 Angry People Took Over Co-op City," *Planning*, July 1977, 27.

173. Jack Newfield and Paul DuBrul, *The Abuse of Power: The Permanent Government and the Fall of New York* (New York: Viking, 1977), 298. Mitchell was a lawyer and Lama an architect. Each got a suspiciously large share of the legal and architectural work on Mitchell-Lama projects.

174. Newfield and DuBrul, *Abuse of Power*, 299.

175. Richard Karp, "No Day of Reckoning: At Co-op City, Only the Taxpayers Are Still on the Hook," *Barron's*, July 25, 1977, 5.

176. Eisenstadt, *Rochdale Village*, 42.

177. Saul, "Co-op City."

178. Eisenstadt, *Rochdale Village*, 42.

179. Karp, "No Day of Reckoning," 5.

180. Newfield and DuBrul, *Abuse of Power*, 303.

181. Newfield and DuBrul, 302.

182. Newfield and DuBrul, 303.

183. Jack Newfield, "How Profiteering and Patronage Helped Create Co-op City's Crisis," *Village Voice*, November 24, 1975, 12.

184. "Community Services Operating Budget 1968," collection 6129, box 5, Kheel Center. For the calculation of the 2020 equivalent see https://www.in2013dollars.com/us/inflation/1968.

185. Newfield, "Profiteering and Patronage," 12.

186. Newfield, 12.

187. Newfield and DuBrul, *Abuse of Power*, 303.

188. OPU to R. K. Bernstein, J. C. Smith, M. Isler, Re: Freedomland Housing Development, October 19, 1965, 5, CPC Goldstone, box 11, NYCMA.

189. Ostroff to Board of Directors of Community Services, September 18, 1969, collection 6129, box 5, Kheel Center.

190. "Co-op Is Like a Family: It Must Live within Income or Find Additional Money," CCT, January 1969, 3.

191. Farrell, "Pioneers," R9.

192. See the following chapter, where I discuss the UHF's failed attempts to get more legislative relief.

193. "Director's Viewpoint: Bernard Cylich," CCT, June 16, 2012, 4; Bernard Cylich, interview with the author, February 27, 2020.

194. Joseph Fried, "Co-op City Weights Repair of Walls," NYT, August 15, 1973, 15.

195. Marcia Schneider, District 11 to Office of School Buildings, Board of Education, November 10, 1980, Board of Ed, series 1115, box 8, folder Community School District 11, NYCMA.

196. Charles Rosen, "Water, Water Everywhere . . . : Community in Crisis: Part II: History of CD Woes," CCT, September 22, 1990, 4.

197. Michael Danielson and Jameson Doig, New York: The Politics of Urban Regional Development (Berkeley: University of California Press, 1982), 275.

198. Ostroff to UHF board of directors, June 3, 1971, collection 6129, box 5, Kheel Center.

199. Ada Louise Huxtable, "A Singularly New York Product," NYT, November 25, 1968, 43.

200. Ulrich Franzen letter, Progressive Architecture, April 1970, 8.

201. "Kibbutz in the Bronx," Newsweek, October 5, 1970.

2. "Everyone Was Seeking a Utopia"

1. Richard Phalon, "Reasons for City's Slow Storm Cleanup Are Thick as the Snow," NYT, February 13, 1969, 37.

2. Phalon, 37.

3. Martin Arnold, "Snow Emergency Ends Here Today: Mayor Sees Refuse Pickup Normal Tomorrow Night," NYT, February 18, 1969, 81. See also "Snow Removal Breakdowns," NYT, February 18, 1969.

4. "Co-op City Residents Come to the Rescue! Hundreds Cared for during the Great Snow!," CCT, February 1969, 1.

5. "Co-op City Is . . ." CCT, May–June 1969, 1.

6. "Building 1 Residents Reminisce about Blizzard," CCT, February 7, 1970, 4.

7. "Co-op City Residents Come to the Rescue!," 2.

8. "Our Community Is on the Move," CCT, July 1967, 1. Emphasis in original.

9. Michael Kessler, "Initial Occupancy Period Closes as Last Family Moves In," CCT, March 25, 1972, 2.

10. "Streets," in Out of Bricks and Mortar: A Community (New York: Riverbay Corporation, n.d.), 13. Theodore Dreiser, Eugene Debs, Paul DeKruif, Daniel DeFoe, Charles Darrow, Gaetano Donezetti.

11. Kenneth H. Brook, "A Defensive Community and Its Elderly Population" (PhD diss., New York University, 1974), 70.

12. "Directory: Co-op City Shopping Center No. 1," *CCT*, January 1969, 3.

13. For a more comprehensive account of these figures see Brook, "Defensive Community," 83–84.

14. "Where Are Butchers, Bakers and Candlestick Makers?," *CCT*, April 4, 1970, 2; Brook, "Defensive Community," 94–96. Brook's numbers were drawn from an unpublished census of initial Co-op City residents conducted by the UHF in 1971. Brook (35) notes that shortly after he studied these records, they were lost. I have not been able to find these records myself.

15. Brook, "Defensive Community," 96.

16. "Where Are Butchers?"; Brook, "Defensive Community," 94–96.

17. "Where Are Butchers?," 2.

18. Brook, "Defensive Community," 89.

19. Brook, 90.

20. Bob Kappstatter and John Quinn, "Co-op City: Problems and Promise," *DN*, November 25, 1968, 48.

21. Brook, "Defensive Community," 99; Meriemil Rodriguez, "Problems Are Tough but Area Solves Them," *DN*, February 11, 1973, 1.

22. "New York—Race and Hispanic Origin for Selected Large Cities and Other Places: Earliest Census to 1990," https://www.census.gov/library/working-papers/2005/demo/POP-twps0076.html.

23. Brook, "Defensive Community," 99; Rodriguez, "Problems Are Tough."

24. Irving Rosenfeld, "The Possible Dream," *CCT*, December 8, 1973, 8.

25. Judith Perez, "'Movin' On Up': Pioneer African-American Families Living in an Integrated Neighborhood in the Bronx, New York," *Bronx County Historical Society Journal* 43 (Fall 2006): 76.

26. Perez, 76.

27. Greg Myers, interview with the author, July 25, 2018.

28. Sonia Sotomayor, *My Beloved World* (New York: Alfred A. Knopf, 2013), 99.

29. Felice Lifshitz, interview with the author, March 27, 2012; Josephine Finkelstein Acre, interview with the author, November 18, 2011.

30. Sotomayor, *Beloved World*, 100–101.

31. Acre interview.

32. Esther Benjamin, interview with the author, March 6, 2012.

33. Marc Bosyk, interview with the author, December 15, 2011.

34. Karen Benjamin, interview with the author, January 25, 2012.

35. Debra Genender, interview with the author, November 6, 2011.

36. Brook, "Defensive Community," 106.

37. Constance Rosenblum, *Boulevard of Dreams: Heady Times, Heartbreak, and Hope along the Grand Concourse in the Bronx* (New York: NYU Press, 2009), 206.

38. Sotomayor, *Beloved World*, 99.

39. Lynn Sjogren, interview with the author, November 22, 2011.

40. William E. Farrell, "In Co-op City, the 'Pioneers' Are Genial," *NYT*, November 9, 1969, R1.

41. Vera Donohue, "Meeting New Friends," *CCT*, September 20, 1969, 6.

42. Anne Sullivan, interview with the author, November 15, 2011.

43. James F. Clarity, "Co-op City, Home to 40,000, Is Given Tempered Praise," *NYT*, May 27, 1971, 41.

44. Matthew Lasner, *High Life: Condo Living in the Suburban Century* (New Haven, CT: Yale University Press, 2012), 150.

45. "A Cooperative from the Ground Up: That's What the United Housing Foundation Is Building in New York City," *Cooperative Housing*, Summer 1965, 11.

46. Minutes of the annual meeting of UHF, June 2, 1966, collection 6129, box 6, Kheel Center.

47. "United Housing Foundation," *Cooperative Housing*, Spring 1966, 7.

48. *Co-op Living: A Guide for Members*, n.d., Bronx County Historical Society, Co-op City vertical files.

49. Report of the Department of Co-operative Education and Activities, January 11, 1971, collection 6129, box 12, Kheel Center.

50. Don Phillips, "Co-op City: A New Community Is Being Born," *CCT*, March 1969, 3.

51. Letter to the editor, *CCT*, September 13, 1969.

52. Sotomayor, *Beloved World*, 100.

53. Genender interview.

54. K. Benjamin interview.

55. E. Benjamin interview.

56. Brook, "Defensive Community," 108.

57. Sullivan interview.

58. Brook, "Defensive Community," 74–75.

59. K. Benjamin interview.

60. "Coming Together the Cooperative Way: Its Origins, Development & Prospects," *New Leader*, April 17, 1972, 28.

61. Brook, "Defensive Community," 109.

62. Sjogren interview.

63. E. Benjamin interview.

64. Sullivan interview.

65. Sjogren interview.

66. Jack Newfield and Paul DuBrul, "How 50,000 Angry People Took Over Co-op City," *Planning Perspectives*, July 1977, 27.

67. Eric Goldstein, *The Price of Whiteness: Jews, Race, and American Identity* (Princeton, NJ: Princeton University Press, 2006), 196; and Deborah Dash Moore, *At Home in America: Second Generation New York Jews* (New York: Columbia University Press, 1981), 240.

68. Jeffrey Gurock, *Jews in Gotham: New York Jews in a Changing City, 1920–2010* (New York: NYU Press, 2012), 143–46. A number of books have examined the conservative turn among ethnic whites, including Jews, in outer-borough New York. See Jonathan Rieder, *Canarsie: Jews and Italians of Brooklyn against Liberalism* (Cambridge, MA: Harvard University Press, 1985), and Joshua Zeitz, *White Ethnic New York: Jews, Catholics, and the Shaping of Postwar Politics* (Chapel Hill: University of North Carolina Press, 2007). On the broader politics of "white ethnic" revival and racial backlash see Matthew Frye Jacobson, *Roots Too: White Ethnic Revival in Post–Civil Rights America* (Cambridge, MA: Harvard University Press, 2006), and Michael Staub, *Torn at the Root: The Crisis of Jewish Liberalism in Postwar America* (New York: Columbia University Press, 2002).

69. Rieder, *Canarsie*, 84.

70. Rieder.

71. It is useful here to compare Co-op City with Canarsie. Unlike the Jewish and Italian homeowners in Canarsie in South Brooklyn, who opposed even middle-class Blacks moving into their neighborhood, because of the fear that they would be followed by poorer Blacks, Co-op City's Jews welcomed middle-class Blacks. Rieder, *Canarsie*, 85.

72. Reggie quoted in Perez, "'Movin' On Up,'" 84. Section 8 subsidies were only introduced in 1974.

73. Bosyk interview.

74. There is a large literature that examines the institutional racism often hidden beneath the rhetoric of racial liberalism; see, among others, Ira Katznelson, *When Affirmative Action Was White: An Untold History of Racial Inequality in Twentieth-Century America* (New York: W. W. Norton, 2005); Karen Miller, *Managing Inequality: Northern Racial Liberalism in Interwar Detroit* (New York: NYU Press, 2014); Mary Poole, *The Segregated Origins of Social Security: African Americans and the Welfare State* (Chapel Hill: University of North Carolina Press, 2006); Richard Rothstein, *The Color of Law: A Forgotten History of How Our Government Segregated America* (New York: W. W. Norton, 2017); Matthew Delmont, *Why Busing Failed: Race, Media, and the National Resistance to School Desegregation* (Berkeley: University of California Press, 2016); Brian Purnell, Jeanne Theoharis, and Komozi Woodard, eds., *The Strange Careers of the Jim Crow North: Segregation and Struggle outside of the South* (New York: NYU Press, 2019).

75. Eli Lederhendler, *New York Jews and the Decline of Urban Ethnicity, 1950–1970* (Syracuse, NY: Syracuse University Press, 2001), 128.

76. Lederhendler, 129.

77. Clarity, "Co-op City, Home to 40,000."

78. Eden Ross Lipson to R. H. Nolte, May 19, 1969, http://www.icwa.org/wp-content/uploads/2015/10/ERL-19.pdf.

79. Perez, "'Movin' On Up.'"

80. Alison quoted in Perez, 75.

81. "Images of Co-op City—the Blacks," *CCT*, January 6, 1973, 4.

82. "Kibbutz in the Bronx," *Newsweek*, October 5, 1970, 90.

83. Sotomayor, *Beloved World*, 103.

84. Sotomayor, 100.

85. Ofonedu quoted in Perez, "'Movin' On Up,'" 76.

86. Sheldon quoted in Perez, 80.

87. Zoe Rosenberg, "New York Narratives: A Bronx Native on Why She's Disenchanted with NYC," Curbed New York, https://ny.curbed.com/2016/3/2/11137020/new-york-narratives-bronx-harlem-gentrification.

88. Bob quoted in Perez, "Movin' On Up,'" 83.

89. "Images of Co-op City—the Blacks."

90. Patrice quoted in Perez, "'Movin' On Up,'" 77.

91. Shirley quoted in Perez, 77.

92. "Images of Co-op City—the Blacks."

93. "Riverbay Gives Residents a Voice," *City News* (hereafter cited as *CN*), August 27, 1970, 1.

94. "Coming Together," 28.

95. "Election 'Racism' Charges; Riverbay President Replies," *CCT*, April 18, 1970, 3.

96. "Blacks Caucus at Co-op City," *CN*, September 11, 1969, 34.

97. Thomas G. Johnson, "The Black Caucus—Who Are We?," *CCT*, February 7, 1970, 8.

98. Johnson, "Black Caucus."

99. Matthew Countryman, *Up South: Civil Rights and Black Power in Philadelphia* (Philadelphia: University of Pennsylvania Press, 2006); Peniel E. Joseph, *Waiting 'Til the Midnight Hour: A Narrative History of Black Power in America* (New York: Henry Holt, 2006); Peniel E. Joseph, *Neighborhood Rebels: Black Power at the Local Level* (New York: Palgrave Macmillan, 2010); Brian Purnell, *Fighting Jim Crow in the County of Kings: The Congress of Racial Equality in Brooklyn* (Lexington: University Press of Kentucky, 2013), chap. 8; Rhonda Y. Williams, *The Politics of Public Housing: Black Women's Struggles against Urban Inequality* (New York: Oxford University Press, 2004).

100. "Council Seeks Representation for Minorities," *CN*, May 14, 1970, 26.

101. "A.C. Moves to Get Minority Groups," *CN*, May 21, 1970, 44.

102. "Leaders Discuss Co-op City," *CN*, April 2, 1970, 25.

103. William Swartz, "Marshall Studies Urban Life from Harlem to Co-op City," *CN*, May 19, 1970, 15.

104. "Council Seeks Representation for Minorities."

105. Julius Kaufman, letter to the editor, *CCT*, February 14, 1970, 2.

106. Editorial Board of the *CCT*, *CCT*, September 30, 1972, 25.

107. "Letter from E. Laufer to Editor," *CCT*, May 2, 1970, 4.

108. "Letter from Paul Leith to Editor," *CCT*, May 2, 1970, 5.

109. "A.C. Moves to Get Minority Groups," *CN*, May 21, 1970, 1.

110. Onnie Williams, "Black Caucus Meets Tuesday," *CCT*, September 18, 1971, 10; "Powell Center's First Community Report," *CCT*, December 16, 1972, 23.

111. Elva Mondesire, letter to the editor, *CCT*, April 18, 1970, 2.

112. Co-op advertisement, *NYT*, October 2, 1966, 360.

113. Co-op advertisement, *NYT*, October 2, 1966, 360.

114. Oscar Newman, *Defensible Space: Crime Prevention through Urban Design* (New York: Macmillan, 1973), 34.

115. Letter to the editor, *CCT*, October 18, 1969, 2.

116. Brooks, "Defensive Community," 89.

117. "Inquiring Photographer," *CN*, May 8, 1969, 18.

118. CSI special board meeting, March 8, 1966, collection 6129, box 6, Kheel Center; "Transportation Needs Explored by UHF," *CCT*, November 1, 1969, 1; "Monorail Proposed from CC to Subway," *CN*, October 22, 1970, 1; "Plan Hydroplanes for CC Commuters," *CN*, June 3, 1971, 1. To this day, there is no train line that directly connects Co-op City with the rest of the city.

119. "Transportation Needs," *CCT*, November 1, 1969, 1.

120. Rodriguez, "Problems Are Tough . . .," February 11, 1973, 1; "Community Says No to Overpass," *CCT*, January 20, 1973, 1.

121. "Q&A," *CCT*, May 1968, 3.

122. Joseph Lelyveld, "Neighborhoods: Baychester Racially Tense beneath Calm Veneer," *NYT*, September 15, 1969, 43.

123. "Project Raises Fear of Welfare Families," *CN*, July 31, 1969, 1.

124. Lelyveld, "Neighborhoods: Baychester Racially Tense," 43. Baychester had been one of the strongholds of Mario Procaccino's white ethnic backlash 1969 mayoral campaign.

125. "Crime in 45th Pct Jumps 34% in August; Assaults Up," *CN*, November 12, 1970, 6.

126. "Crime Up 39% in 45th Pct. Part of General Picture," *CN*, June 25, 1970, 2.

127. "Tenants Council Seeks Attorney to Audit CC," *CN*, March 19, 1970, 14.

128. Mary Morrison, letter to the editor, *CN*, October 16, 1969, 4.

129. *United Housing Foundation: Twenty Years of Accomplishment* (New York: United Housing Foundation, 1971), 21.

130. "Ad: It's a Young Family's World at Co-op City," *NYT*, November 12, 1967, 378; "Ad: If You Have Children, You Will Love the Wonderful New World of Co-op City," *NYT*, June 4, 1967, R9.

131. Letter from Adhoc Committee to Riverbay board, May 28, 1971, collection 6129, box 12, Kheel Center.

132. "'Co-op City Could Be a Disaster," *CN*, June 12, 1969, 47; "Saturday's Cleanup," *CN*, June 12, 1969, 4.

133. Harold Ostroff, "The Impact of Housing Cooperatives in Urban Areas. Speech from the National Association of Housing Cooperatives, February 19, 1966," *Co-op Contact*, Spring 1966, 19.

134. Brook, "Defensive Community," 91.

135. Brook, 5.

136. Letter from Adhoc Committee to Riverbay board, May 28, 1971.

137. K. Benjamin interview.

138. "Dear Sir, Help! Mr. Slick," *CN*, January 6, 1972, 38.

139. Ted Schaefer, "An Experiment between Generations," *CCT*, April 18, 1970, 5.

140. Sjogren interview.

141. John Guerini, "Co-op City Teens Clash with Elders," *CN*, September 4, 1969, 1.

142. A. Horowitz, letter to the editor, *CCT*, May 15, 1971, 17.

143. "Should Residents Sit in Front of Buildings?," *CCT*, August 8, 1970, 4 and 9.

144. Sam Fenster, quoted in "Should Residents Sit in Front of Buildings?," 4.

145. "News from the Advisory Council," *CCT*, January 27, 1973, 4.

146. "The Yesses and Noes of Grass and Shrubs," *CCT*, April 17, 1971, 5.

147. Jack Stryker, letter to the editor, *CN*, April 8, 1971, 10.

148. Brook, "Defensive Community," 109.

149. Schwartz, letter to the editor, *CCT*, May 9, 1970, 2.

150. Ernest Christiano, letter to the editor, *CCT*, June 12, 1971, 2.

151. Rae Schoenberg, letter to the editor, *CCT*, July 31, 1971, 21.

152. Lipson to Nolte, May 19, 1969.

153. Frank Morris, letter to the editor, *CCT*, July 15, 1972, 2.

154. Elba Cabrera, interview no. 289 by Tabitha Kirin, August 5, 1986, Bronx Institute Oral History Project, Special Collections, Leonard Lief Library, Lehman College, CUNY.

155. "Problems Aired at Open Forum," *CCT*, March 21, 1970, 1.

156. "Management to Give Security for Teens," *CN*, March 19, 1970, 1.

157. "Kibbutz in the Bronx."

158. "Problems Aired at Open Forum."

159. "Mrs. Schneider's Statement," *CCT*, November 3, 1973, 3.

160. Hispanic Community, "Images of Co-op City," *CCT*, December 2, 1972, 4.

161. "Images of Co-op City—the Blacks."

162. New York City Board of Education, *The Education Park: What Should It Be: Educational Specifications for the Northeast Bronx Education Park*, August 1966, 1; "Community Leaders Speak on Busing: Co-op City Policy Statement," *CCT*, April 24, 1971, 4.

163. "School Board Seeks Enrollment Advice," *CN*, March 4, 1971, 1.

164. "School Doors Open for 3,000 CC Kids," *CN*, September 10, 1970, 1. The most famous of these was the "Little Yellow Schoolhouse," a building later used by the College of New Rochelle, but other students were educated in rooms in Shopping Center 1.

165. "CQE Calls Meeting Tonight to Map Protest," *CN*, November 25, 1970, 16.

166. "Marshall Speaks Out on Education Budget," *CCT*, June 5, 1971, 4.

167. "CQE Calls Meeting Tonight to Map Protest," 20.

168. "Busing Ordered for CC Schools: 750 Out-of-District Students to Take Priority over Us," *CN*, April 15, 1971, 1. At the time of the order, District 11 would claim that their student population was 56 percent white and 44 percent minority.

169. Bruce Irushalmi, interview with the author, February 17, 2017.

170. "Busing Ordered for CC Schools," 18.

171. Board of Education informal meeting minutes, June 1, 1971, series 1011, NYCMA.

172. See Anker to CSB 11, January 12, 1977, series 1202, box 13, folder CSD District 11, NYCMA. Later in the decade, District 11 officials would resist the Board of Ed's demands for statistics about the integration of its schools.

173. "Claims Board of Ed Uses Scare Tactics," *CN*, April 15, 1971, 1.

174. On the strike and its impact on New York see Jerald Podair, *The Strike That Changed New York* (New Haven, CT: Yale University Press, 2002).

175. Cheryl Greenberg, *Troubling the Waters: Black-Jewish Relations in the American Century* (Princeton, NJ: Princeton University Press, 2006), 231.

176. Peter Eisenstadt, *Rochdale Village: Robert Moses, 6,000 Families, and New York City's Great Experiment in Integrated Housing* (Ithaca, NY: Cornell University Press, 2010), 192 and all of chapter 11. On the hostility of Jewish cooperators to school integration see also the story of a proposal to pair local schools in a majority Jewish Jackson Heights, Queens, cooperative with ones several blocks away in a poorer Black neighborhood that had provoked intense opposition from those who felt they had "worked hard to leave shabby and rundown ghetto[s]" and feared that the proposal would "spoil" their new community. Lasner, *High Life*, 153.

177. "School Chancellor Rescinds Orders to Bus in Students," *CCT*, October 9, 1971, 1.

178. Sullivan interview.

179. "Nesi Promises Seat for Every CC Child," *CN*, April 22, 1971.

180. "1,000 Tell Board: 'No Busing Here,'" *CN*, April 22, 1971, 1.

181. "School Committee States Opposition to Busing," *CN*, April 22, 1971, 2.

182. "Community Speaks on Busing Issue," *CCT*, April 17, 1971, 1.

183. CQE Statement on Racism, *CCT*, April 24, 1971, 4.

184. "1,000 Tell Board," 48.

185. Joseph Laznow, letter to the editor, *CCT*, April 17, 1971, 2.

186. "1,000 Tell Board," 48.

187. Dorothy Hopkins statement, *CCT*, April 24, 1971, 1.

188. "1,000 Tell Board," 48.

189. "1,000 Tell Board."

190. "1,000 Tell Board."

191. "1,000 Tell Board."

192. "1,000 Tell Board."

193. Matthew F. Delmont, *Why Busing Failed: Race, Media, and the National Resistance to School Desegregation* (Berkeley: University of California Press, 2016). See also J. Anthony Lukas, *Common Ground: A Turbulent Decade in the Lives of Three American Families* (New York: Vintage, 1986); Thomas Sugrue, *Sweet Land of Liberty: The Forgotten Struggle for Civil Rights in the North* (New York: Random House, 2008), chap. 13; Rieder, *Canarsie*, chap. 7.

194. Perez, "'Movin' On Up.'"

195. "Scribner Issues New Order on School Busing," *CCT*, May 1, 1971, 1.

196. Board of Education informal meeting minutes, June 1, 1971, series 1011, NYCMA.

197. Board of Education informal meeting minutes, June 8, 1971, series 1011, NYCMA.

198. "School Chancellor Rescinds Orders."

199. Jerry Israel, "H.S. Super Integration Charges Answered by S.B. 11 Chairman," *CCT*, April 28, 1973, 27. The exact number that would constitute such a "tipping point" was not mentioned.

200. Joshua B. Freeman, *Working Class New York: Life and Labor since World War II* (New York: New Press, 2000), 116.

201. William Swartz, "Don Believes in People Who Need People," *CN*, August 13, 1970, 6.

3. "We Remember Picket Lines"

1. Abraham Kazan, "Cooperative Housing in the United States," *Annals of the American Academy of Political and Social Science* 191, no. 1 (1937): 143.

2. Kazan, 137–38.

3. Kazan, 143.

4. "Ostroff Advices Increase Pending State," *CCT*, March 22, 1975, 1.

5. "Thousands Gather to Boost Strike," *CCT*, February 14, 1976, 1.

6. Barbara Selvin, "A Towering Presence," *New York Newsday*, September 7, 1991.

7. "CC Tempers Cool, Heat's Off Merritt," *CN*, June 26, 1969, 1.

8. "Oshins Says: 'Parents Have Good Reason to Be Angry,'" *CN*, September 11, 1969, 1.

9. "Future Section Two Residents Blame Management for Delay," *CN*, June 18, 1970, 2.

10. Robert Fogelson, *The Great Rent Wars: New York, 1917–1929* (New Haven, CT: Yale University Press, 2013), 59–61.

11. Fogelson, 86.

12. Brian Purnell, *Fighting Jim Crow in the County of Kings: The Congress of Racial Equality in Brooklyn* (Lexington: University Press of Kentucky, 2013), 242–43.

13. Roberta Gold, *When Tenants Claimed the City: The Struggle for Citizenship in New York City Housing* (Champaign Urbana: University of Illinois Press, 2014), 114.

14. Peter Eisenstadt, *Rochdale Village: Robert Moses, 6,000 Families, and New York City's Great Experiment in Integrated Housing* (Ithaca, NY: Cornell University Press, 2010), 225.

15. "CC Tenants Council Not Needed: UHF," *CN*, January 29, 1970, 1, 29.

16. "A Look at 16.1% Increase," *CN*, May 21, 1970, 5. This article is a copy of a brief submitted by Gerald Halpern, lawyer for the Tenants Council, to the State Housing Agency to protest the planned carrying charge increase.

17. "CC Director Says: 'They Treat Us Like Children,'" *CN*, January 28, 1971, 1.

18. "CC Tenants Council Not Needed," 1, 29.

19. Irving Rosenfeld, "Dream or Nightmare?," *CCT*, July 29, 1972, 19, 24; "Abraham E. Kazan Dies at 82; Master Co-op Housing Builder," *NYT*, December 22, 1971, 38.

20. "Occupancy Sped Up to Cut $$ Losses," *CN*, August 6, 1970, 1.

21. "How Co-op City Rents Vary 75%," *CN*, April 15, 1971, 1.

22. "Wide Variation in Rental Fees between CC's Sections," *CN*, July 29, 1971, 15.

23. Judith Perez, "'Movin' On Up': Pioneer African-American Families Living in an Integrated Neighborhood in the Bronx, New York," *Bronx County Historical Society Journal* 43 (Fall 2006): 76.

24. "Rent Increase Possible in Early 1973—Ostroff," *CN*, March 25, 1971, 1.

25. "Ostroff Makes Points," *CN*, July 1, 1971, 40.

26. Ostroff to UHF board, June 3, 1971, collection 6129, box 5, Kheel Center.

27. Cynthia Curran, "Administration of Subsidized Housing in New York State—Co-op City: A Case of the Largest Subsidized Cooperative Housing Development in the Nation" (PhD diss., New York University, 1978), 106–7. See appendix table 1 for Co-op City development cost increases, from a 1978 New York State audit.

28. Curran, 110.

29. Curran, 107–9.

30. "Rent Injunction Asked for CC," *CN*, February 8, 1972, 1.

31. Curran, "Administration," 111.

32. "Rent Increase Possible in Early 1973."

33. "Board Meeting Draws 500," *CCT*, December 15, 1973, 1.

34. "Fuel Savings Box Score," *CCT*, December 15, 1972.

35. "Plan Rent Picket against UHF Exec," *CN*, September 9, 1971, 22.

36. "An Open Letter from Ostroff," *CCT*, July 31, 1971, 1.

37. Budget Committee to Riverbay board, June 22, 1971, collection 6129, box 12, Kheel Center.

38. UHF 1973 Annual Report, 1.

39. UHF Annual Meeting minutes, April 24, 1971, collection 61929, box 5, Kheel Center.

40. Board of Directors of Community Services, meeting January 6, 1972, p. 2, collection 6129, box 5, Kheel Center.

41. "A Master Plan for Jersey City," August 27, 1972, collection 6129, box 5, Kheel Center.

42. Community Services, regular board meeting, May 22, 1974, collection 6129, box 17, Kheel Center. For more on how construction loans were used to subsidize operating expenses and carrying charges see Curran, "Administration," 107–10.

43. Bob Varasano, "Inter-Community Relations Committee," CCT, August 14, 1971, 5.

44. "Senior Citizens March on State Legislature," CCT, March 25, 1972, 1.

45. Ostroff to UHF board, September 13, 1973, collection 6129, box 5, Kheel Center; "'Cooperators' Spark Legislative Campaign," CCT, January 27, 1973, 5.

46. Ostroff to Wilson, September 9, 1974, Wilson 1974, reel 27, NYS Archives.

47. Ostroff to Riverbay board, June 18, 1974, collection 6129, box 17, Kheel Center.

48. Minutes, regular meeting board of directors, CSI, July 11, 1972, collection 6129, box 5, Kheel Center.

49. Edward Aronov, "From the Executive Manager," CCT, June 17, 1972, 3.

50. "Urstadt Writes Resident to Support Rent Hike," CN, August 19, 1971, 8.

51. "Conversation with Urstadt: Explains Role of State in Approving Rent Hike," CN, September 16, 1971, 1.

52. "Urstadt Writes Resident to Support Rent Hike."

53. Steven Weisman, "Mitchell-Lama Housing Periled," NYT, December 27, 1970, 48.

54. Steven Weisman, "City Housing Program Still in 'Crisis,'" NYT, October 8, 1972, 14.

55. Betty Romoff, letter to the editor, CCT, July 10, 1971, 6. Emphasis in original.

56. Aronov, "From the Executive Manager."

57. Kenneth H. Brook, "A Defensive Community and Its Elderly Population" (PhD diss., New York University, 1974), 111.

58. On the vulnerability of the middle class (especially middle-class ethnic whites) in this period see Jonathan Rieder, Canarsie: Jews and Italians of Brooklyn against Liberalism (Cambridge, MA: Harvard University Press, 1985).

59. "Coalition Formed: Fight Rent Hike," CN, September 16, 1971, 34.

60. "Ostroff 'Loses His Cool' during Heated Town Hall Meeting," CN, September 16, 1971, 52.

61. "Ostroff 'Loses His Cool.'"

62. Meyer Bernstein, letter to the editor, CCT, May 20, 1972, 14.

63. Lorraine Holtz, letter to the editor, CCT, August 18, 1973, 2.

64. "Ostroff 'Loses His Cool.'"

65. "Link UHF to Profiteering," CN, October 21, 1971, 1.

66. "Says Cracks in Wall Loom as Big $ Problem," CN, October 28, 1971, 1.

67. "OK's Profiteering; Denies Wrongdoing," CN, December 16, 1971, 1.

68. Michael Sicilian, "I'm Sorry, But . . .," CCT, August 14, 1971, 3.

69. Betty Romoff, letter to the editor, CCT, July 10, 1971, 6. Emphasis in original.

70. "Advisory Council President Addresses Tenants Council," CCT, July 10, 1971, 9.

71. Vivian Gornick, "Can the Rent Strikers Beat the Establishment at Co-op City?," Village Voice, November 24, 1975, 12.

72. Minutes, regular board meeting CSI, September 7, 1972, p. 4, collection 6129, Kheel Center.

73. Minutes, regular board meeting CSI, September 7, 1972.

74. "'Cooperators for Co-op City' Is Formed," *CCT*, October 7, 1972, 9.

75. "Cooperators Beware!," *CCT*, October 21, 1972, 4.

76. "AC Collects $14,373: Hopes for Lots More," *CCT*, October 16, 1971, 1.

77. "AC Retains Louis Nizer," *CCT*, November 6, 1971, 1.

78. "Nizer Walks Out," *CCT*, April 22, 1972, 8.

79. "Summary of Law Suit Charges," *CCT*, September 23, 1972, 3.

80. "Rent Rally Draws 2000 & Politicos," *CCT*, November 3, 1973, 1.

81. "AC Hears Oratofsky Urge Demonstration," *CCT*, July 24, 1971, 1.

82. Steering Committees I and II had been formed earlier to fight carrying charge increases, but each collapsed for now unremembered reasons.

83. "Rent Strike Group Moves Forward; Abrams, Dolnick Elected to Lead," *CN*, July 18, 1974, 2; "Steering Unit Sets 'Test' of Rent Strike," *CN*, July 25, 1974, 1. Steering Committees I and II were each short-lived groups about which I could find no records.

84. "Politicians Pledge Their Support for Goals of Steering Committee," *CN*, August 8, 1974, 14.

85. "Assail Ostroff on Fiscal Plan," *CN*, August 8, 1974, 1, 20.

86. "State Calls Rent Hike Only Solution: Riverbay Board Could Vote on Rent Increase in September," *CN*, August 22, 1974, 1.

87. Al Abrams, Seymour Goldberg, Murray Lerner, Lawrence Sivak, and Arthur Taub to Wilson, July 25, 1974, Wilson 1974, reel 27, NYS Archives. Emphasis in original.

88. Wilson to Abrams, August 19, 1974, Wilson 1974, reel 27, NYS Archives.

89. "Rent Collection Hits 85% Mark. Residents Give $3M to Steering Committee," *CN*, September 12, 32.

90. "Quotation of the Week," *CN*, September 12, 1974, 2.

91. Ostroff to Wilson, September 9, 1974, Wilson 1974, reel 27, NYS Archives.

92. Wilson to Ostroff, September 19, 1974, Wilson 1974, reel 27, NYS Archives.

93. "Eye Next Step: A 'Rent Strike,'" *CN*, September 19, 1974, 1.

94. Allan Siegel, "For Voters in Co-op City, Rent Is a Primary Issue," *NYT*, September 6, 1974, 1, 38. On the switch of voters from Howard Samuels to Carey see Curran, "Administration," 127–28.

95. "Carey's Vote in Co-op Led Borough and City," *CN*, November 14, 1974, 2.

96. "Rent Strike Move Boosted Here," *CN*, November 28, 1974, 1.

97. George Schechter, "Co-op City Growing Up," *CCT*, December 21, 1974, 3.

98. Charles Parness, "Why We Resist," *CCT*, May 3, 1975, 5.

99. UHF regular board meeting, September 12, 1974, collection 6129, box 17, Kheel Center.

4. "No Way, We Won't Pay"

1. "Rosen Says No Local Family Will Be Evicted in Rent Strike," *CN*, June 5, 1975, 25.

2. David Medina, "Co-op City Rent Strike Is Backed," *DN*, May 29, 1975, 5.

3. Robert Bailey, *The Crisis Regime: The MAC, the EFCB, and the Political Impact of the New York City Financial Crisis* (Albany: SUNY Press, 1985); Ester Fuchs, *Mayors and Money: Fiscal Policy in New York and Chicago* (Chicago: University of Chicago Press, 1992); Charles Brecher, Raymond Horton, et al., *Mayors and Money: Power Failure: New York City Power and Politics since 1960* (New York: Oxford University Press, 1993); Eric Lichten, *Class, Power and Austerity: The New York City Fiscal Crisis* (South Hadley, MA: Bergin & Garvey, 1986); John Mollenkopf, *A Phoenix in the Ashes: The Rise and Fall of the Koch Coalition in New York City Politics* (Princeton, NJ: Princeton University Press, 1994); Kim Moody, *From Welfare State to Real Estate: Regime Change in New York City, 1974 to the Present* (New York: New Press, 2007); Jack Newfield and Paul DuBrul, *The Abuse of Power: The Permanent Government and the Fall of New York* (New York: Penguin Books, 1978); Kim Phillips-Fein, *Fear City: New York's Fiscal Crisis and the Rise of Austerity Politics* (New York: Metropolitan Books, 2017); Martin Shefter, *Political Crisis/Fiscal Crisis: The Collapse and Revival of New York City* (New York: Basic Books, 1985); Jonathan Soffer, *Ed Koch and the Rebuilding of New York City* (New York: Columbia University Press, 2010); William Tabb, *The Long Default: New York City and the Urban Fiscal Crisis* (New York: Monthly Review, 1982).

4. Joseph Fried, "Co-op City Issue: Subsidized Middle Income Housing," *NYT*, August 12, 1975, 27.

5. Cynthia Curran, "Administration of Subsidized Housing in New York State—Co-op City: A Case of the Largest Subsidized Cooperative Housing Development in the Nation" (PhD diss., New York University, 1978), 35.

6. Phillips-Fein, *Fear City*, 205–55.

7. Newfield and DuBrul, *Abuse of Power*, 304.

8. "Say Good Riddance to Ostroff and UHF," *CN*, June 5, 1975, 32.

9. "Rent Collection Hits 85% Mark. Residents Give $3M to Steering Committee," *CN*, April 7, 1975, 1.

10. "CC Steering Committee Chairman Defends Methods of Operation," *CN*, April 2, 1975, 26.

11. Vivian Gornick, "Can the Rent Strikers Beat the Establishment at Co-op City?," *Village Voice*, November 24, 1975, 11.

12. William Liblick, "Residents Hail Settlement, Support Steering Committee," *CN*, July 8, 1976, 1.

13. "Al Abrams Steps Down as Steering Unit Head," *CN*, January 23, 1975, 1.

14. Ian Frazier, "Utopia, the Bronx: Co-op City and Its People," *New Yorker*, June 26, 2006.

15. Newfield and DuBrul, *Abuse of Power*, 303–4.

16. Joe Klein, "The Temporary Hero of Co-op City," *Rolling Stone*, October 6, 1977.

17. Marge and Steve Glusker, letters to the editor, *CCT*, April 19, 1975, 27.

18. Sewell Chan, "Bronx Odyssey: From Rebel to Executive to Felon," *NYT*, October 10, 2006, B1.

19. Klein, "Temporary Hero of Co-op City."

20. Jeffrey Gurock, *Jews in Gotham: New York Jews in a Changing City, 1920–2010* (New York: NYU Press, 2012), 54.

21. Irving Howe, *World of Our Fathers: The Journey of the Eastern European Jews to America and the Life They Found and Made* (New York: Galahad Books, 1994), 289.

22. Klein, "Temporary Hero of Co-op City."

23. Benjamin and Norma Cirlin, interview with the author, December 27, 2017.

24. Gornick, "Can the Rent Strikers Beat the Establishment?"

25. Benjamin and Norma Cirlin interview.

26. Charles Rosen, "Steering Committee III Reports," CCT, March 15, 1975, 8.

27. "Strike Only Way to Push M-L Bills," CN, March 20, 1975, 1.

28. "Steering Committee Statement," CN, February 6, 1975, 36.

29. Newfield and DuBrul, Abuse of Power, 304.

30. Robert Freidman, "Mieterstreik in New York," in trend 2013, http://www.trend.infopartisan.net/trd0113/t110113.html. Translation by author.

31. Benjamin and Norma Cirlin interview; "Groups Form to Organize for Rent Strike," CN, February 27, 1975, 1, 7.

32. "Groups Form to Organize for Rent Strike," 7.

33. "From the Executive Manager," CCT, March 15, 1975, 1.

34. "Strike Only Way to Push M-L Bills."

35. Aronov to Carey, January 31, 1975; Fred Lzinsky to Carey, February 9, 1975: both in Carey 1975–78, reel 102, NYS Archives. Ostroff to Riverbay board, February 21, 1975, collection 6129, UHF box 17, Kheel Center.

36. "Rent Strike to Start June 1; Move to Pay Essential Bills," CN, May 29, 1975, 29.

37. Aronov to Carey, January 31, 1975; Fred Lzinsky to Carey, February 9, 1975: both in Carey 1975–78, reel 102, NYS Archives. Ostroff to Riverbay board, February 21, 1975, collection 6129, UHF box 17, Kheel Center.

38. "'Save Our Homes' Tell Residents Subcommittee," CN, April 10, 1975, 34.

39. "Action Delayed on Mortgage Bill," CN, April 24, 1975, 1.

40. Although in order to cover the retroactive increase, carrying charges would temporarily be raised to $56.88 per room.

41. "Audit Report on Co-op City (Report A) Interim Report No. 4 on New York State Mitchell-Lama Program," Report No. NY-Auth-12–76 (filed November 3, 1976), 6.

42. "Resident Directors Resign; Rent Collection to Start," CN, May 1, 1975, 1.

43. "Residents Blast Rent Increase Vote; Support Resigning Board Members," CN, May 1, 1975, 2.

44. Rosen letter to Carey, reprinted in CN, May 8, 1975, 8.

45. "Carey Pledges Effort to Pass M-L Bills," CN, May 15, 1975, 1.

46. Harold Ostroff, "Message from the President," CCT, March 22, 1975, 3.

47. "Ostroff Attempt to Frighten CC Called 'UHF Campaign of Fear,'" CN, May 8, 1975, 1.

48. "How to Cope with a $392 Monthly Rent," CN, May 15, 1975, 1.

49. "Rent Strike Called Here. Steering Group to Insure Essential Bills Are Paid," CN, May 22, 1975, 1.

50. "Steering Committee Explains Position on Rent Strike," CN, May 22, 1975, 32. Because the increase was retroactive to April, it was in fact 33 percent rather than 25 percent as originally requested.

51. "Rent Strike to Start June 1; Move to Pay Essential Bills," CN, May 29, 1979, 1.

52. Benjamin Cirlin, follow-up discussion with author, July 9, 2020.

53. Vivian Gornick, "Can the Rent Strikers Beat the Establishment?," 11–12; Newfield and DuBrul, *Abuse of Power*, 307; "Steering Committee Centers," *CCT*, June 21, 1975, 5.

54. Sharon and Charles Landsberg, letter to the editor, *CCT*, August 9, 1975, 2.

55. Freidman, "Mieterstreik in New York."

56. "Challenge State Take-Over; UHF Directors Resign," *CN*, June 5, 1975, 1.

57. UHF regular board meeting, June 12, 1975, collection 6129, box 17, Kheel Archive.

58. UHF regular board meeting, June 12, 1975.

59. "Say Good Riddance to Ostroff and UHF," *CN*, June 5, 1975, 32.

60. "Rosen Says No Local Family Will Be Evicted in Rent Strike," *CN*, June 5, 1975, 35.

61. "Rosen Says No Local Family Will Be Evicted."

62. "Co-op City Managers Move to Halt the Strike," *New York Post*, June 12, 1975.

63. Curran, "Administration," 24.

64. "Co-op City Managers Move to Halt the Strike," *New York Post*, June 12, 1975.

65. Suzanne McAllister to Robert Morgando, June 19, 1975, Carey 1975–78, reel 101, NYS Archives.

66. Hilary Botein, "'Solid Evidence of Union's Present Status': Unions and Housing in Postwar New York" (PhD diss., Columbia University, 2005), 165.

67. Botein, 166; Yonah Freemark," Roosevelt Island: Exception to a City in Crisis," *Journal of Urban History* 37, no. 3 (2011): 370.

68. Joshua B. Freeman, *Working-Class New York: Life and Labor since World War II* (New York: New Press, 2000), 262.

69. Freeman, 259.

70. Freeman, 259.

71. Suzanne McAllister to Robert Morganda / Walter Kicinski, September 25, 1975, Carey 1975–78, reel 102, NYS Archives.

72. Murray Schumach, "Co-op City: A Symptom of Mitchell-Lama Ills," *NYT*, June 18, 1975, 53.

73. Robert Tomasson, "Co-op City Gets a Rent Warning," *NYT*, June 4, 1975, 43.

74. Herbert Freedman to Goodwin, June 6, 1975, Carey 1975–78, Housing, reel 102, NYS Archives.

75. Bernstein to Carey, June 30, 1975, Carey 1975–78, Housing, reel 102, NYS Archives.

76. Jerome Glanzrock to Carey, July 7, 1975; Bernstein to Carey, July 8, 1975; Rosen to Carey, July 8, 1975; Carey to Rosen, May 9, 1975; Bernstein to Carey, July 16, 1975; Hochberg to Carey, August 5, 1975: all in Carey 1975–78, Housing, reel 102, NYS Archives.

77. Carey to Earle McField, June 24, 1975, Carey 1975–78, Housing, reel 102, NYS Archives; "Again! Carey Breaks Pledge to Meet Us," *CN*, February 12, 1976, 1.

78. St. Clair Bourne to David Burke, June 18, 1975, Carey 1975–78, Housing, reel 102, NYS Archives.

79. Murray Schumach, "Co-op City: A Symptom of Mitchell-Lama Ills," *NYT*, June 18, 1975, 43.

80. Infantino letter to all cooperators, August 1, 1975, Carey 1975–78, Housing, reel 102, NYS Archives.

81. DHCR press release, August 4, 1975, Carey 1975–78, Housing, reel 102, NYS Archives.

82. Newfield and DuBrul, *Abuse of Power*, 308.

83. "Strike Leaders Face Jail Time," *CN*, November 13, 1975, 1, 26.

84. Benjamin and Norma Cirlin interview.

85. Michael Horowitz, "Strikers Vow to Resist Court," *CN*, December 30, 1975, 1.

86. "State Grabs Strike Leaders' $, Moves to Stop Bldg. Captains," *CN*, January 8, 1976, 1.

87. Michael Horowitz, "HFA Raises Threat of Mass Evictions," *CN*, November 6, 1975, 1.

88. "Move to Collect $5M Held by Residents," *CN*, October 9, 1975, 1.

89. Terry Raskyn, "Near ½ Co-op City Staff Laid Off," *CN*, January 17, 1976.

90. Newfield and DuBrul, *Abuse of Power*, 308.

91. "State Moves to Foreclose Mortgage on Co-op City," *NYT*, August 5, 1975, 1.

92. "Doing Her Part in Rent Strike," *CN*, June 5, 1975, 1.

93. "Residents Show No Fear of State Foreclosure," *CN*, August 14, 1975, 3.

94. "Spouses of Leaders Ignore Subpoenas," *CN*, January 22, 1976, 31.

95. William Liblick, "Residents Say Huge Fines Won't Stop Rent Strike," *CN*, December 30, 1975, 6.

96. Michael Horowitz, "Appeal Planned Following Fines," *CN*, December 30, 1975, 27.

97. William Liblick, "Residents Stick to Guns in Stands on Rent Hike," *CN*, January 22, 1976, 2.

98. Liblick, "Residents Say Huge Fines Won't Stop Rent Strike."

99. David Friedman, letter to the editor, *CN*, January 22, 1976, 29.

100. Beatrice Safran to Carey, August 19, 1975, Carey 1975–78, Housing, reel 102, NYS Archives.

101. Rosen letter in *NYT*, January 21, 1976, 34.

102. Sandy Satterwhite and Peter Keepnews, "Contempt Trial Resuming in Co-op City Strike," *New York Post*, October 8, 1975; "5,000 Show Support at Court," *CN*, October 9, 1975.

103. Benjamin and Norma Cirlin interview.

104. "Strikers to Keep $5M in Rents," *CN*, October 2, 1975, 26.

105. William Liblick, "Residents Organize to Clean, Patrol CC," *CN*, January 29, 1976, 1, 30.

106. Erika Teutsch to David Burke and Bob Morgando, January 12, 1976, Carey 1975–78, Housing, reel 102, NYS Archives.

107. William Liblick, "Rosen Reveals Secret Discussions with Cuomo," *CN*, January 8, 1976, 33.

108. Gornick, "Can the Rent Strikers Beat the Establishment?," 12.

109. Gornick, 12.

110. Klein, "The Temporary Hero of Co-op City."

111. Lionel Goetz to Rosen, January 19, 1976, Carey 1975–78, Housing, reel 102, NYS Archives.

112. Gornick, "Can the Rent Strikers Beat the Establishment?," 12.

113. Robert Garrett, "Tenants vs the State: The Battle of Co-op City," *New York Post*, January 31, 1975, 23.

114. "Strikers to Keep $5M in Rents," *CN*, October 2, 1975, 1.

115. Michael Horowitz, "HFA Head Calls Strikers 'Selfish,'" *CN*, December 4, 1975, 1.

116. Roger Starr, "Open Letter to Charles Rosen," *CN*, December 11, 1975, 40.

117. Yetta Weinstein, letter to the editor, *CN*, January 15, 1976, 22.

118. Friedman, "Mieterstreik in New York."

119. Barbara Margolis, dir., *On the Line* (1977).

120. Margolis, *On the Line*.

121. Letter to the editor in response to "Open Letter to Charles Rosen," *CN*, December 11, 1975, 40.

122. E. Scharfenberg, "A Rebuttal," *CCT*, February 28, 1976; See also Charles Rosen, "Year End Report: Strikers Winning," *CN*, December 18, 1975, 1, 20.

123. "Rosen Says He Opposes Violence in Rent Strike," *CN*, August 21, 1975; "Schechter Says: Arranged Meeting for 'Common Sense,'" *CN*, November 20, 1975, 34.

124. Michael Agovino, *The Bookmaker: A Memoir of Money, Luck, and Family from the Utopian Outskirts of New York City* (New York: HarperCollins, 2008), 142.

125. Agovino, 143; "Rosen Says He Opposes Violence in Rent Strike."

126. "Caught in Lie: Kaufman Paid Rent Monthly While Supporting Strike," *CN*, August 14, 1975, 1; "Local Reaction: 'He Lied to Us,'" *CN*, September 4, 1975, 1.

127. Co-op Steering Committee III to New Democratic Club of Co-op City, February 2, 1976, Co-op City vertical file, 5.3 3, Bronx County Historical Society. At the same time, the strike leadership itself refused to run for office "to guarantee that all their efforts will be directed only in rent strike activities." Co-op City Steering Committee III notice in *CN*, December 23, 1975, 5.

128. Newfield and DuBrul, *Abuse of Power*, 309–10.

129. There is a rich literature on tenant activism in New York. See Roberta Gold, *When Tenants Claimed the City: The Struggle for Citizenship in New York City Housing* (Urbana-Champaign: University of Illinois Press, 2014); Freeman, *Working-Class New York*; Jared Day, *Urban Castles: Tenement Housing and Landlord Activism in New York, 1890–1943* (New York: Columbia University Press, 1999); Ronald Lawson and Mark Naison, eds., *The Tenant Movement in New York City, 1904–1984* (New Brunswick, NJ: Rutgers University Press, 1986); Robert Fogelson, *The Great Rent Wars: New York, 1917–1929* (New Haven, CT: Yale University Press, 2013).

130. Gold, *When Tenants Claimed the City*, chap. 6.

131. "Steering Unit Sets 'Test' of Rent Strike," *CN*, July 25, 1974, 36. Steering Committees I and II were each short-lived groups about which I could find no records. The rent strike in Rochdale was supported by only a minority of residents and ended after a few months. Peter Eisenstadt, *Rochdale Village: Robert Moses, 6,000 Families, and New York City's Great Experiment in Integrated Housing* (Ithaca, NY: Cornell University Press, 2010), 228.

132. "$3M in August Rents Delivered to HFA," *CN*, August 14, 1975, 2.

133. "City Wide Tenants Unite to Support Co-op City," press release, January 9, 1876, Carey 1975–78, Housing, reel 102, NYS Archives.

134. "$3M in August Rents Delivered to HFA," *CN*, August 14, 1975, 2; Erika Teutsch to David Burke and Bob Morgando, January 12, 1976, Carey 1975–78, Housing, reel 102, NYS Archives.

135. Don Phillips, "Thousands Gather to Boost Strike," *CCT*, February 14, 1976, 1.

136. Margolis, *On the Line.*

137. Phillips, "Thousands Gather to Boost Strike."

138. On these protests see Phillips-Fein, *Fear City,* chaps. 13–15.

139. "Barbaro Answers Starr Charges against Rosen," *CN,* December 23, 1975, 3.

140. "Bella Backs Co-op Strike," *DN,* June 23, 1975, 7.

141. William Liblick, "A Hallahan Denies Harris Request to File Brief in Strike Case," *CN,* December 23, 1975, 2.

142. Phillips, "Thousands Gather to Boost Strike."

143. Francis X. Clines, "A State Financing Agency Warns It Faces Bond Crisis," *NYT,* September 13, 1975, 12; "HFA Being Squeezed by Co-op Obligations," *CN,* September 18, 1975, 2.

144. Belica to Carey, September 3, 1975, Carey 1975–78, Housing, reel 101, NYS Archives.

145. SCIII press release, September 26, 1975, Carey 1975–78, Housing, reel 102, NYS Archives.

146. Clines, "State Financing Agency Warns It Faces Bond Crisis"; "HFA Being Squeezed by Co-op Obligations," *CN,* September 18, 1975, 2.

147. Clines, "State Financing Agency Warns It Faces Bond Crisis," 12.

148. "Bond Problems Seen as Aid to CC," *CN,* October 9, 1975, 1.

149. Linda Greenhouse, "Board of Estimate Blocks Funds to Finance Agency," *NYT,* October 11, 1975, 39.

150. Greenhouse, "Board of Estimate Blocks Funds."

151. Linda Greenhouse, "Estimate Board Rescues State Agency," *NYT,* October 14, 1975, 43.

152. Greenhouse, "Estimate Board Rescues State Agency."

153. "Bond Problems Seen as Aid to CC," *CN,* October 9, 1975, 1.

154. Hugh Carey to Joseph Murphy, chairman HFA, November 26, 1975, Carey 1975–78, Housing, reel 101, NYS Archives.

155. Linda Greenhouse, "State Turns Up Some Funds H.F.A. Needs to Avoid Default," *NYT,* November 8, 1975, 14; Linda Greenhouse, "State Bills Avert Yonkers Default; H.F.A. Also Saved," *NYT,* November 15, 1975, 57.

156. On the federal bailout for New York City see Phillips-Fein, *Fear City,* 200. Ford proposed funding on November 26, and it was signed into law on December 9.

157. Linda Greenhouse, "Albany Approves Rescue Measures for 3 Agencies," *NYT,* December 16, 1975, 1.

158. Carey press release, February 13, 1976, Carey 1975–78, Housing, reel 101, NYS Archives; Steven R. Weisman "State Is Helped by Teachers Fund," *NYT,* February 14, 1976, 52.

159. Steven Weisman, "The Jigsaw Pieces That Salvaged 4 State Construction Agencies," *NYT,* March 21, 1976, 38.

160. Steven R. Weisman, "The New Partnership of the Banks and New York State," *NYT,* March 28, 1976, 151.

161. "Co-op City Choices," *NYT,* May 13, 1976, 33.

162. "Carey to Introduce Capital Grant Bill," *CN,* February 19, 1976, 1.

163. William Liblick, "Rosen Reveals Secret Discussions with Cuomo," *CN,* January 8, 1976, 33.

164. The actual state bailout figure was even higher—$88 million in grants and $140 million in guaranteed loans. Freemark, "Roosevelt Island," 371. See also Richard Ravitch, *So Much to Do: A Full Life of Business, Politics, and Confronting Fiscal Crise* (New York: Public Affairs, 2014), 58–70.

165. Murray Schumach, "Co-op City: A Symptom of Mitchell-Lama Ills," *NYT*, June 18, 1975, 53.

166. "Carey Rejects Cuomo Compromise Plan to End Strike by Co-op City," *NYT*, June 7, 1976, 47.

167. "Proposal to End Rent Strike Given to State," *CN*, September 11, 1975, 29.

168. William Liblick, "Rosen Explains New Proposals to End Strike, Stop Rent Hike," *CN*, September 18, 1975, 1.

169. "Stein Says: Carey Will Not Meet With You!," *CN*, October 2, 1975, 1; "Again! Carey Breaks Pledge to Meet Us."

170. Jim Introne to Robert Morganda / Walter T. Kicinski, September 30, 1975, Carey 1975–78, Housing, reel 102, NYS Archives.

171. Erika Teutsch to David Burke, August 8, 1975, Carey 1975–78, Housing, reel 101, NYS Archives.

172. Suzanne McAllister to Bob Morgando / Walt Kicinski, July 9, 1975, Carey, 1975–78, Housing, reel 102, NYS Archives. See also Suzanne McAllistrer to Walt Kicinski, October 22, 1975, Carey 1975–78, Housing, reel 104, NYS Archives.

173. Walt Kicinski to Bob Morgando / Dave Burke, November 17, 1975, Carey 1975–78, Housing, reel 104, NYS Archives.

174. Erika Teutsch to David Burke, August 8, 1975, Carey 1975–78, Housing, reel 101, NYS Archives.

175. Jim Introne to Robert Morganda / Walter T. Kicinski, September 30, 1975, Carey 1975–78, Housing, reel 102, NYS Archives.

176. Liblick, "Rosen Reveals Secret Discussions with Cuomo," 33; Benjamin and Norma Cirlin interview. Jack Newfield and Paul DuBrul claim that they were the ones to bring Cuomo and Rosen together. Newfield and DuBrul, *Abuse of Power*, 309.

177. Saladin Ambar, *American Cicero: Mario Cuomo and the Defense of Liberalism* (New York: Oxford University Press, 2018).

178. "Strike Talks Continuing, Some Progress Made," *CN*, March 11, 1976, 15.

179. Newfield and DuBrul, *Abuse of Power*, 309.

180. Emanuel Perlmutter, "Co-op City Loses Foreclosure Suit," *NYT*, May 11, 1976, 1.

181. Perlmutter, 1.

182. Steven Weisman, "Carey Bid to Aid H.F.A. Is Set Back," *NYT*, May 13, 1976, 53.

183. Joseph Fried, "Co-op City Strike Ended by Accord," *NYT*, June 30, 1976, 1.

184. "The Co-op City Neurosis," *Wall Street Journal*, May 24, 1976, 16.

185. Association of Government Assisted Housing to Carey, June 1, 1976, Carey 1975–78, Housing, reel 102, NYS Archives.

186. Weisman, "Carey Bid to Aid H.F.A. Is Set Back."

187. "Carey Rejects Cuomo Compromise Plan to End Strike by Co-op City," *NYT*, June 7, 1976, 47.

188. Joseph Fried, "Housing Official Resigns over Co-op City Program," *NYT*, July 8, 1976, 48.

189. Newfield and DuBrul, *Abuse of Power*, 295.

190. Newfield and DuBrul, 296.

191. William Liblick, "Residents Hail Settlement, Support Steering Committee," *CN*, July 8, 1976, 1.

192. Lesley McKillon, "The Strike Is Over," *CCT*, July 3, 1976, 2.

193. "Prosecution Case: 5 Rent Strike Leaders Support Strike after Brust Injunction," *CN*, November 20, 1975, 38.

194. Benjamin and Norma Cirlin interview; Michael Horowitz, "Strikers Free at Last! Amnesty Granted," *CN*, July 29, 1976, 21.

195. Benjamin and Norma Cirlin interview.

196. Betsy Brown, "Who Is Charlie Rosen and Why Does He Think He Can Run Co-op City?," *Sunday News Magazine*, May 29, 1977, 11.

197. "Co-op City Neurosis," *Wall Street Journal*, May 24, 1976, 16.

198. Vivian Gornick, "Can the Rent Strikers Beat the Establishment?," 11.

199. Steven Weisman, "The Jigsaw Pieces That Salvaged 4 State Construction Agencies," *NYT*, March 21, 1976, 38; Linda Greenhouse, "Bills Signed to End 'Moral Obligation' Financing," *NYT*, March 16, 1976, 40; Steven Weisman, "Carey Pressing Plan on Sale of State-Held Mortgages," *NYT*, May 7, 1976, 21.

5. "We Inherited a Mess"

1. Betsy Brown, "Who Is Charlie Rosen and Why Does He Think He Can Run Co-op City?," *Daily News Sunday News Magazine*, May 29, 1977, 5.

2. Brown, 11.

3. Jack Newfield and Paul DuBrul, "How 50,000 Angry People Took Over Co-op City," *Planning*, July 1977, 30.

4. Charles Rosen, "Putting People in the Equation," *CCT*, August 7, 1976, 5.

5. "Feds Take a Look at Power Plant," *CN*, July 29, 1976, 1.

6. "New Board Eyes Cost-Cutting Plans," *CN*, July 22, 1976, 1, 18; Lillian Dobinsky, letter to the editor, *CN*, July 29, 1976, 4.

7. William Liblick, "Residents Blame Mgmt. for Filth in Community," *CN*, September 23, 1976, 3.

8. "Restaurant in the Sky—Co-op City Style," *CN*, January 20, 1977, 14.

9. "1,000 Notices Sent to Pay Back Rent," *CN*, November 24, 1977, 1.

10. "Some Leaders Said to Be 'in Arrears,'" *CN*, August 11, 1977, 1.

11. "Rosen: It's Time to Train New Leadership," *CCT*, January 22, 1977, 19.

12. Gretchen Donant, "DHCR to Approve New Riverbay Post," *CCT*, January 29, 1977, 5.

13. "Anonymous Bldg. Capt. Scores Rosen on $800 a Week Salary," *CN*, February 10, 1977, 1.

14. William Liblick, "Rosen's Riverbay Salary Out of Line, Residents Say," *CN*, February 10, 1977, 21.

15. Joel Dannenberg, "Feelings of Pride and Anguish," *CCT*, April 23, 1977, 19.

16. The initial six-month grace period was extended in January 1977 by an agreement between DHCR and Riverbay. "Foreclosure Averted," *CCT*, January 8, 1977, 1.

17. "Proposal Ending the Co-op City Rent Strike," *CCT*, July 16, 1977, 8. The proposal did not set a limit on how large the funds would be that could be set aside for construction repairs, nor did it include a sunset date on this provision.

18. Michael Horowitz, "Angry Crowd Greets Strike Settlement," *CN*, July 21, 1977, 18.

19. Peter Grad, "Tempers Flare at Strike Pact Meet Sunday," *CCT*, July 23, 1977, 3.

20. "74% Vote 'Yes' to OK Pact," *CCT*, July 23, 1977, 1.

21. Ravitch to Carey, January 21, 1977, letter accompanying Richard Ravitch, *Report and Recommendations with Respect to the Financial Problems Associated with Co-op City and the Mitchell-Lama Program in General, 1977*, GOV 075.0-4 REPRR 201-6732.

22. At the time of Co-op City's construction, cost estimates suggested that the savings for Co-op City's own power plant were minimal, while by buying power from Con Ed, Co-op City would avoid the problems of operating its own facility. Therefore the power plant was never completed, although $28.2 million was still put into its construction. Office of the Comptroller, *Report No. 7: The New York State Mitchell-Lama Program Supervision of Development Costs of Co-op City by the Division of Housing and Community Renewal*, December 29, 1978, 35, Audit Report NY-AUTH-18–78.

23. Ravitch, *Report and Recommendations*, 3.

24. Ravitch to Carey, January 21, 1977, letter accompanying *Report and Recommendations*.

25. Ravitch to Carey, January 21, 1977.

26. Richard Ravitch, *So Much to Do: A Full Life of Business, Politics, and Confronting Fiscal Crises* (New York: Public Affairs, 2014), 112.

27. Ravitch, 112.

28. Office of the State Comptroller, *Certain Operating Matters of Co-op City: Interim Report No. 5 on New York State Mitchell-Lama Program*," April 7, 1977, 7, NY-AUTH-22–77.

29. "Time to Save Middle-Income Housing," *NYT*, March 13, 1978, A20.

30. James Ring Adams, "Subsidized Housing and Politics," *Wall Street Journal*, October 31, 1975.

31. "Surcharge Levied against 1,576 Here," *CN*, February 2, 1978, 25.

32. Office of the State Comptroller, *Certain Operating Matters of Co-op City: Interim Report No. 5*.

33. "Light before Heat at Mitchell-Lamas," *NYT*, April 7, 1977, 28.

34. Riverbay, "A Summary of the Excess Mortgage Charges Imposed on Co-op City," December 10, 1979, 1.

35. Riverbay, "Summary of the Excess Mortgage Charges," 2.

36. Arthur Levitt, *The New York State Mitchell-Lama Program Supervision of Development Costs of Co-op City by the Division of Housing and Community Renewal*, Audit Report NY-AUTH-18–78, December 29, 1978, 16.

37. Levitt, *New York State Mitchell-Lama Program*, 24.

38. Levitt, 29.

39. Levitt, 3–4.

40. Levitt, 5.

41. Levitt, 2–3.

42. Levitt, 33.

43. Benjamin and Norma Cirlin interview.

44. Michael Horowitz and William Liblick, "Unsafe, Unsanitary Conditions at Truman," *CN*, February 3, 1977, 1. Because construction of the Educational Park had been ceded to the UHF (see chap. 1), its construction defects were not covered by the New York City Board of Education.

45. Michael Horowitz, "Sinking Soil Destroys Sidewalks, Gas Lines," *CN*, October 27, 1977.

46. State of New York Commission of Investigation, "The Co-op City Repair Program," March 1983, 25, Rudy Runko, box 5, NYS Archives.

47. Benjamin and Norma Cirlin interview.

48. Benjamin and Norma Cirlin interview.

49. Peter Grad, "Construction Defects—Who'll Pick Up the Tab?," *CCT*, January 20, 1979, 3.

50. State of New York Commission of Investigation, "Co-op City Repair Program."

51. Grad, "Construction Defects," 3.

52. Peter Grad, "HFA Sues Riverbay Over Mortgage," *CCT*, January 13, 1979, 1. State of New York Commission of Investigation, "Co-op City Repair Program."

53. "Koch on Foreclosure: We'll Wait," *CN*, October 25, 1979, 1.

54. Carey to Parness, June 25, 1979, quoted in State of New York Commission of Investigation, "Co-op City Repair Program," 19.

55. Mark Lawton to Wayne Diesel, September 29, 1981, Rudy Runko, box 5, NYS Archives.

56. "Ravitch Plan Seen Creating 2 Classes," *CN*, April 7, 1977, 1.

57. William Liblick, "Ravitch Report Findings Challenged as Unfair," *CN*, March 31, 1977, 3.

58. "Ravitch Plan Seen Creating 2 Classes."

59. Cynthia Curran, "Administration of Subsidized Housing in New York State—Co-op City: A Case of the Largest Subsidized Cooperative Housing Development in the Nation" (PhD diss., New York University, 1978), 133.

60. New York State, *Mitchell-Lama Task Force Report to Governor Carey*, February 28, 1978, 7.

61. New York State, *Mitchell-Lama Task Force Report*, 8.

62. New York State, *Mitchell-Lama Task Force Report*, 10.

63. Theodore Feit to Carey, undated, received July 19, 1977, Carey 1975–78, reel 102, NYS Archives.

64. "Co-op City Exemption," *NYT*, December 27, 1977, 34.

65. Allan Talbot to Carey, May 27, 1976, Carey 1975–78, reel 102, NYS Archives.

66. Eliot Engel, "The Pitfalls of Selective Aid," *CN*, March 15, 1978, 4.

67. Carey to Bernstein, February 14, 1979, Carey 1979–82, reel 18, NYS Archives.

68. Michael Horowitz, "Absolute Power of Harold Ostroff," *CN*, February 20, 1975, 23.

69. Jason Hackworth, *The Neoliberal City: Governance, Ideology, and Development in American Urbanism* (Ithaca, NY: Cornell University Press, 2007), 10. See also Timothy P. R. Weaver, *Blazing the Neoliberal Trail: Urban Political Development in the United States and the United Kingdom* (Philadelphia: University of Pennsylvania Press, 2016); Kim Phillips-Fein, "The History of Neoliberalism," in *Shaped by the State: Toward a New Political History of the Twentieth Century*, ed. Brent Cebul, Lily Geismer, and

Mason B. Williams (Chicago: University of Chicago Press, 2019), 347–62; Ray Forrest and Yosuke Hirayama, "The Financialisation of the Social Project: Embedded Liberalism, Neoliberalism and Home Ownership," *Urban Studies* 52, no. 2 (2015): 233–44. As Michael Heseltine, Margaret Thatcher's secretary of state for the environment, wrote in justification of "Right to Buy," a Thatcherite policy that would allow residents to buy their council (public housing) flats, "There is in this country a deeply ingrained desire for home ownership. The government believes that this spirit should be fostered. It reflects the wishes of the people, ensures the wide spread of wealth through society, encourages a personal desire to improve and modernize one's own home, enables parents to accrue wealth for their children and stimulates the attitudes of independence and self-reliance that are the bedrocks of a free society": "Housing Bill—Provisions and Enactment," in *Keesing's Contemporary Archives*, January 27, 1971, 30644.

70. This is, of course, nothing new in American history. See Nancy Kwak, *A Nation of Homeowners: American Power and the Politics of Housing Aid* (Chicago: University of Chicago Press, 2015), and Lizabeth Cohen, *A Consumers' Republic: The Politics of Mass Consumption in Postwar America* (New York: Vintage Books, 2004). On the continuities between neoliberalism and earlier public/private partnerships see Amy Offner, *Sorting Out the Mixed Economy: The United States, Colombia, and the Rise and Fall of Welfare and Developmental States* (Princeton, NJ: Princeton University Press, 2019).

71. Alice O'Connor, "The Privatized City: The Manhattan Institute, the Urban Crisis and the Conservative Counter-Revolution in New York," *Journal of Urban History* 34, no. 2 (2008): 333–53; Jonathan Soffer, *Ed Koch and the Rebuilding of New York City* (New York: Columbia University Press, 2010), 146–47 and passim. On the messiness and ideological murkiness of New York's neoliberal turn see Benjamin Holtzman, *The Long Crisis: New York City and the Path to Neoliberalism* (New York: Oxford University Press, 2021); Suleiman Osman, "Neoliberalism in New York City from Below," *Labor: Studies in Working-Class History of the Americas* 15, no. 4 (2018): 107–11.

72. Soffer, *Ed Koch*, 146–47.

73. Koch quoted in Ben Holtzman, "Gentrification's First Victims," *Jacobin*, May 2016, https://www.jacobinmag.com/2016/05/gentrification-homeless-broken-windows-police-de-blasio/. See also Benjamin Holtzman, *The Long Crisis: New York City and the Path to Neoliberalism* (New York: Oxford University Press, 2021).

74. Ed Koch, "Text of Address," *NYT*, January 2, 1978.

75. Suleiman Osman, "The Decade of the Neighborhood," in *Rightward Bound: Making America Conservative in the 1970s*, ed. Bruce Shulman and Julian Zelizer (Cambridge, MA: Harvard University Press, 2008), 117.

76. Osman, 115.

77. Marisa Chappell, "The Strange Career of Urban Homesteading: Low-Income Homeownership and the Transformation of American Housing Policy in the Late Twentieth Century," *Journal of Urban History* 46, no. 4 (2020): 757.

78. Osman, "Decade of the Neighborhood," 122.

79. Osman, 115. On the affinity of neoliberals for Jacobs see Timothy P. R. Weaver's discussion of the belief held by the Heritage Foundation's Stuart Butler that enterprise zones were a way to realize Jacobs's "vision of communities": Weaver,

Blazing the Neoliberal Trail, 33–34. On the relationship between private voluntarism and neoliberalism see Holtzman, *Long Crisis*.

80. Holtzman notes that the seemingly low price of $250 for an apartment in Chelsea was, in fact, above market value at the time. Benjamin Holtzman, "Preserving Affordability in Low-Income Housing: HDFC's in Gentrifying New York City," SCARPH 2017, 3.

81. Themis Chronopoulos, "The Rebuilding of the South Bronx after the Fiscal Crisis," *Journal of Urban History* 43, no. 6 (2017): 940. See Lizabeth Cohen, *Saving America's Cities: Ed Logue and the Struggle to Renew Urban America in the Suburban Age* (New York: Macmillan, 2019), chap. 9, for a discussion of the role that urban planner Ed Logue played in the South Bronx Development Organization.

82. Holtzman, *Long Crisis*, chap. 1; Brian Goldstein, *The Roots of Urban Renaissance: Gentrification and the Struggle over Harlem* (Cambridge, MA: Harvard University Press, 2017), chaps. 4 and 5; Chappell, "Strange Career of Urban Homesteading," 747–74.

83. "CERL—Committee to Elect Responsible Leadership," n.d. (1984?), Cuomo, Housing, reel 39, NYS Archives.

84. "CERL Wins Five Seats," *CCT*, March 3, 1979, 1.

85. Michael Horowitz, "How Carey Turns His Back on Us," *CN*, November 29, 1979, 1.

86. "Lies Carey Tells Us," *CN*, November 29, 1979, 4.

87. "City of New York Rent Guidelines Board, Order Number 12, Rent Levels July 1, 1980 through September 30, 1981," TenantNet, City Record, July 7, 1980, http://tenant.net/Rent_Laws/RGBorders/apartment-html/rgb12.html.

88. "The Gathering Storm," *CN*, December 6, 1979, 4.

89. Parness to Robert Steves, November 22, 1979, Carey 1979–82, reel 18, NYS Archives.

90. "Overflow Crowd Tells State: We Won't Pay Twice," *CCT*, January 26, 1980, 1.

91. "Overflow Crowd," 12.

92. "Overflow Crowd," 12.

93. Joel Dannenberg, "To Strike or Not to Strike," *CCT*, February 23, 1980, 32.

94. Michael Horowitz, "Residents Feel Betrayed by State Rent Hike Plan," *CN*, February 21, 1980, 25.

95. Michael Horowitz, "Co-op City's a New Place to Live, But . . ." *CN*, February 22, 1979, 1.

96. Dannenberg, "To Strike or Not to Strike," 32.

97. "Rallies at Carey, Citicorp Offices Focus on 12% Rent Hike Demand," *CCT*, February 16, 1980, 1.

98. "Rallies at Carey, Citicorp Offices."

99. Michael Horowitz, "Economic Rent: Now or in Many Years?," *CN*, February 28, 1980, 1, 21.

100. Charles Parness, "Negotiating Team and State Reach Agreement," *CCT*, March 8, 1980, 1; and "Steering Group to Campaign against Settlement with State," *CN*, March 13, 1980, 30.

101. Edward Regan, "The New York State Mitchell-Lama Program Fiscal Impact of Co-op City Mortgage Modification Agreement," October 14, 1983, MS 5, NY-AUTH-23–82.

102. "Settlement Puts Heat on State," *CN*, March 20, 1980, 1. On HFA thinking see Regan, "New York State Mitchell-Lama Program Fiscal Impact."

103. Parness, "Negotiating Team and State Reach Agreement."

104. "Steering Group to Campaign against Settlement with State," *CN*, March 13, 1980, 1.

105. Michael Horowitz, "Why Vote Approved Stability Package," *CN*, April 3, 1980, 1.

106. "Governor Commends Responsible Action of Co-op City Residents," press release, March 27, 1980, Carey, 1979–82, reel 17, NYS Archives.

107. "There's No 16% Rent Hike, So Why's Rosen Lying," *CN*, January 25, 1979, 4.

108. "Steering Committee III: Where We Stand Information Report 1," *CCT*, January 6, 1979, 10.

109. Nat Kosdan, "Independent Solution," *CCT*, January 13, 1979, 18.

110. Dave Goode, Facebook post, November 14, 2017.

111. Saul Bruh, Facebook post, November 14, 2017.

112. Laurie Berlin-Lambert, Facebook post, November 14, 2017.

113. David Chesler, Facebook post, November 14, 2017.

114. "New York Crime Rates 1960–2019," http://www.disastercenter.com/crime/nycrime.htm.

115. "Crime Rate Low in CC," *CN*, January 18, 1979, 1.

116. "Report from Security Chief Sussman," *CCT*, September 1, 1979, 5.

117. "Crime Drops 25% Here," *CN*, March 16, 1978, 1; "Crime Rate Down in Co-op City," *CCT*, February 7, 1981. See also "Crime Reported Down Here," *CN*, December 22, 1976, 1.

118. On a similar dynamic in the South Brooklyn neighborhood of Canarsie see Jonathan Rieder, *Canarsie: Jews and Italians of Brooklyn against Liberalism* (Cambridge, MA: Harvard University Press, 1985), 68–69.

119. Gary Flanz, Facebook post, January 15, 2019.

120. Marlene Adler, interview with the author, July 25, 2018.

121. Michael Agovino, *The Bookmaker: A Memoir of Money, Luck, and Family from the Utopian Outskirts of New York City* (New York: HarperCollins, 2008), 208.

122. Agovino, 254.

123. Jack Seltzer, "Security Dept. Advises 'Get to Know Your Neighbors,'" *CCT*, April 29, 1977, 5. Emphasis in original.

124. Mitchell Rubinger, "Vandalism Costs," *CCT*, June 25, 1977, 2.

125. Eva Perlman, "Candidate Statement," *CCT*, February 17, 1978.

126. Blanche Polovetz, "Candidate Statement," *CCT*, February 17, 1978.

127. Rieder, *Canarsie*, 96.

128. Wendell Pritchett, *Brownsville, Brooklyn: Blacks, Jews, and the Changing Face of the Ghetto* (Chicago: University of Chicago Press, 2002).

129. As chap. 2 discusses, Co-op City was already significantly more diverse by the time initial move-ins completed in 1972.

130. Bernard Cylich, "Director's Viewpoint," *CCT*, November 23, 2013.

131. Bernard Cylich, "Director's Viewpoint."

132. Phyllis Spiro, Open Housing Center, New York Urban League, to Joseph Goldman, acting commissioner, State Division of Housing, September 7, 1976, Carey 1975–78, Housing, reel 102, NYS Archives.

133. Rosen to Carey, telegram, September 10, 1976, Carey 1975–78, reel 102, NYS Archives.

134. "Apartment Bias Charges Dropped by Urban League," *CN*, December 16, 1976, 2.

135. Robin Herman, "At Co-op City, Home by Dark," *NYT*, January 8, 1982, B1; Toni Mendez, interview with the author, February 6, 2020.

136. "Most Working Residents Can Pay Hike," *CN*, November 18, 1976, 1; Michael Horowitz, "State Releases Income Analysis of CC," *CN*, June 22, 1978, 1.

137. Robin Nurse quoted in Zoe Rosenberg, "New York Narratives: A Bronx Native on Why She's Disenchanted with NYC," Curbed New York, https://ny.curbed.com/2016/3/2/11137020/new-york-narratives-bronx-harlem-gentrification.

138. Joan Williams, "Against Welfare Residents," *CN*, October 7, 1976, 4.

139. Della Brown, "Resist Welfare Tenants," *CN*, October 14, 1976, 4.

140. Rob Peterson, Facebook post, November 14, 2017. Emphasis in original.

141. Sally Fassler Nussbaum, Facebook post, January 11, 2019.

142. Laure Berlin-Lambert, Facebook post, January 11, 2019.

143. Rieder, *Canarsie*, 110.

144. Miles Marshall Lewis, *Scars of the Soul Are Why Kids Wear Bandages When They Don't Have Bruises* (New York: Akashic Books, 2004), 36.

145. James Del Rio, Facebook post, May 17, 2011.

146. Jonathan Valuckas, interview with the author, July 17, 2016.

147. Joseph Goldman, DCHR to Robert Morgando, Governor's Office, September 19, 1977, Carey 1975–78, reel 102, NYS Archives.

148. "Section 5 Residents Prepare Image Uplift . . .," *CCT*, September 3, 1977, 10.

149. "Section 5 Proclamation," *CCT*, October 29, 1977, 12.

150. Adler, interview.

151. "Model Apartment Sales Program Approved, Building 35 Residents Agree," *CCT*, June 3, 1978, 13.

152. "Koch: Vacancies Spread Like Cancer," *CN*, January 26, 1978, 1.

153. Cecil Atkins, "Co-op City's Got It—Let's Flaunt It!," *CCT*, April 9, 1977, 23.

154. "Playground Equipment to Arrive," *CCT*, November 19, 1977.

155. "Board Committee Unveils Model Program to Boost Sales of Co-op Apartments," *CCT*, May 27, 1978.

156. "Dramatic Impact Made by Model Apartments Program," *CCT*, September 30, 1978.

157. "Apartments???," *CCT*, December 2, 1978.

158. "Black Is White," *CCT*, July 28, 1979.

159. Atkins, "Co-op City's Got It!"

160. "Are You Ready for the Fair?," *CCT*, June 24, 1978.

161. "Something Nice Has Taken Root in Co-op City," *CCT*, October 23, 1981, 11.

162. "Koch: Vacancies Spread Like Cancer," 32.

163. Charles Parness, "The President's Report," *CCT*, January 3, 1981, 2.

164. S. Lefkowitz, letter to the editor, *CCT*, January 17, 1981, 4.

165. Abraham Schenck, letter to the editor, *CCT*, January 17, 1981, 4.

166. Henry Mahler, letter to the editor, *CCT*, January 17, 1981, 4.

167. "'Co-op City a Nice Place to Live,' New Ad Campaign Proposed," *CCT*, December 29, 1979, 1.

168. Riverbay Corporation, "City Living the Way It Used to Be," n.d., 3. Note that this was published prior to the carrying charge hikes discussed earlier in this chapter.

169. Riverbay Corporation, "City Living," 9.

170. Riverbay Corporation, "City Living," 3.

171. ". . . She Stops the Buck," *CCT*, September 2, 1978, 13.

6. "Co-op City *Is* the Bronx"

1. "The Birth of a Dream . . .," *CCT*, December 3, 1988, Souvenir Anniversary Pullout, 2.

2. "Birth of a Dream . . .," 3.

3. Tony Illis, "Happy 20th to All," *CCT*, December 3, 1988, 29.

4. Wilana Lerner quote in Sam Howe Verhovek, "Co-op City Sets New Goal: Attract More Whites," *NYT*, November 30, 1987, B1, B6.

5. Campbell Gibson and Kay Jung, "Historical Census Statistics on Population Totals by Race, 1790 to 1990, and by Hispanic Origin, 1970 to 1990, for Large Cities and Other Urban Places in the United States," Census Population Division, Working Paper 76 (2005), table 33: New York—Race and Hispanic Origin for Selected Cities and Other Large Places—Earliest Census to 1990, https://www.census.gov/content/dam/Census/library/working-papers/2005/demo/POP-twps0076.pdf. The totals do not equal 100 percent because of rounding.

6. See appendix, figures 25 and 26.

7. Ari Goldman, "At Co-op City, Worship in Transition," *NYT*, May 31, 1989, B2.

8. "A Celebration of a People," *CCT*, September 15, 1979.

9. Louis Lynch, "African-American Course Growing in Truman H.S.," *CCT*, May 5, 1990, 11; "Black History Celebrations Continue," *CCT*, February 9, 1991, 3.

10. Gregory Meyers, interview with the author, June 20, 2018.

11. Nurse quoted in Zoe Rosenberg, "New York Narratives: A Bronx Native on Why She's Disenchanted with NYC," Curbed New York, https://ny.curbed.com/2016/3/2/11137020/new-york-narratives-bronx-harlem-gentrification.

12. Dean's Table, podcast interview, https://deanstable.com/professor-of-history-aaads-frank-guridy-dt6/.

13. Miles Marshall Lewis, *Scars of the Soul Are Why Kids Wear Bandages When They Don't Have Bruises* (New York: Akashic Books, 2004), 14.

14. Lewis, 14.

15. Michael Agovino, *The Bookmaker: A Memoir of Money, Luck, and Family from the Utopian Outskirts of New York City* (New York: HarperCollins, 2008), 227.

16. Lewis, *Scars of the Soul*, 23.

17. Lewis, 32. Emphasis in original.

18. *Big Fun in the Big Town*, Dutch TV documentary, 1986.

19. Agovino, *Bookmaker*, 201.

20. Toni Mendez, interview with the author, February 6, 2020.

21. Sam Howe Verhovek, "Co-op City Sets New Goal: Attract More Whites," *NYT*, November 30, 1987, B6. An article about PS 153, which drew students from Sections Three and Four, stated that in 1989 the school was 64 percent Black, 19 percent Hispanic, 16 percent non-Hispanic white, and 1 percent Asian: Verena Dobnik,

"Reading Better with Shakespeare in the Bronx," Associated Press, February 17, 1989. A 1993 article described the student population of District 11, of which Co-op City was a part, as 86 percent minority: Sam Dillon, "Ethnic Shifts Are Revealed in Voting for Schools," *NYT*, May 20, 1993, B3.

22. "School Ethnic Survey Released," *CCT*, January 20, 1990, 17.

23. Bruce Irushalmi, interview with the author, February 17, 2017.

24. Lynne Moser, interview with the author, December 14, 2011.

25. Janice Hoetz Goldstein quoted in Nina Wohl, "Co-op City: The Dream and the Reality" (master's thesis, Columbian University, 1995), 41.

26. Derek Alger, "Truman Student Arrested for 2 Racial Bias Attacks," *CN*, January 18, 1992, 1.

27. "3 Local Youths Indicted in Racial Attack on Blacks," *CN*, March 15, 1988, 5.

28. Lewis, *Scars of the Soul*, 119; Steve Schneider, "Teens Air Their Gripes," *CCT*, August 24, 1991, 1.

29. Fay Grad, letter to the editor, *CCT*, July 10, 1982, 6.

30. Shirley Saunders, "Director's Viewpoint: 'Insult to Dinkins Bites Hand That Feeds Us,'" *CCT*, September 8, 1990, 32.

31. "The High Price of Racism," *CCT*, December 19, 1987, 4.

32. Robert Tomasson, "Black Church Charges Co-op City with Racial Bias against It," *NYT*, August 4, 1991, 38.

33. "Church Loses Bid for Theater Space: Commercial Lease Eyed by Board," *CCT*, November 10, 1990, 1, 2.

34. Derek Alger, "Rev. Owens Drops Discrimination Suit," *CN*, January 11, 1992, 1.

35. Sam Howe Verhovek, "Co-op City Sets New Goal: Attract More Whites," *NYT*, November 30, 1987, B1, B6.

36. Shirley Saunders, "A Director's Viewpoint: Angry at N.Y. Times," *CCT*, December 12, 1987, 22.

37. Gladys Luciano, "A Director's Viewpoint: 'The Truth,'" *CCT*, December 19, 1987, 18.

38. Caroline Sozio, "A Director's Viewpoint: False Statement," *CCT*, December 12, 1987, 18.

39. Ellen Esslinger, "N.Y. Times Article Sets off Fireworks," *CCT*, December 12, 1987, 1.

40. Esslinger, 40.

41. Saunders, "A Director's Viewpoint: Angry at N.Y. Times," 22.

42. Harriet Jeffries and Gerald Jeffries, letter to the editor, *CCT*, December 12, 1987, 6.

43. Saunders, "A Director's Viewpoint: Angry at N.Y. Times," 22.

44. Rod Saunders, letter to the editor, *CCT*, December 19, 1987, 6.

45. Tony Illis, "A Director's Viewpoint: Polarizing This Community," *CCT*, December 5, 1987, 22.

46. Ruben Berkowitz, letter to the editor, *CCT*, December 19, 1987, 6.

47. Gretchen Hazell, Mitch Berkowitz, Dave Chernila, and Bernard Cylich, letter to the editor, *CCT*, December 12, 1987, 6.

48. Eva Pellman, "President's Report," *CCT*, December 19, 1987, 2.

49. "President's Report—Eva Pellman," *CCT*, January 23, 1988, 2; "Pellman Out of Race for Board Seat," *CCT*, April 6, 1988, 1. In 1991, Riverbay would approve

a plan to settle Soviet Jews in vacant apartments in Co-op City. However, it was carefully done so as to avoid charges of racial bias—the program was set up as an "affirmative action program for immigrants" from all countries, not merely the USSR. Robert E. Tomasson, "Plan Would Settle Soviet Jews at Co-op City," *NYT*, June 2, 1991, 39.

50. Shirley Saunders, "A Director's Viewpoint: Eliminate Bigotry, Hatred," *CCT*, January 17, 1987, 20.

51. Paul Taylor, "Jackson Evoking Voters' Cheers, Fears: Attitudes in New York Polarized by Race, but Hard to Stereotype," *Washington Post*, April 16, 1988, 1.

52. Susan Chira, "Co-op City: Life Begins to Improve," *NYT*, May 8, 1982, 27.

53. "Racism Discussion Set," *CN*, January 29, 1987, 9; Louis Lynch, "Anti-Bias Rally: Accentuating the Positives," *CCT*, May 23, 1992, 1.

54. Gene Mustain, "Yusuf's Slaying May Sway Vote," *DN*, September 4, 1989, 3; "An Open Letter," *CCT*, September 2, 1989, 1.

55. Donna Murch, "Crack in Los Angeles, Crisis, Militarization, and Black Response in the Late Twentieth-Century War on Drugs," *Journal of American History* 102, no. 1 (2015): 170.

56. Mary Patillo, *Black Picket Fences: Privilege and Peril among the Black Middle Class* (Chicago: University of Chicago Press, 2013), 6.

57. On the racist assumptions about the relationship between blackness and criminality see Khalil Gibran Muhammad, *The Condemnation of Blackness: Race, Crime and the Making of Modern Urban America* (Cambridge, MA: Harvard University Press, 2010).

58. Reiko Hillyer, "The Guardian Angels: Law and Order and Citizen Policing in New York City," *Journal of Urban History* 43, no. 6 (2017): 888. See also Michael Javon Fortner, *Black Silent Majority: The Rockefeller Drug Laws and the Politics of Punishment* (Cambridge, MA: Harvard University Press, 2015). On the history of local Black anticrime activities in New York see Benjamin Holtzman, "Expanding the Thin Blue Line: Resident Patrols and Private Security in Late Twentieth-Century New York," *Modern American History* 3 (2020): 47–67.

59. James Foreman Jr., *Locking Up Our Own: Crime and Punishment in Black America* (New York: Farrar, Straus and Giroux, 2017), 158.

60. This is also not a phenomenon that stopped in the 1980s. In a recent Facebook thread on how Co-op City has changed, one resident wrote, "I've lived here since I was born in 1990. When I was younger, I felt that the neighborhood was cleaner, safer, and really special. Now it feels like any other public housing development." Co-op City Section Five Facebook Group, July 27, 2014.

61. "Anti-Crime Unit in a War on Muggers," *CN*, January 4, 1974, 1.

62. Michael Horowitz, "Co-op City's a Nice Place to Live, But . . ." *CN*, February 22, 1979, 1.

63. "Survey Results: Do You Feel Safe Here?," *CN*, April 25, 1985, 36.

64. See Jonathan Rieder's discussion of a similar dynamic in Canarsie, in *Canarsie: Jews and Italians of Brooklyn against Liberalism* (Cambridge, MA: Harvard University Press, 1985), 90–94.

65. Thomas Raftery and Patrice O'Schaughnessy, "Man Fires on Group, Hits 3," *DN*, May 30, 1989, 7.

66. "Complex Tenants Feeling Insecure," *DN*, March 16, 1990,

67. "Crime Prevention Here," *CN*, November 12, 1988, 4.

68. "Resident: 'We Might as Well Arm Ourselves,'" *CN*, June 20, 1992, 15.

69. "Survey Results: Do You Feel Safe Here?"; "Survey Results: How Residents Rate Co-op's Quality of Life," *CN*, May 2, 1992, 1.

70. Don Terry, "Campaign Stop: Co-op City, the Bronx: A Haven Marred as Drugs Slip In," *NYT*, August 10, 1989, B1.

71. Police Department, City of New York, *CompStat*, vol. 28, no. 18, https://www1.nyc.gov/assets/nypd/downloads/pdf/crime_statistics/cs-en-us-045pct.pdf.

72. "Is Police Picture Turning Blue?," *DN*, October 25, 1987, BX3; Bob Kappstatter, "Stats Signal Safer Streets," *DN*, October 30, 1995, 498; "New York Nabes," *DN*, December 1, 1997, 334. Furthermore, the Forty-Fifth Precinct did not enjoy the drop in crime that other precincts did in the 1990s, so that by 1998, the Forty-Fifth and Forty-Ninth Precincts had nearly identical major crime rates.

73. Derek Alger, "Over 800 Demand More Police, Call for Substation," *CN*, July 18, 1992, 17.

74. Louis Lynch, "Higher Police Visibility for Co-op City? LaForgia Weighs Shift from Plainclothes to Uniforms," *CCT*, July 25, 1992, 2.

75. Jonathan Valukas, interview with the author, July 27, 2016.

76. Agovino, *Bookmaker*, 148. Irushalmi interview; Mendez interview.

77. Marie Brown-Bryant, Facebook post, September 10, 2019.

78. Karen Benjamin, interview with the author, January 25, 2012.

79. Leslie Shatz, Facebook post, September 10, 2019.

80. "Is Truman a Safe School?," *CN*, June 13, 1985, 1.

81. Steve Schneider, "Students' Safety at Risk?," *CCT*, November 17, 1990, 2. On the suspicion that the violence was gang related see Judy Roberson, "Director's Viewpoint: It's Time to Take Back Our Community," *CCT*, November 24, 1990, 25.

82. Mendez interview.

83. Gary Chattman, *Don't Tell Me Not to Believe: One Teacher's Odyssey* (Strategic Book, 2019), 160.

84. Raphael Sugerman, "2 Teens Slashed at Truman HS," *DN*, January 5, 1995, 39.

85. Irushalmi interview.

86. Steve Schneider, "High School Student Beaten by Teen Gang," *CCT*, January 11, 1992, 4.

87. Derek Alger, "Meeting Called at Truman to Discuss Youth Gangs," *CN*, February 1, 1992, 7.

88. Albert Davila, "3 Charges in Bronx Drive-By Killing," *DN*, August 14, 1991, 15; "Most Wanted in the Bronx," *DN*, December 22, 1994, 3; Patrice O'Schaughnessy, "Teen Slain in Rumble," *DN*, March 12, 1990, 47; Robert Gearty, "Looking for Bronx Killer: Case of Mistaken Identity," *DN*, March 22, 1993, 8; Lewis, *Scars of the Soul*, 37; "Teen-Ager Shot after a Dispute at School," *NYT*, December 1989, B2.

89. Irushalmi interview.

90. "Truman Students Broaden Their Horizons," *CCT*, March 5, 1988, 4.

91. Ellen Cosgrove, "New Video Security System for Ed Park," *CCT*, June 5, 1982, 3.

92. "Metal Detectors at Truman High," *CCT*, November 28, 1992.

93. Irushalmi interview.

94. "Reading Test Scores for New York Schools," *NYT*, January 23, 1985, B5. The scores reported were from the April 1984 exam. In part, the location of the district-wide gifted program in Co-op City's IS 181 meant that test scores in that school remained higher than they might otherwise have been. Irushalmi interview.

95. Felicia Lee, "As Scores Fall, Schools Seek Lessons," *NYT*, March 24, 1990, 1, 27.

96. "School Reading Scores: The Good and the Bad," *CCT*, April 4, 1992, 9.

97. Mendez interview.

98. Benjamin and Norma Cirlin interview.

99. Irushalmi interview.

100. I attended Hunter, and the year before I took the test, two students from Co-op City got into Hunter. The year that I did, I was the only student to be accepted.

101. Music and Art merged with the High School for the Performing Arts and obtained the name Fiorello H. LaGuardia High School of Music & Art and the Performing Arts in 1984: https://en.wikipedia.org/wiki/Fiorello_H._LaGuardia_High_School.

102. Oliver Scholars, https://www.oliverscholars.org/. While Prep-for-Prep was started in the Bronx, the majority of Black and Hispanic students who attended elite private schools did so through the Oliver Scholars program.

103. Agovino, *Bookmaker*, 228.

104. Agovino, 225.

105. Agovino, 237.

106. Terry, "Campaign Stop: Co-op City."

107. "Community Home Proposed Near Section 5," *CCT*, March 9, 1991, 3; Mendez interview; Victoria Sammartino, interview with the author, February 7, 2020.

108. Lisa Rein, "Nabes Rap Hot-Sheet Motel," *DN*, August 23, 1998, 5. See also Derek Alger, "Motel Here Houses Homeless Families," *CN*, September 26, 1992, 1.

109. Mendez interview.

110. Bernard Cylich, interview with the author, February 27, 2020.

111. Ruben Klein, "Illegal Tenants Are a Widespread Problem," *CN*, February 8, 1992, 22.

112. Bill Stuttig, "Sublet Amnesty Program Begins Tuesday," *CCT*, February 14, 2004.

113. There is a vast literature on the crack epidemic itself, its media representation, and the policies and responses it engendered, including Philippe Bourgois, *In Search of Respect: Selling Crack in El Barrio* (New York: Cambridge University Press, 1995); David Farber, *Crack: Rock Cocaine, Street Capitalism, and the Decade of Greed* (New York: Cambridge University Press, 2019); Craig Reinarman and Harry Levine, eds., *Crack in America: Demon Drugs and Social Justice* (Berkeley: University of California Press, 1997); Sudhir Venkatesh, *American Project: The Rise and Fall of a Modern Ghetto* (Cambridge, MA: Harvard University Press, 2000).

114. Paul Goldstein, Harry Brownstein, Patrick Ryan, and Patricia Bellucci, "Crack and Homicide in New York City: A Case Study in the Epidemiology of Violence," in Reinarman and Levine, *Crack in America*, 113.

115. Sondra Levin, "Biaggi, Teens in Crack Attack," *CN*, July 17, 1988, 29.

116. "Did CC Teens Find Crack Here?," *CN*, August 28, 1986, 23.

117. "Seize 4 in Big 'Crack' Bust Here," *CCT*, February 7, 1987, 1, 14.

118. "Our Youth Say No to Crack," *CCT*, January 17, 1987, 1.

119. "Dangers of Drug Use: Topic of Presentation," *CN*, April 25, 1987, 37; "Drug Abuse Talk Here," *CN*, April 23, 1988, 3; "Talk on Dope," *CN*, August 21, 1986, 2; Ellen Esslinger, "Urge Kids Be Taught Dope Dangers with A-B-Cs," *CCT*, September 12, 1987, 1; Louis Lynch, "Drug Forum Urges Residents to Help Fight," *CCT*, February 3, 1990, 15; "Drug Workshop Set," *CCT*, April 7, 1990, 1.

120. Terry, "Campaign Stop: Co-op City."

121. V. McDowell, "The Drug War," *DN*, September 22 1986, 28.

122. Louis Lynch, "Drug Workshop Seeks Wider Audience," *CCT*, April 21, 1990, 13.

123. Steve Schneider, "Drug, Sex Items Litter Play Area," *CCT*, November 3, 1990, 3, 4.

124. Saladin Ambar, *American Cicero: Mario Cuomo and the Defense of Liberalism* (New York: Oxford University Press, 2018), 92.

125. Robert Snyder, *Crossing Broadway: Washington Heights and the Promise of New York City* (Ithaca, NY: Cornell University Press, 2015), chap. 5.

126. Noel Wolfe, "Battling Crack: A Study of the Northwest Bronx Community and Clergy Coalition's Tactics," *Journal of Urban History* 43, no. 1 (2017): 18–32.

127. On the particular support of middle-class Black neighborhoods for a punitive approach to the "war on drugs" see Donna Murch, "Crack in Los Angeles: Crisis, Militarization, and Black Response in the Late Twentieth-Century War on Drugs," *Journal of American History* 102, no. 1 (2015): 170.

128. Tony Illis, "Director's Viewpoint: Some Care about Community, Some Don't," *CCT*, November 26, 1988, 29.

129. Tony Illis, "Director's Viewpoint: Genocide in Section 5," *CCT*, February 3, 1990, 30.

130. "Engel Bill Cracks Down on Dealers," *CCT*, July 2, 1988, 25.

131. "Security Suggestion," *CCT*, December 17, 1988, 6; "To Arm or Not to Arm . . . : Question Stirs Debate," *CCT*, October 8, 1988, 1; "Section 5 Kiosk Beefs Up Security," *CCT*, May 5, 1990, 1.

132. "We Demand City Police Step Up War on Crime Here," *CCT*, August 29, 1987, 36.

133. Eileen Alger, "We Want More Police," *CN*, June 11, 1988, 6.

134. Terry, "Campaign Stop: Co-op City."

135. Ellen Esslinger, "Co-op City Plea: Give Us Precinct," *CCT*, September 30, 1989, 1.

136. Iris Herskowitz Baez, "Getting Away with Murder in Section 5," *CN*, May 28, 1988, 11.

137. Baez would also later be convicted in a corruption scandal that would ultimately lead to a six-month prison term. Dorian Block, "Former Co-op City Board President Gets 6 Months in Jail in Plea Deal," *DN*, March 26, 2008.

138. On the greater propensity of middle-class Blacks to opt for a law-and-order strategy than poorer ones see Murch, "Crack in Los Angeles," 170.

139. Tommy Acosta, "We Demand More Cops: 50 Residents Join in City Hall Protest," *CCT*, June 18, 1988, 10.

140. Louis Lynch, "Rallying Cry: 'Give Us More Cops': 600 at Town Hall Meeting: Demonstration Set for Aug," *CCT*, July 18, 1992, 2.

141. "'We Want More Cops,' Rally Tells 45th Precinct," *CN*, August 8, 1992, 6.

142. Shirley Saunders, "Director's Viewpoint: An Update on Security," *CCT*, August 1, 1992, 21.

143. "City Approves TNT Lease Here," *CCT*, January 28, 1989, 16.

144. "Guardian Angel Founder to Speak Here," *CN*, April 2, 1988, 1. On the Guardian Angels and their presence in New York see Hillyer, "Guardian Angels."

145. "'Operation Safety' Launched Here," *CCT*, November 5, 1988, 1.

146. Agovino, *Bookmaker*, 225, 254.

147. Shirley Saunders, "A Director's Viewpoint: Items of Concern to All," *CCT*, September 5, 1987, 16.

148. Ruben Garcia, "Director's Viewpoint: Attack Violence, Don't Run Away," *CCT*, June 27, 1992, 20.

149. "Resident: 'We Might as Well Arm Ourselves.'"

150. "Bronx People in Profile: Roger Dunson," *DN*, November 1, 1993, 26.

151. Steve Schneider, "Community Leaders Call for Teen Programs," *CN*, August 29, 1992, 2.

152. Derek Alger, "Security Meeting: We Want More Protection Here," *CN*, May 7, 1988, 18.

153. Don Terry, "Police Deploy Narcotics Team in Hunts Point," *NYT*, February 16, 1989, B7; "City Approves TNT Lease Here," *CCT*, January 28, 1989, 1.

154. Louis Lynch, "Drug Forum Urges Residents to Help Fight," *CCT*, February 3, 1990, 15. In 1991, the TNT made sixty-three drug arrests in Co-op City but still did not establish consistent patrols there. "Resident: 'We Might as Well Arm Ourselves.'"

155. "Crime Stats Show Drop in Co-op City," *CCT*, September 12, 1992, 1.

156. Derek Alger, "Security Chief Gets Earful from Section 5 Residents," *CN*, June 20, 1992, 14.

157. Raymond Hernandez, "Co-op City; Crime Rate Drops by Half," *NYT*, October 10, 1993, 13, 11.

158. Matthew Purdy, "Discord Rattles Co-op City Towers," *NYT*, July 31, 1995, B1.

7. "The Biggest Housing Bargain in Town"

1. Mario Cuomo to Nat Kosdan, March 15, 1984; Cuomo to Abraham Bernstein, February 1, 1984. "He Served Co-op City!," campaign flyer, Cuomo Housing, reel 39, 1984, NYS Archives.

2. Parness to Cuomo, November 10, 1983, Cuomo Housing, reel 39 (1984), NYS Archives; Gerald Friedman to Cuomo, telegram, February 1, 1983, Cuomo Housing, reel 39 (1984), NYS Archives; Rosen to Cuomo, May 13, 1983, Cuomo Housing, reel 39 (1984), NYS Archives; Cuomo to Jacobs, May 17, 1983, Cuomo Housing, reel 39 (1984), NYS Archives.

3. Cuomo to Jacobs, May 17, 1983, Cuomo Housing, reel 39 (1984), NYS Archives.

4. Tim Sheridan to Charles Parness, December 1, 1983, Cuomo Housing, reel 39 (1984), NYS Archives. Cuomo also rejected an event in February 1986. Ryan to Youth Activities Committee, February 20, 1986, Cuomo Housing 1986, box 20, NYS Archives.

5. John Krinsky, "Neoliberal Times: Intersecting Temporalities and the Neoliberalization of New York City's Public-Sector Labor Relations," *Social Science History* 35, no. 3 (Fall 2011): 381–422; Benjamin Holtzman, *The Long Crisis: New York City and the Path to Neoliberalism* (New York: Oxford University Press, 2021).

6. Nancy Kwak, *A Nation of Homeowners: American Power and the Politics of Housing Aid* (Berkeley: University of California Press, 2015), 202.

7. Marissa Chappell, "The Strange Career of Urban Homesteading: Low-Income Homeownership and the Transformation of American Housing Policy in the Late Twentieth Century," *Journal of Urban History* 46, no. 4 (2020): 757.

8. Jonathan Soffer, *Ed Koch and the Rebuilding of New York City* (New York: Columbia University Press, 2010), 296.

9. Soffer, 261.

10. Cuomo note on memo from William Eimicke to Cuomo, "Urban Homesteading (Attached)," September 13, 1983, Rudy Runko, box 5, NYS Archives.

11. New York State, *1985–86 Enacted Budget Mid-Year FP Update*, 25. https://openbudget.ny.gov/historicalFP/classic/MidYear8586.pdf.

12. Diesel to Cuomo, memo, "State of the State—Housing Programs," January 2, 1985. NYS Archives, Rudy Runko, box 5.

13. Saladin Ambar, *American Cicero: Mario Cuomo and the Defense of American Liberalism* (New York: Oxford University Press, 2018), 43.

14. Ambar, 62.

15. Ambar, 108.

16. Philip Gutis, "Unfettering Mitchell-Lama," *NYT*, February 23, 1986, 8, 1.

17. Since its construction period had only officially concluded in 1972, Co-op City was technically eligible for privatization in 1992. However, several factors led Co-op City residents to resist the siren song of the market. First, while it was clear that residents of centrally located apartments were sitting on increasingly valuable real estate, the potential windfall available in the northeast Bronx was less clear. Second, even advocates of privatization had to admit that Co-op City's reputation for being a "troubled" development, beset by infrastructural and financial problems, meant that it might struggle to find people willing to buy apartments. Third, Co-op City's mortgage stood at over a half billion dollars, making a buyout extremely difficult. Finally, Mitchell-Lama regulations required a vote of two-thirds of cooperative residents in favor of privatization, a nearly insurmountable burden in such a huge development. "Co-op City Council Hosts Buy-Out Forum," *CCT*, July 16, 1988, 4.

18. Holtzman, *Long Crisis*, chap. 2.

19. Even before Co-op City became legally eligible for privatization, some state officials had considered special arrangements that would have allowed cooperators to sell their apartments at market rate. Eimicke to Michael Del Giudice, confidential memo, September 11, 1984, "Co-op City Workout Reorganization," Rudy Runko, box 5, NYS Archives.

20. Statement by William B. Eimicke before the US House of Representatives Subcommittee on Select Revenue of the Committee of Ways and Means, March 3, 1988. In *Low-Income Housing Tax Credits and the Role of Tax Policy in Preserving Low-Income Housing; Hearings before the Subcommittee on Select Revenue of the Committee*

of Ways and Means, House of Representatives, One Hundredth Congress, March 2–3, 1988, vol. 4, 230.

21. "Mitchell-Lama Units to Retain Rent Curbs," *NYT*, April 25, 1986, B3.

22. Elizabeth Kolbert, "Cuomo Sets Rules to Guard Subsidized Housing's Status," *NYT*, July 21, 1987, B3.

23. James Barron, "Koch will Request Mitchell-Lama Site Be Kept Tax Exempt," *NYT*, August 21, 1989, B4.

24. William Eimicke, interview with the author, August 6, 2019.

25. Eimicke interview.

26. Robert Harris to Eimicke, confidential memo, "Options for a Renegotiation of the Co-op City Workout Agreement," August 7, 1984, 3, Rudy Runko, box 5, NYS Archives. The Division of Housing contested these findings until June 1984, when an arbitration panel issued a binding determination that 85 percent of plumbing problems were the responsibility of the state and thus fell under the purview of the repair program, while only 15 percent were Riverbay's responsibility.

27. Edward Regan, "The New York State Mitchell-Lama Program Fiscal Impact of Co-op City Mortgage Modification Agreement," October 14, 1983, 5, NY-AUTH-23–82. The Permanent Repair Program went into effect in October 1981.

28. Regan, "New York State Mitchell-Lama Program Fiscal Impact of Co-op City Mortgage Modification Agreement."

29. State of New York Commission of Investigation, "The Co-op City Repair Program," March 1983, 2, Rudy Runko, box 5, NYS Archives.

30. The program was alternately called the "Co-op City Repair Program" and the "Housing Project Repair Program." Although the program was designed specifically to repair Co-op City's construction defects, it allowed other housing developments to submit requests for repairs, which they did to a much smaller extent than Co-op City. Adding to the confusion, the report covered both the Emergency Repair Program agreed to in 1979 and the Permanent Repair Program that superseded it.

31. State of New York Commission of Investigation, "The Co-op City Repair Program," March 1983, 2, Rudy Runko, box 5, NYS Archives (hereafter "Co-op City Repair Program").

32. "Co-op City Repair Program," 18.

33. "Co-op City Repair Program," 22.

34. "Co-op City Repair Program," 35.

35. "Co-op City Repair Program," 38.

36. "Co-op City Repair Program," 64.

37. Arnold Lubasch, "Co-op City Aide Charged by U.S. with Extortion," *NYT*, February 27, 1986, B4. See also New York State Organized Crime Task Force, *Corruption and Racketeering in the New York City Construction Industry: Final Report to Governor Mario Cuomo from the New York State Organized Crime Task Force* (New York: NYU Press, 1990), 131. All told, ten men wound up being convicted as part of the scandal, serving prison sentences of up to five years and paying over $5 million in back taxes. "Final Three Sentenced in Co-op City Swindle," *CCT*, March 4, 1989, 1.

38. "Co-op City Repair Program," 53.

39. "Co-op City Repair Program," 40.

40. "Co-op City Repair Program," 44.

41. "Co-op City Repair Program," 63.

42. "Co-op City Repair Program," 62.

43. "Co-op City Repair Program," 5.

44. Parness statement, n.d., reproduced in "Co-op City Repair Program," 27.

45. Parness statement, n.d., 5.

46. Parness statement, n.d., 77.

47. "Co-op City Repair Program," 80.

48. Edward Regan, "New York State Housing Finance Agency Supervision of the Co-op City Repair Program," June 13, 1985, MS-2, 84-S-128.

49. Samuel G. Freedman, "Co-op City: A Refuge in Transition," NYT, June 25, 1986, B1. Ferdinand Marcos ruled the Philippines as a dictator until he was ousted in February 1986. His wife, Imelda, was famous for her extravagance, most spectacularly in her huge collection of shoes. Jean-Claude "Baby Doc" Duvalier ruled Haiti until he too, was overthrown by a popular uprising in 1986. His wife was also notorious for her corruption and extravagance.

50. C. Mark Lawton, Division of Budget, to Wayne Diesel, deputy comptroller, September 28, 1981, Rudy Runko, box 5, NYS Archives.

51. Harris to Eimicke, confidential memo, "Options for a Renegotiation of the Co-op City Workout Agreement," August 7, 1984, 3, Rudy Runko, box 5, NYS Archives.

52. Regan, "New York State Mitchell-Lama Program Fiscal Impact of Co-op City Mortgage Modification Agreement," 3.

53. Harris to Eimicke, confidential memo, "Options for a Renegotiation," 11–15.

54. Harris to Eimicke, confidential memo, "Options for a Renegotiation," 11–15.

55. Harris to Eimicke, confidential memo, "Options for a Renegotiation," 4.

56. Harris to Wayne Diesel, budget director, October 10, 1984, attachment "Overall 'HPRP Budget,'" 1, Rudy Runko, box 5, NYS Archives.

57. Eimicke to Del Giudice, confidential memo, "Co-op City Workout Reorganization."

58. Harris to Eimicke, confidential memo, "Options for a Renegotiation," 8. While the memo considered debt forgiveness, it proposed an extremely limited manner, owing to "concerns previously expressed by the Trustee for the bondholders."

59. Frank Ioppolo to Eimicke, memo, July 31, 1985, Rudy Runko, box 5, NYS Archives.

60. Eimicke interview.

61. Charles Parness, "President's Report," CCT, May 15, 1982, 2.

62. Maurice Carroll, "Pact Has Rise in Co-op City Fees," NYT, January 31, 1986, B6. The state also agreed to over $10 million in ongoing subsidy of Co-op City's operating expenses for the four years after the agreement went into effect. And Co-op City agreed to finally end the Nizer lawsuit and all other remaining litigation against the state. "Residual Receipts Agreement. Settlement Agreement," June 20, 1986, Freedom of Information Act.

63. "Order of the Commissioner of Housing and Urban Renewal," n.d., FOIA.

64. Carroll, "Pact Has Rise in Co-op City Fees." The state also agreed to over $10 million in ongoing subsidy of Co-op City's operating expenses for the four years

after the agreement went into effect. "Residual Receipts Agreement. Settlement Agreement."

65. Frank Ioppolo to Eimicke, memo, July 31, 1985.

66. Eimicke letter to Cooperators, February 13, 1986, Cuomo Housing 1986, reel 20, NYS Archives.

67. Cuomo press release, January 30, 1986, Cuomo Housing 1986, reel 20, NYS Archives.

68. Shirley Saunders, "A Director's Viewpoint: For a Better Co-op City," CCT, March 19, 1988, 27.

69. Irving Nusynowitz, Eva Pellman, Sol Friedman, Happy Bell, James Hall, Al Gordon, Tony Illis, and Judy Markfeld to Cuomo, May 7, 1986, Cuomo Housing 1986, reel 20, NYS Archives.

70. Saunders, "Director's Viewpoint: For a Better Co-op City."

71. Harriet Jeffries, "Director's Viewpoint: Summary of Workout Agreements," CCT, April 15, 1989, 29; Louis Lynch, "2,000 Rally Round Board. Throng Tells State: We Won't Pay," CCT, May 4, 1989, 1.

72. "'86 vs. '91," CCT, October 5, 1991, 1.

73. Steve Schneider, "Super Deal. CD's Pact's Fate Depends on Referendum," CCT, September 21, 1991, 2.

74. Matthew Purdy, "Discord Rattles Co-op City Towers," NYT, July 31, 1995, B1.

75. Linda Berk, "President's Message: Carrying Charge Increase Delay," CCT, July 11, 2020, 1.

76. This pattern would be followed a decade later in many American cities. Jason Hackworth, The Neoliberal City: Governance, Ideology, and Development in American Urbanism (Ithaca, NY: Cornell University Press, 2007), 99.

77. Susan Fainstein and Norman Fainstein, "New York City: The Manhattan Business District, 1945–1988," in Unequal Partnerships: The Political Economy of Economic Redevelopment in Postwar America, ed. G. Squires (New Brunswick, NJ: Rutgers University Press, 1989), 59. See also Aaron Shkuda, The Lofts of SoHo: Gentrification, Art, and Industry in New York, 1950–1980 (Chicago: University of Chicago Press, 2016).

78. Brian Goldstein, The Roots of Urban Renaissance: Gentrification and the Struggle over Harlem (Cambridge, MA: Harvard University Press, 2017), 183–90; Robert Snyder, Crossing Broadway: Washington Heights and the Promise of New York City (Ithaca, NY: Cornell University Press, 2015), 137. As Goldstein notes, fears that Harlem would be gentrified in the 1980s were not (yet) matched by much in the way of an actual influx of white, middle-class residents. Goldstein, Roots of Urban Renaissance, 203–4.

79. "Young Family's World," advertisement, NYT, November 12, 1967, 378.

80. Hackworth, Neoliberal City, 83. Some of New York's inner suburbs, such as Nassau and Westchester Counties, experienced notable increases in property values in these years. However, given New York's size, I believe that they are not the functional equivalent of inner-ring suburbs in smaller cities. Moreover, Hackworth argues that in New York, inner-ring suburbs also faced "notable devalorization" (93).

81. John Rennie Short, Bernadette Hanlon, and Thomas Vicino, "The Decline of Inner Suburbs: The New Suburban Gothic in the United States," Geography Compass 1, no. 3 (2007): 645.

82. Short, Hanlon, and Vicino, 641–56.

83. Shawn Kennedy, "About Real Estate—Shopping Center Is Planned for Bronx," *NYT*, April 1, 1987, A24.

84. "Perspectives: Shopping Centers: A Green Light for a South Bronx Venture," *NYT*, January 8, 1989, 10, 5.

85. Estelle Rabinovits letter, *CCT*, February 27, 1988, 6.

86. "Residents Enthused about Shopping Center," *CN*, April 4, 1987, 36.

87. Derek Alger, "Shopping Center: Good or Bad?," *CN*, June 13, 1987, 21.

88. Shirley Saunders, "A Director's Viewpoint: 'Bay Plaza,'" *CCT*, January 31, 1987, 17.

89. Mary Berman, letter to the editor, *CCT*, November 14, 1987, 4.

90. Charles Rosen, "History of Co-op City's CD Problems: A 20-Year Headache; Community in Crisis Part I: That Sinking Feeling," *CCT*, September 15, 1990, 1.

91. Tony Illis, "A Director's Viewpoint: Polarizing This Community," *CCT*, December 5, 1987, 22.

92. "Quality of Life at Stake," *CCT*, November 9, 1991, 3.

93. Larry Barnard, "Director's Viewpoint: Move-In Figures Up; Move-Outs Remain Constant," *CCT*, October 16, 1993, 21.

94. Shirley Saunders, "A Director's Viewpoint: A Difficult Decision," *CCT*, September 26, 1987, 20; Michael Pabon, "Director's Viewpoint: Allegations of Misconduct," *CCT*, July 30, 1988, 22.

95. Phil Laskorski, "Koch for 2 Shelters Here. Riverbay, Civic, Political Groups Vow Battle," *CCT*, February 21, 1987, 1; "Anti-Shelter Rally Tomorrow. Come Out and Be Heard," *CCT*, May 2, 19871, 1; "Confront Cuomo Today on Nukes," *CN*, March 14, 1985, 1; Sam Howe Verhovek, "Democracy, with Gusto, at Co-op City," *NYT*, May 19, 1988, B1.

96. Sam Fenster, "Enough Is Enough," *CCT*, August 8, 1987, 6.

97. Barnard, "Director's Viewpoint: Move-In Figures Up; Move-Outs Remain Constant."

98. Michael Rosenberg, "Director's Viewpoint: Let's Restore Our Good Name," *CCT*, June 18, 1988, 36.

99. Barbara Jones, "Director's Viewpoint: No Gloom or Doom for Co-op City," *CCT*, March 23, 1991, 28.

100. Diana Shaman, "At Co-op City, the Vacancy Sign Is Up," *NYT*, January 17, 1992, A20.

101. Robert E. Tomasson, "Plan Would Settle Soviet Jews at Co-op City," *NYT*, June 2, 1991, 39.

102. "Neighborhood Report: Looking Back, Looking Ahead, Bronx," *NYT*, January 1, 1995, Section 13, 7.

103. When Co-op City residents left, they received the equivalent equity deposit back, minus the cost of any repairs that were necessary to make the apartment ready for the next cooperator.

104. See Holtzman, *Long Crisis*, chap. 2 on the growing appeal of privatization for middle-class tenants.

105. Jerry Cheslow, "A City, Bigger Than Many, within a City," *NYT*, November 20, 1994, R5.

106. Cait Etherington, "The History of Mitchell-Lama Housing; See New Waiting Lists Openings," CityRealty, https://www.cityrealty.com/nyc/market-insight/features/get-to-know/the-history-mitchell-lama-housing-see-new-waiting-lists-openings/19562.

107. "Recent Homeownership Trends in New York City," https://furmancenter.org/files/soc2006/ownershiptrends06_000.pdf. See also "Homeownership Rate for New York," FRED Economic Data, https://fred.stlouisfed.org/series/NYHOWN.

108. JP's (website), Real Estate Charts, http://www.jparsons.net/housingbubble/new_york.html.

109. Owen Mortiz, "The Russians Are Coming and Co-op City Wants 'em," DN, November 4, 1992, 351.

110. "Family Living in Co-op City," DN, May 13, 1994, Real Estate 14.

111. "Family Living at Co op City," 44.

112. "Neighborhood Report: Looking Back, Looking Ahead, Bronx"; "Open House at Co-op City," DN, August 13, 1993, Real Estate 1.

113. Matthew Purdy, "Discord Rattles Co-op City Towers. Feuds and Finances Threaten Stability of Middle-Class Refuge," NYT, July 31, 1995, B1. Former Riverbay president Baez was convicted in 2008 in a corruption scandal stemming from kickbacks she received in the early 2000s. See Dorian Block, "Former Co-op City Board President Gets 6 Months of Jail in Plea Deal," DN, March 26, 2008, https://www.nydailynews.com/new-york/bronx/co-op-city-board-president-6-months-jail-plea-deal-article-1.288650; Miriam Hall and Kyna Doles, "Co-op City Board Sues DHCR, Says It Blotched Investigation into Ex-Management," Real Deal, October 11, 2016, https://therealdeal.com/2016/10/11/co-op-city-board-sues-dhcr-says-it-botched-investigation-into-ex-management. In 2006, Charles Rosen was also convicted of fraud and mismanagement at the Gloria Wise Boys and Girls Club. Sewell Chan, "Bronx Odyssey: From Rebel to Executive to Felon," NYT, October 10, 2006, B1.

114. Riverbay sales flyer, accessed July 15, 2020, https://coopcitynyc.com/img/covid-19/rb_res_sales.pdf. Currently the equity deposit for these apartments would be $16,500 and $35,750 respectively.

115. Michael Gold, "As Market Cools, Median Price for a Manhattan Apartment Drops below $1 Million (to $999,000)," NYT, January 3, 2019, https://www.nytimes.com/2019/01/03/nyregion/manhattan-real-estate-market.html. On average rents see renthop, accessed July 20, 2020, https://www.renthop.com/average-rent-in/new-york-city-ny.

116. Alan Feuer, "Utopia's $500 Million Repair Bill; Co-op City, Once a Working-Class Dream, Is Crumbling," NYT, August 9, 2003, B1.

117. Toriea McCauseland, "Happy 50th Anniversary, Co-op City," CCT, December 15, 2018, 2.

118. Charles Rosen quoted in Jerry Cheslow, "If You're Thinking of Living in / Co-op City; A City, Bigger Than Many, within a City," NYT, November 20, 1994, Sec. 9, 5.

Epilogue

1. Paul Nash, "Fantasia Bronxiana: Freedomland and Co-op City," New York History, 2001, 284.

2. Fred Clarke, "True Pioneers," *Celebrating 50: Co-op City*, December 20, 2018, 17.

3. Niall Ferguson, Charles S. Maier, Erez Manela, and Daniel J. Sargent, eds., *The Shock of the Global: The 1970s in Perspective* (Cambridge, MA: Belknap Press of Harvard University Press, 2010).

4. Eimicke interview.

5. For this exact quote see the ad from Community Protestant Church. See also ads from Amalgamated Bank; Cooperators United for Mitchell-Lama; Building #7 Association; Armienti, DeBellis, Guglielmo & Rhoden LLP; the Coalition of African-American Churches & Community Organizations; the Coalition to Save Affordable Housing; Direct Energy; the Building #24 Association; the Building #15A Shareholders Association; and the Co-op City Branch of the NAACP.

6. Michelle Marbury, "Section 4 Partnership: Bit by Bit, Putting It Together," *CCT*, August 22, 2020, 15.

7. Ballotpedia, "New York's 16th Congressional District Election, 2020 (June 23 Democratic Primary)," https://ballotpedia.org/New_York%27s_16th_Congressional_District_election,_2020_(June_23_Democratic_primary).

8. Jesse McKinley, "Jamaal Bowman Proves Ocasio-Cortez Was No Fluke," *NYT*, July 17, 2020, https://www.nytimes.com/2020/07/17/nyregion/jamaal-bowman-eliot-engel.html.

9. "The Jewish Vote Canvass for Jamaal Bowman," eventbrite, https://www.eventbrite.com/e/the-jewish-vote-canvass-for-jamaal-bowman-co-op-city-am-shift-tickets-96986415981. On the support of some of Co-op City's Black elite for Engel see Rod Saunders, "Director's Viewpoint," *CCT*, June 20, 2020, 8.

10. Julia Ioffe, "'This Year's A.O.C., Jamaal Bowman Says He's Ready to Fight," *GQ*, August 3, 2020, https://www.gq.com/story/jamaal-bowman-for-congress.

11. Jamal Bowman, interview with the author, August 24, 2020.

12. C. J. Hughes, "Co-op City for Affordability and Open Spaces," *NYT*, February 24, 2016, https://www.nytimes.com/2016/02/28/realestate/co-op-city-for-affordability-and-open-spaces.html.

13. "Douglas Elliman Wins Bid to Manage Co-op City," Real Deal, May 5, 2016, https://therealdeal.com/2016/05/05/douglas-elliman-wins-bid-to-manage-co-op-city/.

14. Jason Chirevas, "DHCR Approves Carrying Charge Increases for 2019, 2020," *CCT*, August 17, 2019, 1.

15. Jason Chirevas, "MTA's Byford: Bus Redesign 'Not Set in Stone,'" *CCT*, June 29, 2019, 1.

16. Toreia McCauseland, "Sisters Organize Black Lives Matter Protest in Co-op City," *CCT*, June 13, 2020, 9.

17. Hughes, "Co-op City for Affordability and Open Spaces." In comparison, the same census found that New York City's percentage of Black residents was 26 percent; Hispanic residents, 29 percent; and non-Hispanic whites, 33 percent; and in the Bronx, 36 percent of residents were Black, 54 percent were Hispanic, and 11 percent were non-Hispanic whites: https://en.wikipedia.org/wiki/Demographic_history_of_New_York_City.

18. Police Department, City of New York, *CompStat* report for the Forty-Fifth Precinct, the week of June 29–July 5, 2020, vol. 27, no. 27, https://www1.nyc.gov/assets/nypd/downloads/pdf/crime_statistics/cs-en-us-045pct.pdf.

19. See GreatSchools.org, https://www.greatschools.org/search/search.zipcode?sort=rating&zip=10475.

20. "Synopsis of the History of Co-op City," *Celebrating 50*, 2.

INDEX

Page numbers in italics refer to figures.

Abrams, Al, 112
Abrams, Robert, 139
Abzug, Bella, 138
affordable housing, 7, 8, 9, 23, 33, 160, 162, 206–7, 220–22. *See also* New York State Limited-Profit Housing Companies Act
African Americans. *See* Blacks
"Afro-American culture night," 87
Agovino, Michael, 135, 171, 185, 186, 198, 202
Amalgamated Clothing Workers of America (ACWA), 6
Amalgamated Houses, 6, 7, 8, 14
American Institute of Architects (AIA), 28, 29, 32, 33, 59
Aronov, Edward, 106, 112, 121
austerity policies
    New York City fiscal crisis, 13, 15, 16, 20, 128, 209
    New York City resistance, 137, 164, 206
    New York State and, 146, 209, 222, 224
    See also Municipal Assistance Corporation

Badillo, Herman, 22, 38, 44, 46
Baez, Iris Herskowitz, 201, 202, 218, 220, 280n137
Ballard, William, 43
Barbaro, Frank, 138
Bauer, Catherine, 6
Baychester, 81, 87, 197
Beame, Abraham, 1, 3, 111, 128
Belica, Paul, 127, 134, 139, 142
Benedict, Jane, 136
Bernstein, Abraham, 129, 160, 162
Biaggi, Mario, 199
blackout (1977), 1, 2, 3
Blacks, 17, 19
    fragility of middle class, 193
    tough-on-crime measures, 194
    in West Bronx, 41, 42

Blacks, Co-op City
    applicants, 66
    Black Heritage Festival, 183
    fear of crime, 182
    Four MCs rap group, *185*
    at groundbreaking, 46
    majority Black community, 226–27
    racial diversity, 74–75, 190
    rappers and street parties, 184
Borstelmann, Thomas, 16
Boston Secor Houses, 3, 50, 81, 88, 92, 93
Bowman, Jamaal, 227, 228
Bronx, *2*
    Co-op City authentic part, 185–86
    racism in, 187
    tactical narcotics team (TNT) 203, 202, 203
    urban decay, 3, 225
Bronxdale projects, 67
Bronx Planning Commission, 43, 81

Cabrera, Elba, 86
Caesar, Ron, 187, 215
Calandra, John, 90, 122
Canarsie, 171, 174, 253n71
Carey, Hugh
    candidate promises, 113, 131, 134
    carrying charges increases, 166, 167, 169
    construction defect repairs, 160, 209
    Co-op City debt burden, 122, 123
    Federal Reserve help, 140
    federal Treasury help, 128
    on Goodwin's inflexibility, 141, 142
    HFA bond trouble, 138, 139
    HFA rescue package, 140
    Mitchell-Lama task force, 153, 154, 156, 161
    negotiation agreement, 144
    rent strike neutrality, 129, 136

Cavaglieri, Giorgio, 28, 29
Chavez, Cesar, 138
Cirlin, Benjamin, 120, 124, 131, 132, 135, 145, 148, 159, 198
"Citizens Concerned about Co-op City," 46
Citizens Housing and Planning Council, 47
City University of New York (CUNY), 8, 20, 117, 137
Citywide Tenants United, 136
Committee for Excellence in Architecture, 28
Committee for Quality Education (CQE), 88–92
Committee to Elect Responsible Leadership (CERL), 166, 168, 169, 171, 176, 177, 179, 211
Community Services Incorporated (CSI), 55, 56, 57, 150
Concourse Village, 41
Consolidated Edison (Con Ed), 1, 56, 104, 131, 154, 269n22
Co-op City, 23
    advertising, 34, 45, 46, 47, 68, 79, 83, 188, 216
    applicants for residence, 34, 35, 36, 41, 42, 43
    construction, 36, 63, 104
    cost-cutting measures, 148, 149, 150, 151, 154
    demographics of, 4, 19, 48, 65–66, 172, 173, 182–83, 186, 229, 288n17
    discriminatory policies, 172–73
    groundbreaking ceremony, 22, 46
    history of, 12–13, 18, 26
    illegal sublets, 199
    income limits and rent proposal, 155, 156, 157
    layout and street names, 63, 64, 65, 70
    Model Apartment Program, 176
    site history, 24–25, 36
    snowstorm (1969), 61
    state audit, 123, 158, 159
    twentieth anniversary, 181–82
Co-op City, apartment amenities, 29, 68, 69, 205
    air conditioning, 23, 26, 68
    Bay Plaza shopping mall, 217
    community, 59, 70–72
    co-operative stores, 30
    walkable commercial hub, 29–30, 32
Co-op City, crime
    crime wave, 5
    drug trafficking, 82, 195, 199–201
    escape from crime-ridden neighborhoods, 67–68, 80, 82–83

Guardian Angels, 202
    laundry room safety, 196, 201
    "Operation Safety," 202
    police presence, 12, 83, 182, 193, 194, 201–3
    racism and racial incidents, 192–96
    reason to leave, 169–75
    safety of, 170, 203–4, 226, 229, 277n60, 278n72
Co-op City, critics of, 14–15, 18, 22, 24, 59
    architecture, 27–29, 31, 93
    effect on neighborhoods, 38, 41, 42, 43
    social makeup, 32
Co-op City Advisory Council, 76, 77, 78, 79, 101, 106, 109, 110, 111
Co-op City Black Caucus, 18
    activities of, 79
    Advisory Council and, 76–77
    busing plan, 91
    Section Five image problem, 175–87
    "Valley" neighborhood dance incident, 86–87
Co-op City Fair, 94
Co-op City finances, 107
    carrying charges increases, 97–98, 99, 102, 103, 107, 122–23, 168–69, 212, 225
    construction costs, 52–54, 57, 97, 102–3
    construction defect repairs, 5, 57–58, 109, 149, 153, 159
    construction loans and, 121–22
    differential carrying charges, 102
    Emergency Repair Program (ERP), 160, 209–10
    heating and electric bills, 103–4
    income verification, 153, 156, 157
    mortgage, 5, 27, 179
    original estimate, 26–27
    Permanent Repair Program, 209, 211, 283n26, 283n30
    state and city government and, 106, 110, 112, 165–66, 179, 205–7, 212–14
    tax abatement, 57
    tax arrears, 166, 167, 212–13
    vacancies and applications, 176–77
    vacancy problems, 176, 205, 206, 215, 219, 220, 221, 222, 286n103
    workout agreements, 215–16, 222
Co-op City lawsuits
    state government and, 110–11
    against UHF, 110–11
Co-op City News, 169
    crack vials in Section Five, 199–200
    crime and safety, 82, 195
    differential carrying charges, 102

open space use, 85
rent strike letters, 134, 135
rent strike results, 167
rent strike support, 123, 135–36
vandalism cleanup, 151
welfare family rumors, 173–74
Co-op City residents
    activists and joiners, 99–100
    Carey and, 113
    carrying charges or rent, 162–63
    city purchase of units, 49
    community building, 62
    equity payment and carrying charges, 47,
        57, 108, 236n21
    nonvoting shares, 98
    optimism, 72–74, 149, 172, 206, 223
    organization by, 4–5
    orientation meetings, 69–70, 71
    privatization and, 222, 282nn17–18
    public relations, 160–63, 176–78
    racial stress, 62–63
    Soviet Jews resettlement, 219, 276n49
    views of UHF, 108, 109, 113–14
    welfare family rumors, 49, 108
Co-op City Section One, 3, 63, 66, 80, 84,
    102
Co-op City Section Four, 201
Co-op City Section Five, 63, 66, 102, 175,
    226
Co-op City's Security Department, 171, 200
Co-op City Tenants Council, 82, 101–2
Co-op City Times, 99
    applicants for residence, 46
    architecture or community, 29
    on Bay Plaza shopping mall, 217
    benefits of cooperative, 70
    carrying charges increase, 57, 97
    on Charles Rosen, 119
    commercial space, 31
    on construction defects, 218
    Co-op City resident letters, 219
    Co-op City residents, 62
    crime reporting, 82, 195
    Dinkin's visit ignored, 187
    educational draw, 87
    goal of Co-op City, 33
    integration rates, 76
    public space use, 84, 85
    Riverbay advertising plan, 189–90
    Riverbay and racial harmony, 192
    Rosen resignation letter, 152
    SCIII and CERL arguments, 169
    snowstorm (1969), 61
    transportation issues, 80–81

twentieth anniversary supplement, 181
    vacancies and applications, 176, 177
    vandalism and graffiti, 86
Co-op Contact, 28, 45
cooperative housing, 4, 9, 249n173
    goal of, 12
    limited dividend housing and, 6
    social relations and, 96–98
    See also United Housing Foundation
Cooperative Housing, 31, 32, 47
Cooperator, 45
Cooperators for Co-op City, 110
Co-op Living, 70
Coordinating Council of Committees, 168
Corde Corporation, 50
corruption
    City-Wide Plumbing, 210
    Mitchell-Lama projects and, 54–56
    noncompetitive bids, 210–11
    power plant, 56
    A-PRO, 210–11
    Rey Caulking, 210
    Riverbay excuses, 211
    scandals, 219
    State Investigation Commission, 55, 210,
        211, 283n37
    UHF organizational structure, 56
Council of Community Organizations, 168
Cuomo, Mario, 142, 143, 144, 146, 148, 200,
    206, 207, 208, 209, 215, 225, 267n176
Cylich, Bernie, 57, 58

Daily News, 112, 200
Dannenberg, Joel, 152, 153, 167, 177
Death and Life of Great American Cities, The
    (Jacobs), 13–14
De Blasio, Bill, 222
Department of Housing and Community
    Renewal (DHCR)
    carrying charges increases, 111, 112, 214,
        215, 228
    construction costs, 54, 103, 158
    equity deposit, 221
    financial problems, 162
    income verification, 156, 157
    oversight failures, 158, 161, 178
    Permanent Repair Program, 210, 211
    Rosen hire, 152
    suit to end strike, 129
    threats against strikers, 130, 141
    UHF member resignation, 125
    vacancy crisis and, 222
    view of rent strike, 134
    See also Goodwin, Lee

Dinkins, David, 187
Dolnick, Larry, 119
DuBrul, Paul, 72, 144, 161

economic rent, 155, 156, 157, 166, 168, 212, 213, 214, 284n58
"Educational Park," 50–52, 83. *See also* Committee for Quality Education; Northeast Bronx Educational Park
Eimicke, William, 207, 208, 209, 213, 214, 215, 225
Eisland, June, 201
elderly
    attraction to Co-op City, 83, 84, 230
    Concourse neighborhoods, 42, 43
    crime and, 43, 80, 171
    leaving Co-op City, 183
    race and, 86, 183
    rent strike and, 130
    sociability and, 71
    socializing, 71, 72
Electchester, 7
Energy Research Development Administration (ERDA), 150–51
Engel, Eliot, 119, 161, 201, 227

families with children, 83, 84, 107, 119
Farband Cooperative, 6
Ford, Gerald, 128, 140
Freedomland amusement park, 25, 26, 27, 38, 55, 223

gentrification, 5, 16–17, 216–17
Goodwin, Lee, 111, 112, 113, 126, 128–29, 130, 134, 138, 141, 142, 144
Grand Concourse, 1, 37, 38, 39, 40, 41, 42, 43, 48, 66, 68, 225, 246n81
Guridy, Frank, 184

Harry S. Truman High School, 58, 88, 93, 159, 183, 186–88, 196–99, 203
Hawkins, Yusuf, 192
Hazell, Gretchen, 204
Heritage Foundation, 15
HFA mortgage bonds
    bailouts of, 139, 141
    carrying charges increase, 113
    construction cost financing, 97
    construction costs deduction, 159–60
    default worries, 138, 139, 140
    foreclosure, 127, 128, 129, 142, 143, 153
    interest rate, 52–53, 103, 107, 138
    maturing notes, 140

moral obligation bonds, 10, 20, 127, 146
    rent strike and, 127
    Rosen's view of, 117, 120–21
    state government and, 141, 207, 212
Hispanics. *See* Latinos
Hochberg, Alan, 111, 122, 136
homeownership, 164, 165, 207, 209, 220

Illis, Tony, 182, 188, 190, 201–2, 218, 219
Infantino, Robert, 129
inner-ring suburbs, 217, 285n80
International Ladies Garment Workers Union (ILGWU), 6
Irushalmi, Bruce, 186, 197

Jacobs, Jane, 13, 14, 15, 16, 29, 30, 32, 178
Jeffries, Harriet, 189, 202, 215
Jessor, Hermann, 26, 27, 29, 52
Jewish people, at Co-op City, 4
Jews
    at Co-op City, 44, 66, 183
    ethnically mixed neighborhood, 72–76
    integration without crime, 49
    leaving Co-op City, 174, 226
    migration from neighborhoods, 38–39
    socialist views, 119
    unionists, 6
    in West Bronx, 39, 40
    West Bronx exodus, 38, 41, 42, 43, 44, 66–67
    See also Grand Concourse
Johnson, Lyndon, 22

Kaufman, Stephen, 111, 135, 136, 265n127
Kazan, Abraham
    on construction costs, 54, 55
    cooperative proponent, 7, 96, 117, 118
    CSI founder, 55
    groundbreaking ceremony, 22, 23
    retirement party, 56
    Robert Moses and, 10, 11, 14
    UHF founder, 6, 8, 97
    urban integration proponent, 46
Koch, Edward, 160, 164, 165, 176, 207–8
Kristoff, Frank, 157

Lama, Alfred, 9, 54, 249n173
Latinos, 44
    at Co-op City, 66, 72, 87, 172, 182, 188, 189
    in New York City, 173, 183
    racial diversity, 44, 46, 74–75, 229

in South Bronx, 41
Truman High school, 186
in West Bronx, 41, 42
legislation, federal. *See* National Housing
    Acts
legislation, state. *See* New York State
    Housing Law; New York State Limited-
    Profit Housing Companies Act; State
    Redevelopment Companies Law
Lerner, Wilana, 188
Levitt, Arthur, Sr., 146, 157, 158, 159,
    173
Lewis, Miles Marshall, 184, 185, 186
Lieb, Steve, 203
Liebman, Herman, 69, 71
Lindsay, John, 37, 44, 46, 57, 58, 60
Lower Manhattan Expressway, 13, 25

Manhattan Institute, 15, 16
Marshall, Ed, 78, 89
Metropolitan Life Insurance Company, 7,
    10–11, 238n50
Mitchell, MacNeil, 9, 54, 249n173
Mitchell-Lama Council, 136
Mitchell-Lama projects, 65
    equity deposit requirement, 34, 286n103
    fiscal problems, 117
    free riders surcharge, 157
    goal of affordable housing, 154, 155
    limited-equity housing, 9–10, 220
    means test, 131
    middle class retention, 38, 65
    mortgages, 97
    privatization of, 208–9, 282n17
    state and city government and, 107, 117,
        209
    state purchase legislation, 47
    task force, 143, 153, 154, 155, 160, 161
Mitchell-Lama Task Force, 143
moral obligation bonds. *See* HFA mortgage
    bonds
Moses, Robert, 10, 11, 12, 13, 14, 22, 23, 26,
    27, 33, 37, 238n60, 238n62
Municipal Assistance Corporation (MAC),
    128, 137, 142, 164
My Beloved World (Sotomayor), 67–68
Myers, Greg, 184

National Housing Acts, 7, 9, 11, 237n44
Native Americans, 243n11
neoliberalism, 15, 16, 18, 21, 163, 164, 204,
    205, 206, 222, 225, 282n17
Newfield, Jack, 72, 144

Newsweek, 59
New York City, 164, 171
    federal bailout, 140
    fiscal crisis, 116–17, 128
    homeownership programs, 165
    homesteader programs, 163
    snowstorm (1969), 60–61
New York City Board of Education, 50,
    52
New York City Board of Estimate, 26
New York City Office of the Aging, 80
New York City Planning Commission
    (CPC), 57
    Concourse applicants, 43, 44
    ethnic diversity issue, 32, 33
    opposition to Co-op City, 24
    parking facility costs, 54
    plan approval, 29, 33, 34, 37
    site benefits, 38
    transportation issues, 27
New York City Public Housing Authority
    (NYCHA), 7, 8, 9, 11, 50, 81, 108, 175
New York City Rent Guidelines Board,
    166
New York Post, 134
New York State
    Affordable Housing Ownership Program,
        207
    co-op residents on debt burden, 122
    fiscal problems, 117
    Low-Income Housing Trust Fund
        Program, 207
    Mitchell-Lama subcommittee, 122
    rent strike and, 128
    Rosen's view of, 120–21
New York State Commission of
    Investigations, 210
New York State Housing Finance
    Agency (HFA)
    carrying charges increases, 113
    carrying charges petitions, 168
    construction defect repairs, 159, 160, 209,
        211, 215
    Co-op City mortgage, 27
    creation of, 10
    economic rent, 156
    near default, 115
    Permanent Repair Program, 210
    rent strike and, 120, 127, 224
    SCIII and, 111, 144, 149
    state role in mismanagement, 167
    See also HFA mortgage bonds
New York State Housing Law (1926), 6, 7

New York State Limited-Profit Housing
    Companies Act (1955). *See* Mitchell-
    Lama projects
New York Times
    construction contract, 24
    Co-op City criticism, 59
    Co-op City finances, 131
    Co-op City freeloaders, 161, 162
    Co-op City praise, 22
    Co-op City teenagers, 74
    Co-op City welfare rumors, 49
    drug trafficking, 200
    Grand Concourse, 41
    HFA finances, 140
    income verification, 157
    marketing plan for diversity, 188–90
Nizer, Louis, 56, 110
Northeast Bronx Committee for
    Neighborhood Schools, 90
Northeast Bronx Educational Park, *51*
    busing plan, 88, 89, 90, 91, 92, 93
    construction defects and delays, 58, 88,
        270n44
    cost savings, 51
    educational draw, 50, 52, 87
    racial integration, 88
    reading level decline, 197–98
    test scores, 230
    See also Harry S. Truman High School

O'Dwyer, William, 7
On the Line (documentary), 134–35
Ostroff, Harold
    called Caesar, 101
    carrying charges increases, 106, 111,
        122, 126
    commercial cooperatives, 30
    community democracy, 32, 47, 70
    construction costs, 52, 53, 54, 102,
        103
    on cooperative housing goal, 11, 12
    on CSI board, 55
    defeat on cooperative housing, 59
    diversity issues, 66, 78, 86
    on Educational Park, 52
    families with children, 83
    on fiscal responsibility, 97
    groundbreaking ceremony, 22
    middle class retention, 37, 48
    rent increases, 104, 109, 110, 113,
        114
    on rent strike, 123
    on Riverbay board of directors, 76
    state legislative lobbying, 105

state mortgage assistance request, 112
tower in a park model, 28, 29
welfare family rumors, 108

Pabon, Michael, 202
Parkchester, 7
Parness, Charles, 113, 166, 167, 168–69, 177,
    211, 214, 215, 284n49
Parness, Sandra, 211
Pellman, Eva, 171, 188, 189, 190, 191
Penn South, 8
Perkins + Will, 58, 159, 209
Peter Cooper Village, 7
Phillips, Don, 29, 61, 70, 71, 84, 94
Potofsky, Jacob, 22, 30, 46, 55, 56, 126
power plant, 26, 56, 104, 150, 154, 236n8,
    269n22
Progressive Architecture, 59
public housing, 7, 9, 11, 58, 271n69
public space use, 84–85, 93–94
Puerto Ricans. *See* Latinos

Queensview Cooperative, 8

racial inequities, 17
racial integration, 46–49, 66
racial liberalism, 19, 72, 73, 74, 226
racism
    busing issues, 90, 91, 92
    at Co-op City, 76, 173, 174
    hiring discrimination, 187
    racial harmony, 191–92, 225–26
    racial inequities, 17
Ravitch, Richard, 154, 155, 156, 160, 161,
    166
Reagan, Ronald, 207
rent strike (1975–76)
    beginnings of, 115
    carrying charges increases, 122–23
    cooperator control, 115, 118, 145, 147,
        149
    court action against, 129–31
    Cuomo negotiation plan, 142–44
    escrow checks, *124*
    eviction threats, 130
    final settlement, 153–54, 268n16, 269n17
    mass support, 110, 111, 131, *132*, 136–38
    model of cooperation, 118
    nonsupporters, 135
    organizing for, 121
    SCIII deadline approval, 122
    settlement critics, 143
    settlement critics or proponents, 145
    victory claim, 144, 214

See also Department of Housing and
   Community Renewal; Rosen, Charles;
   Steering Committee III
rent strikes, 3, 5, 10, 20
   CORE and Bedford-Stuyvesant, 100
   history of, 100, 136
   Rochdale Village, 136
   service delays (1969), 99
   state government and, 112, 113, 168
rent strikes, Co-op City, 101, 102
Riverbay Corporation
   Advisory Council and, 76
   affordable housing, 21
   board of directors composition, 144, 183
   carrying charges misrepresentation, 158,
      159
   Class A shares, 98
   construction repair costs, 159–60
   Co-op City management, 56
   DHCR opinion of, 134
   discrimination controversies, 187–88
   Douglas Elliman Property Management,
      228
   EBASCO construction management,
      210–11, 283n37
   escrow checks, 112, 125
   income verification, 153, 155, 157
   infighting and politics, 219
   lawsuit against UHF, 110–11
   maintenance worker contract, 151
   marketing and affordability, 52, 112, 123,
      155, 178, 212, 221
   marketing plan for diversity, 188–91
   Memo of Settlement, 214–15, 284n62
   mortgage and tax payments, 160
   rent increase, 122–23
   rent raise opposition, 108
   Tenants Council and, 101
   vacancies and applications, 78, 178
   wait list policies, 172–73, 188
   white flight anxiety, 149
   See also Committee to Elect Responsible
      Leadership; Rosen, Charles; Steering
      Committee III
Riverton Houses, 7
Rochdale Pioneers, integration of, 33
Rochdale Village
   integrated education, 49, 90
   integration of, 45, 46
   management fired, 101
   rent strike, 136, 265n131
   UHF project, 8, 23, 32
Rockefeller, Nelson, 9, 10, 22, 23, 33, 38,
   117, 127

Rohatyn, Felix, 128
Rosen, Charles
   background of, 119–20
   Carey and, 129
   celebrity status, 132, *133*
   cost-cutting measures, 149, 150
   critics of, 134
   at DHCR, 152
   Dreiser Loop Community Center, 115,
      116, 126
   escrow checks location, 145
   governance challenges, 224
   HFA mortgage bonds bailout, 139
   infrastructure problems, 218
   negotiations, 142, 143
   rent strike agreement, 153
   rent strike and, 5
   rent strike purpose, 126, 141
   rent strike tactics, 120, 121, 124, 130, 131
   Riverbay president, 173
   Teamsters accusation, 55
   UHF corruption, 56, 57
   UHF model failure, 117, 118, 120
   victory speech, 144
   view of Ostroff, 123
   See also HFA mortgage bonds; Steering
      Committee III
Rosenberg, Michael, 219

Saunders, Rod, 190
Saunders, Shirley, 187, 189, 190, 191, 202, 218
Schechter, George, 14, 26, 29, 56, 77, 78, 91,
   101, 102, 104, 113
schools and education
   busing issues, 89, 90, 186 (*see also*
      Northeast Bronx Educational Park)
   integration experiment, 50, 52
   integration issues, 256n176, 275n21
   magnet schools, 279n101
   Ocean Hill-Brownsville, 89
   Oliver Scholars program, 198, 279n102
   test scores, 198, 279n94
   See also Harry S. Truman High School
Scribner, Harvey, 88, 89, 93
Shapiro, Al, 181, 199, 201
Shiffman, Ronald, 160, 161, 162
Sholem Aleichem Houses, 6
Sicilian, Michael, 109
Sivak, Larry, 113
Smith, Esther, 124, 144, 180, 183
Sotomayor, Sonia, 67, 68, 75
Sozio, Caroline, 189
Spanish-American Society, 79, 87, 92
Starr, Roger, 38, 134, 161

State of New York Mortgage Agency
  (SONYMA), 207
State Redevelopment Companies Law,
  238n50
Steering Committee III (SCIII)
  bondholders leverage, 146
  carrying charges increases, 112, 120, 123
  CERL and, 169
  construction defect repairs, 159
  cost-cutting measures, 148, 149, 150–51
  court action against, 129–31
  escrow checks, 20, 112, 124, 129, 144,
    145, 151
  formation and purpose, 111
  Goodwin and, 128, 129
  makeup of, 124–25
  negotiations, 142, 143, 146
  organizing for rent strike, 121, 125
  progress post-strike, 152, 153
  rent strike purpose, 126, 141
  rent strike vote, 123, 124, 262n50
  Rosen as leader, 118–19
  state legislature testimony, 122
  UHF view of, 113
  vacancy problems, 176
  vandalism cleanup, 151
  victory claim, 144
  See also HFA mortgage bonds
Steering Committees I and II, 260n83,
  265n131
Steiner, George, 210
Stuyvesant Town, 7
Sunnyside Gardens, 6
Sweet, Robert, 38, 43, 44
Szold, Robert, 55, 126

Taub, Arthur, 91, 92, 163
Teamsters' Pension Fund, 25, 55
teenagers
  boredom of, 83–84
  public space use, 85
  racism and, 86
  "Stop the Violence Teen Club," 203
  vandalism and graffiti, 86
  See also Harry S. Truman High School
Tenant Interim Lease Program, 165,
  272n80
Teutsch, Erika, 131
Tolopko, Frank, 169
transportation
  bus and subway access, 80–81
  highway overpass, 81
  planning issues, 27
Trump Village, 55, 172

Tuomey, Gerald, 203, 204
Twin Pines project, 105

United Federation of Teachers (UFT), 89,
  90, 91, 92, 100
United Housing Foundation (UHF)
  community building, 62
  community life, 70
  construction funds, 121
  cooperative housing developer, 3
  corruption investigation, 109–10
  critics of, 14
  development costs, 232
  economic homogeneity, 47, 73
  goal of Co-op City, 4, 22, 29, 31–32, 69
  increased costs, 105, 106
  limited-equity housing, 237n39
  limited-income housing, 8, 32–33, 238n49
  loan assistance, 47, 248n141
  mission statement, 12
  Mitchell-Lama projects, 10
  nondiscriminatory housing policy, 45–46,
    47–48
  shared ownership, 33, 97
  site purchase, 25–26
  state legislature and, 105, 106, 224
  tenant relations, 101, 109–10, 113
  tenement replacement, 11
  vertical construction model, 11, 13, 26, 28
  views of rent strike, 125–26
  See also Amalgamated Houses;
    Community Services Incorporated;
    Rochdale Village
Urban Development Corporation (UDC),
  117, 126, 127, 128, 139, 141, 154,
  267n164
urban homesteading, 163, 207
Urban League, 172
urban liberalism, 8, 15, 16, 18, 19, 20, 21,
  118, 137, 209, 227, 228
urban renewal, 13–16, 164
Urstadt, Charles J., 106, 107

Van Arsdale, Harry, Jr., 7, 22
Village Voice, 133, 135, 145–46

Wagner, Robert, 26, 33
Wall Street Journal, 126, 143, 145–46
Webb & Knapp, 25, 55
west Bronx. See Jews; Latinos
white flight, 2, 5, 17, 37, 38, 44
Wilson, Malcolm, 105, 112, 113

Zeckendorf, William, 25, 55